Mother Russia

Mother Russia

The Feminine Myth in Russian Culture

JOANNA HUBBS

Indiana University Press

BLOOMINGTON AND INDIANAPOLIS

First Midland Book Edition 1993

© 1988 by Joanna Hubbs

All rights reserved

Manufactured in the United States of America

Library of Congress Cataloging-in-Publication Data
Hubbs, Joanna, 1939-
Mother Russia: the feminine myth in Russian culture / by Joanna Hubbs.
p.   cm.
Bibliography: p.
Includes index.
ISBN 0-253-33860-3
1. Mother-goddesses—Soviet Union.   2. Mythology, Slavic.
3. Soviet Union—Religion.   4. Soviet Union—Civilization.
I. Title.
BL940.S65H83   1988   87-37469
291.2'11'0947—dc19   CIP

ISBN 0–253–20842–4 (pbk.)
3 4 5 6 7 99 98 97 96 95 94 93

To Clay

with love

CONTENTS

ILLUSTRATIONS FOLLOW P. 123

Acknowledgments

I wish to thank Lorna Peterson, Leonard Glick, Ethel Dunn, Maria Banerjee, and Richard Stites for their encouragement over the past eight years of research and writing.

I am especially grateful to Richard Pope for his careful reading of the manuscript and for his invaluable suggestions for revision.

My thanks to the library staff of Hampshire College, particularly to Mike Kurrier, Serena Weaver, and John Gunther.

Illustrations 7, 8, and 10, from Marija Gimbutas, *The Goddesses and Gods of Old Europe*, copyright 1974, 1982 by Thames and Hudson Ltd., are reproduced by permission of the University of California Press.

Russia as Mother

Russia herself, as has been observed, is a woman nation.

—S. GRAHAM, *Undiscovered Russia*

Khan Batu fixed his eyes
On a red-faced peasant *baba*

And with primeval melancholy
The Khan at the moment recalled
That though he had slaughtered so many
He had understood nothing at all.

For those peasants, buffoons
And simpletons at first seeming
Are like dolls within a doll
Secrets within secrets concealing.

—Y. YEVTUSHENKO, "A Russian
Toy—Roly-Poly"[1]

Who is not familiar with the round and brightly colored Matrioshka doll? She is the most common of all Russian toys. Not simply decorative, she is also a puzzle, a child's game. Broken apart at the stomach, she spills out many identical dolls, one inside the other in descending order, until the tiny center doll appears as though it were her youngest. One containing many, she seems ever-fertile, this rosy-cheeked peasant Matrioshka wearing a *babushka* (scarf). Her egg-shaped form, all head and torso, is wrapped in a brightly painted peasant dress called a *sarafan*. The first syllable of her name, a diminutive of Matriona, means "mother." Her red, yellow, blue, and green garments suggest the colors of blood, sunlight, ripe wheat, sky, water, flowers, and luxuriant plants.

A number of legends are associated with the Matrioshka. She is linked with the ancient Ugrian goddess Jumala of the Urals, who was thought to contain all things within her body. The Vikings, merchant-warriors and probable founders of the Russian state in the ninth century, looked for this original Matrioshka because, like the El Dorado of a later age, she was thought to be made of solid gold. Sixteenth-century German geographers' maps show a "Golden Woman" then still believed to exist in the little-known kingdom of Muscovy. She was described by the German Baron von Herberstein in 1549 as a statue with a hollow "singing" interior found in a sacred forest and containing three figures, one inside the other. Her Ugrian worshippers left offerings of value—usually gold—on a tree. When enough gold had been collected by her guards, it was melted down, and a new shell was made for the goddess. Like the precious frames which enfold the sacred icons of the Mother of God in Russia, the goddess's blessings were sought by a gift in kind: wealth for wealth. In 1584 another foreigner, the English ambassador to the Muscovite court Giles Fletcher, sent an expedition to the Urals in search of this ancient and precious figure. The searches have continued: In 1967, an old hunter living in the town of Tiumen' told modern treasure-seekers that the Golden Woman had been taken away and hidden so that her wealth might never be found, her image never desecrated.[2] The mysterious "Golden Woman" sought by foreigners for her material value remains elusive, her wealth symbolic and undiscovered.

The oldest existing Matrioshka dolls (from the nineteenth century) contain first a girl in a *sarafan* and kerchief carrying a black rooster under her arm, then a boy, then another girl, and finally a baby in swaddling clothes. Over the years, the identity and costumes of the figures have varied. Some represent a group of boyars or boyarinas (Muscovite nobles and their wives); others are clerks, falconers, and warriors; still others open up to reveal a series of fairytale characters. Today the Matrioshka is commonly a woman or a girl who contains only her own images within her body. The ancient goddess now appears simply as a doll, her mystery reduced to a brightly colored puzzle for small children. But the doll is also a popular symbol of Russia's rich folk heritage.

More than a doll and a relic from a forgotten past, Matrioshka remains a symbolic embodiment of "Mother Russia."

Just as the doll is to be found everywhere, so too Russia's epithet, passing into popular habit of mind, has been taken for granted. The doll is mute, and the epithet is sentimentalized. My task here is to make the doll speak: to show how the epithet, like its embodiment, is not merely ornamental but contains Russia's vision of herself as a nation. Matrioshka's ancient significance is clouded, but the habit of mind which sees the mother as the "nest" where her children can find refuge and identity remains strong. This is apparent in the "umbilical" love of Russia as motherland by her Soviet children.[3] But the unusually deep attachment to the country as mother is everywhere to be found, most strikingly, perhaps, in the representation in popular tradition of the Russian countryside, which seems to recall prodigal children to their primordial home.[4] The historical Mother Russia and the mythological Mother Earth unite in the creative power still attributed to the land. What is named by the peasant in proverb, song, folklore, and folk art is evoked nostalgically by writers, artists, and intellectuals.

For centuries, Russia had a predominantly agrarian culture. The land was called Mother, and her physical features—natural or man-made—were also given maternal epithets. Rivers which run through the immense steppes are still called "little mothers": *Matushka* Don, *Matushka* Dnieper. Most important of all is *Matushka* Volga, whose sacred nature is celebrated in the first recorded folk song and in a popular ballad as "Our Dear Mother" and "Our Natal Mother."[5] There is still no road to her source in the northern marshes. Travelers must make their way on foot and experience the sense of the sacred on approaching the mother of rivers.[6] If nature was mother, so too were the very monuments built to testify to a measure of human power—cities, roads, churches.[7] Russia's cultural evolution was marked by a movement from Mother Kiev, the city which is popularly called the birthgiver, to Mother Moscow, which nourished Russia's growth and is identified with her heart. Only later in her history, by force of autocratic fiat, did Russia move her capital to Saint Petersburg, so that she might show a masculine face to the West. "Piter" is indeed a masculine city, planned, symmetrical, and built on pylons sunk deep into the barren marshes of the north. A foreign city with a foreign name, this tsar-built monument to masculine power stands as a challenge to the maternal soil, facing the Baltic with its back to the motherland.

In the peasant tradition, however, all things are borne by the earth and derive from her fertility. The soil is the great *baba* (woman), the giant Matrioshka who enfolds the historical

Mother Russia. The soil is sacred: The peasants implore "Mother Moist Earth" for aid in their lives. She seems to need no mate. She is self-moistened, self-inseminated. A recent Russian exile, like others before him, nostalgically evoked his land's fertility and the feelings of the peasantry associated with it:

> Far beyond the meadows the forest began. Between them lay the wheat fields of the peasants. They were fat, rich fields soft to the foot, breathing the odor of fruitfulness and sustenance. That odor interpreted the Russian phrase *Matushka Zemlia*, Mother Earth, giving suck from bountiful breasts to countless children. When the peasants spoke of *Matushka Zemlia*, their eyes, usually dull and expressionless, were flooded with love, like the eyes of children who see their mother at a distance.[8]

The unbroken and monotonous countryside of rolling steppes is gentle, enveloping. Nature, wrote the historian of religion G. P. Fedotov, is embracing, and man is "unwilling to master her."[9] She is the good mother; but she is also the destroyer, giving with one hand to take with the other, her bounties unevenly distributed. The land, immensely fertile in the Ukrainian steppes, the cradle of Russian history, resists cultivation in the forested north, where Russian culture anchored itself. The climate there is harsh, and in winter nature seems to devour her own creation. She eats away at the store of the peasants' hard-won grain; she makes the livestock listless; she confines the peasantry to their huts, where they huddle around the earthen *mat' pech'* (mother stove). Then, as suddenly as the first autumn frost, spring comes without warning, and the land is flooded by melting snow: "Mother Spring" arrives in a cascade of flowers and buds, which emerge miraculously from under the frozen ground.[10]

The contours of the land and its seasonal cycles have suggested maternity to intellectuals and city-dwellers, as well as to peasants and country gentry. But their visions of it have differed. For the peasant the earth is home, and as such defines the boundaries of life, labor, and community by binding her children to the round of the seasons. *Matushka Rus'* (Little Mother Russia) is simply the historical name of the land which the peasants perceived as "married" to *Batiushka Tsar'* (Little Father Tsar). Mother Russia in peasant thought contains the succession of historical tsars who ruled from her center. For centuries the peasants said, "Your fatherland is your mother," as though to underscore her all-absorbing nature and to puncture the patriarchal pride of the tsars.[11]

The intellectual, no longer living close to the soil, evokes the maternal land as an idealized Paradise Lost, a longed-for place of communion and collectivity. Mother Earth and Mother Russia both express creative power. The first is associated with a feminine myth believed by the peasantry; the second suggests the accommodation of that religious conception of the soil to the constraints of history. The link between the two "mothers" was explored with intense emotion and anguish by the nineteenth-century Russian intelligentsia. Compelled to define the limits of self-expression against the backdrop of a suffering motherland crushed by autocracy, Russian writers and thinkers assumed the role of the true champions of Mother Russia. She represented for them the image of an all-enveloping Matrioshka, whose children lived within her confines and depended upon their bond with her for function and identity in the spiritual as well as the physical sense. As the fertile earth, she gave birth to folklore, ritual, dance, and song, described as Dionysiac in their emotional range, variety, and abundance.[12] Russia as motherland has been the source and object of much art, literature, and speculative thought. But as the Russia who calls for self-sacrificing champions, she also represents suffering and constraint. Her dual nature as the fount of creativity and its limit assumes metaphysical as well as social and psychological dimensions, raising the question of the proper relationship of the individual to the whole.

The mid-nineteenth-century Slavophile poet F. I. Tiutchev in an often-quoted poem warned his contemporaries that "one cannot understand Russia by reason alone / or measure her by a common yardstick." The yardstick was fashioned in the West, but Russia had a "peculiar nature" in which, lacking the proper perspective for judgment, one must "simply believe."[13] The mystical and nationalistic thrust of this poem reflects the poet's intuition that to grasp the course of Russia's development, one must first come to terms with the prevailing myth or religious disposition that pervades the structure of the state.

Characterizing his country's culture for the West, the twentieth-century Russian philosopher N. Berdiaev argued unequivocably that the "fundamental category in Russia is motherhood."[14] Yet despite considerable evidence to support his contention, no one has explored the nature and sources of the national obsession or sought out the origins and cultural influence of the myth of the feminine divinity from which the motherland derives its very epithet. Tracing the worship of maternity and fertility, my study of Mother Russia will look closely at the bond between the mother, perceived as the land, and her children—peasantry, gentry, intelligentsia, and tsars. Through the prism of this myth, I hope to illuminate many of the beliefs, aspirations, and conflicts which underlie Russian cultural, social, and political life; which give shape to her institutions and historical evolution; and which express the "peculiar" Russian character. Such a project requires investigation of sources often overlooked by historians of Russia. By reading the texts of prehistoric artifacts, archaic myths, folktales, epics, and rituals of the Eastern Slavs and then relating these to the testimony of modern literature, I will demonstrate that together they form a substratum of meaning informing Russian culture as a whole and creating over the centuries a unifying national ethos.[15]

This book is divided into two parts. The first examines the myth of divine maternity, and the second explores the masculine response to it. Part One, "Mothers," uses evidence drawn from archeology, anthropology, and ethnography to recreate the image and suggest the role of the female divinity among the Great Russians, the Ukrainians, and the Belorussians. Part Two, "Mothers' Sons," considers the impact of the myth of Russia and earth as mother upon Russian culture as a whole. Although the institution of the autocracy and the ideologies justifying its existence have fascinated scholars for centuries, less attention has been given to the peasants' conceptions of the maternal land which challenge the despotic and military order of the tsars.[16]

The history of the rise and development of the institution of autocracy does not itself shed light on the psychological impact of its hold upon gentry and peasantry alike. By the nineteenth century, the historical record was amplified by a literary canon. It became the self-imposed task of the Russian intelligentsia to express the distortions of the psyche and the social order created by the empire of tsars. The last section of "Mothers' Sons" focuses on Russia's first literary genius, Alexander Pushkin, who formulated the "problem" which subsequent writers and artists would explore—that of the individual's relationship to the motherland. Re-examining Pushkin's work in the light of the themes of devotion to a sacred maternity or femininity and of opposition to the oppressive hegemony created by the tsars leads us to a new appreciation of the historical, social, and psychological contradictions which the great poet and his successors expressed to their contemporaries. In conclusion, we will see how the "siren call" of the land as mother continued to be heard in the works of writers before and after the 1917 Revolution.

"Mothers" and "Mothers' Sons" reflect on the clash of feminine and masculine mythologies, with their respective origins in agrarian and warrior conceptions of nature. The analysis presented here will point to certain fundamental elements in the relations of men and women played out in the "body politic" as peasant and ruler, Mother Russia and Father Tsar. Finally, this study will begin to reconstruct and explore the impact of a hidden and yet still vital mythology crucial to a deeper understanding of the Russian people—a mythology in which woman plays a central role.

PART ONE

Mothers

CHAPTER ONE

The First Mothers

At every step in studying Russian popular religion one meets the constant longing for a great divine female power. . . . Is it too daring to hypothesize, on the basis of this religious propensity, the scattered elements of the cult of the Great Goddess who once had reigned upon the immense Russian plains?

—G. P. FEDOTOV, *The Russian Religious Mind*[1]

In a well-known Russian folktale called "Go I Know Not Whither, Bring Back I Know Not What," we glimpse a hunters' goddess of creation who has no name and who lives everywhere. She assumes the form of virgin, mother, and old woman and gives to those who know how to approach her, as sons or as bridegrooms, the magical power to create wealth and fertility. Although it refers to a kingdom, the story carries an echo of the world of ancient hunters dominated by feminine power. The hunter-hero is surrounded on all sides by women; his dove-bride confers the kingdom upon him; the good mother of animals and princesses grants him the gift of wealth and authority; the protective wife temporarily holds at bay the evil witch Baba Yaga. In contrast, his master, an unmarried king, is protected only by his men. The king invokes the witch out of greed and in return she brings him destruction. The hunter, surrounded by women and living harmoniously within their laws, is victorious.[2]

This folktale carries forward motifs common in ancient Eurasian mythologies which show a divine force empowering the hunter, hero, or king. In tracing through the surviving artifacts which reflect the presence of this female divinity-first in the hunting and gathering period of the Paleolithic, and then in the Neolithic, when horticulture, farming, and herding developed-we begin to see the broad significance of the complex goddess.

Paleolithic Genesis: The Mistress of Animals

Russia was the cradleland for the female statuettes (called Venuses by archeologists) made by mammoth hunters who roamed the Eurasian steppes during the Ice Age. From Siberia to the Ukraine, archeological sites have yielded a profusion of such figurines, carved with abstract markings-meanders, chevrons, lozenges, and parallel lines-and linked to animals and the hearth fire. Did these Venuses, slender and clothed in animal skins, or naked and corpulent, represent all-powerful goddesses, clan mothers, or amuletic idols?[3] Their significance in the lives of these hunting peoples cannot be incontrovertibly determined. However, in their representations as young girls or mothers, they suggest that female fertility was seen as the essential expression of divinity.[4]

In western Europe, where the cult or use of the figurines was diffused from the East in the later Paleolithic, cave paintings offer a compelling image of the womb of a Great Mother Goddess who creates and nurtures all life.[5] Located beneath clusters of stalactites resembling breasts, images of composite animals, drawn within the form of a bird-headed woman, suggest the flux from which all individuals-animal as well as human-emerge. The cave as the womb of the universal creatrix was most probably a shrine to invoke fertility and the locus for initiation rites into its divine mysteries. Although some shrines are decorated to indicate the outlines of a woman's body so that entry into the cave is analogous to entry into the womb, the Venuses found inside are not specifically sexual in nature; rather, they convey a cult of maternity. Perhaps that is why the carved phalli and the images of animal-masked men, caught in a sacred dance, indicate a notion of engulfment *in utero* rather than an assertion of masculine potency.[6]

Mistress of Animals, mother of humanity, the Ice Age "goddess" also appears to rule the sky and the earth. The twenty-thousand-year-old Venus of Laussel, who carries a moon-shaped animal tusk horn in her hand, anticipates the Greek huntress Artemis, a lunar divinity served by colleges of priestesses.[7] There is indeed evidence to suggest that the oldest form of religious veneration, shamanism, discovered among the Nordic hunting tribes, was once dominated by women. Women are still prototypes and guides in initiation and choose the "elect." Women are seen as the sources of shamanic power among Siberian and other northern peoples who continue to worship a parthenogenetic mistress of all life, mother of fire and ruler over earth and sky.[8]

The link between the Paleolithic *cultus* and the Neolithic religion of a universal genetrix is vividly documented in two sites: the Anatolian Çatal Hüyük and the Balkan-Ukrainian Tripol'e. Dating from 7000 B.C., the settlement of Çatal Hüyük reflects a society in transition from hunting to horticulture, farming, and stockbreeding. Figurines of the steppes as well as stalactites from the caves in the nearby Taurus Mountains appear in numerous house-shrines dedicated to a triune goddess.[9] In her sanctuaries she is depicted as an insect, a butterfly, a bird; or as a whirling figure, spinner of rain, perhaps; or as a pregnant and birth-giving mother; or as a chthonian deity, the vulture goddess surrounded by human and animal skulls. Sometimes the divinity is represented as twin goddesses-a mother-daughter dyad, like the later Demeter and Kore, accompanied by a youth-the future Attis or Tammuz. Consistent with Paleolithic practice, the shrines, decorated with animal heads and horns (often emerging out of breasts as well as wombs), portray the man-hunter as contingent and identified with the beast. With the introduction of agriculture, the domestic bull supplants the wild animal, and the male is sacrificed to placate the female divinity, like the later dying and reviving youth-consorts of the Great Mother Goddesses in Eurasian mythologies. Women are thought to have overseen her cult. They are buried inside the shrines, often together with mirrors, which, in later times, indicated oracular powers.[10]

The divinity so strikingly represented in her diverse manifestations at Çatal Hüyük appears throughout Europe, the Middle East, and Africa in the image of the "Eye Goddess." Between the seventh and the third millennia, her worship was highly developed in the region between the Aegean and the western Ukraine.[11] The artifacts of the culture called Tripol'e (Three Fields) after a site near Kiev, reflect, like the Anatolian settlement, a gradual evolution from hunting to agriculture. In her earliest manifestations, the female deity appears in zoomorphic form. The hunters' goddess who regenerates and transforms all things is revealed through creatures who undergo metamorphosis: frogs, butterflies, deer (who shed their horns), bears (who hibernate), or snakes (who slough their skin and burrow phallically into the earth to emerge umbilically out of it). Earthbound as a serpent, skybound as a bird, the goddess seems to spin all creation out of her earthly womb and nourish it from her heavenly breast.[12]

Painted cultic vessels allow us to reconstruct this Great Goddess and to trace the gradual restriction of her powers from an omnipotent hunters' deity to a sedentary Mother Earth. On early and breast-shaped vessels, she is identified by a double-yolk egg ideogram surrounded by water signs. She is the all-seeing and all-creating Bird and Eye Goddess encircled by snakes (meanders) to delimit the sphere of the birth-giving earth, and by deer-horn crescents to suggest the sky and the growth-stimulating moon. By the third millennium, the abstract representations of the divinity ruling over the three spheres of nature—sometimes indicated by three lines symbolizing sky, earth, and water or underworld—are humanized. She loses her original androgyny, and her powers are circumscribed by masculine figures. Now she is depicted as a woman enclosed between earth and sky. Male figures, each linked to one sphere of nature, appear like newly emerging deities, carved from her body. Their arrival heralds the introduction of plow agriculture and the assertion of masculine power and potency: The bull enters the field; the plowman spills the seeds. In figurine form, the corpulent goddess, decorated with lozenges (ideograms of the female sex organ) into which a dot or a grain is impressed, suggests the planted earth.[13]

However, women continue to be the goddess's chief priestesses, accompanying her in her slow transformation. Female figurines gathered inside miniature house-shrines perform magical rites as grinders of grain and keepers of the hearth. They remain linked to the fertility of the earth, as well as to that of animals and human beings. Associated with spindle whorls, they also may spin out rain. On the Tripol'e cultic vessels, breasts appear to sprout from basins, and jars held high by female figurines are decorated with parallel lines to indicate rainfall.[14]

Around 3500 B.C., the peaceable Tripol'e farming settlements, probably organized into matriclans, were destroyed by Indo-European nomadic herders. These intruders attempted to impose upon the settled populations a patriarchal structure.[15] For them the male was the protector of the herd and its grazing territories and, by extension, the life of the clan itself. From the third to the first millennium, a protracted struggle took place between the farming cultures and the invading herders. The inhabitants of the settlements absorbed the foreign male divinities into the cult of their Mother Goddesses, assimilated, perhaps, to the bull or the horse consorts who served her.

The new gods of the Indo-Europeans only emphasized patriarchal elements already apparent with the advent of plow agriculture. In taking over certain functions of the all-powerful female divinity, they translated them into symbols of physical prowess, thereby challenging the values of the woman-centered family, clan, and agrarian community with those affirming the centrality of the tribe and eventually the state. The gods appear to be terrible in their majesty and aggressiveness. When they fertilize the earth, they do so violently, wounding her with hammers, swords, lightning bolts, or meteorites. Armed warriors assert their power over nature and surround its mistress.[16] But the conflict between the two forms of divinity, feminine and masculine, was a protracted one, never concluded.

Serpent Maidens and Amazons: Scythians and Sarmatians on the Russian Steppes

The cult of the goddess shared by Eurasian Paleolithic and Neolithic peoples and found in the Ukraine at Tripol'e continued to dominate even the patriarchal Scythians who ruled the Russian steppes during the first millennium (700–200 B.C.).[17] A powerful female divinity presided over tribal chieftains or kings, as well as over the priesthood, and legitimized their authority. At the same time, she seems to have "authorized" the gradual transformation of matriclans into patriclans and patriarchal states. She appears in this self-abnegating role in Herodotus's account of the Scythian origin myth, which the sixth-century historian heard from Greek settlers on the Black Sea: Herakles ("Glory of Hera"), herding the cows of King Geryon, stopped to rest at the mouth of the Dnieper River.[18] While he slept, the mares who pulled his chariot were stolen by a monstrous half-serpent maiden who lived in a cave and called herself the Mistress of the Woodland. She promised to release them only if Herakles became her lover. When the hero complied, she asked him whether the three sons whom she would bear should remain in her kingdom or go with their father. Herakles instructed her to raise the boys herself. Upon reaching manhood, they were to be submitted to a test: Whoever managed to bend Herakles' bow and gird himself with his girdle (stolen from the Amazon Queen Hippolyte) would rule his mother's land. Scythes thus became Scythia's first king and the "law of the father" was imposed upon the "land of the mother."[19]

This myth may well refer to a process of social and cultural accommodation between the Scythian invaders and the native population; for the area of south Russia inhabited by the Sauromatians, Meotians, Sindians, and Taurians was dominated by the cult of the Great Goddess, related perhaps to the one worshipped at Tripol'e.[20] In the sixth century, the Greek merchants who colonized the area around the Black Sea assimilated her to their Athena (a goddess linked with both bird and serpent) and Demeter-Kore, the parthenogenetic earth mother. She was also identified with Artemis.[21] The native population, which had absorbed successive waves of invaders and had turned to the Greek merchants for protection, was associated with the man-slaying Amazons, "Moon Maidens," who venerated the huntress goddess. These warrior women, dressed in animal skins, were organized in matriclans and were said to mate once a year and to kill their male offspring.[22] The Sauromatians regarded themselves as direct descendants of the Amazons' intermarriage or accommodation with the Scythian invaders. According to Herodotus, they continued to maintain the customs of their mothers. Archeologists have confirmed Herodotus's observations with the excavation of graves containing armed women and the discovery of temples to a Great Goddess served by armed priestesses.[23] A connection has also been made between the people of the Black Sea region and a culture of farmers and herders, presided over by armed clan mothers, which spread from the Urals to the Ukraine in the sixth century B.C.[24] The mythical conflict between the Greeks, the Scythians, and the Amazons refers, perhaps, to the clash between the ancient matriclans of hunters and horticulturalists and the emergent patriclans of cultures dominated by herding and plow agriculture.

Thus, while the serpentine Woodland Goddess recalls Tripol'e predecessors in the area of the Ukraine, she is attributed the role of the ancestress of the Scythian pastoralists and is made to legitimize authority in their own traditions. She appears as a serpent-tailed maiden amid the stylized animal figurines which the Greeks made for their Scythian customers. The Mistress of the Woodland empowers warriors, like the supreme deity of the Altaic Pazyryks (to whom the Scythians are related), represented as an awesome woman sitting majestically on her throne, holding the Tree of Life, and towering over the horsemen before her. (Illustration 17.) In her chthonian aspect, the Woodland Goddess may also be related to the *kamennye baby*, "stone women," whose rounded Matrioshka-like forms are found over barrows in the territory of Scythian settlement. Engraved with serpent and animal images, they hold a rhyton or horn and are flanked by horsemen.[25]

Herodotus reports that the Scythians worshipped a Great

Goddess called Hestia or Tabiti. This chief divinity was accompanied by a male and female couple, identified with Zeus or Papeus and Earth or Api, his wife. The gods of the second order of importance were associated with Apollo, Celestial Aphrodite, Herakles, and Ares.[26] Just as the Hellenic myth of Scythian origin suggested the accommodation of matriclan to patriclan, so too in the Scythian religious pantheon two views of female power are apparent. The authority of a supreme goddess, Mistress of Animals (to whom the horse was particularly sacred) and clan mother, is limited by a male-female couple who divide up sky and earth. The assertion of masculine power is more pronounced in the grouping of the gods and goddesses of the second order: Celestial Aphrodite is surrounded.

The discordant nature of the Scythian divine hierarchy, with its reversal of male and female hegemony, is apparent in the peculiar form of the Scythian priesthood, as well. Here again we find the arrogation of feminine authority by a masculine band over which the goddess still rules and to whom she gives power. There were, Herodotus reports, many soothsayers, called *Enarees* in Scythia, claiming to have been taught their art by Aphrodite. They wore women's dress, spoke in high-pitched voices, and performed women's work. Before assuming their functions, the initiates into this priesthood—which resembles that of certain Siberian shamans—incurred a "female sickness." Their role was to look after the well-being of the clan and preserve the health of kings and chieftains. They appeared to imitate the functions of clan mothers and priestesses and derived their authority from a feminine source.[27]

The Sarmatians, who replaced the Scythians as rulers of the Russian steppes by the third century B.C., appear to have had stronger ties with matriclan cultures than their predecessors. Some archeologists argue that they represented an eastern branch of the Sauromatians of south Russia, who were linked, as we have seen, to the Amazons.[28] The period of Sarmatian rule (ending in the third century A.D.) left a number of artifacts testifying to the veneration of a Great Goddess who, like the Scythian Hestia-Tabiti or the Woodland Mistress, armed warriors. Carved or incised mirrors suggest the oracular functions of her priestesses, and tripod altars, often decorated with "Scythian" animal designs, were used for sacrifices to her. Mistress of Animals, she is also represented as a Tree of Life (Illustration no. 13); worshipped in forests and groves, she resembles the Ice Age divinities of the hunters.[29]

While representations of the Great Goddess in her all-powerful form continued through the first millennium, her chief functions, encroached upon by the male divinities of the Scythian tribal confederation, were taken over by the gods of the state. This process is apparent among the inhabitants of the Hellenic Bosphoran kingdom in south Russia, with whom the Sarmatians traded.[30] At the end of the first millenium, the Persian Empire had become both an irresistible magnet and a coercive force to the merchants and artisans of the Black Sea cities. "Iranization" coincided with the appearance of the sun god Mithra's image on Bosphoran coins and plaques. The god of kings and military elites rides high in the heavens in his war chariot. Below him stands the figure of the goddess with her arms raised to him (*orante*), as though she were now the suppliant rather than the parthenogenetic deity of her previous manifestations, encompassing her creation. Sometimes she is replaced altogether by Ahura Mazda, the supreme deity of the Iranians, the god of light. By the first century A.D., the god, as supreme judge and oath-taker, accompanies her to administer the rites of communion to her male worshippers. The inhabitants of the Bosphoran kingdom may already have assimilated her to the Iranian goddess of the elite, Anahita, the "Lady of the Lake," the mistress of moisture akin to Aphrodite and Ishtar. She no longer controls creation. Her overlord, Ahura Mazda, the principle of light, had prevailed over the forces of fertility associated with earth and darkness. Although Anahita's archaic powers assure the growth of all things and are invoked by those who seek fame and wealth, her functions are circumscribed.[31]

Among the Slavs who came to dominate the Ukraine and central and north Russia in the course of the first millennium A.D., the denigration of an all-powerful goddess occurred considerably later. In the second and third centuries, the Dacians, associated with Slavic tribes and settled on the lower Danube, depict her worshipped by horsemen and surrounded by celestial spheres, birds, animals, and double-entwined serpents. She rules over the three zones of nature as a Tree of Life goddess flanked by votaries. In the third or fourth centuries, we see, in the region of the Dnieper, the figure of a woman with arms upraised (*orante*) approached by suppliants and with the heads of sacrificed horned animals around her. From the fourth to the sixth centuries in the lower Don, the jewelry of the Antes (another tribe linked to the Slavs) displays the image of the goddess accompanied by horses, birds, and snakes. From around the fifth century she makes her appearance amid the artifacts of a people now identified with the early Slavs. An Eastern Slavic buckle shows her schematized as a lozenge-headed woman. This archaic image of fertility is echoed in a Slavic stone relief depicting a human figure kneeling before a diamond-shaped ideogram of the goddess and accompanied by a deer, its antlers entwined in a tree. By the tenth century she appears in the north of Russia as a vertical stream of diamonds topped by a lozenge shape with horses, deer, bears, and circles or sun disks on either side of her. She is the Tree of Life goddess in the form of a pillar.

Archeologists argue that contact with Sarmatian and Iranian peoples influenced the religious outlook of the Slavic tribes.[32] However, their veneration of a female divinity, schematized to underscore her fertility function and surrounded by animals still associated with hunters, suggests the merging of a preexisting and archaic goddess with the horse or warrior female deity who empowers armed men. The transformation of a goddess, morphologically linked to Ice Age and Tripol'e figurines and ornamental motifs, into a warrior god becomes apparent when we examine the few sources describing the religion of the ancient Slavs.

Water Nymphs and the Mothers Called Fate: The Religion of the Slavs

According to the sixth-century Byzantine historian Procopius, the pagan Slavs worshipped "both river and tree nymphs and some other kind of spirits, and they sacrifice to all these and make their divinations in connection with these sacrifices." They had no temples; in their rituals, in forest groves and by the shores of rivers and lakes, they invoked vampires or werewolves, called Upirs. In all this, the Slavs resembled a number of Germanic tribes described several centuries earlier by the Roman historian Tacitus. Their holy places were groves and woods, he wrote, and they venerated a goddess he likened to the Isis of the Egyptians. Among the tribes in closest proximity to the area later inhabited by the Western Slavs, Tacitus mentions peoples who worshipped the Mother of the Gods and wore as an emblem of the cult the masks of boars, which served them instead of armor.[33]

Forest and river nymphs, werewolves, and boar-masked worshippers all suggest Paleolithic images of hunters in the guise of animals in the cave—womb of the Great Mother. But when we move forward from Procopius's description to the twelfth century, long after the expansion of the Slavs, we find that, much as in the Bosphoran kingdom, the god appears to have arrogated the Great Goddess's powers: His form is superimposed on her traditional image. The Western Slavs now worshipped a warrior and fertility god who was attended by priests and armed men. The new god's temples were located in urban centers or in citadels.

The shrine of Svantovit on the island of Rüngen was a military stronghold dedicated to the pillar god—his shape mirroring that of the Tree of Life goddess found in the north of Russia in the tenth century. Described by the twelfth-century Danish historian Saxo Grammaticus as Janus-like but with four faces rather than two, the sword- and phallic-like idol seems to have replaced the ancient all-seeing Eye Goddess. (His sacred white horse suggests that he usurped her role as the patron of horses, as well.) Since his protective warrior functions were associated with fertility, the walls of his temple were hung with the horns of bulls—reminiscent of the vulture goddess's altar at Çatal Hüyük. However, on one side of a statue of Svantovit discovered in the nineteenth century near the river Zbrucz on the Russo-Gallacian border, he appears in the guise of a goddess with breasts, carrying a rhyton in his right hand, resembling the one held by the Great Goddess depicted on Scythian artifacts or by the *kamennye baby* guarding Scythian barrows. At "his" feet stand a woman and a child; below the woman, a male figure squats with upraised arms. Other faces show male figures, one accompanied by a horse. Underneath each stands a woman alone, without a child. Saxo's description of Svantovit's oracular role emphasizes the incorporation of feminine power into masculine authority. Every year his priests filled the god's horn with mead, so that he might predict the abundance of the year's harvest, and his white horse might foretell the fortunes of war. The male, as bringer of fertility in the annual ceremony, reversed the archaic pattern of Indo-European rites in which a goddess, or a goddess as mare, empowered a king to give wealth to his people. Indeed, the ancient rituals which Saxo describes were still practiced in individual households among the Western Slavs as late as the present century: On the last day of each year, women cooked and baked a huge quantity of food and lit candles before icons in the corner sacred to the ancestors. The family table became an altar. The husband sat behind the *pech'* (oven), while the wife piled so much food on the table that the husband was hidden from view. Then he was asked to predict the next year's harvest.[34]

While the worship of Svantovit and the other polycephalous gods among the Western Slavs was associated with temples, priests, and armed men, there persisted another religious rite more closely related to Procopius's account of the veneration of nymphs. This second religion, clearly more archaic, appears to have had no organized priesthood. It revolved around the goddess called Zhiva (from *zhit'*, "to live") by the Elbe Slavs and was mentioned by the Saxon priest Helmhold in the twelfth century. The ceremonies were performed by the whole community in the depths of the forest and in the places where land and water met. It is thought that, as in later Russian peasant rituals, the women, both young and old, officiated. Among the Western Slavs, the two cults, masculine and feminine, sometimes appeared contiguously, their juxtaposition underscoring the imposition of warrior values over those of feminine fertility, emphasizing the well-being of family and community.[35]

The practice of *dvoeverie* (two faiths), which would characterize later Russian culture, resulted most certainly from the aggressive expansion of the Slavic tribes and reflected the conflict of hierarchically oriented warrior elites with the still-matrifocal clans they were to protect. In the sixth century B.C., Herodotus mentioned tribes by the names of Neuri, Budini, or "Scythian plowmen," whom historians would later identify with the proto-Slavs. In the sixth century A.D., the Gothic historian Jordanes and the Byzantine Procopius referred to them as Venedi and Sclaveni and also identified them with the Antes. By the ninth century, the Slavs had spread into central Europe after occupying much of the territory of the Sarmatians. In the course of their expansion, they appear to have united with Finno-Ugric peoples of the north of Russia, whose customs suggest the veneration of feminine divinities as well as traces of matrilinity.[36]

Scholars believe that the Slavs, like the Scythians and the Sarmatians before them, were of Indo-European stock and had settled north of the Carpathian Mountains and the middle Dnieper. There they had withstood the invasions of the Goths, the Alans, and the Antes from the east. By the sixth century, they in turn asserted their power over the area. The social structure of the Slavs, it is argued, was always patriarchal.[37] There is, however, some compelling evidence to suggest that the confederation of tribes made up of hunters and farmers was not uniformly or indeed predominantly patrilineal and patrilocal but preserved, like the Finno-Ugric peoples, matrilineal customs despite contacts with and conquest by patriarchal cultures.[38]

Descriptions of the Slavs in ecclesiastical chronicles are, not surprisingly, hostile to their pagan practices. The first of these, the twelfth-century *Primary Chronicle* attributed to the monk Nestor, calls the Poliane the most civilized of the pagan Slavs. The name of these founders of Kiev is a word associated with *pole* (field). *Polianitsy* were Amazonian heroines of the Russian epic who rivaled their masculine counterparts in strength and valor. Nestor writes that the Poliane, who worshipped their ancestors in forest groves and by lakes, were highly reverent toward women, showing respect, as in matrilineal custom, for their wives' brothers. Bridegrooms did not seek their brides; instead, the girls were taken to them.[39] All this suggests matrilineal traditions; but the taking of the bride to the groom would seem to indicate a movement toward patrilocal residence.[40] Nonetheless, through the centuries, the structure of the great Russian family, the archaic extended family, has continued to offer evidence of vestiginal matrilineal succession and rights. Unlike those of other Indo-Europeans, the extended family of the ancient Slavs was never headed by a despotic father. The Slavic great family was an egalitarian institution; decisions regarding the repartition of the land, for example, were arrived at by all members. Although men and women served as elders, a role that appears to have been largely administrative and adjudicative, women's possessions were not subject to distribution and could be handed down from mother to daughter.[41]

The most striking evidence, however, for archaic feminine authority in the family and community is in the religious rites of ancient—and modern—Russian peasant women. The word for family in Russia, *sem'ia*, means "seed" as well as the union of the *suprugi*, man and wife. The cult of ancestors, central to the Russian peasant tradition, has from the earliest times been overseen by women. Both in the family and in the village, the peasant woman was, and remained to this century, the chief priestess of all rites of passage. She officiated as well over the seasonal ceremonies linked to the bringing of nature's fertility from field and forest into the community and the family itself. Feminine power seemed to radiate from the domestic hearth fire, the *pech'*. In the flames, tended by women, the ancestral spirits hovered; their goodwill was the source of the family's prosperity.

Scholars describe the religion of the ancient Slavs as animistic, lacking a divine hierarchy characteristic of the cults of ruling elites. Nor was there an organized priesthood. Instead, when Christian missionaries and chroniclers attacked pagan beliefs, they most often attacked the women who appeared to be priestesses officiating over fertility rites practiced in the countryside and in the home.[42] Chroniclers, who confirm Procopius's earlier observations, refer to the river, lake, and forest nymphs as *bereginy* (*bereg* means "shore") and say that they appear to be the most ancient of divinities among the pagans. The *bereginy* represent the most primitive form of the hunting and fertility goddess. And in the descriptions of their habitat, the movement from the hunt to farming is clearly discernible: The name *beregina* means "earth" as well as "shore," the place where land and water meet.[43] Their cult is associated with birch trees, the first to flower in the spring. When these divinities appear in later Russian folklore as *rusalki* or *vily*, living in water, on land, and in trees, they assume the transformational powers of these most archaic goddesses. In folk art they appear as half-women and half-fish, serpent-tailed maidens, or *ptitsy-siriny*, bird maidens associated with the popular fairytale figure of the magical Firebird.[44] In the form of birds they recall manifestations of female fertility in the caves of the Ice Age. They also echo the hybrid goddesses of Tripol'e.

The *bereginy* of the ancient Slavs were "domesticated" as goddesses of fate called *rozhanitsy* and associated with the *rod* (clan or extended family). Sometimes they are identified as one goddess; more often they are seen as multiple, like the Norns of the Germanic peoples, the Moirae of the Greeks, and the Parcae of the Romans—the Fates. According to the Christian chroniclers, these divinities were particularly dangerous because peasant women continued to worship them in secret. Their sacred place was the bathhouse, where fire and water symbolized both purification and generation. The bathhouse was a *bozhena* (from *bog*, "god") or "temple" in Russian folklore, the traditional locus of all prophecy, sorcery, and magical cures. Marriage rituals in the bathhouse were as important as church ceremonies. The bathhouse and the *rozhanitsy* were the center of the cult of the family, and in Kievan and Muscovite Russia, old women were censured by the priesthood most particularly for the special feasts which they prepared in honor of the goddesses of fate who presided over childbirth.[45]

Of the male spirits or deities among the early Slavs, only two names survive: The first is Rod, whom the early Christian chroniclers call the consort of the *rozhanitsy*. This suggests the missionary church's need to provide patriarchal deities for the Slavic family, which was so apparently dominated by female divinities and their priestesses. The "god" Rod may well be the result of a confusion on the chroniclers' part with the word for "ancestors," *roditeli*, drawn from the word for "family" or "clan."[46] There is no further mention in Russian lore of that fabricated divinity. The Upir, on the other hand, described as a vampire or werewolf and connected in folklore with wise women and witches, refers most certainly to a votary or priest of the animal or moon goddess. Werewolves are thought to turn into vampires after their death. Indeed, among the Celts—whose mythology retains strong vestiges of the cult of a Mother Goddess—wolves, vampires, werewolves, swans, and serpent women are all said to issue from a goddess.[47] In Slavic lore, the future vampire is said to be born with a caul over his head. The caul symbolizes the regenerative powers of the serpent skin, which gives the vampire the transformative abilities of the womb. But in order to become a werewolf, the aspirant needs to invoke the moon. Upirs were probably shamans empowered by a *beregina* or *bereginy*, as Mistress of Animals and of the moon. Certainly, the Slavic priesthood in the Varangian period, the *volkhvy*, were etymologically linked with the werewolf and thus with the goddess.[48]

The masculinization of female divinities—seen so strikingly in the idol and cult of Svantovit among the Western Slavs—and the custom of giving them male counterparts or rivals continued through the centuries and is evident in the folklore of the Eastern Slavs: The *leshii* (woodsprite), *vodianoi* (watersprite), *bannik* (bathhouse spirit), and *domovoi* (house spirit) all appear to share and even supplant the role of the *rozhanitsy*, *bereginy*, *vily*, and *rusalki*. Sometimes they are even given families to rule. But their generic names and restricted powers suggest a process of incomplete usurpation.[49] Indeed, the presence of the archaic nymphs first associated with the religion of the early Slavs continues to infuse the folk tradition. So does the name and cult of one particular goddess—Mokosh.

Mother Mokosh and Lord Perun: The Religion of the Varangians

The kingdom of the Varangians, the founders of the Russian state, first established in Novgorod, in the north, moved south to anchor itself in Kiev by the ninth century. The origins of the Varangians are as much at issue as are those of the Slavs. Were they native Slavic warrior-merchant clans who emerged out of the marshes of the north or the steppes of the east to rule over the farming and hunting populations? Or were they Viking merchants and warriors who entered Russia to use her network of rivers to reach the wealth of Byzantium?[50] The Russian *Primary Chronicle* states that the Varangians were called into the land of Kiev by local tribes to end warring in the Ukrainian steppes and to provide protection from the invasions of Turkic peoples who, like their predecessors, the Huns and the Goths, had swept over the area. In 980, shortly before the Christianization of the state, the prince of Kiev, Vladimir, set up an official pantheon which included Iranian and Scandinavian as well as Finnish and Slavic divinities, apparently to provide divine sanction for the Varangian ruling class.[51] The male gods crowded out the only goddess, Mokosh, but her antiquity and popularity with the native population must have obliged Vladimir to include her. In fact, the author of one sixteenth-century text suggests that there existed only three main divinities: Perun, Khors, and Mokosh. Mokosh, he argues, may well have been worshipped long before Perun and long after Vladimir's destruction of the idols.[52] In addition to the deities mentioned by the chronicler, the Varangians acknowledged a group of gods called the Svarevichi, the sons of the sun god, Svarog, son in turn of Dazhbog, elevated to the Vladimir pantheon. Linked with fire and sunlight, the Svarevichi are said to have been of Iranian origin.[53]

The Varangian pantheon united "military" gods with gods of fertility. Yet in looking for the remnants of their cult in folklore, we find that in most cases the peasantry believed these masculine divinities to be goddess-borne or to derive their functions from earlier feminine prototypes. Thus, the god of fire, Svarog, whose features may have been drawn from the Iranian sun and warrior deity Indra, betrays vestiges of his role in the sphere of the mothers.[54] That role is recalled in the folklore of the South Slavs, where he is associated by function with the all-powerful *vily* and shares their ability to turn into an animal or a bird. But the *vily* appeared long before their male companion. They are said to have originally been closely united with human beings, whom they taught to farm and to bury the dead. During this golden age, the earth produced in great abundance. But because of sin giving rise to warfare, humanity became detached from these original mothers, who disappeared, weeping, from the earth and now reappear riding through the forest on stags—an image recalling their roles amid hunting and horticultural peoples. As Fates who predict the future, they may protect like sisters and mothers, or they may tempt and lure men to their deaths—angered, perhaps, at their denigration.[55]

In the myth of the South Slavic peasantry, Svarog appears as a later god to assume the powers of the primordial mothers disaffected by men's actions. But in folklore there remains no trace of Svarog's father, Dazhbog, associated also with fertility and wealth and placed high on the Kievan acropolis to rule over the land as a sun god. Instead, the sun is represented in Finnish and Ukrainian folklore as a beautiful maiden or a woman described as "red" ("red" and "beautiful" are drawn from the same root, *kras*) and addressed as *rodnaia matushka* (birth mother).[56] And when the sun is masculine in Slavic folklore, it is a *son* god, accompanied, like the Svarog of the South Slavs, by maidens or mothers. Among the Western Slavs, the mother of the sun, *Matushka Krasnogo Solntsa* (Mother of the Red Sun), contains him. In Great Russian folklore, the sun is sometimes seen to ride through the skies on his horse (like Mithra on Sarmatian and Bosphoran coins), but at dusk he returns as an old man to a maternal earth, from which he rises again as a child in the morning. His attendants are women. The Morning Star (Zorya or Zarya) gives him birth; and the Evening Star takes him to his death. Sometimes the women are seen as three Fates or sisters who guard the sun's abode and the whole universe like mothers defending their child's cradle.[57]

Perhaps the most archaic of the Varangian gods of Iranian origin is the bird-dog Simargl (or Senmurv or Simurg), who is often mentioned with the goddess Mokosh.[58] The protector of the home and the family, Simargl in his hybrid nature reflects the ancient depiction of the Mistress of Animals found in many cultures. He has been linked to the Sumerian goddess Ishtar before she became anthropomorphized, when she still appeared in the shape of a bird, a fish, or a tree. Indeed, in the folklore of the Ukraine, this creature sits upon a tree on an island guarded by a fish; among the tenth-century Slavs, he appears on women's jewelry, together with the *bereginy* or flanking a Tree of Life. In Russian folk art, the dog and bird, who have female heads, are sometimes associated with the Tree of Life and are often carved on spindles and earrings or are painted on ceramic bowls—women's objects.[59] On nineteenth-century ceremonial towels, the bird-woman is called the *ptitsa-sirin* and is surrounded by all manner of vegetation and animal life. Simargl is also connected with the Firebird—a female bird who helps heroes, like the Senmurv of Persian myth. The Firebird is variously represented as a beautiful maiden, the mother of all birds, the sun, and the hearth fire.[60]

Chief of the Varangian pantheon is a god, Perun, whose name stands for violence and battle. Through war, he appears to "fertilize" the land and to bring riches. Perun is the patron of the ruling princes of Kiev, linked to the Scandinavian warlike Thor, warrior god and king of all creation.[61] He stands at the center; his symbol is the oak tree, thought to attract lightning. Perun, like Zeus, "inseminates" the earth in the violent passion of the thunderstorm, but his tree may also indicate another form of passion: the death of the year or fertility god. The Norse Tree of Life, Yggdrasill, upon which Thor (Perun's prototype) once hanged, is guarded by the Fates, the mothers who sit at its roots and determine the births and deaths of gods and mortals. In Russian folklore this motif is repeated in riddles and charms about certain magical oak trees associated with the cross upon which the Christian Dying and Reviving God was crucified.[62]

Perun, the oak god, resembles the reborn vegetation divinity, and even if his power to induce fertility with the thunderbolt suggests the reversal of an archaic agrarian and dependent role vis-à-vis an earth mother, there is something of the (sacrificial) bull in the warrior Perun. Like the Persian cloud Parajana in the *Rig Veda*, he is envisioned as a bellowing bull who impregnates the earth with rain after "violating" it with his thunder hammer or axe. He is like the ox who pulls the "earth-opening" plow, and for that fertilizing function the Russian and Slavic peasants remember him under the Christian name of Elias the rainmaker. Among the South Slavs, his sacred marriage with the earth was reenacted by a young virgin adorned with flowers whirling ecstatically in a ring of women who "watered her" as she danced. Invoking the rain to moisten and fructify the soil, she bore the name of Perun himself.[63]

Perun, however, contends with another Varangian deity, Volos or Veles, who was particularly venerated by merchants. Volos is the god of cattle and the giver of wealth, who appears both as a youth and as an old man. He is a divinity of the underworld, also associated with Priapic cults. Indeed, his worship shows a closeness to peasant beliefs in earth's productivity in opposition to princely power expressed through the sky god, Perun, who rules from on high. Volos is linked to Artemis as her consort, and of all the Varangian gods he stands closest to the goddess Mokosh, the patron of horses. He is remembered in Russian folklore in the figure of Saint Nicholas, who shares many of the functions of Mary, the Mother of God.[64]

The Vladimir pantheon thus reveals male divinities whose powers refer to the fertility of the land and whose origins are traceable to archaic feminine ones. Only one goddess, however, is permitted into this masculine band: Mokosh. She is now only a goddess of women, but there is evidence to suggest an adversarial role in regard to Perun and other male Varangian divinities. Her cult continued among Russian women to the present century. It resisted the imprecations of the Christian missionaries who thundered in their sermons and chronicles against the old women who sacrificed to Mokosh, the *rozhanitsy*, and the *vily*, as well as to the bird of Simargl.[65]

Mokosh may originally have been the goddess of Finno-Ugric tribes, linked perhaps to the *kamennye baby* of the first millennium as a clan mother. Finnish tribes still have a divinity called Moksha, related functionally to the Vogul Golden *Baba*, who holds a child in her arms and is called the "Giver of Life." Was the hollow goddess whom the Ugrians worshipped in the forests the original Matrioshka, a manifestation of Mokosh herself?[66] The thirteenth-century *Novgorod Chronicle* mentions a Golden *Baba* to whom Finns and Ugrians sacrificed in the city of Perm. Among the northwestern Siberians, the Vostiaks, there is a silver image of the goddess much like the Golden *Baba* who is said to be the guardian of animals and the source of earth's fertility. Both the Finnish Vostiaks and the Vogul peoples have a myth of the goddess's denigration which suggests the origin of Mokosh's conflict with the Varangian gods. She was, they say, thrown down to earth from her heavenly home by male divinities. Like Mokosh herself, she is thought to visit women in their houses to help them when they honor her.[67]

Despite her Finnish-sounding name, some scholars regard Mokosh as an autochthonous goddess of the Poliane and of other tribes who settled in the region of Kiev. If she was originally a northern divinity, her functions may simply have been assimilated to those of native female deities in south Russia. Whatever her origins, Mokosh left a mark on all of Russia. Villages are named after her; her name, which appears related to the word for "moist" (*mokryi*), may have been adapted to the cult of the Russian Mother Moist Earth. In her behavior as a wanderer and a spinner, she resembles the Christian divinities Mary and Paraskeva. But her cult is most marked in the north. In Novgorod she is remembered as the goddess with a great head, identified with the spindle. She spins flax and wool, and women bring her ceremonial towels embroidered with the image of a goddess surrounded by her whole living creation.[68]

Mokosh possesses all aspects of the Mother Goddess. She is "moist," as if to suggest her oneness with the waters of the skies and the earth; she roams the land, as did Demeter, to fructify the soil; she is a spinner like the Fates, linked with the generation and maintenance of life; she is the goddess of women, of childbirth, and of animals. The horse, symbol of the warrior's might, is sacred to her. She seems to have no consort. Yet all her powers have been denigrated in the divine pantheon of the Kievan princes. Perhaps she was associated from the very start with the peasantry's worship of Mother Moist Earth, whose epithet reflects the name of the goddess.

Not surprisingly, there is little information about Mother Moist Earth in the clerical documents of the early centuries of Varangian rule. Throughout the Middle Ages, missionaries fought against the veneration of the soil. But despite the church's attempts to assimilate the worship of earth to that of Mary, the fusion was never accepted by the peasants. In the fourteenth century, Gregory of Smolensk, an ecclesiastical chronicler, boasted of hearing stories about the earth complaining that her children had been lost to the Mother of God. However, until the last century, a popular proverb suggested the failure of the Christian missionaries to make that identification complete and thereby "erase" the pagan cult: "Your first mother is Mary; your second mother is the earth; and your third mother is your own mother."[69]

The earth, regarded as a maternal body creating and nourishing her children, was perceived by Slavs and Varangians alike as the source of political authority, as well as fertility. The Varangian rulers were required to accept the religion of the earth and the cult of ancestors dwelling in it in order to legitimize their power over her "children." Like the Scythian and Sarmatian kings or heroes represented on plaques and ornaments taking oaths or paying tribute to a Great Goddess, Varangian princes passed down authority from father to son through pledges to the maternal earth and the recognition of their family (*rod*) filiation with or birth from the soil.[70]

In accepting the cult of the female divinity of the populace they ruled, the Varangians may also have been obliged to adopt the Slavic and Finnish priestly caste which appeared in the north of Russia at the courts of the princes.[71] The *volkhvy*—whose name associates them with wolves and werewolves and Upirs, epigones of the Mistress of Animals—assumed the powers of seers and predicters of the harvest, like the priests of Svantovit among the Western Slavs. They appear to have mediated between the functions of defense and fertility, between rulers and peasantry, a role which seems to have placed them in conflict with women and which reveals their closer allegiance to the warrior and ruling classes. An eleventh-century clerical account dealing with the rites of the *volkhvy* makes this quite clear and suggests that the relationship of ruler to ruled, man to woman's fertility, soldier to farmer, was one of violent struggle: After a failed harvest in 1070, the rulers of the town of Rostov-Suzdal called the *volkhvy* to help them find the source of the disaster in which the earth refused to yield her wealth. The *volkhvy* summoned the most distinguished women of the city and blamed them for the crop failure, as well as for the scarcity of honey and game. When all the women had been brought, the *volkhvy* went among them, stabbing each one in the back and drawing from them meat and fish and other produce. "Thus they killed many women and appropriated their property," concludes the chronicler.[72]

The act of taking food in the form of murder and symbolic rape may also be linked to the use of the plow, which "cuts" the earth before it is sowed. But it has other implications. Quite possibly the "distinguished women" of Rostov-Suzdal were the priestesses of a domestic fertility cult; the shaman-priests may have been engaged in the conflict over the management of that fertility. The *volkhvy* serve the princes; in their conquest over the women, they make explicit the rapine which appears to unite rulers and ruled. Woman is "killed" as the earth is subdued and the peasantry made to serve the state. At the same time, it is clear that women are seen to control the productivity of the earth and animal life, a control which the *volkhvy* wish to take from them.[73]

The battling between two priesthoods is obliquely demonstrated in a legend about the death of Prince Oleg, successor to the first Varangian ruler, Riurik.[74] The writer of the eleventh-century *Primary Chronicle* describes Oleg as a sorcerer and seer, a *volkhv* who identified himself with the foreign ruling elite. In the legend he was told by magicians that he would die through the intermediary of a horse. Wishing to prove them wrong, he refused to mount his favorite steed. When it died, he made fun of the seers who had been mistaken, but he was then killed by a serpent emerging out of the skull of the animal.

We know little about the magicians who predicted Oleg's death. They are referred to as "baggage" in the eleventh-century chronicle, a term used most often to abuse old women, *baby*, who worshipped their domestic divinities. These magicians may have been priestesses challenged by the *volkhv* Oleg and his Varangian allies, a supposition made plausible by the existence of similar legends among the Norse and the English in which a man dies as a result of scorning a woman.[75] In the Norse account, the hero Oddr belittles the power of a seeress. In England, a knight is cursed by a witch when he taunts her for her prediction, and perishes when a snake darts out of the bones of the horse. The Danes associate horse and snake with the goddess of death, Hel or Hela, who rides a horse, a nightmare, and whose appearance is prophetic.[76]

The goddess and her priestesses could be eliminated neither by the pagan *volkhvy*, nor by the Varangian rulers, nor by the

Christian priesthood which began to serve them by the eleventh century. Instead, her generative force, associated with land and human fertility and underlying all wealth and political power, was appropriated by the male ruling elite. It was masculinized and entrapped: Mokosh was surrounded; the *volkhvy* encircled the recalcitrant women.[77] Consequently, the religion of the mothers moved underground, into the home or as secret rites at rivers and in groves, fields, and gardens. The cult of the Mother Goddess in her various forms and functions was carried into the religious folk tradition of the peasantry.

CHAPTER TWO

Reconstructing the Russian Great Goddess:
Rusalki and Baba Yaga

> She looked at him and shook her hair,
> Threw kisses, laughed
> And like a child,
> Cried to the monk: "Come to me here. . . ."
>
> —A. PUSHKIN, *Rusalka*[1]

In the north of Russian during the winter Koliada festival, a folksong is sung about a girl who sits inside a white tent in a meadow embroidering a napkin as she awaits her future husband:

> And the first thing she embroidered was the moon,
> The shining moon and then the stars.
> Then she made the beautiful sun,
> The beautiful sun and the warmed clouds.
> And after them the wet pine trees in the forest,
> The wet pines in the forest with wild animals around them,
> And then the shining sea with its waves. . . .[2]

The girl of the song creates all nature like a goddess; then she populates it, becoming fertile by embroidering herself a husband, who comes to seek her in the ship. The napkin which she sews in her "temple" in the meadow is like those offered by peasant girls in northern Russia to an all-encompassing female divinity, whose features are found in the folklore figures of the *rusalka*, the witch Baba Yaga, and Mother Moist Earth. The goddess of the embroideries is triune, her image and functions expressing the unfolding of feminine life as virgin, mother, and wise old woman. Their ages correspond to the cycle of the seasons: spring, summer, winter. Each aspect contains all the others; together they display a metaphysic in which human existence is spun out of the context of a creativity associated with a feminine cosmic order.

Nineteenth-century embroideries from the north of Russia bring together a rich store of images and motifs, out of which we can begin to reconstruct the figure of a Great Goddess in her many incarnations and begin to understand the role of women in her cult. Her image appears in both naturalistic detail and abstract designs upon sacerdotal towels spun and embroidered by peasant women for specific cultic purposes. At weddings these napkins adorned the head of the bride to invoke her fertility; in death they were placed around the bones of the exhumed ancestors to implore their aid. In springtime, girls decorated early-flowering trees—the birch, preeminently—with ritual towels to invoke the productivity of nature; in the house, the embroidered image of the goddess covered the loaf of bread placed upon the domestic altar for the ancestors.[3]

The embroidery goddess is the patron of woman as spinner. In folk belief, spinning is associated with birth-giving and nurture. It provides the visible basis for a cosmology suggesting the continuous creativity of the divinity spinning all living things out of her own body. The religious symbolism of the spun and embroidered votive towels was learned by heart by peasant women, who passed their knowledge to each other as they worked.[4] Spinning and sewing, sowing and dancing, they performed the functions of teachers and priestesses in a domestic and ancient cult. Like their Paleolithic and Neolithic predecessors, they worshipped and safeguarded the image of the goddess to ensure the well-being of family and community and linked their own work to a symbolic stimulation of human and natural fertility.[5]

The representation of the embroidered female divinity remains constant in its general outlines. Whether in naturalistic or abstract form, she stands at the center of a cultic scene, with her hands raised, *orante*. Her receptive figure forms the outline of the womb of earth and the breast of heaven. Above her head swirl the celestial spheres; below her feet lie plants and reptiles. In her upraised hands, she sometimes holds a chalice; often she carries flowers, birds, and the moon and sun disks as though she had just created them. The heavens and the earth both seem to frame her body and to emanate from it. As the mistress of the social order, she is flanked by horsemen or male and female votaries. Sometimes she is shown holding the horses' reins, which appear "umbilically" attached to her hands. Often she reveals herself as the carrier of male sexual organs. Male potency is accorded only through her graces. In some embroideries, she stands in a house-temple with horsemen flanking the Tree of Life at her feet, or she presides over an altar upon which rests the head of a bull while two stags frame her divine figure. Even in the nineteenth-century images, she remains the mistress of hunters and warriors, who implore her blessing.

Clearly, the peasant women who evoke the goddess deny the hegemony of their male masters and political rulers and declare the subordination of the social order to the feminine cosmic one.[6] This stress upon feminine power is even more pronounced in the abstract and geometric figuration of the goddess, which emphasized her fertility and her centricity in family and community life. The goddess of the raised arms surrounded by horsemen, animals, plants, and stars is found in central Russia in her naturalistic form. In the north, on the other hand, her shape is abstracted into meanders, lozenges, squares, and circles. As the central divinity, flanked by her worshippers and presiding over the whole universe, she is depicted in these embroideries of the north as a column of lozenges or a column topped by a lozenge face representing the female sex organ.[7] The goddess as column is also the goddess as the Tree of Life, represented with a human face amid the foliage or as a three-pronged flower, each prong with a feminine face. The tripartite schema which characterizes her is used also to reveal her presence in everyday life. She is the samovar flanked by drinkers below and above her; she is the boyarina surrounded on three sides by her guests.[8]

The figure of the goddess in the embroidery of Russian peasant women recalls, as we have seen, that of Scythian, Sarmatian, Dacian, Antes, and early Slavic art. When she emerges in the north in the tenth century, her image combines the attributes of a hunters' and horticulturalists' deity with that of a farming and warrior culture: She has been abstracted and surrounded by deer as well as horses.[9] Transformed into a totemic pillar, the diamond shapes which are her ideogram now appear to symbolize not only the female sex organ but also the sun. Sometimes she is shown as a bear. But in the bronze idols unearthed from the tenth-century grave of Kostroma, we find a striking synthesis of southern and northern forms: A goddess stands inside a temple. She is encircled by horses who contain diamond shapes; on their backs stand human figures with their arms raised to the sky. Inside the temple, the image of the goddess is that of a diamond-headed column.[10] One Soviet archeologist, B. A. Rybakov, writes of this "tsaritsa of all creation" (who remains nameless): From the seventh to the tenth century, temples were erected for her, and horsemen rode to her with their weapons as offerings. Everything blossomed and grew around her. Animals and birds flocked to her side, and out of her body grew the flowering Tree of Life. She was surrounded by sun symbols. The sun disk was in her head, and sometimes she was represented by it alone. Rybakov likens her to the West Slavic goddess Zhiva, and links her in her earliest form with the *bereginy*.[11]

The embroidery goddess is without name, but her image combines all the archaic forms of female divinity. In her abstracted form, she symbolizes the creative forces that move all nature into activity. The ancient figure of the hybrid divine woman who can transform herself into every living thing and penetrate all spheres of the cosmos is found in the tripartite division of her epiphany represented on the embroidered ritual towels; these are offered to her under her first known name among the Slavs— that of the water and tree nymph, *beregina* and, later, *rusalka*.[12]

In reconstruction the figure of the Russian Great Goddess as the *rusalka*, the witch Baba Yaga, and Mother Earth, we will follow her through each of her traditional and ancient roles: She is the Mistress of Animals; the clan mother of the hearth, the source and center of the social group; the ruler of earth, of water, and of vegetation, expressed as the Tree of Life; the queen of the underworld and of the heavens with all their spheres; and the controller of the weather. In each of her functions, woman is her priestess.

Rusalka, Vila, and *Sirin:*
The Great Goddess as Virgin

The *rusalka* in Russian lore is a maiden; she is a spinner who regulates human and animal fertility, the cycle of the seasons, the moon, and the weather. In her image as *sirin* (siren), she appears to reaffirm and to retain over time the powers of the Scythian snake goddess and Mistress of the Woodland.[13] While by the nineteenth century the epiphany of the Great Mother Goddess was principally to be found on embroidered votive napkins, the *sirin*'s form, from the eleventh century to the present, decorated objects made of wood, stone, and metal. Amuletic, she seems to lend her protective powers to the spindle, to the walls of houses, to doorways and locks, as well as to the clothing and adornment of the inhabitants of the *izba* (house).[14] In this she represents the magic of the *rusalka* in everyday life. Indeed, the *rusalka's* activity as a spinner makes her the guardian of the well-being of the whole community, like the peasant women, who were once thought to assume her role when they spun and embroidered votive napkins. In ancient times, the ritual of spinning was performed in a woven tent in a field—as in the ballad which introduces this chapter. The thread spun in the tent was to surround the courtyard and meadow, protecting its inhabitants from sickness and bringing abundance from the field into the village.[15] The *rusalka-sirin* in her most ancient form as a multiple divinity appears to embody the fertilizing powers of the Paleolithic clan mothers.

Sometimes shown alone as a lovely maiden, more frequently the *rusalka* is one of a group of girls; in folktales, she is one of the many daughters of a sea or bird king. Her mysterious and underworld nature was feared, and wherever she revealed herself, in forest groves or by the water, she was not to be angered or disturbed. Accounts of her appearances are legion. Typical is that of a peasant from Saratov on the Volga who told of going at night into the forest where it was known that a *rusalka* lived. Walking toward a pond in the middle of a grove, he suddenly saw the water stir, swirl, and move as though someone were bathing. Coming closer, he was astonished by the sudden emergence of a beautiful girl, who went to the edge of the pool, sat down and began to comb her long hair in the moonlight. When the moon went behind a cloud, she called to it: "Moon shine, shine moon," and it obeyed her wishes.[16] The peasant telling the story of his encounter saw himself in mortal danger, for the nymphs were thought to drown all who ventured into their territory.

Sometimes, particularly in the area of the Ukraine, the *rusalki* were thought to perch in trees. In spring when the sap rose, they would move into the branches, where they combed their hair and wove linen garments, which they washed and dried on the boughs. They called to the village girls for gifts; in response, young women greeted these bringers of fertility by decorating birches with ribbons and votive towels. But when the *rusalki* sang and called to men, luring them into their midst, the sacrificial nature of these divine nymphs became apparent. The unwary male who listened to their songs or was led by curiosity to spy on them would, like the young hunter Actaeon who happened upon Artemis and her nymphs while they were bathing, be destroyed.

The *rusalki* lived without men. In the Ukraine they were linked primarily with water; in Belorussia, with forest and field.

In fertile areas, they were imagined as beautiful naked maidens. In Great Russia, where the land is harsher, they appeared as large-breasted Amazons. In the north, they were hideous and hairy. Their names, too, differed in each region. They were called *mavki, navki, faraony,* and *vodianiani.*[17] As *rusalki* they gave their name to rivers. Scholars associate them with the ancient pagan spring holiday of the Rusalia, linked to the Roman Rosalia, or feast of the roses, when Adonis, the young lover of Cybele, was sacrificed to her and mourned by maidens.[18]

These mistresses of the natural order performed many functions. Among the southern Slavs, where they were called *vily,* they controlled the weather, lured the unwary to their realm by lighting midnight fires, transformed themselves into swans, geese, or ducks, or assumed the form of "fish" women like the *siriny;* they were also portrayed as huntress and warrior maidens and were linked to Artemis.[19] Like the Greek goddesses, they helped and hindered heroes of South Slavic lore. Guardians of life-giving waters like the *rusalki* and the *rozhanitsy,* they were goddesses of fate who were also patrons of warriors. Akin to the German Valkyries or swan maidens, who chose the dead in battle and wove the web of war made of men's guts through which a shuttle of arrows passed, the *vily* and *rusalki* were also related to the destructive half-fish, half-woman German Lorelei, who lured men to her watery home, as well as to the French Ondine, the Celtic Melusina, the Greek Sirens and Harpies, and the Scandinavian Volsi.[20]

Every incarnation of the water nymphs suggests the archaic image of the bird-headed transformational goddess who accompanies humanity from the period of the hunt to that of horticulture, herding—and warfare.[21] She is the goddess who creates parthenogenetically by bringing moisture to the earth from below and above, unaided by male consorts. She is one yet multiple, chooses her mate like the shamanic Mistress of Animals, and confers power (military or otherwise) on the male, whom, like the Great Goddesses of the Neolithic, she then destroys. She is virginal like Artemis, and yet the giver of life and death.

This goddess appears to have been served among the early Slavs, as among other peoples, by a feminine priesthood. Artifacts from the twelfth and thirteenth centuries found around Kiev show that the Slavic *bereginy,* like the Russian *rusalki,* were emulated in their moisture-making functions by young girls, whirling in long-sleeved blouses (like the goddess at Çatal Hüyük), who played the part of rainmakers, bringers of fertility.[22] The very name for "girl" in Russian, *deva,* suggests linguistic ties with Indian and Persian religious and mythological figures of feminine divinity. The Indian virgin goddess Devi (whose name means simply "goddess"), accompanied by her maidens, was originally the preeminent ruler of the religious pantheon.[23] *Div* or *deva* in Sanskrit means "light" and "pure"; among the Russians, *deva*, the girl, is evoked together with the sun by the epithet *krasnyi*, meaning "red" or "beautiful." But among the patriarchal Persians, the once heavenly maidens called *devi* who proliferated on earth were banned to hell and pestered humanity from this underground abode.[24] Indeed, the Russian Alkonost', the half-woman and half-bird of folktale, a *sirin-rusalka* who torments the damned, may have her origin in the Persian myth. The *rusalki*, however, continued to exercise hegemony over the natural order and showed their vindictiveness against the human race, like the underground *devi*, by withholding their life-giving functions and stressing their destructive powers when their worship was disregarded.[25]

The *vily*, like the *rusalki*, no longer living in the community, could be brought back into it only by their priestesses, the peasant girls. Their defiant isolation informed the widespread belief among the Russian peasantry that the *rusalki* were the souls of girls who had drowned themselves because of desertion by a lover or rejection by a parent. Perhaps the anger of the *rusalki* in Russian folk belief, which in its expression indicates the vindictiveness of the dead improperly venerated by the living, more specifically reflected the suppressed fury of peasant women whose lives and cults were treated with rough disrespect by men, who were nonetheless fearful of their magic. The denigration of feminine power may therefore account for the stress upon the death-dealing function of the *rusalki*—as well as that of their European and Asian sisters, whose vengeance most often falls upon male victims. Indeed, the *vily, rusalki, mavki*, and *faraony* of Russian lore are good to those who respect them, giving them health and wealth; evil comes only to those who ignore their power.[26]

As a consequence, the most apparent role of the *rusalka* is that of the mistress of the underworld who lures the living to her realm and punishes them by inflicting premature death on those who scorn her powers. The ancient feast of the Radunitsa, which commemorates the dead, was dedicated to the *rusalki* and concerned the destructive aspects of rebirth and fertility, which the spring festival, the Rusalia, attempted to overcome. Just as the Rusalia was a feast of women and girls, so too was the Radunitsa; and just as the *rusalki* were identified with the girls bringing fertility from forest to village in the spring, so too were the female ancestors associated with these divinities who lured the individual out of the community and into the chthonian depths of forest—and grave.[27]

The land of the dead in Russian lore has feminine names or associations: Rai, Nava, Peklo. Rai is the place where the sun sets and rises and where the spirits of the dead and those who will receive life dwell. It is also the abode of the horrible bird-woman Alkonost', whose song tortures evil souls and gives them no rest. Nava refers to the ocean traversed by the dead and bears another name for the *rusalki, navki*. Peklo is associated with the *pech'*, mother *pech'* or stove, and suggests the warmth of home and the mother rather than the torments of a Christian hell from whose mythology it derives. But the *rusalki* as souls and mistresses of the dead, the alembic through which death is transformed into life, were more closely linked with water than with the all-consuming fire. Controlling the waters of life and death, they gave wisdom to those who drank from their fount.[28]

Just as the sap rises in the spring, when, according to peasant belief, the *rusalki* rose from their winter watery and gravelike dwellings to the trees, and then in early summer danced into the fields covering all in greenery, so analogously the existence of the living community was nourished by the goodwill of the dead borne by and reborn through these mistresses of life and death. The image of the *rusalki* as the maternal womb which takes back human, animal, and plant life to confound it in the waters of death in order to create anew, through the uterine waters of life, refers to the Slavic belief in the transmigration of souls. Strikingly reminiscent of the faith of northern hunters is the so-called animism of the ancient Slavs, retained to the present day by the Russian peasantry. According to this creed, the animal dead assume human form, and inversely, people can take the form of animals. A Russian peasant declares that "a body may be inhabited by a soul; it can be a wolf, a snake, or a bear."[29] But it is an animism dominated by the divine mothers. It can have no hierarchical religious forms, for its overriding mythos is that of the constant transformation of all life, envisioned as an endless round of births, deaths, and rebirths through the maternal body of nature. And indeed, in their hybrid form, the *rusalki* as spirits of the original clan mother or first ancestress who dwell in the trees bringing the waters of life and death are also regarded as Mistresses of Animals.

As we have seen, the *rusalka*, like her ancient Slavic predecessor, the *beregina*, assumed in folk art the form of the half-woman and half-bird or fish-*sirin*. The *sirin* herself was often depicted holding a branch, and sometimes accompanied by a horse or a lion who looked up to her. Tenth-century Slavic jewelry showed her as a dragon or lion-tailed creature with the wings of a bird. In short, she was confounded with her creation. The *rusalki*, *mavki*, *vily*, *bereginy*, and *siriny* were identified with specific animals—the "sun" lion, the deer, the horse, as well as birds, fish, and snakes. In popular imagination, the hair of the nymphs was a Medusa-like tangle of serpents; in combing it out, the water snakes were "milked" for their rain. The deer of the hunters was symbolically tied to the snake: The shedding of the horns of the deer and of the serpent's skin as an act of rebirth and renewal testified to the ever-generative nature of the *rusalki* themselves. Indeed, in Bulgarian lore, the *vila* rides a deer with a snake as her bridle. While the linkage of wild animal to snake suggests the archaic divinities' transformation from hunting to horticultural goddesses whose serpent-hair brings rain and rebirth, the patronage of the horse by the *rusalki* and their namesakes shows their integration into the herding and warrior cults. Among the Altaic herders, the horse was sometimes masked ritually as a deer to indicate that it had replaced the wild animal in the economy of these hunters; among the Scythians, the bones of horses and deer were intermingled as though to make apparent that changed relationship. And among the Russians, the head of a horse placed atop the roof of the *izba* is thought to have replaced the antlers of a deer.[30]

The *rusalki* and *vily*, mistresses of the horse like the Greek goddesses Artemis, Athena, and the horse-headed Demeter, could turn themselves into any animal, bird, or reptile. Most frequently they changed into horses or were accompanied by them. In fact, during the feast of the Rusalia in many parts of Russia, the effigy of the *rusalka* was followed by that of a horse, and peasants claimed to have seen fish-tailed nymphs riding on horseback through forest and field. The association with the horse clearly identifies the *rusalka* with the goddess of the embroideries and her predecessors and suggests the rule of the female divinity over the male sphere. Indeed, those who disrespected the *rusalka* suffered the loss of their horses and livestock, with whom the Russian male peasant linked his own "potency" in village and field. The tiny *konik* (horsehead) crowning the roof of the *izba* emerged out of a rhombus shape, the symbol of the female, whose body was assimilable to the house.[31] The male *konik* therefore appeared as though thrust out of a house—a womb built of logs. The peasant house was a treehouse. The image of its patroness as *sirin* decorated its walls, windows, or doors. She was the guardian of horses, but she was also the mistress of the Tree of Life. The tree was the analogue of the *rusalka* as it was that of the embroidery goddess: When girls went to the forest to seek out the wood nymph, they decorated and sacrificed the birch tree and addressed her as *rusalka*.

The tree protected the animal. Its function as a symbol of female divinity and generation appeared to bridge the transitions between hunting, gathering, horticultural, farming, and herding economies. In Russia the veneration of the birch tree, the most holy of trees, the first to flower in the spring, is still widespread. It has penetrated the rites of the Soviet state. Scholars contend that it was once totemic in the hunting and horticultural communities of the ancient Slavs. It surely bound together the feminine population in what appeared once to be matrilocal and matrilineal associations. Clear traces of this female bonding as the basis of all community life can be found in the Rusalia and Semik rituals of spring and early summer performed by peasant women in the forests. Through the worship of the *rusalka* as tree and water goddess, the women secured the well-being and productivity of the village and its fields.[32]

The tree sheltered the animals, and the human collectivity was united under its aegis. But through the *rusalki*, the birch was also the locus for the coming together of the living and the dead, the communion of animal, plant, and human life. The *sirin* often stares out at the world from a thicket of plants and trees, like the Paleolithic images of the bird-headed women who are barely distinguishable from the animal forms imprinted on their bodies. The tree, however, is the umbilicus symbolically uniting all life, seen and unseen, dead and living. Its roots, invisible beneath the ground, thrust the trunk and foliage upward to the skies like the phallus emerging out of the womb of the earth nourished by underground sources and suggesting the interconnectedness of the three spheres of nature: the subterranean, the earthly, and the heavenly. The seasonal death and rebirth of the tree appear as stark reminders of individual mortality and the immortal recreative power of nature. As the Norse tree Yggdrasill was ruled by the three Fates, the Norns who watered its roots, so too the Russian birch had an oracular nature.[33] The *rusalki* who sat on its branches and watered it were, like the Fates, spinners; they decided who died and who would be reborn, who prospered and who perished, who married and who would be barren. The tree was the spindle out of which they spun out human life. Just as they united the living with the dead, so too they raised the water from the ground into the skies, making rain.

The *rusalki* were rulers of the skies, as well as the earth and its inhabitants. Rain, called "milk from heaven," and clouds, perceived as cows or breasts by the Indo-Europeans, were directed by the *rusalki*, who rode upon clouds in the form of birds. If, however, out of anger at their worshippers they were too assiduous in combing their hair to make rain, they caused floods.[34] they also produced winds and controlled the phases of the moon, like Artemis. In the Ukraine they may have been linked to the moon maidens, the *poludnitsy*, who directed the rays of the sun to ensure the fertility of the fields. Reminders of the archaic solar identity of the *rusalki* can be found in the woodcarving of the north, where the *sirin* is shown with a horse and a great-maned lion, epigones of the sun who appear to emerge from her hybrid body. The link of the *rusalki* with the "fire from heaven" is found in Ukrainian charms and sayings, where the sun is a female divinity linked with water and addressed as "Mother Hot Sun" and "Mother Holy Water." But the most compelling identification of the *rusalka* with the rays of the sun is in the much-loved Russian folktale of the magical Firebird.[35]

The function of the *ruslaki* as bringers of forest fertility into the fields was emphasized in folk ritual. In the Russian village, that was perhaps their most important function, accomplished under great duress. In the Ukraine, the escorting of the *rusalki* into the planted field could be performed by women alone. The nymphs' resistance referred perhaps to the historical movement from horticulture to farming, which met with considerable disapproval from the women of the community, since it displaced their work in the fields and substituted the plow and the bullock or horse for the hoe.

In leading the *rusalki* out of the forest, the peasant women seemed to play out the challenge to feminine hegemony. The image of the *rusalki* is still that of the goddesses of the hunters, living alone and choosing their mates to affirm the control of nature over human efforts to capture its power. In Bulgarian lore, where that memory of transition from hunting to farming deities is still preserved, the *rusalki* or *vily* come into the fields out of the forest and pour out the fertilizing dew from their hunting horns.[36] But just as farming directs the forces of nature (in the South Slavic myths, the *vily* are chased away with whips and shouts, suggesting the entry of the bull or horse into the field) through an act of violence performed by plow and bullock on the body of the earth, so too the women of the community, in close contact with that generative nature, were obliged to ensure its compliance with human will, even at the cost of self-mutilation.

This process is strikingly illustrated in a spring rite played out in the farming communities of the Ukraine called "Leading Back the *Rusalka*." During the Rusalia festival, two straw dolls representing the *rusalki* were made. There were, in effigy, inhabitants no longer of the forest but of the fields. These dolls were taken out of the village and into the surrounding fields, where the women split into two opposing camps—girls and mothers. The girls defended the dolls, while the mothers attacked them in a series of round dances, *khorovody*, mimicking war, gradually moving the whole group into the open field. There the dolls were finally torn from the protection of the girls by the women, and their dismembered bodies were spread over the ground. During their ritual lament, the girls loosened their hair to resemble the *rusalki* and fell to the earth, feigning death. The "dangerous" liberty of the girls in the community was thus tamed to serve its reproductive needs through an act of violence by the mothers as instruments of the patriarchal collectivity.[37]

Though the *rusalka* represented nature uncontrolled, she also stood for feminine power in the village and the overwhelming importance of the girls as potential mothers in the maintenance of family life. For the *rusalki*, though virginal, were also represented as protective clan mothers. The universal image of the *sirin-rusalka* inside the peasant house suggests a vital underground pagan cult maintaining the solidarity of peasant women. The cult of the *rusalki* expressed women's desire for freedom and control. As spirits of unbaptized children or drowned girls who were freed by death from the constraints of patriarchal marriage, the *rusalki* remained forever young and at liberty, challengers to the social and religious order.[38] Like the image of the embroidered goddess, the belief in and worship of the *rusalki* implies the subjection of the male-dominated social order to the more archaic and significant feminine one. The *rusalki* and their priestesses, the village women, not only exerted control over human, animal, and plant fertility but protected the social group, as well.

The *sirin*, found often in the icon corner decorated with a tree bough, was the Tree of Life goddess who sheltered the family, while the tree maidens, *rusalki*, initiated girls and youths into the mysteries of family life.[39] They instructed young women to take up spinning and weaving and foretold whether they would or would not marry. They intimidated both girls and boys. Girls could be pressed into their service by drowning and becoming one of their host; young men were taught not to disregard the force of the feminine but rather to tremble at its numinous power over them.

In the dark domain of forest and water, where nature overrules the social order, the tricks of the *rusalki* once may have been associated with masculine rites of passage. The cautionary tales of those who spied on the mysteries of the nymphs reminded young men of the magical power of the feminine and bore echoes of matrilocal and matrilineal marriage customs. Young men went to meet them in the depths of the forest (symbolically associated with their bewitched circle dance—the womb). There the *rusalki* demanded to be served by these "transient" mates and punished any assertion of power over them.[40] The sexual initiation was therefore also an initiation into the knowledge that nature dominates man's lives and actions.

The *rusalki* personified the regeneration and rebirth of nature and suggested the cult of the maiden goddess Artemis. Their virginal or youthful attributes echoed the ancient belief in the parthenogenetic powers of nature herself, and their multitude seemed to underscore the critical role of the community of young women "priestesses" upon whose potential fertility the life of the village depended. But while the *rusalki* expressed the force of life in the form of independent but fecund young women who dwelled outside the human and most particularly male control, the image of the ancient and all-seeing elder, once a mother and now past childbearing age, represented another and equally archaic form through which nature was embodied. The witch Baba Yaga dwells without a mate in the depths of the forest.

Baba Yaga: The Great Goddess as Elder

Like the nymphs, the Russian witch has been associated by scholars with the goddess of the embroideries: "Surrounded by the personification of the four elements, in each hand the goddess holds one or more birds; at her feet there are also birds, as well as other animals and plants. Later this same goddess is pictured with horses on either side. This motif occurs in folktales in the figure of the benevolent Yaga who offers the hero the gift of a winged horse as well as the figure of the *Khoziaika lesa* [hostess or mother of the forest]."[41]

The *rusalki* are manifest in daily life through their image, the *siriny*, and embody through cautionary tales the peasant's fear of the untamed forest. But they appear in the folklore tradition under multiple disguises: beautiful virgins, the twelve daughters of a king, swan maidens, and even the composite figure of the Firebird. Baba Yaga, on the other hand, dominates the storytelling tradition and remains clearly identifiable in it. Her mastery over nature and humanity is expressed more vividly in the *persona* of the wise old woman, good or evil according to the manner in which she is approached. Like the old women of the village, from whom the population of witches is largely drawn, she displays a knowledge of nature and society that appears to exceed that of the young virgins, eternal daughters, the *rusalki*, who merely *embody* the force of life. Multiple, like their nature and productions, the maidens suggest the many seeds which fall to earth but do not always attain their full cycle of growth. But Yaga is like the withered flower pod brimming with new seed. She is the expression of realized potential, the fulfillment of the cycle of life associated with woman. She has known all things: virginity (she has no consort), motherhood (her children in plant and animal form are legion), and old age (she gathers all things into her abode to die). In her the cycles of feminine life are brought to completion, and yet she contains them all. The *rusalki* in their virginal nature and springtime appearances are the Artemis-Kore to her Demeter-Hekate, spring to her winter, sexual desire and love to her own iron rule over sexual union. The *rusalki* lure through their movements—spinning, dancing, and singing; Yaga cooks and eats and gathers all into her oven maw in order to create anew. They are connected with uterine waters; she with consuming fire.

The wisdom of Yaga bridges the domains of nature and society in ways in which the activities of the *rusalki* cannot. Like the young peasant girls whose freedom of movement in the community challenges the bondage of the mothers, the *rusalki* hover uneasily over the social bonds of the village, preferring the liberty of forest, trees, and water to the constraints imposed by man. Baba Yaga, the old one, has lived in both spheres. Though like the divine virgins she dwells in the forest far from human life, she does so, as a "social" being, in a hut. And what an extraordinary abode it is! Standing in a clearing in the middle of a dark forest, shaped like a peasant *izba*, the hut has curious supports: It moves on hens' feet. Its door is turned toward the forest and away from the nearest village. The picket fence which surrounds it strikes horror in all who approach: Made of human bones rather than wooden posts, each "spike" is crowned with a human skull whose eyes flash in the dark. The house itself appears to be composed of parts of the human body, with legs for doorposts, hands for bolts, and a mouth with sharp teeth as a lock.[42]

But if she appears in her forbidding aspects as Hekate, the mother of the dead, the underground aspect of Artemis the hunting goddess, Yaga is also the horse-headed Demeter, the self-sufficient mother without a mate, and her hut is the hut of plenty. A proverb summarizes this other aspect in invoking Yaga's house: "*Izbushka* [on hens' feet]; *pirogi* [pies] underneath, and covered with *bliny* [pancakes].''[43] In her house, which is dominated by the oven like that of any peasant, cooking and eating are an act of life-affirmation, fertility, and abundance, as well as one through which nature destroys her creation. The hut is filled with animal servants and cleaned by a virgin. In short, Yaga's house confounds human, animal, and plant life. Its fire creates and consumes. The living and the dead commingle; the moon and the sun, the evening and morning star, begin and end their heavenly course from her abode.[44]

Baba Yaga, like the *rusalki*, is a spinner; her house is sometimes represented standing on a spindle. The thread is made of the bones and entrails of the dead as the hut turns round and round on its bird feet. It is both the universal egg, the womb of all creation, and the hen, or the mother bird which carries it. The spinner and cook who inhabits it is a skinny hag with a withered face and a wild tangle of hair—a characteristic power she shares with the *rusalki*—which crowns her head like the serpent-locks of the Medusa. Her nose and breasts are iron, and her mouth is a cavelike horror of iron teeth: She is vampiric; human fingers float in her food. She freezes the blood of those who behold her. On the other hand, she can be a kindly old woman whose hair looks like rye, or a luxuriant garden. Sometimes she wears a married woman's headdress, a horned *povoinik* which gives her the appearance of being crowned with a bull's horns or the crescent moon.[45] Her hat links her to the Neolithic goddesses and priestesses of Çatal Hüyük and Tripol'e, to Isis of the Egyptians, and to the Greek moon goddess Artemis-Hekate adorned with the silver sphere. She can be both good and evil in her aspects, beautiful as well as hideous, young as well as old. She can be one, and she can also appear as a triune goddess. Above all she is alone, surrounded by a number of magical implements through which she works her transformational powers.

With her golden spindle, Baba Yaga is often seen in her triune form as the three Fates to whom the hero or heroine turns in order to determine his or her destiny. She rides in a mortar and pushes herself with a pestle, sweeping her tracks with a birch broom. The symbolism of the mortar and pestle is both complex and deceptively simple: It is used not only to grind grain but also to prepare the flax which women use in spinning cloth. Mortar and pestle are the instruments of destruction and of nurture and protection (clothing). In their symbolic form, they represent the human sexual organs, womb and phallus. Birth, generation, nurture, and death are all conjoined here. As she sweeps through the skies, seated in her womb-mortar, propelling herself with the pestle-phallus, the old witch creates life; and with the inverted birch tree (which links her here to the *rusalki*), the Tree of Life, she destroys. The tree hides her passage from the view of the mortal. No human must break through the veil of her mysterious activities. She punishes the overcurious who would learn the secret of her paradoxical nature. Yaga is a mother, but a cannibal mother. She whose children are many—from her forty mare-daughters to the tangle of reptiles and animals and astral bodies which inhabit her abode—is also the hungry one who devours them.

The spindle, mortar, and pestle from the world of women carry a "feminine" metaphysic. But Yaga also appropriates from the world of men. She has a magical transforming wand. She rules over the masculine generative organ and directs it. She is a horse goddess and has a fire-breathing flying horse, which she gives to those youths who please her. She has a self-cutting sword, whose power she awards to the warrior. And she keeps a self-playing musical instrument, the *gusli*, used in ancient *Rus'* by male wandering minstrels, who appear to gain their powers from her. She confers these instruments of the male world as gifts which hinder or help the progress of youths who seek her out. She also offers the deserving the most potent of all magical objects from the world of women: mirrors, votive towels, scarves, rings, and balls of yarn to permit her worshippers to reach their goal of finding a mate. She presides over her mysteries of union, communion, and cannibalistic death from her hot *pech'* and will entrap and devour those who challenge her order or approach her rashly.

Although Baba Yaga may appear as a wise old woman, a lovely maiden, or three sisters, she is just as frequently seen in her role as the evil one. Feminine power, which she personifies, is regarded with fear. Indeed, the widowed old women of the village, alone like the mateless Yaga, suggest the dispensability of the male in their world and make apparent the greater longevity of the female, regarded as a magical quality. Women are seen as potential witches, and Baba Yaga is their patron goddess.[46] She represents the epiphany of the female elder.

"The power of witchcraft belongs particularly to old women," wrote Briffault in his monumental study *The Mothers*. "For it is a common notion that such a power is counteracted by child-bearing, so that a mother is not so dangerous as a woman past child-bearing age or a young unmarried woman." Among the Russians, witches are usually, if not always, in the guise of old women and thought to be immortal.[47] The word *ved'ma* (witch) comes from the word for "to know." Witches bore the general characteristics of Yaga herself, including her transformational powers. Like the village girls who embodied the *rusalki* to bring fertility into the village and the fields, the old women of the community performed the function of priestesses by assuming the persona of the divine mistress of the universe. Like her, witches were said to control the weather. They could devour the moon and the sun and bring disease, crop failure, and death. They regulated the flow of cows' milk as well as the rainfall. Witches, like the Eurasian horse goddess, also appeared in charge of the male phallic symbol of power, the horse, which they caused to gallop all night to make it worthless for work in the morning. Linked to wolves and vampires, they performed their chief mischief in midsummer, at the very time when the good wise women of the village wandered into the fields and forests at night to pick medicinal plants which would protect the community.[48] Unlike male sorcerers, the *kolduny*, successors surely to the Slavic shamans, the *volkhvy*, witches, hid their secrets; and no man could be initiated into their knowledge unless he was linked to them by blood.

The fear of Yaga and her witch followers may be as much related to the patriarchal denigration of their cult as to the dark elements which they embodied. Just as the *rusalki* turn into destroyers of men as a result of a dismissal, so too the evil nature of Baba Yaga as witch may refer to the grudge harbored by women against those who controlled religious and social life. The name Yaga gives a hint of divine anger. Though some linguists and folklorists have traced its etymology to the Sanskrit for "snake" and to the Russian word *est'*, "to eat," other derivations emphasize her resentful nature: Related to the Polish name for Yaga, Jezda, signifying an association with nightmares, the Slavic word *enga* means "grudge"; and the term for "brawling" is *iagat'*. This sense of denigration may be reinforced by her epithet *baba*. All married women are referred to by this derogatory name. Yet the word was originally associated with the Hittite goddess Kubaba, who evolved into the All-Mother Cybele of the Phrygians.[49]

Each of the meanings of the name Baba (the once "goddess" and now "hag") Yaga is reflected in the image and actions of the mistress of witches. As the protean goddess, she is interchangeable with the serpent and is associated with it in folktales. As the cannibal witch, she is also the wolf goddess who eats all who try to enter her sphere. Her association with nightmares and illness reflects her role as the goddess of the underworld and the guide to initiation—for illness and dreams are most frequently linked with initiatory rituals. And her reputation for grudging and brawling comes from the conflicts which her votaries engaged in to protect her from the hostility of the church and menfolk.

The denigration of the power of witches by the church in Russia, as elsewhere, testified to the tenacity of the ancient woman-centered fertility rites. "You still cling to pagan customs and believe in witchcraft," thundered the bishop of Vladimir, Serapion, in the thirteenth century. "You pray to them and ask for gifts as though they ruled the earth by permitting rain, sunshine, and by making the land fertile."[50] Moving their divinities into the safety of the family and the community of women who handed down the rituals and mysteries in the form of folktales and folk art, the Russian *baby* acted much like their sisters in both the East and the West. From this underground realm, the wrathful attributes of such denigrated goddesses were further accentuated.[51] At the same time, under the protection of feminine votaries, the figures of the *rusalki*, like that of Yaga, asserted their hegemony over all creation.

The "sacred text" through which the female divinity was revealed to her Russian worshippers is the folktale told originally at ritual periods in the life of the community. In this "liturgy," the powers and attributes of the Great Goddess Baba Yaga are vividly evoked. The folktale suggests her archaic nature as goddess of the Paleolithic hunters, as mistress of the herds and herders, as horse goddess, and as the deity of farmers. Her persona unites all aspects of fertility: that which comes from the earth, that which comes from the skies, and that which replenishes the human community. She is the mistress of the soil and its productions; she is the one who dwells in the heavens and controls the planets' round; and she is the guardian of the hearth, the ever-vigilant mother of the human collectivity. In folktales Baba Yaga is found in all these forms. But her oldest is that of the shamanic Mistress of Animals, the ancient bird goddess whose abode on hens' feet is as one with her own body. Associated with the eagle, the raven, and the crow—the birds of nordic shaman-hunters—she is represented as the benign genetrix who helps the hero reach his bride, but who punishes all manifestations of greed on his part by her own voracious nature. This motif is quite apparent in a popular fairytale called "The Sea King and Vasilisa the Wise," where Baba Yaga assumes the form of the hunter's bird mother and is closely linked in this function with the equally archaic *rusalki*.[52]

In the story of a king's sacrifice of his son to an eagle in return for wealth and the youth's rescue by a wise Vasilisa, the masculine figures appear as either voracious mortals or supernatural agents of feminine power. The wishes of mortals are fulfilled only when they obey the mistress of creation, who operates through her eagle and Sea King "sons," as well as appears in her benign shape as forest mother or divine virgin, the true reward of the compliant prince. Human greed is answered with nature's rapacity in the form of the hungry eagle and Sea King. Human compliance and humility are rewarded with the treasure of love, marriage, and fertility. At the same time, masculine desire for power is analogous with evil and subordinated to feminine magic and generosity. The story seems to underline the greater efficacity of the witch (Yaga-Vasilisa) over the male shaman or sorcerer (eagle and Sea King). We are reminded that they derive their power from feminine sources. The eagle can confer gifts only through his Yaga mother; the Sea King dies at the hands of Vasilisa, his more powerful daughter.

Not only the bird mother and the mistress of hunters, Baba Yaga is also the guardian of the horse and patroness of herders and warriors.[53] Like the Scythian serpent goddess, Yaga presides over a herd of mares who are her daughters; but unlike her ancient analogue, she can transform herself into a mare, as well. In the story "The Chestnut Grey," the male hero is initiated from childhood (the "Simpleton") to maturity (the "Wise Prince") by passing through the head of the mare-witch. In another tale, "Zamoryshchek and Baba Yaga," she represents both her benign and evil aspects as the horse goddess:[54] An old and barren couple are given the miraculous gift of many children when forty sons hatch from forty eggs. The sons grow up to labor in their parents' fields, but one day they discover that the hay they bale is being consumed by an unknown thief. The miscreant, a mare, is trapped by the youngest of the sons, the valiant Zamoryshchek. She then appears as the good Yaga and gives the young man foals for his brothers to ride in their quest for brides. The brothers, led by Zamoryshchek on the Yaga-mare, set off on their journey and meet another Baba Yaga, who offers them her forty daughters to marry. The good mare-Yaga, in her aspect as mother who unites girls and youths, warns the brothers of the evil Yaga's trick: The daughters would kill them. The youths slaughter their brides and escape to find real princesses to marry.

Baba Yaga in the form of a mare allows herself to be tamed by the brothers, but for the purposes of marriage. Indeed, the gift of a horse as the instrument of Yaga's will to unite male and female is a common motif in a number of stories and seems to contradict the patriarchal association of warrior and steed. In the tale "Maria Morena," the Amazon queen, the warrior ethos is actively undermined: The hero must journey to the house of Baba Yaga for a horse which will help him win his captive bride. Here, too, the witch is presented as the owner of mares and is herself pictured as a rider who flies through the skies on her steed. The youth discovers that her house is surrounded by a fence of human skulls. One stake alone is bare; it awaits his head. Baba Yaga challenges him to look after her mares while she is gone; if he fails, his head will adorn the fence like that of other valiant champions. In this tale she is represented like the goddess of the embroideries, holding the bridles of the horsemen who come to her as suppliants. The youth must control the mares so that he can win a magic steed, which will in turn take him to his bride. Again the rites of human fertility are emphasized over those of warriors who must submit to the natural order.[55]

Baba Yaga as the bird and horse mistress refers respectively, then, to the culture of the hunters and that of warriors and herders of horses. As the transformational goddess, she is the guide and initiator of the male into the mysteries of the female world of fertility. Like the divinity represented on Russian embroideries, she is the deity of agriculturalists and warriors both but continues, quite emphatically, to personify her older and parthenogenetic transformational nature. She is, for example, the frog princess, a popular and well-loved figure who whirls all things out of her sleeves and confers political authority (the kingdom) on her mate; as the cow and fish, she symbolizes her complete autonomy as birth-giver. In her association with the bear (who is sometimes seen as the master of the forest in her stead) and the serpent, she demands human sacrifice of her worshippers; in return for life she requires death.[56]

The link of Yaga with the snake in the shape of a serpentine dragon emphasizes her function as self-inseminated creatrix and "phallic" or destructive mother. Her snake or dragon "servants" or homologues kidnap maidens and challenge youths; they threaten to take back or interfere with the fertility she has created out of her own body. Indeed, the Russian contribution to dragonlore is to be found in the clear connection made between the monster and the witch. The dragon appears to symbolize the winter and underworld nature of Yaga, which the peasantry associate with a masculine aggressiveness and destruction. The dragon Koshchei, whose name is derived from *kost'*, "bone," suggests the grave. And though he is called "Immortal," he is bedeviled by a "death" known only to the good Yaga, who protects those who know how to approach her. The other fabled monster is called Chudo-Yudo, a fire-breathing dragon with many heads whose appearance suggests a distant echo of Medusa's serpentine locks. Both Chudo-Yudo and Koshchei are male; both are aggressive and evil.[57] Unlike the eagle and bear, who suggest a nurturing as well as chthonian nature, these serpents seem to express Baba Yaga's phallic aspect alone and associate it with destruction—but a destruction over which the witch has complete control.

As Mistress of Animals, Baba Yaga oversees the fertility of land and human community, but she is also the queen of the skies and mother of the planets. Both the skin-sloughing serpent Chudo-Yudo and his "mother" Baba Yaga guard the magic waters of life and death. Snake and witch are linked by the Russian peasantry with rain and are invoked in times of drought. Just as serpents were believed to suck the milk of cows and eat eggs out of nests, so snakes and witches both appear as devourers of the skies, stealing the dew and the rain, and the clouds on which they were supposed to ride. The witch was thought to gobble up the moon and the sun, like Yaga herself.[58] The serpent and Baba Yaga connect heaven and earth, the underworld and the skies, in their rainmaking role. They control all spheres of nature, the air as well as water. The moon, the sun, the winds, and the rains are their servants. But the moon in particular, that planet sacred to the archaic goddess Artemis, is linked in Russian folk tradition to Baba Yaga as it is to the maiden *rusalki*. The moon is seen to be horned like a bull and gradually consumed by a serpent, the two servants of the Neolithic goddess. Among Russian peasants, that moon is the body of Baba Yaga herself, the cannibal witch who eats away at her own body while she regulates the fertility of plant and woman, "waxing" and "waning" in rhythm to the lunar cycle like the tides. The hut of Baba Yaga is the abode of this moon goddess and turns on its chicken leg or spindle axis in conjunction with the phases of the moon. When the moon is full, the opening points to the west, and the charnel hut is accessible to the living. The Yaga who sits in the house is like the full moon, pregnant and healthy. But when the night skies show only a crescent like the horns of a headless sacrificed bull, Yaga no longer lives in the hut. It is as empty as her barren belly.[59]

The waxing and waning moon not only refers to the full and empty hut-belly of the witch; it stands for Baba Yaga's transformation from the lovely spinner Vasilisa the Wise to the decrepit hag with a withered leg representing the dying crescent. The change of the moon also suggests the decomposition of the body, as the self-devouring goddess moves from generation to death. The moon is perceived by the Russian peasant like the Firebird, the Phoenix, continually reborn from its ashes: "Baba Yaga, broken leg, feeds the whole world but is herself hungry," goes a Russian riddle to name the plow.[60] As plow the goddess of fertility wounds her own body, the soil, to produce food; so too the witch of the moon consumes herself to provide the world with abundance.

The notion of life issuing out of death which lies behind the image of the self-consuming moon deity (whose mortar and pestle stress the interconnectedness of fertility and destruction, nurture and generation) is also found in the role of Baba Yaga as Fate. The phases of the moon are represented as three Fates. The Greek Moirae symbolize the waxing, full, and waning moon—creation, unfolding, and destruction. The Muses, the Erynnes, the Gorgons, and the Graeae are also three in number and linked to the moon. The spinner is the one who sees all and knows all, linked perhaps to the archaic Eye Goddess. Indeed, Baba Yaga says to the skulls which adorn her picket fence and whose eyes glow in the light of the moon, "Skuzh mne glaz"—"Tell me eyes."[61]

Moon-rain-fertility-woman-serpent mean periodic death and regeneration in the lore of Baba Yaga and the moon divinities of Europe. The serpent, as servant and homologue, is also uroboric. He is phallus and umbilicus, the guardian of the womb as well as the "instrument" which opens it. Like Baba Yaga, he chases the moon and the sun in order to regenerate them through death or reentry into the "maw" of the Great Mother. Among the dominant motifs in Russian folklore is that of masculine intervention in and regulation of feminine "cosmic" powers. The male, whether youth, prince, serpent (phallus-umbilicus), animal, or bird, is ever the "organ" of a female force and can contend with it only when he is armed by it. This "instrumental" male activity is illustrated in the story of "The Witch and the Sister of the Sun": Chased by Baba Yaga, the hero is both the symbol of the sun itself and a priest or king who must save himself from the clutches of the underworld goddess by uniting with his feminine half, the sun maiden. But to protect himself and save the world from Yaga's voracious appetite, he must be empowered by the maiden and then restore a proper balance between life and death through a "sacred marriage" with her.[62]

The Yaga-serpent—who guards the waters of life and death, and as a wolf goddess swallows the sun, brings or withholds rain, and is resurrected like the moon when she sheds her old form or skin—is also a clan mother, the guardian of the house. The Russian *pech'* is connected to the outside world by a stove-pipe appropriately called a "serpent" or "snake." It was believed that the house snake stood vigil over all the members of the household. Should it be killed, misfortune would befall everyone, but particularly the mistress of the house. Furthermore, the house snake was thought to entwine itself around the *izba* like an uroboric umbilicus, the guardian of the womb.[63] Just as "mother *pech'*" stands at the center of the house and is surrounded by the serpent, so too Baba Yaga reflects the image of the ancient clan mother who brings fertility to the household like the good mother, uniting the past to the future generations.

The center of Baba Yaga's hut is the *pech'*. All who come to her house ask to be fed or are sacrificed to it. When the *pech'* is not in use, it becomes the bed for Baba Yaga, who fills the whole house with her body, suggesting the physical as well as psychological centricity of the peasant grandmother who sleeps atop the stove. The stove is the repository of dead souls, the ancestors. Like the Hittite goddess Salgusa, Baba Yaga guards the bones of the dead and through the alembic-oven makes new souls.[64]

Baba Yaga's priestess is the grandmother who oversees a number of generations from the heights of her perch on the oven. Old women organize their younger followers to protect the house from disease or the village from the plague, which is thought to be caused by divine anger. One often-described ritual for the exorcism of cattle plague involves both women and girls: When illness descends on the village, the old and young women gather at night and walk seminaked in procession around the community, armed with brooms, pokers, tongs, and shovels. They follow a plow held by a widow accompanied by young virgins or pregnant women. The procession is completed by the old *baby*. The song they sing invokes the evil of the *rusalki* of the forest, inimical to the domestic herd, which is specifically guarded by Baba Yaga.[65]

Protective but possessive mother, Baba Yaga hovers over the entry of the infant into the world and threatens to "steal it," take it back to her domain.[66] She sends souls to earth and re-calls them. She has the keys to all spheres of nature and power over all souls. Baba Yaga, the cannibal witch, eats children. Her cannibalism recalls ancient memories of human, particularly child, sacrifice. She appears, in folklore, as a successor to the vulture-headed chthonian goddess of Çatal Hüyük worshipped in the house-sanctuary, where bones of women and children are found commingled. The witch Medea, like the Hittite witch Wisuriyanza, who succeeded the archaic Neolothic divinity, the Semitic Lilith, and the Greek Gello, all demand, like Baba Yaga, the offering of a child in return for wealth and fertility.[67] Indeed, Yaga as a birth- and death-giver resembles the Matrioshka doll. Each spills its "children" out of its body; but the doll commands by virtue of its very form that they be returned to it, with the smallest at the center.

The double function of Baba Yaga as genetrix and cannibal witch expresses the fundamental paradox of nature. At no time is that contradiction clearer than during the period from child-hood to adolescence or adulthood when the child must break with a mother who both clings to it and wishes for her child to grow as an individual. All the stories of witch figures contending with youths or maidens are in essence tales and rituals of initia-tion.[68] In them Baba Yaga's dual nature is always suggested: She is a good mother who saves her son from the evil witch; she is the lovely girl who delivers the hero from dragons or is herself delivered by him, expelling her evil nature; she is the wise old woman who guides the youth or girl to his or her goal; she is three princesses or three hags who can either shelter or destroy. She is both the prize and the perils of the journey. The tale of "Ivashko and the Wise Woman" illustrates most directly the pri-mordial dualism of the nurturing and the over-possessive mother: The child Ivashko is enticed by a Yaga who imitates his mother's voice to lure him to her hut. The cannibal witch is also the castrat-ing mother who tries to gnaw down the tree where he hides. The youth is saved by the magic of his own good mother, who comes to his aid by sending a flock of swans and geese—the virginal *rusalki*, or marriageable peasant girls identified with them—to carry him home. When Ivashko returns, he finds his mother cook-ing *bliny*, and they sit down to eat.[69]

The story of Ivashko is a male puberty ritual in which the child is both helped and hindered by the mothers and must pass a test before he can accede to manhood. It is also a tale which com-pares that "escape" into puberty with the emergence of the sun out of the womb of earth. The cooking of the round *bliny* is a ritual and occurs at key periods in the sun's yearly course through the skies. It is thought to help its "sexual" vitality. Individual and cosmic order are united in the folktale: The image of the sun born daily from the earth and absorbed back into it at night, bloody at birth (sunrise) and at death (sunset), is analogous to human life and is associated particularly with the male rites of passage from the world of the mothers. Only with maternal aid, however, can the youth succeed and restrain her possessive cannibalistic and castrating nature. The hut of Baba Yaga becomes the puberty initiation hut in which the importance of food to the child is related to his emergent sexuality: The youth threatened by the image of being shoved into the fire of the oven and becoming food—and consort—for the witch-mother saves himself sometimes by substituting Baba Yaga's daughter in his stead.[70]

Ivashko's tale illustrates a male initiatory ritual in an abbreviated form; but the initiations are considerably more complex, usually taking the form of a journey, and differ in form for boys and for girls. Indeed, the house of Yaga is as much an initiatory hut for the young woman as it is for her brother. For the youth, the quest which leads him to the hut involves the need to find the waters of life for an aging father-king; or to enter into conflict with a Firebird or dragon ravaging the country; or to search for a bride—though usually all these motifs are united for that purpose. The young man asserts his masculinity on the way to his union with a girl.[71]

The girl's quest begins when she is pushed out of the house by a wicked stepmother, often related to Baba Yaga, and involves the performance of some domestic chore—spinning, cleaning, cooking, finding a light, feeding animals. In some stories, the death of the parents leaves the girl with a younger brother she must protect. In each case, the journey moves the girl or boy through the three realms of nature: the upper world of sun, moon, and birds, and middle world of the living, and the underworld of the ancestral spirits in Yaga's hut. And in each case the initiate is given magic feminine implements which will move him or her from one world to the next: balls of yarn, dolls, scarves, rings, mirrors. They are also helped by animal, bird, and reptile guides—most often by those who live in two spheres and can mediate between the world of the living and that of the dead. The guides who help them are generally female: "Woman in the picture language of the myth and folktale," writes Wosien in her analysis of Russian fairytales, "represents the totality of what can be known to man. Hence the predominance of female initiators and helpers along the way."[72]

If the path to male maturity passes through the hut of Baba Yaga, whose magic or wisdom must be absorbed, the rites of initiation for women place even greater stress upon docility and obedience in the face of maternal and "natural" power. The girl must learn to imitate in the most exacting manner the tasks which will be her lot when she assumes the role of mother and old woman herself. The power she must obey is also the power which she will one day exercise, not through the mediation of a woman, as for the boy, but alone, as the incarnation of the mistress of creation, *rusalka* and Baba Yaga both.

The girl in the folklore of Baba Yaga must perform specific domestic and farming chores which assume symbolic and ritual significance. For example, she feeds the many forms of life which inhabit the hut. In so doing she learns how to worship and take care of the ancestral spirits and stands vigil over the well-being of the family, her first duty. She then learns how to spin properly and how to weave, how to prepare food and cook it, and how to keep the house in order—in short, how to govern the domestic economy, which represents the cosmic one in microcosm. Most important, she tends to the oven to acquire the secret of fertility and generation. She learns to be a bride: There are still masks of Baba Yaga in Russia which were used ritually to announce to girls the date of their weddings, but only after the girls had correctly answered a series of riddles concerning the mysteries of reproduction.[73]

The most popular of the Baba Yaga stories also deals most specifically with female initiation. It is in its many variants the tale of Vasilisa the Fair or the Wise, or Maryshia, as she is variously called: Vasilisa is the daughter of a merchant. Her mother dies when the girl is still a child, leaving Vasilisa to assume the role of her dead parent. But the mother leaves a magic doll which helps her whenever Vasilisa feeds it. The father is not privy to this magic; it passes from mother to daughter and teaches the ritual magic of feeding to the girl.

The merchant marries another woman with two daughters. She is the evil sister of Baba Yaga and jealous of Vasilisa's beauty—a theme found in the ancient myth of Psyche and Aphrodite, of Cinderella, and of Snow White. She gives Vasilisa all the work to do, but for each impossible task the doll comes to the girl's aid, and she feeds it the best things that she can find (like the food presented to the souls of the dead by peasant women).

Thanks to the doll, her life is easy, but when she reaches marriage-able age, the family moves to the edge of the forest in which stands the hut of Baba Yaga. One evening as the stepmother and three girls sit spinning, the lamp goes out, and the stepmother sends Vasilisa into the forest to get light (knowledge) from the witch: "She walked with fear and trembling. Suddenly a horse-man galloped past her; his face was white, he was dressed in white, his horse was white, and his horse's trappings were white—daybreak came into the woods." She meets another horseman clad in red. Then, reaching the terrifying hut, she is passed by a black-cloaked horseman. Night falls, and the eyes of the skulls on the picket fence light up. Yaga appears in her mortar and pestle; but Vasilisa, protected by her amuletic doll, is not attacked. Instead, when she tells the witch that she is in quest of light, Baba Yaga puts her to work.

Vasilisa's first labor is to prepare food from the oven. When-ever she opens up the *pech'*, all kinds of victuals come pouring out, and the girl serves her mistress. But when she tries to give the remains of the feast to her protective doll, she is refused. For the doll and Yaga are one, and Yaga has already been fed. At sun-rise, Yaga, as the sun, leaves in her mortar and pestle. And Vasilisa continues to perform her tasks. At night, when she has completed her work, Baba Yaga tells her to talk. The girl first asks the identity of the horsemen she met on her way. Baba Yaga answers: The white horseman is "my bright day"; the red horse-man is "my red sun"; and the black horseman is "my dark night." "And all of them," she adds, "are my faithful servants." Vasilisa is still curious but asks no more. She is wise with the wisdom of her mother and her amuletic doll. "It is well," says Yaga, "that you ask only about what you have seen outside my house; I do not like to have my dirty linen washed in public and I eat the overcurious." Vasilisa responds that she is helped by the blessing of her mother. And it is only then, after the proper ritual reply, that Baba Yaga gives the girl what she seeks. The light is taken from a skull as though to stress the relationship of life and death, the ultimate mystery: "Get thee gone blessed daughter. I want no blessed ones in my house," says the witch to the initiate, who now emerges from the realm of the ancestors where Baba Yaga rules over the living.

The light, brought home inside the skull, immediately burns the stepmother and daughters. Vasilisa buries the skull respect-fully. She is now ready to become betrothed, like spring, emerg-ing from the kingdom of winter. She leaves the house of the dead stepmother and in her wanderings meets a kindly old woman, who takes her in and gives her work as a weaver and spin-ner. She is now fully "ordained" as a priestess of Baba Yaga, the maiden who would become a bride, a mother, and herself a witch in her old age. When she has finished spinning and weaving, she sees that she has enough cloth to fashion a shirt for the king. The king, curious about the mysterious seamstress, finds her in the courtyard of the old *baba* and immediately falls in love. They marry, and Vasilisa brings the old woman, her father, and the amuletic doll to live with her.[74]

We are back to the song with which we began our chapter. In it, a young girl embroiders her groom on the linen towel she has made while she sits in a tent pitched in a field. As the vir-ginal priestess of the benign Baba Yaga and the "tamed" *rusalka* of the forest, Vasilisa in the folktale is like the embroidery god-dess flanked by horsemen and votaries with all creation revolv-ing around her head and feet. The magical spinner, who embod-ies the archaic water and wood nymphs and the chthonian witch, has lured her groom into the web she made. But in this initi-atory tale, her journey has only begun. Like the goddesses she rep-resents, she has traveled alone, without the need of a mate, accom-panied only by the amuletic power of the ancestral female doll. Only when we examine the third incarnation of the embroidery goddess, that of Mother Earth, do we come to understand the anal-ogy made by the Russian peasantry between feminine existence—as virgin, mother, and old woman—and that of the natural order as a whole.

CHAPTER THREE

Reconstructing the Russian Great Goddess: Mother Earth

> Mother Earth, like love and sex, is a mystery: for her own secret purposes she divided mankind into male and female; she lures men irresistibly; the peasants kiss the earth like sons, carry her with them as an amulet, talk softly to her, cast spells in her name and charm love and hatred, sun and day. . . .
> It is for woman to take the part of Mother Earth.
>
> —B. Pilnyak, "Mother Earth"[1]

The worship of Mother Earth among the peasantry was once so widespread that the eminent Russian historian George Fedotov saw it as the core of Russian religion, in which "converge the most secret and deep religious feelings of the folk."[2] The *rusalki-siriny* in peasant belief are perhaps most of all amuletic, protective, like the invisible spirits of the ancestors gathered together in the body of a clan and nature mother. Their good graces must be actively sought, or evil befalls the community. Baba Yaga is a guide, an initiator, the source of human and divine wisdom, and the embodiment of the laws of nature as parthenogenetic mother. Her "liturgy" stresses that she has no need of human intervention to stimulate the cycle of life she has created. Like the *rusalki* she is invisible, yet her presence is everywhere. Mother Earth, on the other hand, is clearly visible as the very soil upon which all things live. She regulates the life of the village through the rituals of the agrarian calendar. In the image of the embroidered goddess, Mother Earth represents the principle of fruitfulness. She mediates between the potentiality of the virgin-*rusalki* and the all-encompassing and awesome power of Baba Yaga. She embodies the protective and benign aspect of the feminine-natural cycle as a sacred womb, protecting its human children.

The appearance of the cult of Mother Earth in the area of Russia coincided with the advent of intensive plow agriculture. At the same time, it came to absorb aspects of hunters' and horticulturalists' veneration associated with the *rusalka* and Yaga, the maid-mother dyad. Its origins, as we have seen, can be traced to the grain-impressed female figurines found at Tripol'e and the denigration of the all-powerful hunters' goddess to a passive planted earth. This denigration is apparent in the pantheon of the Scythians, whose Mother Earth and Father Sky divide up the attributes of the Great Goddess Tabiti. Among the Slavs, Mother Earth, associated with moisture, appears to be related to Mokosh and the moon goddesses Artemis and Semele (mother of Dionysus, the fertility god), with their regulatory powers over the waters. But while Mokosh is quite clearly linked to the archaic hunting moon goddess through spinning, childbirth, patronage of animals, and rain, thus resembling the *rusalka* or Baba Yaga, Mother Earth, in whom we glimpse only the vestiges of these ancient powers, has no particular image.[3]

The Russian Mother Moist Earth incorporates three mythologems. The first is expressed among the Greeks through the figures of Kore and Demeter. Kore, the daughter, assumes the guise of the Queen of the Underworld in Hades' kingdom when the god separates her by force from her mother. Subsequently she becomes the embodiment of spring and fertility when she is reunited with the Earth Goddess. The Kore-Demeter myth, underscoring the primordial importance of the mother-daughter bond in the continuation of life, is expressed in Russian folklore through the relationship of the maiden *rusalki* and the old mother Baba Yaga. The *rusalki* are linked with the (female) ancestors in order to bring fertility; Yaga has a young girl as her helper. It is an archaic, woman-centered, hunters' and horticulturalists' myth which emphasizes the parthenogenetic aspects of earth's creativity prior to masculine intervention.

The second mythologem is that of a Great Mother Goddess and her consort, the Dying God. Here the male takes on the functions of Kore, the daughter, in his relationship to a still all-powerful female divinity. In his characterization of the general outlines of the worship surrounding the Great Mother Goddess in agrarian cultures, the historian of religion E. O. James observes:

It was the Goddess, however, who was the dominant force in this act of renewal, whatever form it took. The Young God died in the rotation of the seasons and had to be rescued by her from the nether regions. Moreover it was she who resuscitated him and in so doing brought about the revival of life in nature and in mankind. . . . She was the embodiment of creative power in all its fulness; he was the personification of the decline and revival of vegetation and of all generative force.[4]

The male, in this second mythologem, is utterly dependent upon the Goddess.

The third mythologem, centered on male and female Divine Twins, resembles that of the Greek Apollo and Artemis born of the Great Mother Goddess Leto. In this, perhaps the least ancient, mythologem, a parthenogenetic divinity—the virgin huntress Artemis, mistress of animals—shares her power with an equally mighty masculine challenger, the sun god who dominates the heavens in his war chariot. Like Mithra on Bosphoran coins, who divides creation with a Great Goddess, Apollo rules the day, leaving the night to his sister. In the veneration of Mother Earth in Russia, the first two myths are dominant. The third appears in the attribution of male and female names to various deities invoked in the course of the agrarian cycle.

The mythologem of Kore-Demeter, Yaga-*rusalka*, underscoring the notion that earth can produce without aid from a consort, was expressed among the Russians in the veneration of earth as mother, and in the apparent lack of a strong father god to vie with the attachment felt by the peasantry for the maternal soil. The Russian Mother Moist Earth was self-moistened, self-inseminated. Man was her son rather than her master and perished like all her productions; woman was her daughter and in her own role as mother played the more significant part in the cult: She was like Kore to Demeter. In Greek mythology, the Mother Goddess assumes the archetypal form of earth's maternity.[5] In the myth of mother and daughter, the male is the divider and the death-dealer whose actions are punished.

Demeter, alone or with her daughter, is husbandless in the etiological Greek myth. She incarnates the bond of mother and child. Hades appears out of the underworld to carry Kore away in what appears to be a patrilocal wedding or "bride capture." Humanity pays for the abduction by the coming of winter and of death. Only when she is reunited with her child does the mother become benign. The myth suggests that death, barrenness, and suffering are associated with the division of the virginal and maternal feminine. It may also refer, in Greece as well as in Russia, to the patriarchal denigration of the parthenogenetic deity in her dual aspect, resulting in the figures of an angry Demeter and despairing Kore, of a wrathful Yaga and dangerous *rusalki*. The myth may also be connected to the intrusion of man in the cultivation of the soil through the use of the plow—an act perceived as one of violence and rape. Certainly in Russia, as elsewhere, plowing was surrounded by expiatory rituals, and in agrarian rites virgins and mothers had to be united to make the earth produce. When, however, the land was barren or animals were afflicted with disease, the cause of these misfortunes was attributed to woman's anger.

Earth as Clan Mother

Before turning to the rites of the agrarian calendar through which the three mythologems were most vividly expressed, we need to see how the cult of earth as parthenogenetic mother was expressed in the beliefs of the Russian peasantry. Baba Yaga and the *rusalki* lived in all spheres as the dialectical forces of life, moving amid the realms of nature like the shuttle flying through the web of creation, ever changing its contours. Mother Earth was the loom itself in all its solidity; she was also the maternal breast and womb: the black and fruitful soil. As such she was thought to carry the family, the village, and the nation, which she nurtured and protected—and ruled—like a mother.

"Mother Earth," wrote Fedotov, "becomes clearer to us against the background of the *gens* religion." Through her the individual and the tribal ancestors were united and made whole; she conferred identity upon each person: "The sacred motherhood of the earth is intimately akin to the worship of the parents. The double mystery of birth and death is experienced as well in the life of the *rod* as it is in the yearly cycle of the earth." She was the genetrix of the family and the clan. "Earth is to each mother and father," goes a popular expression. And she herself was sometimes described as a person: Stones were her body; roots were her bones; the living trees and grasses were her hair. When her children were in danger, she moaned and cried. She wailed for them in times of famine and trembled for their sins. She sheltered the dead in her womb: The Russian peasant envisioned the underworld of the ancestors as a house heated against the dampness of Mother Moist Earth by a *pech'*. And those who were not buried in the native maternal soil went to a kind of limbo—like people who lose touch with their family.[6]

In perpetuating the archaic image of the clan mother, the cult of Mother Earth also incorporated that of the mother as guardian of domestic animals, which, like the soil, were "cultivated" for human needs. The life of animal and plant is sustained by the earth, and there is a homology between them: "Bread is alive, like cattle," goes one proverb; "When spring comes, the first hen's egg holds the harvest." Similarly, there is a homology between beast and mankind. Among the Russian peasantry, animals, thought to have souls, were placed in graves to rejoin their Mother Earth in death. In the Ukraine to the beginning of this century, a dead cow was given the same rites as a person, and the killing of animals for any but sacrificial purposes was hedged in with a number of taboos.[7]

Mother Moist Earth was served by women. Ceremonies suggest that the earth's priestesses could, like midwives, give birth to rain, by forcing it from the earth's womb, thereby releasing the "amniotic fluid" trapped within. The act of birth would, as with the human mother, stimulate the nurturing breast of heaven.[8] Other customs further underscore women's relation to earth's parthenogenetic powers: Rain was predicted in Vladimir Province by women going to sleep in fields and gardens dressed only in their shifts to hear directly from Mother Earth when she would send relief. Indeed, water itself was addressed by peasants in many parts of Russia as "mother." Rivers, called "mothers," were not to be polluted; to throw anything into them save rocks from the fields would cause them to become "heavy and difficult, like women in labor." The linkage between "Mother Water" and "Mother Earth" was emphasized in the custom of washing the newly born (seen to emerge from earth), as well as the dead before they were put back into the soil from which they came.[9]

Mother Earth was perceived, then, as a cosmic egg containing humanity between the breast of the sky and the womb of the soil. The planets which whirl in the heavens were regarded as a family, a *rod*, inhabiting this sphere like the living below and the ancestors underground. In north Russian songs sung at weddings and during the seasonal fertility festivities, sun, moon, and stars were called familiarly: "My Father the Bright Moon" and "My Mother the Bright Sun." Significantly, as if to underscore matrilocal custom, they were often made to look down on the earth from the *terem* (women's quarters, a term from the period of the Mongol invasion). The sky was not filled with masculine divinities; rather, it was the home of the family, and thus the realm of the feminine.[10]

Mother Earth was not only assimilated to the biological

mother who gives birth, she was also the basis of the social community and oversaw its order. In that she differed from the *rusalki* and Baba Yaga, whose sphere was nature and the purely biological cycle of fertility. Like the embroidery goddess, she held the reins of the horsemen incarnating the social order. Like the Scythian goddess, to whom warriors and kings came for the confirmation of their power, she was also the oath-taker. All sins were to be confessed to her: Like the Fates, she predicted how individuals, families, or nations would develop. Mother Earth foretold both the abundance of the harvest and the course of political events. She was the judge of last appeal. The question of land ownership was disputed in her "court." When conflicts over land occurred, the judge who was appointed the "voice" of Mother Earth was required to eat some soil before pronouncing his verdict. Each party was obliged to walk around the border of the disputed lot with a clod of earth on his or her head so that Mother Earth herself might determine who was in the right (and though the church tried, it failed to substitute the icon for the soil). Like the matriarch, the earth imposed her order over that of the patriarchal society of the village, and like a mother whose judgment and goodwill were treasured, she was kissed by the peasantry who venerated her.[11] But of all the roles attributed to the earth, that of public confession was the most politically subversive, for it challenged the order both of the church and of the state.

The confession to earth was first associated with the heretical dissent from the church of the *Strigol'niki*, a fourteenth-century sect in Novgorod. Whether the sect originated in the West or derived from archaic peasant tradition, its members confessed sins to the earth rather than to the clergy. Though the sect itself died out, this custom continued. But the earth was not a lenient judge: She did not forgive murder. She rejected vampires, evil witches, or those damned by their parents. Those who confessed and those who wished to re-enter her body had to be clean: The dead or dying were washed before they met her.[12] The law of Mother Earth was the law of the *rod*; her justice was that of the mother; and the mother of the family was the executrix of her order in the family and in the village.

The role of earth's priestesses was to bind together the life of the fields, the barn, and the household. The mothers mediated also between the untamed potential fertility of the forest maidens, the *rusalki*, and the awesome and destructive power of the elders, the Yagas. The mothers protected against their evil and disruptive elements to make the *rod* strong. As the earth was cultivated to feed humanity and thereby reveal her benign nature, so too the mother had to be counted upon in the patriarchal peasant community as its bulwark against her anger. Since woman had a special relationship to the soil, she repaired the damage done by man when he "wounded" the earth with his plow. Victory over the earth was at best precarious and ever subject to reversal. In one legend she is represented as eating those who "eat" her.[13] Thus, plowing or hurting the earth was hedged in with taboos. When male sinners confessed to earth, it was with the knowledge that they had sinned against her: "I ask your mercy," they began the ritual incantation, "I tore at your breast with a sharp plow." Among the Ukrainians, "he who strikes the earth beats his own mother." And in other regions one heard that "it is a sin to beat the earth—she is our mother." Children were admonished not to poke in the soil, and in Belorussia one could not dig on the twenty-fifth of March, when the earth was pregnant, or she would retaliate with famine and drought.[14]

Mother Earth was "tamed" much like the woman married in patrilocal and patrilineal custom. Unlike the virginal *rusalki* and the old Baba Yaga, who lived without mates and resisted all forcible control with violent retribution, Mother Earth and the mother, her priestess, served masters, out of love for their offspring. "The husband is the head, but the wife is the soul," declared the peasants, and "Where the whole family is to be found, so too is the soul." Like the earth owned by masters and often abused, the mother, nonetheless, represented the totemic center of village life, its soul. "Mother gives birth so that the earth will not swallow all mankind," another proverb explains. In her role as priestess of earth, the mother united the sacrificial rites to the ancestors with the cultivation of the soil. The proverb "Whatever is born in the fields is prepared at home" implies the reciprocal aspect of the mother's relationship to the Moist Earth. Grain was called "Mother Rye," and the gruel prepared at home was called "Mother Kasha."[15]

While the *pech'* was the mother's domain, it did not symbolize the destructive aspects of Baba Yaga's furnace; rather, it served the family like the heat of maternal love. "During the day my *pech'* heats me, and at night my mother," said peasants to evoke the nature of protective love. She was the sun as well as the spirit of the *pech'*, without which the family would perish: "It is warm in the sun; it is good by the mother." She alone protected: "A real mother is like a stone fence."[16] The mother at her *pech'*, like Yaga in the form of the tamed Mother Earth, held the keys to all nature's vitality. Within her *izba*-temple, the mistress of the hearth officiated over the Slavic cult of fire and sun. The dwelling was divided into a male and a female half. The ancestors, who were thought to dwell in the *pech'*, were also invoked in front of the icon corner in the feminine part of the house. The table beneath the icons held sacrifices to the dead in the form of bread, usually covered by a votive towel upon which the image of the embroidery goddess was imprinted. The napkin, considered more powerful than the icons themselves, was endowed with special healing and fertility powers, while the bread symbolized the dead ancestors.[17]

Mothers and the Rites of Birth and Death

The bathhouse, the temple of the pagan *rozhanitsy*, was the passage through which the child was ushered into life. The baby was born on the ground or on a straw mattress so that it might pass directly from the earth to the human mother. Fire from the *pech'* and cleansing water greeted it. Then it was baptized by women into the pagan cult of the *rozhanitsy* and Mother Earth. Only when the mother reentered the house did the midwives present the child to the man, "wrapped in the father's shirt so that the father would love it." The bond of mother to child was stressed over that to the father, whose role was secondary in the determination of the child's fate.[18]

As priestesses of the *rozhanitsy* and Mother Earth, mothers protected their infants from all dangers. Among the Russian peasantry, there was a firm belief that a mother controlled a child's development and growth by conferring a particular fate upon it. If the newborn should die, it was buried under the house or icon corner so that it would be linked directly with the ancestors and the maternal body of the house. As the child grew, the mother cast her spells upon it with lullabies: The word *baiat'* (to sing these songs) also means "to charm." She raised it with incantations in the same manner as she invoked the fertility of the earth, with songs and rituals intended to make plants flourish. At the same time, she punished those children who resisted her laws. Even when the child left, she continued her vigilance, assimilating her role to that of Mother Earth and casting spells in her name: "Say goodbye to your family, fall to Mother Moist Earth, and go to sleep." In fact, the young moved from mother to mother.[19]

The mother and Mother Earth determined the fate of the child and protected it by healing. When medicinal plants were picked at midsummer, the women sometimes lay down upon the earth to invoke her powers more directly. The mothers protected the entire community against diseases also called "mothers." The sick were taken by women to the place where it was thought that the "evil mother" disease had "caught" them to ask earth for forgiveness.[20]

Women, communicating between the living and the dead, performed the rituals associated with birth, healing, and fertility and also prepared the dying and dead to reenter the maternal womb of the earth. In so doing, they assimilated themselves to the seasonal cycle, stressing nature's rebirth out of death. Among the ancient Slavs, caves as well as hills were chosen for burial sites, and coffins were carved out of tree trunks to facilitate "reawakening." Women officiated over these last rites. Among the peasantry in Vladimir Province, as in other places, it was customary for the dying to ask earth permission to reenter her body with the ritual invocation, "Mother Moist Earth, forgive me and take me."[21] Those about to expire were placed on straw or on the ground as when they had entered the world—in order to facilitate their return to the earth and reincarnation out of it. They were washed with water from earthenware pots, which were then disposed of in the fields or placed in the coffin together with some straw. Water and straw had greeted the child as it entered the world. Women then led the funeral processions through village and fields and threw bread or *pirogi* into the grave. When the mourners returned home, they put their hands inside the open *pech'* to affirm the link between the spirits of the dead and the fertility of the fields and to reunite the recently deceased with the ancestors. Death was regarded as a rebirth into the earth, and graves as the "watchtowers" where Mother Moist Earth stood vigil through her army of underworld children over those living on her surface. In spring and fall, feasts for the dead coincided with regeneration and fruition. Food, too, was brought to the deceased, to thank them for their goodwill, and families feasted upon the ground with *bliny*, eggs, beer, and *pirogi*.[22]

The rites of birth and death played out by the mothers reaffirmed the union of earth with all her children, living and dead. This bond was symbolized by the "living" mother *pech'*, the ancestral abode and locus of a fire cult which guaranteed fruitfulness. The cult of Mother Earth centered on the communal life of the village and the well-being of the family and emphasized the need for the individual to conform to the immutable cycle of existence. Woman was the priestess as well as the giver of life, which she took back (in the course of funerary rites) so that the cycle might begin anew. When we look closely at the yearly agrarian rituals in traditional Russian village life, we will see how that dynamic of female transformational power was played out.

Agrarian Rites and Festivals

The great drama of life and death which the Greeks transformed into art as comedy and tragedy was performed in Russia by priestesses, in the service not of Dionysus, the god of fertility, but of Mother Earth herself.[23] Agrarian festivals have been described by a number of Russian and Soviet ethnologists from the nineteenth century to the present. Yet, it appears that no one has observed that the cycle invoking fertility derives from the process of feminine growth and maturation contained in the image of the triune goddess. It has not been noted that the three mythologems—Demeter-Kore, the Great Mother Goddess and the Dying God, and the Divine Twins—are interwoven into the very fabric of the agricultural rites, celebrating birth, marriage, and death in nature and, by analogy, in the community.

The Russian agrarian tradition features a fertility god, likened to the Greek Dionysus. He is called Iarilo, the "Ardent Sun," or Kupalo, linked with water, or Kostromo-Kostrobunko, associated with grain, or Lado, whose name is invoked as a refrain in folksongs. But unlike the Greeks, the Russians also attribute feminine names to these deities: Iarilo becomes Iarila; Kupalo, Kupala; Lado and Kostromo, Lada and Kostroma. The three mythologems are thus simultaneously evoked: Demeter and Kore revolve around the divinities represented as women; the Great Mother Goddess and her youthful son-consort are evident in the sacrificial role played by the god; and the division of male and female powers, Divine Twins in the service of fertility, is implicit in their representation under the same name.

The three mythologems appear together in sharpest focus in the deities called Lado and Lada, whose names are a common refrain in the songs and chants of girls and women planting, harvesting, or performing wedding rituals. Lada has been linked to a Latvian goddess, as well as to the Golden *Baba* of the Ugrians. She is also thought to derive from the Finnish-Slavic Mokosh and the Great Mother Goddess of the northern Letts and Mordvins. Some see in her the Scandinavian goddess of fire, of the hearth, and of herds, Loduna. But Lada may also have a southern origin and can be related to the Carian and ancient Lydian names for the "Divine Lady" who becomes Leto, the mother of the Divine Twins Artemis and Apollo.[24] In connection with the goddess who mothers twins, the Poles, who worshipped Zizilia and Didilia, divinities of love and fertility, also venerated Lada, linked to the Leda of the Greeks and to the Scythian Tabiti-Hestia. Lada was regarded by one seventeenth-century chronicler as the mother of Lel and Polel, associated by the author with Castor and Pollux—and the Greek Leda. In Lithuanian songs, Lada alone is addressed as a Great Goddess, "Mother Lada," the deity of the sun, accompanied by her son or consort Dido.[25]

The worship of Lada and Lado in Russia is mentioned in fifteenth- to eighteenth-century monastic texts, which refer to girls' invoking a phallic god called Lado or Ladon or Dido/Dida and a goddess they name Lada. One eighteenth-century English traveler observed that Lada/Lado were not "twins" but a goddess and son-consort: "On Thursday before Whitsuntide" the peasant girls around Moscow "celebrate the festival of the Slavonian goddess Lada and her son Dida by singing, dancing, and decorating a birch tree with garlands and ribbons which they afterwards throw with great solemnity into a river and learn, from the figures the ribbons assume in the current, who they shall wed and what their fates will be in marriage."[26] The worship of Lada-Dida was performed during the period of the Rusalia, when the *rusalki* were invoked by young women, like Kores welcoming the fruitful mother Demeter.

The word *lad* and the verb *ladit'* offer another clue to the nature of the goddess and the role of the girls in her ritual, particularly during the springtime cult of the *rusalki*. *Lad* means "harmony," and the verb *ladit'* means "to become on good terms with someone." This was precisely the function of the young women when in spring they brought the fertility of the forest into the village and fields by welcoming the *rusalki*. If Lada suggests the abstract concept of harmony, as well as the goddess of harmony herself, then her companion Ladon has a more specific etymological derivation. The term means both "threshing floor" and "palm of the hand." It has been argued that the name of Lada's "mate" may be linked to a ceremony surrounding the Dying Fertility God, and to a practice associated by the ancient Slavs with threshing—scourging youths to test their endurance and stimulate their growth, a ritual performed by the worshippers of Artemis.[27]

In the songs of Russian peasant girls, the assimilation of Lado with grain and the harvesting and preparation of it was common: "Oi millet, oi Lid-Lado we have sown," they chanted, "and millet we will thresh, Oi Lid-Lado, we will thresh." The goddess Lada, whose name is also interchangeable with Liuli, is the mistress of growth who uses the young and old women as her agents: "Where young women go flowers bloom, Oi Liuli [Lada], Where old women go mushrooms grow, Oi Liuli [Lada]." Young women look like flowers, and old women like wrinkled mushrooms. But children and youths are assimilated to the cultivated grain and are the "products" of the "domesticated" or "tamed" mothers: "Where children go, the rye is thick, O Liuli." In appealing to the goddess, the singers seemed to evoke the triune aspect of the feminine as maid, mother, and elder for the purpose of stimulating growth and providing nurture for the whole community.[28] Lado, Ladon, and Dido as the son or twinlike companions of the goddess all derive their name from her. They play out their roles in her cycle, vividly illustrated in the festivals which delineated the year's activities for the peasantry.

The Russian agrarian cycle originally began in March, but under the influence of the Orthodox church, the new year became associated with the winter solstice and assimilated to the birth of the "son" god Christ. Solstice ceremonies, which began around the twelfth of December, were called Sviatki (*svet* means "light") and Koliada (from *kolo*, "wheel"), indicating the sun.[29] The period of Shrovetide or Carnival at the end of February to mark the end of Lent was called Maslenitsa (from *maslo*, "butter"). "Bringing in the Spring" or "Bringing in the Cuckoo" fell between the twenty-second and the twenty-fifth of March. Then came the festival of the dead, Radunitsa (from *rad*, meaning "gladness"), which occurred after Easter. The notion of rebirth was most forcefully evoked in the ceremonies of the Rusaliia, Semik, and Troitsa, a week-long cycle of rituals lasting from Whitsun to the Intercession of the Trinity. The chief summer festival in June, on Saint John the Baptist's Day, was called Kupalo, Kostromo, or Kostrobunko, depending upon the province. Together with the winter Koliada, Kupalo divided the year in two, since it fell on the summer solstice and emphasized water and fire rites. (*Kupat'*, from which the feast derives its name, means "to bathe.") Petrovki, or St. Peter's Day, referred to as "Goodbye to Spring," followed. After the harvest in early September began the Bab'e Leto, "Women's Summer," corresponding with the birthday of the Mother of God. The yearly cycle culminated in October with a celebration of the harvest and with the promise of marriage: Pokrovskaia Subbota, or the "Saturday of Protection" (or "Intercession").

Sviatki and Koliada

The Koliada festivities united the community through the worship of ancestors in order to invoke the promise of rebirth. Ceremonies linked humanity with the natural order and the sun with the maternal earth through the mediation of women. Young women foretold their own futures and, thereby, that of the village and fields. Symbolically assimilated to the Fates as spinners, they created life and lured their mates; as mummers they represented the souls of the deceased, who demanded gifts in return for favors; and through the reenactment of a ritual drama revolving around death and rebirth, girls and women assured the well-being of the community.

Koliada was thought by Russian peasants to be a time of "half-light" when the living and the dead communed and the promise of new life emerged out of the frozen ground. The sun, slowly waning in its orbit, seemed to die. Festivities held at this time had to stimulate its procreative power. Koliada, the holiday of the solstice, was celebrated for the community as a whole by young girls and women. Their actions evoked the *rusalki* and Baba Yaga; images of Demeter and Kore suggested the conjunction of life and death through the mother-daughter duality. Starting with Sviatki, young women predicted their futures, and old women performed the rites of feeding the dead.

The word *Koliada* is thought to have originated in the Greek festival of Kalanda, Romanized as Calandae, marking the start of the new year. Clearly the missionaries among the Slavs assimilated their festivals to those with which they were familiar through experience or through Roman texts. In the Volga region, Koliada appears to have borne a more archaic name, Ovsen' or Vinograd ("garden" or "vineyard"), attributed to the name of a goddess. She may be linked to Vesna (from Ovsen'), goddess of spring, or to Lada, the sun goddess of the north, for in ancient times it was said that a young woman called Koliada was driven in a sleigh and accompanied by followers who sang that the female sun, Koliada, was born.[30] Songs about Koliada were often accompanied by the refrain of "Oi Lada," "Oi Lado," or "Oi Lado-Lada."

The festival of Koliada could be personified as female or male; it could be a newly born child, a mother, an old woman, a daughter, or an old man or youth. Koliada was most of all thought to be a symbol of the sun surrounded by the forces of darkness, which had to be cast off with the help of humanity—particularly women. The festival of Koliada, like that of Christ, was a festival of birth; but the forces of darkness were those of the maternal womb, which had to be escaped.[31] In his male aspect, Koliada was often linked with Saint Nicholas, the Christian saint who replaced the worship of Artemis-Diana among the peoples of the Black Sea. He assumed the goddess's functions as the helper of women in childbearing and the bringer of fertility. "Nicholas walks in the cellar," goes one Koliada song, "Nicholas seeks what is not filled / What is not filled / Is not covered / Nicholas wants to fill up." But in another version of this song, Koliada is a goddess who brings wealth.[32] In the following song, the goddess assumes both male and female duties: "Koliada came in a carriage . . . / Koliada brought an axe. / Koliada felled an oak. / Koliada fixed the yard. / Koliada heated the bath. / Koliada made kasha [gruel]. / Koliada fed the children / And put them to bed / And covered them up. / The children got up / And gave her a kopek." Sometimes in Koliada songs she appears with gruel "to feed the wife so that she gives birth to children." Her fertility is brought from the fields into the human community. "Koliada, where were you earlier?" asks one song. And she replies, "I was spending the night in the fields. / Now I come to you."[33]

The Koliada festival was preceded by a ceremony suggesting the control which women exercised over the forces of human generation and nature's production. The young women gathered at the house of a widow to spin, like the *rusalki*, Yaga, and the Fates. The widow, joined by older women, told folktales. While the girls were occupied with their work, the youths of the village were encouraged or "lured" to visit and court them. The young women appeared to pick their mates rather than the other way around: "She ate her dinner / She went to the door / She stood at the door / And chose her husband" is a Koliada song which refers both to the ritual of the maskers which follows and to that during which young women received young men at the widow's house. Another song stresses the independence of the young women being courted and identifies them with the *rusalki* as tree goddesses: "There stood a curly birch / Crowned by a *terem*. / And the roots of the birch are made of steel / Its branches of silver; its trunk of gold. / There sat a beautiful maiden. / She sewed a towel . . . with gold and silver."[34] In the song, the youth—like those who come to visit the spinners—arrives and tries to "cut down the tree," but the maiden refuses him. She will descend of her own free will when the time comes.

The ritual of courting was preceded by yet another, reflecting the assertive role of young women in courtship and associating the choice with the prediction of crop and animal fertility.

Prior to Koliada, young women gathered in the bathhouse or even in the icon corner for *gadanie* (fortunetelling). They placed a handkerchief or an embroidered towel over a bowl of water in which they had dropped gold jewelry; then they sang while removing the objects hidden in the bowl. Whoever drew the desired object, a ring, would marry; others would not, and could even die in the following year. During the "casting of lots," the young women sang to evoke both human and crop fertility: "We keep gold on the Holy Eve.... Gold fell on the poppy seeds / And they flowered into poppies. / White fire burst forth out of them / And turned into snow."[35] The golden objects in the bowl covered with the votive towel symbolized the union of sun and water, male and female, in the domain of the goddess of fertility, to whom the young women turned in their prophetic functions. A mirror (so frequently found accompanying the remains of Scythian and Sarmatian priestesses or queens, as well as women at Çatal Hüyük) was used by the young women to reflect the image of the future groom.[36]

The rituals of *gadanie* were linked to the chief Koliada ceremonial of the maskers' round, occurring on Christmas Eve and, with regional differences, organized around singing and requests for gifts. The maskers, representing ancestral spirits, granted prosperity to every family in the village, invoking the name of Lado-Lada in their blessing. The composition of the mummers varied in each locality. In some areas, they were made up chiefly of young women, who, like the *rusalki*, were associated with birds. Like the Bulgarians, who linked the Koliada (Kulada) with the appearance of the *vily*, the Russian maskers went from door to door. In some areas they were led by a young woman in white on a sleigh, like a snow goddess or winter *rusalka*, followed by mummers seated in a cradle of sleighs, singing and playing musical instruments. In other regions the group of mummers might represent the personae of a mother goddess and her son-consort, or the members of a family, the living and the dead united during the winter solstice.[37]

The archaic masking ceremonies, traceable to the ancient Greeks, symbolically united all life at a "chaotic" time when the sun dips and leaves the sky before being "reborn" again from the earth. Social bonds were temporarily dissolved: Men dressed as women, and women as men; people assumed the form of animals; the dead and the living intermingled. The Russian *koliadki* (mummers) also invoked the transformational powers of nature. When the *koliadki* included both sexes, men were disguised as horses, bulls, goats, bears, and wolves; women dressed as gypsies, priests, or officials.[38] As in the Ice Age and the early Neolithic, men identified with animals, and women with an anthropomorphized goddess. Among the Great Russians, some groups led a "mare" with a child riding on its back, but the animal was more commonly a goat or a bull. In the course of the Koliada processions, the death and rebirth of these sacrificial animals were acted out. Women's control over the beast as a Dying and Reviving God found clear expression in other dramas performed in many parts of Russia. One involved a youth who was masked as a bull to chase and butt girls. In return, the young women joined forces to "kill" and "revive" him. Another ceremony, that of the "corpse," assimilated the animal to the human male: A male corpse would be removed from his birchwood coffin and brought into the *izba*. A woman dressed as a priest officiated over a pagan mass with a bast shoe in her hand. After the "priest's" incantations, one of the assembly of girls was required to kiss the cadaver. The kiss ensured the amity of the deceased while at the same time reviving the vigor of the earth. In this parody of the Orthodox mass, it appeared that women and girls "raised the dead."[39]

The festivities of Koliada, which had begun with the lighting of bonfires to help the sun in its dangerous journey through the darkness, were brought to a close by the burning of a yule log in a symbolic unification of the living with the ancestors dwelling in the *pech'*. In fact, the yule log, over which older women most frequently officiated, appeared to bring the sun's vitality into the house. Thus, while Koliada had been ushered in by girls representing the *rusalki* with their promise of marriage and abundance, it was the Yaga-like elders who completed the ceremonies by burning the log and preparing a special feast for the dead. Placing the "male" Badnik (as the log was called in Novgorod Province) into the flames of the oven suggested a rite of sexual stimulation, as well as one of death and rebirth assimilated to earth's fertility. The whole family would pray to the log: "Let the rye grow, let our cattle and children increase." The yule log symbolized not only the sun but also the ancestors in the earth, and determined the well-being of the collectivity.[40]

The day after Koliada, in Kursk Province as in other places, Bab'e Kasha, or "Lady Gruel," arrived. The family ate a special meal of *kut'ia* prepared by women in the bathhouse in order to receive the blessings of a good harvest directly from the ancestral spirits. The *kut'ia* was made of ritually symbolic foods, eggs and grain, suggesting rebirth. In Belorussia, this ceremonial feast centered on a rite in which the whole family drank out of a single

horned vessel like that represented in images of the ancient Paleolithic and Neolithic goddesses.[41]

Maslenitsa

The rites of the winter solstice were devoted to nature as virgin and chthonian mother, the transformational goddess. Maslenitsa was a festival to awaken the earth. Despite regional differences, the common patterns of celebration consisted in making a
straw doll called Maslenitsa, or naming a woman to play the
part, and selecting and decorating a tree. *Bliny* were cooked for
ceremonies of remembrance of the dead. The festivities culminated with special games involving newlyweds sledding down
artificially constructed hills. The best spinners would also descend, on their spinning benches. Those who slid the farthest
were assured of the best crop of flax in the forthcoming year.
Maslenitsa's name, *maslo* (butter), associated her with Lent. In
Tula her role was assumed by a woman in a sleigh with loosened
hair decorated with flax and carrying dried flowers in her out-
stretched arms. Preceded by a child on a horse, symbol of the
rising sun, and accompanied by young girls and women, Maslenitsa was pulled by men through the village or town. In other areas
the goddess was occasionally impersonated by a man called the
sun, sitting on a *pech'*, and driven through the streets on an immense sleigh. The ceremony of leading the Maslenitsa in from
the cemetery was performed with laughter, sometimes provoked
by the doll's companion, a woman parodying a priest. But the
ritual was essentially erotic rather than satiric, intended to stimulate the still-dormant earth.[42]

As the spring mother goddess with her child the sun, Maslenitsa was welcomed with an offering of food. The newly born sun
needed vitality, and the mother would reward gifts with gifts.
Maslenitsa's great welcome was only the prelude to the drama
she initiated. Her stay in the community signaled the beginning
of erotic and birth-giving rites. Most of all, it was a time for the
popular dramas performed by the *skoromokhy*, ancient itinerant
mummers and musicians persecuted by the church; and for the
round dance (*khorovod*).[43] The *khorovod* was linked to the work of
spinning and weaving; but during Maslenitsa, it was also associated with the sexually luring dance of the *rusalki* and *vily*, who at-
tracted the sun's growing ardor. The word itself refers to the ancient Slavic sun god, Khor, but its origins may be more archaic,
referring also to a lunar ritual—which would explain why *bliny*
were prepared by moonlight. As a moon dance, the *khorovod*

evoked the cult of the dead and referred symbolically to the period of the hunt when animals were gradually encircled before being killed. Thus, in certain areas of Russia, hares and deer, sacred to the lunar divinities, were placed in the center of the circle. But more often it was youths or youths and young women who performed and leaped, encircled by mature women invoking the fertilizing power of the moon with seductive motions.[44]

The rituals which greeted Maslenitsa and "fattened" her were followed by sinister ones. The pregnant and well-fed-mother, "serenaded" with bawdy songs, was led out of the community to be delivered of her child in the fields. In central Russia, three youths carried the doll, and the most beautiful girls were chosen to surround it. Once in the field, the doll was pulled apart. Food emerged from her body, and her remains were burned or scattered over the fields. (In the Ukraine and Belorussia, a girl or woman called Koliada acted out the role of the goddess.) Why was the doll destroyed? Frazer, noting similiar ceremonies in western Europe, attributed them to the chasing away of winter in the guise of a witch.[45] But other symbolic and more complex patterns can be found in the Maslenitsa ritual. They suggest that nature as mother feeds her young with blood from the womb and milk from the breast. Maslenitsa, then, recalls the notion that life and death are conjoined: As death led to life in the Koliada rites, so life led to death in those of Maslenitsa. In the next spring festival, young and old women joined forces to bring maternity from the land of the dead into that of the living.

Greeting Spring and Radunitsa

In early March, young women greeted spring by calling on the souls of the dead, in the form of birds and insects: "O you little bee / ardent bee / fly across the sea / get the keys, the golden keys / lock up winter / freezing winter / and unlock summer . . . filled with grain." The chorus of young women who sang these songs held tree boughs in their hands with pastry birds entwined in the leaves. Such birds would decorate trees, barns, and orchards, as well as the earth itself. The young women would also call up the female cuckoo, a *psychopomp* or spirit of the dead linked to the goddess Zhiva. March had been the month of the goddess Cybele of the Phrygians, the time when she was thought to have given birth to her son-consort Attis. Among the Bulgarians, that memory may have been preserved in "Mother March," when women temporarily asserted power over men. It might also explain the timing of the Christian feast of the Annunciation. In Russia, Lada's name was invoked, and *khorovody* were performed near springs and lakes.[46]

Maslenitsa, the "fat" Mother, had been awakened at the cemetery and led into the fields to nourish the soil with her fertile body. But in the spring rituals, fertility was sought in the forest, where the *rusalki* dwelled and where the promise of nature's reawakening was discovered in the budding branches of the birch tree. The *rusalki* moved from the frozen waters into the trees and took flight in the form of birds welcomed by young women. The duality of mother and daughter not only is underscored in the spring rites but also appears uninterrupted by a male or a Hades figure. While Maslenitsa evoked impending maternity, the "Greeting of Spring" seemed to welcome the mother accompanied by her newly born progeny—Demeter together with Kore delivered from the underworld, or the *rusalki* released from Yaga's realm: "My spring, where is your daughter?" one song asks and answers, "She sits in the garden / She sews a shirt."[47]

In some parts of Great Russia, spring was personified by a goddess called Vesnianka. When the young women of the village greeted her with songs and dances, the ritual was also called a *vesnianka*. But unlike the Christian festival of Easter, which begins with death and is followed by rebirth, this ritual reversed the process. The rebirth of nature in the form of mother and daughter united was succeeded by rites honoring the dead. The holiday of Krasnaia Gora (Red/Beautiful Mountain), which took place in flat Novgorod as well as in Tula and other hillier areas of Russia, referred, according to some researchers, to the ancient Slavic custom of burying the deceased on hilltops or inclines where churches and monasteries now stand.[48]

Krasnaia Gora occurred at sunset when young women and men gathered to dance, holding bread and eggs and singing about the advent of spring. Often young women would perform this ritual alone, dancing around one individual who stood at the center of the ring with ritual bread and an egg which had been dyed red. Turning toward the setting sun, thought to be going to the land of the ancestors, she addressed it as the feminine *Vesna* (spring). The hill, the sun, the red-painted eggs, and spring itself, as well as the young woman who prayed to her, were linked by the adjective *krasnoe* (red/beautiful). Standing on the hillside, between the sky and earth, the girl appeared to mediate between the earthly "womb," home of the ancestors, and the sky, the breast of the goddess who "fed" humanity with sunlight and rain. With her companions, she attempted to stimulate the sun's ardor by luring it into the circle, for it was believed that during the period of Krasnia Gora the sun, too, danced, waiting to be born.[49]

While the young women evoked and encouraged the vitality of sun and spring, old women sacrificed to it. In Smolensk they took food and young children to the hilltop and brought with them dolls called *Vesna*. The rites of the hill were linked with a holiday for the dead, Radunitsa, which was held the day after Easter and was closely followed by the Navii Den', the day of the *navy-rusalki*, when water nymphs moved into the trees. In Kievan Russia, Radunitsa was also called Babilskoe Prazdnik (Women's Day) and was devoted to honoring the *rod* with a feast (*trizda*), prepared and celebrated by women in honor of the deceased. The ritual of painting eggs red, purple, or brown took place during Radunitsa. Eggs were placed at grave sites to symbolize rebirth as new blood circulating out of the ground to revive nature. Radunitsa, a pagan holiday, was incorporated into the Easter rites. It was thought that if a family proclaimed to the dead that "Christ is risen," the dead would answer from their graves, like the congregation in church, "Indeed He is risen!"[50]

Rusaliia, Semik, and Troitsa

From Easter or Radunitsa to Whitsuntide or Rusaliia, the dead souls welcomed to the earth by young and old women were thought to linger in trees, fields, and gardens, bringing life and vigor. The Rusaliia (Trinity Week or *Zelenie Sviatki*), originally in honor of the fertility god Adonis, occurred when the god was thought to emerge out of the earth. While Rusaliia is still celebrated in that way by Greek peasants, for the Russians the holiday involved bringing the *rusalki* (or *navy* or *vily*) from the forest onto cultivated land and into the village.[51] It was a ritual presided over by the female deity as the Tree of Life.

With the first warmth of spring, the peasants would say "Roditeli vzochuli" ("The ancestors are awake"). Young women would carry birch branches from the forest into the community. These boughs were in some areas called *rusalki*; in other areas, the rite of bringing in the greenery was performed by a girl dressed in white, her hair loosened and flowers woven into it. She was accompanied by a little girl, sometimes naked, called "the *rusalka's* daughter," illustrating the myth of Demeter and Kore reunited. Sometimes the two were accompanied by youths costumed as a horse, with the child sitting on their back. In other areas, a procession of singing girls brought a *rusalka* doll decorated with ribbons and votive towels into the village.[52]

Rusaliia was above all the festival of women. In the Ukraine on the eve of Rusaliia, when the nymphs were thought to rise up into the trees, no one dared bathe for fear of offending the newly risen ancestral spirits, who would retaliate with floods or cattle plagues. Moreover, young men risked being seduced and killed if they ventured into the nymphs' territory in the forest. The girls played a mediatory role: They were to secure the goodwill of the *rusalki* by bringing them into the village, and in return sacrificed to them in order to protect the community. "A *rusalka* sat on the curving road / on the curved branch of the birch tree. / The *rusalka* asked for bread and salt," begins one holiday song.[53]

The central ritual of the Rusaliia week was Semik, celebrated on the seventh Thursday after Easter. Its root, *sem'*, identifies it with the words for "seed," "sperm," and "family" (as well as "seven"). More than any other of the yearly festivals, it affirmed the solidarity of the feminine community, which asserted its own order over that of the prevailing social one. In the evening, girls went into the woods to pick a Semik birch and mark it, sometimes tying its tips together as if to trap the rising sap to energize the fields and village where it would be carried. Next morning, the girls would go to the birch with eggs and beer, offerings of food for the dead. They would decorate the tree with ribbons and towels called the *"rusalka's* shirt," which the nymph had requested.[54]

The clothing of the *rusalka* tree was a prelude to the major ceremony of Semik called *kumstvo*, designed to assure the solidarity of the village as a whole and to reaffirm its link with the deceased. Young girls wore garlands, sometimes threading in stalks of dried wheat or rye, out of the boughs of the birch tree which stood over the ritual like a goddess. When the garlands were ready, the girls would embrace one another through them, pledging eternal blood ties, *kumstvo*, on behalf of their families (for *kum* means "cousin").[55]

The symbolism of *kumstvo* was complex. The braided tree branches perhaps represented the braiding of the girls' hair to "trap" their own fertility and tame it until they married. The Semik rite, over which the birch tree presided totemically (like the ancient clan mother or Scythian goddess who guaranteed pledges and protected social harmony, rewarding it with fertility), involved the unification of all nature and humanity. *Kumstvo* was a prelude to the prediction of marriage on the part of the young women. They pledged themselves to the birch, which was to be tamed like them for the benefit of the cultivated land and the continuation of the human community. But until the tree was brought from "wild" nature into the village by her priest-esses, no man was allowed to witness these sacred rites. In Vladi-mir Province and in Mogilev, if a man appeared to disturb the cere-monies, he would be destroyed like Euripides' Pentheus by these Russian Bacchantes. But unlike their Greek predecessors, the girls based their assertion of feminine superiority on blood and family ties grounded in feminine authority.[56]

The pledging of solidarity on behalf of the community repre-sented one symbolic level of *kumstvo*; another suggested that the young women assumed in their own persons the totemic attri-butes of the tree: Kissing through the braided and circular boughs, they became possessed with the fertilizing powers of earth, as well as the ancestral family spirits. Identified with these powers, they could now cut down the Semik tree and take it into the village and the fields. Houses and churches were decorated with the holy birch so that the whole community assumed a fes-tive air, itself transformed into a forest and infused with its vital-ity. At the same time, the young women brought the Semik, deco-rated like a goddess, into a house to be entertained by the villagers. The Semik goddess, ruler of the dead souls, was fed like the deceased. During her rule, the girl-priestesses who had ef-fectuated the exchange from village to forest and forest to village would themselves begin to select mates, like alluring *rusalki*. They invited men to come and stroll with them, to drink vodka and eat eggs.[57]

After the visitor called Semik or Rusalka had been enter-tained like her predecessor Maslenitsa, she too was turned out of the village to spread out her own gifts to her worshippers. But while Maslenitsa was dismembered and scattered over the fields, Semik or Rusalka was drowned in order to provide the needed rainfall for the sprouting crops. Young women would take the dec-orated birch to the river and ceremonially undress her while sing-ing songs in which the tree pleaded with them not to send her away: "I was curly, I was well-dressed, / But now I stand naked. / All my clothes have been taken away, / All my leaves have been torn away. / You friends take me away, / Throw me in the fast river." While the rite of the tree's stripping was performed, the young women loosened their hair like the *rusalki* and sang: "I will throw my garland into the water / so that the wheat grows thick." If the garland sank, its owner would perish in the course of the year and would thereby join the *rusalka*, her *kuma*; if it floated, she would marry. In either case she would be a source of natural abundance.[58]

The end of Semik marked the beginning of Troitsa Day, Trinity Sunday, in the Orthodox church. Called "Mother Troitsa," this day completed the Rusalia festivities. In *khorovody*, a young woman would stand in the center of the ring both to predict marriage and to complain of bad luck. On "Mother Troitsa," young women identified themselves in song with the cultivated garden (marriage and maternity) into which a youth would come. Or they would represent themselves as a tree growing in the middle of a fertile field. In concluding the week-long holiday with the evocation of "Mother Troitsa," the young women reflected on their passage from maidenhood to motherhood through the prediction of marriage. Combining the roles of daughter and mother, they revealed the governing motif of the Rusalia as an echo of the rites of Demeter and Kore.[59]

Ivan Kupalo

The feast of midsummer called Ivan Kupalo was the celebration of Mother Moist Earth and of married women. Involving the whole community, it was led by the mothers to celebrate growth in field, garden, and forest, symbolically linked to their sons and mates. As in the rites of midwinter, the divinities were both feminine and masculine, merging the mythology of the Great Mother and the Dying God with that of the parthenogenetic goddess and the male-female Divine Twins. Occurring at the time of the summer equinox, Kupalo expressed the relationship of the sun to the earth as mother and as consort. It celebrated sexual union, symbolized in ceremonies involving fire and water with ritual bathing by men and women in lakes and rivers. A time also of "haeterism," female-led orgy, Kupalo emphasized the reproductive powers of the family under the aegis of the mother and assimilated these to the natural order.

The oldest reports of this festival come from church chronicles of the twelfth century, where it is confused with the Rusalia. The chronicles describe the oldest peasant girls' being dressed as brides and led to the river, where they would dance and "jump" and worship the goddess, telling fortunes and returning to the community to sprinkle the houses with the sanctified river water. Later, bonfires were lit, and the villagers jumped over the flames.[60]

The rituals changed little over time; the use of fire and water was always central. Kupalo is derived from *kupat'*, "to bathe." One seventeenth-century chronicler referred to Kupalo as a Slavic deity associated with Lado and linked by him to

Ceres, the Roman Demeter. But the source of the name remains a puzzle. Some researchers have argued that it evolved from a corruption of the name of the Phrygian Kybele or Cybele, and indeed in southeast and southwest Russia, Kupalo had a female counterpart called Kupal'nitsa. Whatever the etymology and historical source of the name, it was assimilated by the Russian peasantry to John the Baptist. The sexual "games" central to the festival and involving communal bathing were linked to the saint's baptism of Christ. Kupalo acquired his "Christian" name, Ivan (John), from that association.[61]

In some areas, the festival assumed other names. In Vladimir, Kupalo was Lado accompanied by Lada; in Murom, he was called Kostromo and/or Kostroma; in Kostromo province, on the other hand, the sun god Iarilo and goddess Iarila were worshipped. This dual form, as we saw in the evocation of Lado and Lada, suggests not only the juxtaposition of two myths (of Divine Twins and of a mother-son consort dyad), but also the androgyny of Mother Moist Earth, herself patroness of the maternal family, uniting male and female in her reproductive rites. Hence, in some areas the effigies of Kupalo and Kupala, Iarilo and Iarila, Lado and Lada were burned together and were frequently called by the Christian names Ivan (John) and Maria, suggesting again the union of the mother figure (Mary) and the sacrificed son (John the Baptist) surrogate. At the same time, they are represented as brother and sister or Divine Twins who bathe together in an incestuous union symbolizing the production of abundance. Their union occurs in water, field, or fire—especially the flames of the oven.[62]

The marriage between brother and sister, performed in a context dominated by the maternal, suggests matrilineal views of that union. Songs and ballads decry the incest but do not deny its benefits, the production of wealth and protection against ill health. Ivan and Maria consummate their marriage without knowing their true relationship. As a result, they are turned into a flower called Ivan-da-Maria: "How is it that a sister goes after a brother," asks one such Kupalo song. "A sister does not go after her brother," singers chide. "We will go into the fields / we will knock down the grass . . . for it is the brother with his sister."[63] At the same time, the flower is woven into wreaths and taken home by the celebrants as a medicinal cure. The brother-sister relationship refers to the proper role of the male in a maternal social and cosmic order: He must subordinate himself to the law of the sister, wife, and mother. This is apparent when we look at the ways in which Kupalo reflects the sun as a Dying and Reviving God and appears as a later substitute for the archaic parthenogenetic goddess.

Effigies of Kupalo were made exclusively by women, who wove and braided straw to create "their child" (or chose a tree to represent him, as for the *rusalka* at Semik). The link of Semik with Kupalo is found in customs around Chernigov and in Volynia, Podulia, and the Ukraine. Girls went to the forest to select and decorate a Kupalo tree, brought it into the village, and destroyed it by burning or drowning. The straw effigy, most frequently called Iarilo in the north and east, was closely associated with the sun. In the course of the midsummer festivities, it was rolled into a lake, suggesting both a mother's womb and the sexual union of youth and young woman.[64]

Iarilo is the clearest image of the Dying God. His name means "spring" and, as Iuru, "ardent." He has been linked with the Sanskrit Ari, the Greek Eros, and the Roman Priapus. His symbol is that of the auroch bull, and the signs of his worship can still be found in the names of cities and men (Iaroslav, Iaropolk, Iaromirov).[65] In one legend he assumes the role of the bridegroom of Mother Earth: Iarilo came to her and said, "Mother Moist Earth, love me, the god of light, be my beloved, and I'll cover you with blue seas and golden sands, and green grass, and red and blue flowers, and you will bear me an unending number of children." When he leaves her, the earth laments, not so much as a bride but like a mother: "I cry not for myself," she is heard to say, "but for my children." Iarilo promises to protect them all with his fire. This is not Eros speaking but the warrior ruler who protects the *rod*, and his beloved is no virginal beauty but an ancient mother.[66]

The legend, with its strong patriarchal overtones, betrays its matrifocal and archaic source in the still-apparent hegemony of the Mother Goddess. Iarilo incarnated in the sun wheel also indicates his function as the youthful son and consort of the mother. In Belorussia, a handsome youth dressed in a white shirt and mounted on a white horse carried a garland of flowers and a sheaf of grain. When he reached the fields, he walked barefoot to make the crops grow. But this fertilizing function was ephemeral; immediately thereafter, in the form of an effigy, he was torn up or burned by women. Sometimes Iarilo was represented only in the form of a huge phallus placed in a coffin, accompanied in procession by an old man and followed by wailing women like Isis mourning Osiris; Kybele, Adonis; Ishtar, Tammuz. Indeed, in the region where Iarilo was worshipped, women made and decorated the effigy or surrounded the youth, accompanying him on his journey to the earth as her lover and to his "death" as her son.[67]

Iarilo, the Dying God surrounded by women, is doubled by a goddess bearing the same name: Iarila, Kostroma, and Kupala. She is both a sun and an earth divinity and appears as maiden and mother, Kore and Demeter. In Belorussia, Iarila was a young and lovely maiden dressed, like her male counterpart, in white, carrying flowers, with her hair loosened, riding a white horse. But unlike him, though she bore a sheaf of wheat, she held in her other hand a mask—a "human head." Like the Indian Durga-Kali and Baba Yaga in her incarnation as Vasilisa the Fair, she brought with her the symbols of life and death, light and darkness, youth and old age. Girls danced and sang around her.[68]

The figure of Kostroma in the solstice rites, the "twin" of Kostromo, whose name, derived from *kostra*, means "flax," also has archaic attributes like Iarila the sun goddess. Kostroma is both an evil witch and a good mother; she is also the dying and reborn daughter. The image of the archaic triune goddess is most completely expressed through her. Unlike the passive Iarilo or Kostromo, she has a will of her own: "In our wheat field sits a witch," goes one song about her. "Go away from our wheat. / Our wheat is holy, blessed." The goddess is a chthonian mother who must be appeased to yield her bounty. Indeed, on Ivan Kupalo Night, witches were thought to go about the land and light the darkness with magical fires. They placed silver in the waters and made the trees talk. In Belorussia, Baba Yaga was said to go about with her sisterhood of witches draining off the energies of the sun with their magical fires, plucking plants from the soil, and turning the power of the earth against humanity.[69] But the night of Saint John's was also the night of "female haeterism," a time to pick medicinal plants and bring back the incestuous Ivan-da-Maria magic flower to the community.

While Kostroma is both benign and dangerous, she is also represented as the dying and reborn daughter, a Kore-Demeter figure. In certain children's games in the province of Kursk, Kostroma is described as a girl and a mother, as bread and *pech'*, as flax and spinner. Her death is merely a sleep from which she reawakens reinvigorated. In one song, the ancient image of the Tree of Life goddess is vividly evoked. "Under the birch / Lay our Kostroma. / She has been killed; but was not killed, / Covered with crepe. / A lovely girl came to her / Uncovered the crepe, / Looked into her face and asked: / 'Do you sleep, dear Kostroma, / Do you feel nothing? / Your horse the crow flies in the field.' / The beautiful girl brought water / and asked the rain-giver: / 'Give us rain, Lady, / much rain / So that the grass grows / and blunts Kostroma's braid.' / Behind the river / Kostroma braids the hay. / She throws her braid / In the midst of the haymakers.''[70]

The fertility goddess Kostroma, unlike her male counterpart Kostromo or Iarilo, lies under her birch in a state between life and death, "killed but not killed." Her sleep can be disturbed only by her priestess, the lovely girl who thereby awakens nature's maternal body. Her somnolent condition refers both to the need for human (female) stimulation of nature's forces and to the fact that "killed but not killed," she must cannibalize her own body for humankind: She is killed—as the hay is mowed—and yet she is not dead, for she is the force which mows the hay. In cutting the hay, Kostroma cuts her braid; and in the process of cutting the braid she moves, like village girls, from the realm of the self-sufficient virgin (the parthenogenetic one) to the realm of the married and nurturing mother. Indeed, after solstice and after the harvest which followed, the girls too would be wed, their braids cut off and their magical potential for luring their mates fulfilled in the production of children. Kupalo/Kostromo/Iarilo festivities announced and celebrated the sacredness of sexual union under the aegis of the mothers. In the months that followed, the weddings of young women, the spring *rusalki*, were arranged.

Petrov Den', Bab'e Leto, and Pokrovskaia Subbota

In autumn the *rusalki* reappeared to announce their return to the underworld. After the sexual-fertility rites of Kupalo came a women's festival called "Goodbye to Spring," Christianized under the name of Petrov Den', "Saint Peter's Day." Both towns-women and country girls would go outside, where swings had been set up for them to imitate the behavior of the *rusalki* in the tree boughs, swinging back and forth as though imparting the magic of "feminine power" to the soil. They sang about the declining vitality of the sun, about the ancestral spirits in the underworld, and about the water and tree nymphs who were withdrawing to their winter dwellings. On the eve of Petrov Den', villagers began an all-night vigil to watch the sun, called Lado, "leap out" from the earth as though born at dawn. The day's activities, the "dance of the sun," and the swinging of the girls and women in the fields and gardens, indicated that the sacred union at the summer solstice would result in the birth of crops. For indeed Petrov

Den', presided over by women, preceded the harvest, called the *stradnaia pora*, or "time of suffering"—their own hard labor and that of the grain cut and "killed" by scythes. Just before the harvest, women and girls, singing, brought garlands of wheat or rye into the house so that the wealth of the fields might act to stimulate human fertility, as well. [71]

Though harvesting was done by men, women, and girls, it was "sung" by the women. Often the mistress of the house went out into the fields to encourage her daughters and daughters-in-law. When the reaping ended, the women would lean over backward into the field and sing to Mother Moist Earth: "Wheat field, wheat field, / I reaped you [I was sorry for you], / And I lost my strength for you." Their own suffering was the sacrificial gift to the agony of the cut crops. [72]

The feast of Bab'e Leto, "Women's Summer," began on the first of September, Saint Simon's Day. It was marked by several significant events in the household: Old fires, thought to be exhausted (like the waning sun), were extinguished, and new ones honoring the ancestors were lit by the mistress of the household. The dead were remembered and their prophetic powers heeded. Spinning began, new beer was brewed, and, most important, marriages were arranged. "It is time, mother, to reap the grain," goes one harvest song; "it is time to give away the girl." [73] In October the yearly cycle was completed with the *Pokrovskaia Subbota*, the Day of Protection or Intercession, when girls appealed to ancestral spirits and to the Mother of God (behind whom stood the shadow of the Slavic birth goddess Mokosh in the guise of the apocryphal Saint Paraskeva) for a happy marriage. But the marriage meant a change for them from wild and free *rusalka* to tamed or cultivated mother—earth; from their own to their husband's family and to exploitation. The culmination of the year's cycle in wedding plans was not a joyful one.

The Reluctant Bride

> Oh my mother, dear
> I don't want to marry
> Oi Liuli, Liuli, Liuli
> I don't want to marry. [74]

For her wedding, the bride often made and wore a ritual votive towel or handkerchief embroidered with the image of the goddess. But the social reality was quite at odds with such an assertion of female power. Just as Russia had for centuries been in the grip of autocracy, so too the family by the nineteenth century had become a microcosm of the state. Most of the songs related to the agrarian festivals—dances, divinations, dirges, incantations, love and marriage feasts—had been created and sung by women. Perhaps the richly emotional and heavily modulated, "generous" nature of Russian folk melody reflects the need for emotional release from a life of hard labor and oppression. This is apparent in the large numbers of wedding songs suffused with poignancy, melancholy, and even bitterness.

The life of the married peasant woman was indeed a bitter one. Numerous disparaging proverbs testify to the scorn with which men treated her in an attempt to deny her overwhelming importance in the economy of village and family. Marriage was advantageous to the young man: It raised his prestige and provided for his heirs. But a married woman lost all freedom. She was often beaten, and suffered as a workhorse and the carrier of too many children. But while men made light of women's work, intelligence, and temperament, proverbs indicate that they did so with some misgivings: "Beat a wife and you will become wise," but "Who beats the *baba* will soon become poor." "A man is not a man if his wife rules," a husband is warned of woman's potential power and independence. But should his wife die, her husband is described as an orphan rather than the father of his children.[75] She is a wife, but she is above all a mother. Indeed, in his study of Slavic matriarchal institutions, the Italian scholar E. Gasparini observes that among no other peoples was so much attention paid to the internal life of women; and among no other were the economy and rites of family and village, of field and garden, so regulated by and assimilated to the feminine cycle. It is no exaggeration to note that the Russian village was like the wheel turned by a female donkey. If women conceded to men the exercise of public power, they had been the source of tribal (*rod*) institutions for millennia.[76]

In an earlier chapter, we noted vestiges of matrilineal and matrilocal custom in the Russian family. In observing the powerful roles and critical functions of women in rites of increase and protection, we find further confirmation of ancient woman-centered social orders. The particular stress upon virginity among the Slavs may stem from an Indo-European patriarchal demand, but more probably it refers back to the hunters' parthenogenetic figure of a goddess like the *rusalka* with hegemony over the forces of nature and the human collectivity dependent upon them. The wedding songs—or plaints—of the Russian bride, expressing her reluctance to marry and lose her freedom, may be based only partly upon her knowledge of the hardship which she would be forced to endure. They may also refer to a distant period when matrilocal weddings did not deprive the bride of the security of her family or of the freedom she continued to prize.

The word for "to marry," *voditi zhenu*, means literally to "bring a wife." Its patrilocal sense is unequivocal. But there is an analogous archaic expression, *uzheti muzha*, "to lead a husband," and *vysvatat' dlia docheri zhenikha*, "to find a husband for a daughter," which both imply matrilocal custom. The word *rod*, designating the family together with its ancestors, from *rodit'*, "to give birth," suggests that the birth-giver or woman is the totemic center of those related by blood. Furthermore, *rod* is used only to indicate the bride's family. The denigration of paternity also indicated the continuing pull of ingrained and ancient matrifocal institutions. No law of primogeniture ensured the peasant's male line. To add to the denial of the father's role in his blood relationship to the child was the importance, particularly in the Ukraine, accorded to brothers and uncles, typical of matrilineal and matrilocal custom. They played the central role in the weddings of their sisters and nieces. Finally, despite church condemnation, the belief that any child of the mother was legitimate and that no dishonor fell on women who gave birth shortly after marriage indicates how little the paternity of the male was honored. The contrasting attachment of the children to the mother is markedly at odds with the subordination of the father in the affective life of the family.[77] Sons could not leave their mothers without being blessed by them.

If the mother was the "soul" of family life, the young woman was the Amazon whose vitality provided the basis for its future regeneration: In folktales, as we have seen, she often chooses her bridegroom or confers upon him a kingdom or a treasure. In the agrarian rituals, girls foretold their future mates. In fact, particularly in the Ukraine, young women were allowed considerable liberty of action before their weddings and the right to choose their husbands. (A seventeenth-century French traveler was so struck by this freedom that he reported with amazement: "Among the common customs of this nation, one finds girls making love to young men who please them.")[78] A girl could bring a young man to her mother's house, and he was permitted to live with her before being persuaded that he should take her for his bride. Young Ukrainian women's initiative in courtship is reflected in the many riddles they asked to lure their "prey." When young men were invited to sit with the spinning girls during the Koliada celebrations, the widow played the role of chief Bacchante to these aggressive seductresses, leading the spinners in lewd and sexually explicit songs and ballads. If the marriage did not last, the young woman was free to return to her maternal family, the protection of which was accorded to the bride in the gift of a family icon.[79]

The ceremonies surrounding the wedding were called in Russia "the game," and the marriage was a ritual "played" out. It was perhaps the most significant event of village life, uniting the whole community through the honoring of the dead and the promise of new life. The bridegroom and the bride, as well as their attendants, assumed the parts of folkloric characters: He was the prince, she the princess, he the falcon, she the swan, he the warrior, she the treasure. The bride was frequently associated with the pagan goddess whose image decorated her bridal costume, and her mother appeared in the guise of the Yaga, both benign and evil.

The celebration of a wedding in the Ukraine took the form of a conflict. The bride's attendants sang (commenting on the action like the chorus in Greek drama), asked riddles, uttered magical incantations, danced, and "charmed" the company like a group of *rusalki*. The groom's party formed a military band to help the youth capture his reluctant and heavily guarded bride. But the victory was won through the help of the mothers. The marriage game displayed the most vivid matrifocal aspects. As in other parts of Russia, the ceremony was divided into specific acts: Matchmaking was followed by the lamentation of the fiancée, which was succeeded by a ceremony in the bathhouse where the future bride bemoaned the loss of her virginity. The reception for the bride was given by the groom, but the ceremony of the wedding morn took place in the house of the bride, who was "attacked" by the groom's party. The wedding game finished when the husband took his wife to his parents' home.[80]

The matchmaking prelude often involved a *voplesnitsa* (wailer) who played the part of the mistress of ceremonies for the entire "wedding game." Her persona projected the power of the mothers, who arranged their children's alliances. In Vologodsk Province, for example, the mother told her son exactly what to do: "You go, my son, to marry / Go to the great courtyard. / Don't let the horse go ahead of you. / Give the horse some food. / Stop and feed him well. ... / You will arrive, my son, in a white room. / Don't stand, my son, under the icons, / Stand, my child, instead among the fields / And bow to them like a lord."[81]

While the mothers compelled their sons to marry, the young women's songs about their prospective grooms, less than enthusiastic, reflected the custom of arranged weddings. The fiancé was likened to an invading force, the future bride to the land or a garden or orchard about to be despoiled. Sometimes he was presented as the warrior, and sometimes as the hunter. But in Ukrainian songs reflecting the traces of more archaic custom, the bride is not at all hesitant to marry: She chases her mate, advised by her mother to catch "the falcon bright in the open field." When he "perches on her hand / She brings him to her mother." Elsewhere the mother leads her daughter out of the *terem* to pick her husband from a group of youths.[82] Once the match was made or the girl had chosen and the mother had agreed, the bride's family went to the *pech'* to ask for the blessing of the ancestors. At that moment the prospective groom and his party would arrive with bread and salt—playing the role of the hunters who had spied out the tracks of their prey. The girl, seeking refuge behind the *pech'* or in the icon corner, would begin to lament.

The bride's lament is one of the richest forms of ancient peasant poetry. Though in the Ukraine both the mother and the daughter needed to consent to the match, and brought out the embroidered votive towel with the image of the goddess upon it to seal the oath and bind the couple, the young woman nonetheless proceeded to beseech the members of the family for their aid in preventing her from being taken out of the household. As in matrilineal custom, she implored her brother to defend her against the groom.[83]

Several days after the matchmaking and the groom's proposal and entry into the bride's house, there occurred a ritual called a *devushnik*, in which the fiancée and her attendants went to the bathhouse to mourn the loss of the future bride's braid, the symbol of her freedom and virginity. The ritual identified the young woman with the *rusalka* and suggested her independence from the world of men. During the *devushnik* (from *deva*, "girl"), the fiancée was given a special ribbon set with beads called a *krasota* (beauty), representing her braid. In song she deplores not just the loss of her freedom, but her link with both the forest and the magical maiden *rusalki* who inhabit it. The *krasota* was often dedicated to the birch tree, where it was ceremoniously hung. The bride was herself assimilated to the birch tree. In the bathhouse, she abandoned the divinity of the tree to dedicate herself to the cultivated maternal earth. Bowing to the ground, she called on Mother Moist Earth, Lada, or Mary and recited: "Take my body, earth ... and give birth to grass. / Oh, choose me, rain / Oh, choose me, Mother Moist Earth, / I with my beautiful *krasota*."[84]

On the wedding day, the bride was surrounded by her own female army of Amazonian followers called a *druzhina* (military group), like the "warriors" following the groom. The young man left for his "campaign" only after he had been blessed by his mother, thereby guaranteeing the success of his mission. The mother dressed in a fur coat, worn inside out, and a man's fur hat; "mounted" on a rake or fork, she ran around the courtyard and house "sowing" grain and money. Thus she appears as an animal mistress and an androgynous Yaga, planting her own seed or son into the fertile field represented by the bride. Indeed, the coins she threw on the earth had been collected for that purpose since her son's childhood. As she "rode," the whole *druzhina* (male band) followed her, singing: "Sow, mother, sow oats / for our whole clan / so our harvest may be rich / and Ivashko's clan handsome." Before setting out for the house of the bride, the groom, together with the male group, would be blessed with bread by his mother, who was described in the accompanying ritual incantation as she who "had borne him, clothed him with the moon, bound him with the sun."[85]

The groom's mother passed her son to another mother. For when the expedition arrived at the home of the bride, it was met by her mother, clad in the same ceremonial clothing as the youth's own parent. The passage from mother to mother, suggesting the tenacity of matrifocal customs, was not effectuated without conflict. When the bridegroom reached the house of the bride, he found it barricaded and was obliged to order his entourage to take their swords and capture the resistant young woman hiding behind her own "soldiers." The battle for the girl was sabotaged from within her own camp. In the Ukraine, men "sold" the bride and tried to escape as though ashamed of their treacherous actions. The uncle of the bride took over the "traitor-father's" role and, as in matrilineal custom, assumed the function of the chief male representative of the family.[86]

Only after the "laying down of the law" by the female chorus who accompanied the bride was the mother of the bride charged with cutting her braid and replacing it with the headdress of a married woman, the *kika* or *kokoshnik*, or, in the Ukraine, *namika*. The girl resisted, calling her mother an enemy, while a contest took place between the women of the groom and the women of the bride: The first called for compliance, the second for resistance. The mothers then "domesticated" the sacrificed segment of braid: It was anointed with honey and butter and covered with money and bread. The wedding cake was decorated with a twig to indicate that the service to the grain-growing Mother Moist Earth must replace that of the independent tree goddess.[87]

The ritual of bringing the bride into the husband's house was in many ways similar to that of escorting in the *rusalka* or Kupala doll or effigy: "Bring in buckwheat / black, full, and abundant. / We bring in a daughter-in-law / young and rich," sang the women of the husband's family.[88] The new wife was likened throughout the wedding and welcoming rites to the *rusalka*, the witch, and the fruitful Mother Earth who would regenerate the family and fill the larder, as well. The search and cleansing custom to which she was subjected was intended to purge the stranger of hostile intentions and unite the two families in a peaceful bond.

In Ukrainian wedding customs, the conflict of matrilocal and patrilocal traditions was vividly played out: The bride had to be overcome with violence; patriarchal rule had to be enforced by the ritual of bride capture in the face of a still-strong maternal family. The ceremonies surrounding marriage strikingly evoked the historical conflict between warrior-herders and agrarian populations discussed in earlier chapters. The mythology of the hunters and farmers survived in the assimilation of the bride to the *rusalka*, the fruitful maternal earth, and Yaga; the intervention of the male retained echoes of a Hades-like rape and military combat.

The patriarchal nature of the wedding rites was further accentuated through the influence of the church. While in the Ukraine the Christian ceremony was performed only as an afterthought because of the still-influential community of women, in north Russia, where the clergy had been more effective in enforcing orthodoxy, the bride was taken to the church. The church wedding subsumed and absorbed pagan fertility rituals. The role of the father was considerably strengthened, and the songs which referred to the "plowing" of the bride by the groom were of a violent nature. The bride was obliged to show every sign of submission, awaiting her fiancé in the icon corner without the moral support of a female chorus. In some areas the bride's passivity was emphasized: The groom would step on her foot, sometimes making it bleed. While in the Ukraine there had been an emphasis on the passage of the groom from mother to mother, in the north this too was reversed: The bride was transferred like a captive from father to father. The bride welcomed to the patriarchal household was obliged to show her subservience to the new husband as she had to the fathers: After retiring to the nuptial chamber, she was required to remove her husband's boots—the boots which had just walked on her.[89]

The cult of Mother Earth, as revealed in the rituals of the agrarian calendar, assimilated the cycle of the seasons to the life of woman passing from girlhood to motherhood and old age. It evoked mythological images of the *rusalka*, Mother Moist Earth, and Baba Yaga resembling those of the Greek myth of Kore and Demeter and the Near Eastern myth of the Great Mother Goddess and her son-consort the Dying God. It also evoked the presence of the Divine Twins (Apollo-Artemis), but did so under the aegis of the Mother Goddess. Songs, incantations, and marriage customs stressed the suffering of the cultivated earth assimilated to the peasant mother, in contrast to the freedom and awesome power of earlier divinities embodied by independent village maidens and elders. The emphatic plaints concerning earth's burdensome functions and the married woman's life of toil, clearly indicate the position of women in a patriarchal family.

The patrilineal and patrilocal wedding rites (most pronounced in the north of Russia) which cut the mother off from the daughter echo the disintegration of the union of Kore and Demeter by Hades' intrusion. Hades may well have represented the effects of patriarchal marriage customs resulting in the anger of the matriclan, whose patron was the earth mother Demeter. In his chariot, he was surely a symbol for the warrior state and its divine pantheon in conflict with the agrarian village or clan community. In Russia, the Varangian state had almost from its origins united with the Orthodox church to create a framework of power. Just as the relationship of the rulers to the ruled and the warriors to the peasants was one of material exploitation, so that of the church to its members demanded the submission of all spiritual life to the authority of a masculine clergy. But the women of Kievan *Rus'*, like the reluctant brides of peasant custom, fought the incursion of the Christian priesthood into the domestic realm over which they ruled. In attempting to break the women's resistance to conversion, the church was obliged, in Russia as elsewhere, to create a feminine divinity to vie with the all-powerful pagan goddesses. She was Mary, the Mother of God. But while she assumed the functions of earlier deities, she was never fully assimilated to them. Hers was a cult apart.

CHAPTER FOUR

The Coming of Christianity: Mary and Paraskeva-Piatnitsa

> A church procession was coming up the hill for Borodino. First along the dusty road came the infantry in ranks, bareheaded and with arms reversed. From behind them came the sound of church singing. . . . "They are bringing her, our Protectress! . . . the Iberian Mother of God!' someone cried.
>
> —L. Tolstoi, *War and Peace*[1]

Unlike the image of the pagan Slavic and Russian Great Goddess, that of the Orthodox Mary has a historical and urban origin. She entered Kiev in the tenth century and became the principal vehicle for the conversion of the population to an alien and essentially masculine faith, rooted not in the fertility of the soil or the forest but in the principles of paternal authority, punishment, and filial love.[2]

Christianization: The Resistance of the "God-Accursed Hags"

The Grand Prince Vladimir of Kiev imposed Byzantine Christianity upon his subjects in 988–989. The Byzantine linkage of church and state appealed to the ambitious trader-prince as a means to convince the Kievan urban elite as well as the peasantry that his rule was supported by divine sanction. What Vladimir attempted to impose by fiat was said to have been embraced with love and enthusiasm much earlier by his grandmother,

Olga, hailed by the monk-chroniclers as the "Grandmother of the Russian Land." What little we know about Olga the historical figure is to be found in the *Primary Chronicle* and in the accounts of the Byzantines who observed with interest her trading journeys to their city, accompanied by Varangian warrior-merchants.[3] After the death of Riurik, the founder of the dynasty whose kingdom embraced both Novgorod and Kiev, his relative Oleg became ruler. Like his predecessor, Oleg continued to make trips to Byzantium, to exchange the raw materials of the north for the luxurious products of Byzantine craftsmen. Oleg's daughter Olga appears to have assumed the throne after the murder of her husband, Igor, a hated and quarrelsome prince killed by enemy Derevlians, one of the group of Slavic tribes Kiev was attempting to subdue. The author of the *Primary Chronicle*, who, deliberately perhaps, confounds "fact" with myth or folktale to popularize this first convert, a widow and a mother, gives an account of Olga's reign that sounds more like folklore than Christian hagiography: Courted by the Derevlians' Prince Mal, who is eager to marry her to acquire the Kievan kingdom, Olga begins to assert her power and independence through a series of tricks performed upon her enemies. Like many folktales, the story of "Olga's Revenge" is divided into three acts. In the first the Derevlians send messages to Olga accusing the murdered Igor of behaving like a "ravenous wolf" rather than the peaceable ruler, their own Prince Mal.[4] Olga counters this indictment of her husband by telling the messengers to send other envoys in order to begin talks concerning an eventual marriage alliance. Her palace, the future site of the Church of the Mother of God in Kiev, is the scene of the first revenge.

Olga's Kievan subjects bring the Derevlian envoys into her presence in ships, as she had ordered. The Derevlians, "puffed up with pride," are immediately pushed into a deep trench and buried alive. The burial in a ship recalls the barrow funerals of the Scandinavians. But could this mockery of Varangian-Scandinavian custom as punishment rather than reward refer to an attempt to reassert the traditions of a native Slavic and matrifocal populace to which Olga's ancestry has been traced? Certainly the burial in earth suggests the theme of vengeance of an underworld divinity or her priestess over those who attempt to "marry her" only to rule.[5]

Olga's next action makes such a conjecture plausible. She invites her enemies to a feast where she will negotiate the proposed marriage. When the envoys are welcomed and asked to refresh themselves before the meal by taking a bath in the bathhouse, Olga orders her men to set the building on fire. In the first "sacrifice," earth swallows male pride; in the second, the feminine asserts power through a fire in the bathhouse—the temple of the *rozhanitsy*. Yaga's oven and the witch's cauldron engulf those who wish to capture this angry and most reluctant widow as bride. She buries men through both inhumation and cremation; her elements are fire, earth, and water.

While in the first two "acts" Olga decimated the leaders of the Derevlians on her own soil, in the final one she assumes military power. Announcing that she plans to come to their land to prepare a funeral meal over the grave of her husband, Olga invites the Derevlians to a feast. When they are drunk, her followers slaughter them. On her husband's grave, she assumes the role of the commander of soldiers and becomes an Amazon queen, an aggressor rather than a victim.

As though to crush all aspects of masculine hegemony, Olga's victory over the Derevlians must be complete. She asks for three pigeons and three sparrows from every enemy house as a tribute. When she places firebrands in their claws and releases them, her army of birds, like one commanded by a folklore *bogatyria* or queen, descends on each household.

Olga's chronicler describes her reign as the consolidation of her conquest. She goes through the land of the Derevlians "establishing laws and tribute" and trading actively with the Byzantines.[6] She increases both the extent and the wealth of the founder Riurik's empire. But in the course of one of her trips to Byzantium, she is converted to Christianity. The image the Christian author of the *Primary Chronicle* gives us is that of a pagan goddess, a brave Amazon, a Yaga-like widow whose awesome power and dangerous anger destroy all who bar her path. Accompanied only by a youthful and ineffectual son, she is a *baba* freed of a husband's restraints who protects her land and avenges her *rod* more effectively than a man. In short, this woman, who rules over the elements as well as over men, praised by the chronicler as "wiser than any man," appears to be a mighty goddess who creates and destroys rulers and whose will directs both nature and the social order.[7]

By making Olga the "Grandmother of the Russian Land" and describing her barbaric might, the author of the *Primary Chronicle* suggested to Kievan readers that his new religion was not antithetical to beliefs in feminine power. Rather, Christianity is represented as a natural evolution from pagan belief. It would at the same time glorify the strong woman (like Olga), and yet subject her barbaric rule to the hegemony of the "just" male god. Olga, the first Christian, becomes the clan mother and protectress of the new religious order. As the original ancestress, she will, like Mary, intercede with the stern and omnipotent Father God and His Sacrificed Son for the well-being of the Russian land. Olga's legend "commands" other women to follow her path. In short, through the myth and image of the Amazon queen, the church and state sought to drive the message of conversion to the very homes of their subjects and to the still-recalcitrant mothers who ruled over their families in this private domain.

Though Olga became the first convert, the new religion would be imposed through her grandson. Vladimir enforced the new faith as brutally as his grandmother had treated her enemies. In adopting Byzantine Christianity and thus facilitating commercial ties between Kiev and the empire, Vladimir also assumed the role of the church's agent. At the same time, the church identified itself with the secular state to gain assistance in its missionary activities and became closely associated by the populace with a political rather than a spiritual institution.[8] The first groups constrained to follow in the steps of their rulers were Vladimir's court and the townspeople of Kiev. Until the twelfth century, Christianity remained the religion of the upper classes, who, at least in the accounts of the clerical chroniclers, seemed to acquiesce to conversion. One large segment of the population, however, proved so intractable that even these missionary apologists could not claim victory over them. The women of Kiev, like their peasant sisters, resisted the imposition of Christianity with great stubbornness.

The recalcitrance of Russian women appears as a curious phenomenon. Christianity, the religion of love, seemed to support women and family in the Roman Empire against the tyranny of the state; and the number of female martyrs shows the extent to which the church was successful in its efforts to persuade women to devote their energies to a new gospel opposed to an imperial warrior ethos. But in the Russian conversion, there were no women martyrs, and later only a few would emerge. What could have been the cause of this apparent disaffection with the church?

The introduction of Christianity into Russia, wrote one scholar of the history of matrifocal institutions, was a fateful factor in bringing about "a state of shameful subjection for the Russian woman."[9] The *Primary Chronicle*'s emphasis on the barbarism and brutality of the tribes living in the area of Kiev prior to the coming of the Varangians may well have been an attempt to

discredit matrifocal or matrilineal customs of the native population by the patriarchal rulers and the Christian chroniclers who
served them. A prominent historian of Russia's early development suggests that some proto-Slavic tribes were matriarchal
and remained so into the medieval period. For while the story of
Olga indicates clear acquiescence to the rule of a powerful
woman, it is also evident from the historical record that the
women of Kiev enjoyed considerable freedom and respect. They
could own property, run businesses, and trade (like Olga herself); they were educated and were regarded as the equals of men.[10]

Women were also protected from patriarchal constraints in
the legal tradition. The laws of Kiev, compiled by Vladimir
Monomakh in the eleventh-century *Russkaia pravda*, reflect upon
the important role accorded to women's brothers and indicate
the continuance of matrilineal and matrilocal custom. But the elevated status of women in Kievan society was attributed by chroniclers and later historians to the coming of Christianity rather
than to a reflection of archaic custom. Canon law was described
by the church's apologists as a defense of women against patriarchal barbarism by forbidding the observance of Slavic tribal marriages, which the clergy described as "polygamous" and rooted
in the ritual of bride capture. By playing a central role in the education of women and assuming the guardianship of widows and or-
phans, the church, encouraged by Kievan princes, sought to
break the hold of women on family life and thereby shatter the
bonds of the native population's matrifocal order.

The religion of the *rod*, administered by women, was attacked by the church and undermined by the state. The official divinities, Perun and his male "band" of gods to which the grand
prince and his retinue had adhered, might come and go, but the
mother-centered family seems to have been perceived by the
pagan Slavs as the microcosm of the divine order whose patron
was the fertility goddess. The fight against the women of Kiev
was led by Vladimir himself in the name of the church. Pressing
for conversion, he saw the need to redirect the allegiance of his
subjects from the sphere of the home to that of the state—and to
the Father God in whose name he ruled. He began by attempting to remove children from their mothers in order to instruct
them in his own schools. The women cried for their children "as
for the dead," observes the author of the *Primary Chronicle* with
a certain complacency.[11]

The result of this concerted effort by the grand prince and
the missionaries was the beginning of a divided family in Kiev.
Centuries of opposition to Christianity on the part of women and

peasants would result in *dvoeverie,* "two faiths," which split the nation into a Christianized upper class and a rural population with strong attachments to paganism. While Vladimir's male followers answered the call of their prince to rally to the new creed, their wives refused to comply. The clergy fought back by damning all those whose wives continued to exercise the pagan faith. In so doing, they hoped to coerce husbands into obliging their wives to espouse Christianity for the good of the whole family: "If the wife is clean, her husband will be clean," the missionaries told their male converts.[12] But the women held back, not only because they feared losing their power, but also because of the church's denigration of the feminine in dogma and rite.

Byzantine Christianity, no less than Roman Catholicism, was misogynous.[13] Perhaps because the newly established church in the East found itself vulnerable to the fertility religions of the Near East, it regarded women as the source of all spiritual taint in much the same manner as the Hebrew prophets excoriated the religion of the "Whore of Babylon," fearing the attraction of the Great Goddess cult to their people. The Byzantine clergy's fear was associated too with a strong ascetic impulse and a concomitant suspicion of family life where woman could assert her will.

The monastic ideal of celibacy was set against the necessary evil of marriage. In the teachings of the Byzantine clergy, the cycle of reproduction, which lay at the very center of peasant beliefs, was hedged in by sin. Only the man who protected himself from the urgings of his flesh and the will of his wife could be saved. He must rule over her and master his bestial nature. Saint Augustine's call for the replacement of an earthly ideal by a spiritual one appeared to justify the church fathers in their attack against the female sex. Woman was Eve the rebel, who betrayed her maker and defied the laws of the male god. Thundered Tertullian in the second century to his female audience,

> Do you realize that Eve is you? The curse of God pronounced on your sex weighs still on the world. Guilty you must bear its hardships. You are the devil's gateway, you desecrated the fatal tree, you first betrayed the law of God, you who softened up with your cajoling words the man against whom the devil could not prevail by force. The image of God, the man Adam, you broke him, it was child's play for you. *You* deserved death, and it was the son of God who had to die."[14]

His words were echoed by those of the fourth-century Byzantine patriarch Saint John Chrysostom, a leading father of the Orthodox church, who blamed Eve and her descendants for leading the male astray. Clearly, the religion of the fertility goddesses, against whom these tirades were in some measure directed, maintained its female votaries—particularly among the Slavs.[15]

The condemnation of woman as the incarnation of Eve is especially apparent in the writings of the Slavic missionaries which attack the rituals of the family. Kievan literature abounds in satirical homilies, selected for translation from the Greek and directed against women. "On Good and Bad Women" is the title of one such attack, in which the evil wife is depicted as rebellious and self-willed. Another author writes that "no wild beast can equal a malicious and bitter-tongued woman." She betrays man and will not obey him; like Delilah, who cut off Samson's hair, she deprives him of all power. "I have seen lions and bears tamed by kind treatment," he continues, "but a bad woman elevates herself while being tamed and rages while blamed." The "tamed" woman is represented by our author as a good and submissive wife enjoying the trust of her husband, who, according to the Apostle Paul, must take advice from her. "Such a wife is always good. . . . She gets up at night and distributes sufficient food to the servants. . . . And she gives to the poor the fruits of her toil."[16]

The wife's obedience must have been obtained with considerable difficulty, for women continued to be cursed with such persistence that clerical anathema found its way into many proverbs deprecating the *baba* in village life. The women, whom the missionaries came to call "those cursed by God," continued to the twentieth century to be cursed by their menfolk.[17] The clerical assault on a woman as Eve and rebel, coupled with the state's attempts to impose its patriarchal will on the family, resulted in a general denigration of women in Russian life but testified paradoxically to their power and stubborn resistance to male authority.

Woman was to be trained by her Byzantine teachers in a school modeled on the monastery. The tainted and evil Eve must be transformed into the gentle and submissive Mother of God, Mary, in whose divine maternity the church saw a hope for the cleansing of woman's evil. But since that motherhood was miraculous, and Mary the only one of her sex who had been chosen, others could only aspire vainly to her status.[18] The father was to be the teacher and leader of the family in the same way as the elder headed the monastery. He was responsible for its salvation and was consequently the director of its proper conduct. Like the *pater potestas* of the Roman family, the Christian husband was the sole authority in its midst.

By the sixteenth century, this monastic rule was codified in the *Domostroi* (Law of the Home), written by the priest Sylvestor. The wife was called the abbotess who guided the family in the worship of God incarnate in the person of her husband. The author of the *Domostroi* outlines the organization of household tasks with minute precision. Nothing is left to the will of sinful woman. In performing her duties, the wife is to be an obedient subject of the church and the state.

The assimilation of family life to the monastic ideal made of it, theoretically, a masculine enclave in which the husband was bound to fight with the woman of the household. The war between the sexes was exacerbated, and the divisions within the family were exaggerated. Moreover, such an organization was so clearly at odds with the archaic worship of the *rod* and the importance accorded to the mother by the peasantry that the new domestic order decreed by church and tsar could be achieved only by something in the nature of a military campaign: The power of woman as wife and mother had to be subdued by her husband, the representative of the state. The resulting domestic situation led over time to the patriarchal wedding rituals of the peasantry, which in turn reflected the increasing authority of the despotic ruler over the village and family organization.

The "God-cursed women" (*baby bogomerzkiia*) continued, nonetheless, to fight tenaciously against conversion and to practice their ancient rites despite continuous condemnation. They asserted woman's superior powers over the social order as prophetesses, healers, or "Fates" who controlled the destiny of their offspring and whose advice was sought by the community. Like the townswomen and their peasant sisters, the wives of the upper classes regarded the clergy with repugnance. "Do you call on the idol-worshipping women to whom not only the rich but the poor women go?" asked one indignant clerical writer, hoping to shame his readers.[19]

From the eleventh century, exasperated missionaries had declared: "Listen not to an evil woman," and insisted that "they who cleave to her shall die in hell." Their anger did not abate until the seventeenth century. In confessing their reluctant converts, they would anxiously ask them: "In your thoughts did you want to go to a witch or to an evil woman for advice?"[20] But their attempts to intervene in the pagan rituals of their female parishioners, interrogating girls about fortune telling or old women about feasts prepared for the *rozhanitsy*, were to little avail. Such practices survived to the present century.

While the process of Christianization proceeded with less

overt opposition among the aristocratic families of Kiev, on whom the grand prince could exert personal pressure, the wives of the boyars, like peasant women, tended their ancient customs in secret and kept alive the worship of female divinities by embroidering their images on linen and clothing and calling upon "witches" to cure disease, "christen" children, prepare feasts for the dead, and invoke fertility. They continued to tell stories invoking the goddess in all her aspects. Through their tales, they passed their faith on to their children. At the same time, in an attempt to counter the masculinized dogma of the church, noblewomen and peasants introduced their essentially feminine vision of the cosmic order into the teachings of the church. This is most striking in the body of popular "Spiritual Verses," called *Dukhovnye stikhi*, whose subject is Christian myth and apocrypha, much of which revolves around the Mother of God. Here the sinful nature of woman is not unremittingly underscored as it is in church dogma. The cycle called "The Lament of Adam and Eve" even contains a singular account of Eve's confession which replaces the Christian image of the powerless and evil woman with that of an omnipotent goddess fallen from her once lofty status.[21]

While the women may have reconstructed Christian myth to suit their needs and concentrated on paganizing the benign image of Mary rather than dealing with that of sinful Eve, the church, in turn, revised pagan stories in the light of its gospel or created new tales out of the old genre. This kind of revision is strikingly illustrated in the popular folktale called "The Story of Saint Nicholas." Based on the figure of a fourth-century bishop of Myra on the Black Sea, Nicholas's cult is thought to have replaced that of the Lykean Artemis, the patron of animal and human fertility who protected sailors. The saint was made to assume the archaic goddess's functions as the bringer of wealth and the patron of men, boys, and sailors, whom he saved from danger. In the Russian hierarchy of saints, Nicholas's place directly under the Mother of God testifies to the continuing importance of the fertility function usurped from the Virgin Huntress herself. (Lykean Artemis became a demon in Christian mythology, predicting shipwrecks and bringing on miscarriage in women.)[22]

In the Russian folktale, Saint Nicholas saves male individuals, particularly merchants, from the evil female: When Ivan, the son of a merchant, placed under the protection of Nicholas by his father, is obliged to keep vigil over the body of a king's daughter, a witch, the saint has the youth read the Holy Psalms over the grave. With the help of Nicholas, Ivan captures the evil girl and forces her to pray to the Mother of God and to God himself. Although she is resurrected and given in marriage to Ivan by her father, she is not yet purged of her evil. The saint throws the princess into a bonfire and pulls her apart. After her torn body disgorges legions of frogs, snakes, and other reptiles, Nicholas puts the limbs together again, and baptizes them with sea water. He makes the sign of the cross, and the princess arises, transformed into a good and obedient wife. Ivan assumes the throne after the tsar's death.[23]

This folktale provides us with a revealing insight into the clergy's missionary activity among Russian women and girls. Only through marriage in the church under the patronage of the male guardian saint could they finally be coerced into wifely obedience and the acceptance of patriarchal and Christian authority. It is notable that Ivan gains the throne only through a matrilocal wedding to the once evil princess, who has been divested of pagan power and can do him no harm. Saint Nicholas performs all the functions once attributed to pagan women: veneration of the dead, protection of the young against evil forces, union through marriage, and the creation of material wealth—by means of trade rather than the cultivation of the soil.

Since Russian women resisted the image of the evil Eve, preferring that of the Holy Mother, Mary, the church saw that its missionary work should be directed toward encouraging Marial worship. And since women could not be drawn to the new faith through vilification, another tactic was tried: the identification of Christianity with the good wife. The story of "Peter and Fevroniia, Wonderworkers of Murom," attributed to the monk Ermolai-Erazm, dates from the fifteenth century in its written form, but it is certainly much older and is based upon archaic folktales, from which it borrows its characters and motifs. In this work of the Russian medieval period, the didactic purpose is clear: Russian women can be drawn to the practice of the church by showing them their pagan goddess assuming Christian guise.[24]

In the city of Murom, known for its resistance to missionaries, the righteous Christian ruler Paul is tried by the devil, who appeared as a serpent to seduce his wife, called the "Dark Princess."[25] While the woman saw that the serpent was a demon, those around her could not distinguish him from her husband. When she tells Paul about the serpent's visits to her bedchamber, he advises her to find out from the serpent what will be the manner of his death (a common folkloric motif, particularly in stories about the serpent Koshchei and Baba Yaga). The serpent tells her that Paul's brother Peter will kill him. And indeed, when Peter is summoned to fight the serpent to the death, it looks as if he has murdered his own brother—so well did the devil assume Paul's appearance. Thereafter, we hear nothing more about the "Dark Princess," whose dealing with the devil brought her brother-in-law to apparent fratricide.

Tainted by the serpent's blood, and covered with sores, Peter leaves the kingdom in search of a cure for himself and for his land plagued by fratricidal strife. His sister-in-law, an incompletely converted woman, had been the source of discord and disease. With his retinue, he reaches a village called Charity and is carried inside a deserted house, where he finds himself before a beautiful and half-naked maiden who sits weaving: "Before her a hare was jumping and playing about." (The hare was sacred to Artemis as moon goddess.) Like a *rusalka* or the young peasant women who invoked her, the girl tells Peter a riddle: "It is indeed unfortunate when the yard is without ears and the house without eyes."[26] As the Wise Vasilisa of folklore, she informs Peter that she lives alone, having sent her family to "view death." Her parents are in the graveyard; her brother has gone to climb a tree—the Tree of Life.

Peter, carried into the maiden's abode on a bier as though already dead, is cured by the Wise Maiden, but only on the condition that he marry her. Like the Scythian Mistress of the Woodland, she makes demands of her suppliants: "I am the physician who is able to cure your prince, but I do not desire any part of his wealth. However, if I do not become his wife I shall have no reason to cure him."[27] Peter, after going back on his promise and falling ill again, finally agrees to marry this enchantress, who presents herself to him as a peasant girl far below his station. The marriage of prince and peasant, pagan and Christian, results, as in the folktale of Saint Nicholas, in the disappearance of woman's evil and vengeful nature.

But the story does not end here. When Peter brings his bride back to the city of Murom, the boyars, angered by his union with a peasant, accuse Fevroniia—the name she gave herself as Peter's wife—of bad manners at the feast table. Fevroniia then begins to perform miracles, turning crumbs from the table into frankincense and myrrh. The boyars, fearful of her power and goodness, complain that she rules over their wives and demand that she leave the court. But Fevroniia agrees to leave only if her husband accompanies her. The couple and their retinue depart on a boat. Peter worries about their exile, but the all-knowing and wise Fevroniia quiets his fears with another miracle:

> That same evening the servants began to prepare dinner for the prince. They cut down branches of some trees and making a spit put the kettle on. Princess Fevroniia who was walking along the shore, came upon these branches that had been cut from the trees. Seeing them, she said, "Bless them, for before morning these branches will grow into great trees with rich foliage." And so it happened, for when the travelers got up in the morning they found that these branches had grown into great trees with rich foliage.[28]

Identifying herself as the pagan tree goddess, Fevroniia predicts the outcome of their exile. Indeed, a fratricidal war has broken out among the boyars—the boughs separated from the tree—and they beg Peter and his enchantress bride to return and rule over them. While the first veiled fratricide by Peter occurs in response to the rejection of the serpent and the "Dark Princess," the second leads to general war as a result of the ejection of the goddess of the Tree of Life. Fevroniia, christened through her marriage with Peter, returns with her consort to the city and rules over the population like a good mother: "They treated all as if they were their own children."[29]

The account of their deaths emphasizes the political and social equality of Fevroniia and Peter as corulers in their kingdom and suggests the divine omniscience and spiritual superiority of the wife: Just before Peter's death, Fevroniia sits embroidering the figures of saints—rather than the goddess—on towels and covers. Hearing the news of her husband's death, she behaves like one of the three Fates: She "placed the needle in the coverlet and wound up the thread." She dies with him by her own will, during the feast of Kupalo/Kupala.[30] The boyars bury Peter in the cathedral and place Fevroniia's body in a grave outside the city to underscore her peasant and pagan character; but the following morning, her grave is discovered next to that of Peter in the Cathedral of the Mother of God.

The assimilation of the fertility goddess under the name of Fevroniia to an apocryphal saint married to a sainted Christian ruler was intended to indicate that the pagan rituals of the peasantry and their continued worship of female divinities were not incompatible with the teachings of the church. But the most effective and compelling of these efforts to "tame" pagan cults by placing them under the aegis, and hence control, of the clergy involved the worship of Mary called the *Bogoroditsa*, or "Birth-Giver of God."

The Cult of Mary

In Kiev as early as the eleventh century, the epithet "Wise," used to characterize both Vasilisa of folklore and Fevroniia of Christian fable, was given to the Mother of God. There is no doubt that the proselytizing clergy regarded Mary as the proper successor to the archaic goddesses. A minor figure in primitive Christian dogma, she was not included in the Trinity, nor was her role as a holy woman emphasized after Christ's birth. Her cult emerged in response to the failure of missionary efforts among populations worshipping female divinities, and her image reflected the demands of a patriarchal church for a docile virgin and merciful mother obedient to masculine authority.

When the eleventh-century Byzantine builders of Saint Sophia in Kiev placed over the altar an immense image of the Mother of God with arms raised (*orante*), they represented her in the form of the archaic goddesses whose outlines are found on the artifacts of Scythian and Slavic religious culture. The figure of Mary in Russia was impressed upon preexisting maternal authority, both religious and familial. Despite the church's demand that the father be the family leader, the continued centricity of the mother could not be overcome.[31] In linking Mary to mother divinities and Christ her son to their dying and reviving consorts, the church stressed the superiority of Mary's cult over others. It was precisely under such conditions that the veneration of the Virgin had originated in the fourth century.

The church had not initially allocated a central place to Mary in dogma or liturgical rites. But efforts to create an exclusively male faith based on the ethic of maternal love, nonresistance to violence, and altruism were bound to fail. The early church had taken the notion of divine maternal love from the cults of such Mother Goddesses as Isis, while at the same time it aggressively repudiated these same religions. Clement of Alexandria in the third century had Christ declare that "I have come to destroy the work of the female." However, to their consternation, the church fathers soon found themselves obliged to accommodate those very features of the pagan fertility religions which they denounced in order to attract converts.[32] At the Council of Ephesus (431), the church officially adopted the cult of Mary as the Mother of Christ.

When the clergy gathered in the city where Artemis-Diana was still worshipped, the patriarch of Constantinople, Nestorius, feared that the title of *Theotokos*, Mother of God, brought

Christ's mother too close to that of the ancient female divinities. The Western church would later delete this attribute. However, from the fifth century onward, the cult of Mary became so popular that the calendar year in the West as in the East was soon marked by her feasts.[33]

The Western church's stress on the virginity of Mary was certainly not intended as a concession to the parthenogenetic powers of the archaic goddesses; on the contrary, it indicated her subjection to the masculine prowess of the inseminating sky father-god.[34] The sacred womb of the Great Mother Goddesses became with Mary a vessel for God's seed. Mary the Everlasting Virgin carried her immaculateness not as a symbol of power but rather as the sign of God's grace. It marked her humility and dependence upon the male for salvation and placed her under the authority of her own son, whom she had made incarnate. In short, though the cult of Mary was modeled on that of the archaic Mother Goddesses and therefore was assimilated to them, the church fathers at Ephesus safeguarded themselves against the resurgence of pagan beliefs by placing all of Mary's attributes under the strict control of the male. No longer flanked, like the ancient deities, by her consort-son and her servants, Mary was now herself a votary. Her maternal love was but a shadow of the Father's: "So you, Lord-God, are the Great Mother!" exclaimed Saint Anselm, summarizing the process of usurpation which had occurred.[35]

The myth (and image) of Mary, which elevated divine virginity and condemned individual mothers, allowed for the absorption and weakening of fertility cults. But the implicit denigration of motherhood was not so easily accepted by the Greek Orthodox clergy who had named Mary *Theotokos*. The Mother of God was a mother rather than the virgin worshipped in the Western church. While the Roman church underscored the Passion and Death of God, the Eastern church worshipped his Resurrection—the ever-renewing cycle evident in the natural world. Greek Orthodoxy had accommodated the Hellenistic mysteries of Demeter and Kore at Eleusis to the liturgy of the Mass, stressing the birth, death, and rebirth of Christ as the Dying and Reviving God.[36] Further, it emphasized the centricity of birth and Christ's incarnation through his mother. Nor did the Orthodox church fully accept the notion of Immaculate Conception. Heirs to the Arian heresy, banned from Byzantium at the Council of Nicea in 325, the Greeks maintained the full humanity of Christ and consequently found this view difficult to reconcile with the virginity of the mother. Christ's closeness to and immanence in mankind, together with his birth from a mother, linked him more clearly, too, with the consorts of the pagan goddesses.

The *Theotokos* of the Byzantines became the *Bogoroditsa*, or "Birth-Giver of God," among the Russians. There the importance of Mary's motherhood soon became a central tenet of the faith. More weight was placed upon Mary than on her son, the God-child. In fact, the Russian Mother of God is not merely the vessel for the Lord; she is the universal mother and mistress of all things.[37] The transformation of the *Theotokos* into the powerful *Bogoroditsa* appears to have begun with the first stages of Christianization. Hoping to entice converts by prominently displaying the image of Mary and proclaiming her attributes, the missionaries of the new faith found that in time Mary resembled less the subservient divinity of the male Christian religion than the pagan goddess whose worship she had been created to supersede.

In the Beginning Was Mother Church

The cathedral in Kiev, designed by Byzantine architects, was named after their Saint Sophia. Sophia, the Greek word for "wisdom," referred to the feminine aspect of God and may have filtered into Christian dogma from the religion of Isis.[38] Subsequent churches which spread across the Russian landscape were often named for the Mother of God as well as for Sophia, as though to identify the new religion with its feminine patroness. Both Mary and Sophia are "Wise Maidens," easily assimilated to the divinities found in folklore. Over the altar in the Kievan Saint Sophia, the sixteen-foot image of the Mother of God with upraised arms suggests quite clearly the figure of the pagan goddess of peasant embroidery in her temple. The church building itself appears as an immanent part of the Virgin's body; worshippers entering the sacred space were "reborn" through their physical as well as spiritual contact with the Great Mother and her son (pictured smaller than Mary in the central cupola of the cathedral).

Russian church builders, working on the Byzantine model, were subsequently influenced by Armenian and Georgian architecture and elaborated upon the style of their teachers by elongating the drum of the domes (representing Christ and his Apostles) and giving them the now-characteristic Russian onion shape.[39] Through the Kievan period and succeeding centuries, the Russian countryside was dotted by innumerable single-domed chapels and multi-domed churches whose golden cupolas shone against the landscape like miniature suns or, when painted deepest blue and "sprinkled" with stars, suggested the Virgin's mantle as the sky.

Morphologically, the lines of these churches suggest the union of male and female: Elongated drums are capped by cupolas growing out of the feminine body of the building. But the terminology of ecclesiastic architecture stressed the analogy with the female body. The dome was called the head; the drum, the neck; the gable, the shoulder; and the vaulting below the drum, the bosom. In northern churches, the domes were modified to suit the exigencies of wood, and they received the name of *kokoshniki*, feminine headdresses. The liturgical analogy of the church edifice as the place within which sky and earth, heaven and humanity, are conjoined suggests too the union of mother and child, male and female, in the context of the maternal body.

The interior of the church was designed to impress upon the worshipper the feeling of an "affective embrace" in which all senses were engaged. Standing together under the "sky" of the cupolas, the congregation pressed against each other rather than being separated by rows and seats as in the West. In fact, the churches of Russia were frequently named for the Mother of God's *Pokrov* (Protection or Intercession): "To enter a Russian church," says the modern writer Tertz, "is rather like creeping under a blanket or throwing a fur coat over one's head ... the church is less a building than a cloak of protection."[40]

In Russia as elsewhere, the proliferation of churches bearing the name of the Mother of God testified to the church's acknowledgment of the power of female divinity. Not only were the temples of God named for his wife and mother, but like numerous monasteries they were placed under her guardianship. The first Russian monastery, the tenth-century Pecherskaia Lavra of Kiev, was a honeycomb of caves connected by tunnels bored into the limestone cliffs above the city and was thought to be watched over by Mary herself. In the *Dukhovnye stikhi*, the Holy Virgin, the church building, and the Tree of Life in the form of the cross are intimately identified: "On the Holy Cypress tree / Stood the Little Apostolic Church. / And in it / Slept the Little Mother Mary on her throne."[41]

Like the *baba* dominating the household from her *pech'* or oven-throne, Mary as the soul of the church sleeps atop her Tree of Life. In Russia as in Europe, the church, so frequently linked with Mary, was the center of town and village life. In Novgorod, where another Saint Sophia was built in the eleventh century, the city and church were one: "Where Saint Sophia stands, there is Novgorod."[42] In Moscow, the church to Mary built in the Kremlin in the fifteenth century and called the Dormition was regarded as the heart of the capital. The edifice was the symbol of Mary's protection and power, and in the liturgy of the church, the prayers to her permeate the daily rituals, as they do the yearly religious holidays. In hymns to the "Most Clean and Pure," Mary is called the bride as well as the birth-giver of Christ.[43] She is maternal love incarnate, while Sophia represents the spiritual creative force out of which the universe was engendered. Mary the mother appeals to the hearts of her votaries; her cult is not in doctrine and theological debate but in image and rite found in the symbolism of the icon.

The Icons of the Mother of God

The practice of icon painting may have originated with Syrian and Egyptian death portraits in the centuries before the birth of Christ, but the Christian worship of icons goes back to the sixth and seventh centuries in Byzantium and is linked with the development of monasticism. In the eighth century, a conflict broke out over the veneration of these images. A group hostile to their continued use, the Iconoclasts, wished to diminish the power of the monastic orders by divesting them of their "miracle-working" icons. But they were defeated, and the cult of icons was fully endorsed by the Second Council of Nicea in 787. Consequently, when the Slavs were converted by Vladimir in the tenth century, the missionaries brought these images with them to introduce the worship of their gods and goddesses to the pagan populace. Russian artists continued to copy the style of their Byzantine preceptors, emphasizing an emotional intensity of color and form.

It would be hard to overestimate the importance of the icon in Russian culture as the continuous reminder of divine caring and involvement in human affairs. The image of Mary, represented as mother and ruler, was so popular that her icon became totemic: Over it and before it, oaths were sworn and conflicts resolved; Russian principalities placed themselves under its protective power; armies and populations prayed to it when they set out for war or were attacked.[44]

The wooden icon itself was thought to embody the Goddess as the Tree of Life. In religious songs, the Mother of God is assimilated to that tree. But the representation of Mary is remarkably varied and numbers over three hundred styles. She is often confounded with "Sophia, the Wisdom of God"; she is the "Ever-Burning Bush" bringing light and fertility to the world; and she is the "Invincible Wall" of protective power. But the most popular of her icons is that of the kind and sorrowful mother with face bent over her tiny child, whose body she seems to engulf: the "Lady of Sorrows" and the "Lady of Tenderness" (*Umilenie*).

As the goddess of the embroideries, Mary is accompanied by animals and encircled with flowers and grain sheafs; birds fly over her, and swans swim at her feet; planets revolve around her head; and saints, princes, warriors, and tsars turn toward her in supplication. In short, Mary is the Tree of Life goddess depicted in various stages of her maternity. As the Virgin *Orans* she stands with her arms raised, and in a circle, filling her upper torso, Christ the infant, dwarfed by her immense figure, imitates the gesture of his mother. As virgin and mother, the source of all power, she unites heaven and earth. In icons which represent her as the *rusalka* and Yaga or Wise Woman, she is surrounded by animal, bird, fish, and plant life. She gives fishermen their catch, beekeepers their honey. As mistress of the forest, she gives hunters their prey.[45] Although she is pictured pregnant, nursing her child, and alone and bereft of her son, Mary never ages. The icons of Christ, on the other hand, show him moving through the life cycle and dying sacrificed in the form of a mature male.

The icons of Mary were always deemed miraculous, those of her son rarely so. She is thought to be immanent in creation, helping her earthly children. Christ, on the other hand, is a distant and stern judge of human evil. Active in saving her children from harm and limiting God the Father's despotic powers over them, Mary is characterized by mercy and compassion; her son is linked closely with his vengeful father: "We have no other help or representation . . . save You, oh Mother of all sorrows and of all family burdens," begins a prayer to the Pokrov icon.[46] In fact, her icon came to be regarded as identical with the mother herself and was decorated in much the same manner as the *rusalka* or Semik tree and the Kupalo-Kupala and other fertility effigies, in order to invoke her aid and protection. From her wooden image, the Holy Mary of the Tree seemed to the believer to communicate directly with her votaries.

From the eleventh century, Russian religious history is filled with accounts of the appearances of Mary's icons. The first missionaries clearly recognized that the most effective way to introduce the image of their most convincing divinity was to associate her with pagan holy trees and water. In order to identify

Mary with the *rusalki* or *vily*, the clergy placed her icon on branches or in vegetation. In 1060, the miraculous Eletskoi icon of Chernigov appeared in a forest. In 1182 a Ukrainian girl brought the Kupiatitskaia icon out of the woods, and in 1191 shepherds found the Zhirovitskoi icon on a tree. The cherished Pskov icon was found in a lake in 1420, and in 1442 the Makar'evskaia appeared near a sacred spring. Mary's miracle-working images were discovered in similar sites through the eighteenth century.[47] The most popular and representative styles in which the attributes of Mary were communicated to her votaries were those of the "Lady of Tender Mercy" (*Umilenie*), "Mary *Orans*" (or *Orante*), and the Goddess surrounded by her human and animal creation. In each of these three forms, she declares her power over the earth, the heavens, and the underworld.

The "Lady of Tender Mercy": Mary as Mistress of the Hearth and Clan Mother

The most sacred of all icons, the *Umilenie* Virgin of Vladimir, a twelfth-century Byzantine icon commissioned by the son of Vladimir Monomakh to evoke a sense of protective maternal love, was credited with the Russian victory over the Mongols in the sixteenth century and henceforth was called the Lady of Kazan, after the place where the battle had occurred (Illustration no. 27). The icon of the Mother of God enfolding her child was referred to as the pallium of Russia, its protective mantle. Three holidays commemorated its powers, reminding the faithful of three successive conflicts with the Tatars. In 1521 the miraculous icon, taken to Moscow from its home in the principality of Vladimir, which by the thirteenth century had displaced Kiev as the principal Russian city, was placed in the Cathedral of the Assumption. Long before the move to the aegis of the Muscovite tsardom, it had become the symbol of national unity, credited with saving Russia's principal cities from enemies.[48] In effect, Mary of the Vladimir *Umilenie* was the patron not only of Russia but of soldiers who fought in her name. However, the use of the miracle-working icons for protection in battle was restricted to defensive actions. The goddess of warriors armed her worshippers with the power of the ancestral dead and demanded that they perform their duties by fighting to protect the soil and the family. She did not tolerate internecine warfare leaving the land defenseless. Like the embroidery goddess holding the reins of the warriors who flank her, she gave only to those who defended the order of nature, to men who, like monks, humbled themselves before the laws of charity and protective maternal love associated with feminine virtues.[49]

The icons of the Mother of God were above all amuletic. The image of mother and child is already seen on baked amulets found in the early Middle Ages in Kiev resembling those unearthed in the ancient settlements of Tripol'e (and the later Greek and Roman representations of Isis and Demeter). Mary, the Merciful One, the *Umilenie*, is the most common of all icons found in the icon corner of countless Russian houses, where she functions as the watchful and protective mother linking the living to the dead. Her eyes, filled with sorrow and foreboding, reveal her linkage with the ancient Fates: She knows the destiny of the child whose body she seems to cover with her head. While she looks mournfully at the viewer, her tiny son turns his imploring gaze upward to her immense head.

In the popular mind, Mary, uniting the living with the dead, was the guardian of the family rather than the savior of the nation, and was thus linked with the pagan rites of the hearth or family fire and with water and birth, that is, with the *rozhanitsy*, the Slavic Mokosh, the *rusalki*, and the Yaga. The peasantry attributed to Mary the full complement of destructive and regenerative qualities of the feminine which the Christian church had denied or eliminated in its creation of her image.

In her role as the mistress of the hearth and of fire, Mary resembles the fate-giving Yaga. Though hers is thought to be the fire from heaven, and her icon is used to protect the house from burning, she is nonetheless represented as the *baba* who sits at the *pech'*, the domain of the ancestors.[50] In peasant lore, the role of the mistress of the house is associated with three old women, Fates, who are sometimes interchangeable with Mary as the guardians of the family fires. In the *Dukhovnye stikhi* they are called three "wives": Alleluiah, Miloserdnia, and Miloslaviia. The popular legend of the flight of the Mother of God from Jerusalem describes Mary's meeting a certain "wife" called both Miloslaviia and Miloserdnia who offers to hide the infant Jesus and save him from Herod's men; in so doing she sacrifices her own child by throwing him into the *pech'*. When the pursuers leave, she is satisfied that she has killed the infant: "To the fiery *pech'* she came / 'Has my treasure already burned?' / She opened the iron door, / Out of the *pech'* grass grew, / And in the grass flowers blossomed, / And in the flowers, the child played."[51]

The pagan sacrifice is justified—and purified—by Mary's miracle of transmutation. But this miracle occurs only through the

altruism of the "good" wife who burns her own offspring to protect the divine child. Through Mary's association with Miloslaviia/
Miloserdnia, the triple chthonian aspects of Yaga are acknowledged and linked with the Christian mother's sacrificial love.[52]
Furthermore, Mary's relationship to Christ is represented as that
of a mother who foresees and mourns her son's death.

While at Christmas, the time of birth, Mary is hailed in liturgy as well as in popular lore as the "Tsaritsa of All Mankind,"
the "Heavenly Star," the "Mistress of Earth and Heaven" who
brings Christ, the Sun, to the world, in the Koliada festivities
she was the goddess who saw his fate like a peasant girl telling fortunes. In a cycle of poems in the *Dukhovnye stikhi* called "The
Dream of the Mother of God," she predicts her child's death:
"Under the Holy Cypress I slept / And I saw much in my
dream. / I gave birth to a son ... / In the river I washed him. /
They brought forth a miraculous cross, / And Christ said: / 'Ai,
Mother, You Mother Mary, / Holy Mother of God ... / I will sleep
[die] on that cross."[53] But the mother who claims the body of
the sacrificed son—washed in the waters of the maternal river
Jordan and hung on the frame of the Tree of Life—is Mother Earth.
The Birth-Giver of God bears her child so that Mother Moist Earth
may take him back. The pagan cycle is the more significant one,
and Christ appears as the seasonal fertility god, the paradigm
for all perishable humanity.[54]

Like the Sumerian goddess Inanna, the Egyptian Isis, the
Phrygian Cybele, Mary laments the death of her son-consort:
Christmas leads in the Christian calendar to Easter, the time of
death and resurrection. But the rebirth of God is preceded on
Good Friday in the *Dukhovnye stikhi* by Mary's cry of pain: "Oh
son, ruler of all beauty. / What is left of all my grief, / The sky
weeps with all creation. / The sun hides and all is in shadow. /
The moon shines on your spilled blood, / All light goes out."[55]
Christ the Sun is dying, and with him the bright day. Mary the
mother takes him from the "tree" and places him in the "dark
grave." She buries her son with the help of three "wives"—her
chthonian "triplication"—in a scene depicted with intense emotion in a number of icons. One in particular, from the sixteenth
century in north Russia, shows the descent from the cross as the
sorrow of Mary cradling her son's head and enveloping his figure in hers like the "Lady of Tender Mercy."[56]

Mary the mother who mourns is, in popular belief, the mistress of the ancestors. Kievan medallion amulets from the eleventh to the thirteenth centuries show on one side the Mother of
God holding her child, and on the reverse the head of Medusa.

The symbolism is plain: The birth-giving mother is also the guardian of the dead. The most famous of the apocryphal stories surrounding Mary's underworld role is "The Descent of the Mother of God into Hell." Versions of this tale, echoing the Sumerian goddess Inanna's harrowing of hell in quest of her lover, Tammuz, existed in the Greek version from the ninth century. The account was never popularized in the West, but it entered the folkloric canon of eastern Europe.[57]

"The Descent of the Mother of God into Hell" begins when Mary learns about the torments of sinners in the underworld and, like the ancient Mother Goddesses, descends to share in the pain of her children. She first notices the tree of the underworld, where those who cause dissension in the family are tortured. This is indeed a great transgression in the religions of the pagan goddesses.[58] The Birth-Giver listens to the entire list of sins. The most severely punished are women—priests' wives who remarry after the deaths of their husbands, and nuns who fornicate. But Mary acts with compassion rather than the vindictiveness of God and Christ toward those unfortunates. The sinners appeal to her as an intercessor and protector for the Christian people. Regarded as the mediator between the despotism of the Divine Father and Son and the sinfulness of the children (like a good wife in a patriarchal family), she begs them to mitigate the harshness of their laws.

Mary's implicit criticism of a religion of the ruler-despot does not initially have any effect on Christ, represented as the copy of his father, the "stern judge." Only the chorus of saints and holy men under the protection of the Virgin can appease the anger of the male divinities. Finally Christ is sent to proclaim a period of clemency for the damned, like a newly crowned ruler who releases prisoners in celebration of his acquisition of power: "You will have Good Thursday to Holy Pentecost, day and night, to rest and to praise the Father, the Son, and the Holy Ghost."[59] No reference is made to the Mother of God, whose will and powers had changed the law, yet the Lord must bend his will to hers. For indeed, these days are the period in the Russian agrarian calendar when the ancestors, under the aegis of the *rusalki*, come up to the earth and reside in the villages with their families.

The Christian apocrypha represent Mary in traditional patriarchal fashion as a benevolent, interceding, and hence dependent mother; but the peasantry give her an all-powerful, heavenly, *and* underworld role: while in the *Dukhovnye stikhi* she is Yaga at the *pech'*, in folktales she is assimilated to the child-taking and child-giving Yaga who rules her human children without a consort or son. In one story, an old man and an old woman bear a daughter but can find no godmother for her. Finally, an old woman offers her services and, revealing herself to be Mary, the Mother of God, takes the child to heaven. But the girl commits a sin by picking three sacred lilies. The Holy Virgin casts the sinner out of heaven and into the forest. After some time, the girl is discovered by a prince, out hunting, who mistakes her for a *rusalka*. Despite the danger she represents, like Hades, he carries her off. Attempting to evade him, the girl turns herself into a tree. But the prince captures her and takes her back to his kingdom, where she bears three sons, each with the moon and the stars upon his forehead, and each born while the father is absent—to stress the parthenogenetic birth in which Mary the Great Mother filled the womb of her sinful goddaughter.

Mary demands that the three children be sent to her in order to expiate the sin committed by the mother, and she takes the girl back to heaven with her, as well. The prince, looking for his *rusalka* bride in the depths of the woods, sees a fire and finds that the animals surrounding it will not allow him to approach the flames. In the middle of the circle, guarded by all manner of beasts, sits Mary, her goddaughter, and the three heavenly sons. The girl (as the Wise Maiden) now implores Mary, the Yaga, to let the husband enter their company. One goddess is the mistress of the heavens; the other, the woodland divinity. Keepers of the fire on earth, they also contain the moon, sun, and stars as their three sons. Mary permits the prince to take his sons with him—just as the Scythian serpent goddess had offered hers to Herakles—but she takes the bride to heaven.[60] The men, father and sons, remain on earth; the women retire to another realm, which is both heaven and the woodland clearing sacred to Yaga and the *rusalka*.

The meaning of the story is clear: Children are from the mother alone; only through a rejection of masculine bonds, which "capture" the feminine, can woman "wipe clean" the sin of disobeying the mistress of all life. Mary and her goddaughter, like Demeter and Kore, are also the clan and hearth mother Baba Yaga and *rusalka*. In fact, the folktale reverses the account of Eve's sin and presents the Mother of God as the supreme being who reveals the eternally profane nature of man. No father god appears in this tale—only sons, the prince and his own children. Marriage among mortals debases woman because it is "forced." Just as unequivocally, the famous icon of the Mother of God called the *Bogoroditsa Orans* (Birth-Giver *Orans*) asserts the maternal law over the entire cosmos—society, earth, underworld, and the heavens.

Mary *Orans*: Mistress of the Heavens

The image of the goddess with upraised arms has, as we have seen, a long history: In Paleolithic cave paintings, at Çatal Hüyük, in Tripol'e figurines, and in the Russian embroidery goddess, the gesture suggests both receptivity and prayer.[61] The Iaroslav Virgin *Orans*, called the "Lady of the Sign," an imposingly tall figure, dates from the twelfth century. (Illustration no. 12.) Above her haloed head are two bright spheres from which gaze two angels holding circular objects in their hands. On her breast in a circle of light rests the haloed Christ Child raising his arms to his mother. Here is an awesome Christian evocation of the goddess of all creation. Like the Tripol'e bird mother, she carries the mandalic egg-child in her body; irradiated by the sun and the moon, she is at the same time the source of their light.

The Virgin *Orans* bonds the skies and the earth. The sun, moon, and angels are all contained in shining spheres like those which surround Christ and his mother's head. Her body, a long column evoking the Tree of Life, is "rooted" in an intricate oval dark red carpet and seems to emerge out of the earth. Carrier of Christ as the sun in her breast, she is the sky goddess rising from the underworld. Her arms are raised not merely in a gesture of praise to a higher power, but to encompass. The expression of omniscient sadness, like that of the icon of the "Lady of Tender Mercy," links her to the Fates. In other icons, her nature as the ruler of the heavens is more pronounced: She is seated on a throne in the sky holding the Christ Child on her lap while the saints and rulers cluster around her feet on the earth below.[62] But as the Virgin *Orans*, she expresses most vividly her epiphany as the goddess who rules over all realms of nature from on high and is identified with the heavenly spheres.

In folklore, Mary is frequently associated with the act of birth and pictured as the dawn star opening the gates through which the solar disk emerges: the genetrix of the sun. Her mantle, like that of Isis, is the sky which covers the earth and her child, the sun, with a starry veil. As the dawn star and the moon goddess combined, Mary does not so much reflect the power of the sun as she gives it birth and nurture. Like Artemis, the moon goddess, she too is called the *Stella Maris*, the star of the seas.[63] But she is a sun divinity as well as the mother of the sun, clothed in her light-blue mantle of the sky. Russian iconographers depict her clothed in the "beautiful-red" ascribed to both the sun and the maiden. The attribute of sun-son bearer, as mother and daughter or twin sisters, is vividly portrayed in an apocryphal story called "The Tale of Mary and Martha of Murom," a city whose resistant pagan tradition gave us the account of Fevroniia, the All-Wise Maiden.

Two pious widowed sisters, Mary and Martha, meet each other daily on the road from Byzantium to Murom. One day an angel appears in their sleep, giving gold to Mary and silver to Martha. Gold symbolizes the sun and the Holy Cross; silver, the moon or the church. The angel instructs the widows to offer these gifts to the first three men they meet on their way to see each other. The sisters awake and set out for their daily walk, encountering the three strangers as the angel had predicted. They tell the men to use their gifts for the construction of a church to the Archangel Michael which would house the Holy Golden Cross entrusted to the city of Murom.[64]

The church and the cross became the source of many miracles. While the journey of the two sisters has been regarded as a parable for the political union between two cities, Murom and Byzantium, personified by widows, it was perhaps an analogy for the daily movement of the sun and moon. This cycle was interrupted by the church in order to inhibit the belief in the independent actions of the feminine sky deities and replace the pagan sisters with the image of the Christian Mother Church, clad in silver like the moon and containing inside her the Golden and Holy Cross, her sun-son.

In Orthodox liturgy as well as in pagan lore, the Mother of God is the mistress of all the planets in the heavens. The prayer to the icon of the Birth-Giver of Iversk describes her as: "Light of all / Highest of all creation . . . / Holy star / Bright moon / Beautiful sun. / Blessed in miracles / Life comes from your flesh / Even in your icon / There is astonishing power. / Sun comes from your rays / Your radiance fills the stars."[65]

Mary, mistress of the skies, is assimilated to the heavenly maidens, the *rusalki*, and depicted as the Wise Maiden. She is found in this form in a number of protective charms to help children, travelers, hunters, fishermen, and sailors. One such invocation begins, "On the sea-ocean, on the island of Buyan [a reference to the sky rather than the seas] there lies a white and hot stone. On this stone . . . stands a throne; and on that throne sits a beautiful maiden. This is not a maiden but the Most Holy

Mother of God. She sews and sews with a golden needle and a thin thread."[66] The maiden who sews is like the *rusalka* or the Wise Vasilisa. The white stone upon which her throne rests may be the moon; its heat suggests the sun, as well.[67] In other charms, the link of moon and sun is more apparent. The heavenly and Wise Maiden, Mary, seated on a "white and burning stone," is often associated with the swan (who pulls Apollo's chariot); in invocations like the one above, she gives her suppliant a feather from a bird which she holds on her lap. Other incantations address her as a goddess who sits upon a golden stool, sews with a golden thread, and holds the golden keys to heaven. There she is identified as the sun and as the mother of the sun, as well—the opener of the skies and the birth-giver—and is invoked to help women in labor. One charm directs her to "take your golden keys and open for me the door of flesh and let the child out into the light and freedom.[68]

Mary the Swan, like the *rusalki*, is also the source of sky fertility in the form of rain. She holds the golden keys of lightning, which precedes the storm. Mary the Thunderer (*Gramovitsa*) appears in a column of fire previously attributed to the ancient Perun. She is responsible for the rainbow linking heaven and earth and lets the rain flow over it to cover the fields. Sometimes she, too, uses the multicolored bridge to descend to earth. In her nature as rain-giver, Mary appears as the moon goddess Artemis—the source of dew, moisture, and fertility—who also helped women in childbirth to release the waters of the womb.[69]

Mary-*Rusalka*: Tree Goddess, Mistress of Animals and Birds

Mary is the Tree of Life upon which her son hangs. Her association with the Tree of Life is made explicit in a number of icons. One from the sixteenth century shows her before the cross, which is painted to look like a tree with the moon and the stars, and angels, perched like *siriny-rusalki*, in its branches. Another icon, the seventeenth-century Vladimir Mother of God (illustration no. 15), represents Mary as the totemic Tree Goddess and mother of the Russian state in whose "foliage" Russian rulers "blossom." Like the *rusalki*, she appears as the original ancestress, the clan mother. The birch sacred to the pagan divinities is identified with her, as well; and we have seen how the discovery of her icons on trees and by water linked her to the archaic nymphs. So too does the conjunction of Rusalia with Trinity Day, when the Mother of God is worshipped. In certain areas, during Troitsa and Semik, the sacred and decorated tree was thrown into the river with the icon of Mary upon it.[70]

Mary the Tree Goddess is, like the pagan nymphs and the Slavic Mokosh, represented as a spinner, and through her spinning, like them, she makes rain. The first image of the Mother of God holding a distaff is found in a twelfth-century fresco of the Kievan Saint Sophia. The "Ustiug Annunciation" icon of the same period shows her with a ball of red thread and an image of Christ etched upon her breast as though spun from it. She is evoked in charms as spinning alone or together with two others, her "sisters."[71] She is one of the three Fates, a spinner—but one connected to the *rusalki* as a bird goddess, as well.

The icon of the Virgin, called the *Golubitskima*, shows her with doves or pigeons. She is the clan mother protecting the domestic hearth. As "Mary the Swan" she is portrayed with swans at her feet, and in charms or incantations, she is described holding a swan on her lap. Like nymphs of the woodlands, swan maidens who change their shape and penetrate all the realms of nature, Mary, too, can move from the heavens to earth and to the underworld.[72] In Greek mythology, the water bird pulling the sun god's chariot is sacred to Aphrodite, representing both the grace of the goddess of love and her hideous nature as the ancient Fates, the Graeae. The dove, which is also Mary's symbol, evoked both the purity of the goddess of love and her link with the virgin deity, Artemis. The Pleiades, once the nymph companions of the huntress goddess, were turned into doves to save them from the fury of hunters. Russian folklore, as we have seen, contains a number of stories in which the dove princess aids her pursuer in return for proper veneration. Thus, we see that by infusing the image of Mary with the accumulated power of the bird and spinner symbols, her Russian worshippers, with the acquiescence of the church, revised the persona of Mary to conform to their most cherished and archaic divinities.

Lady of the birds, Mary is the Mistress of Animals, as well. Icons show her encircled by all manner of beasts, insects, and even fish. She grants game to hunters who appeal to her through charms. She is made to call to all her animal children, like the benign Yaga of fairytales, who communicates with all living things and provides for those who honor her. She is the patron of fishermen; they appeal to her generosity before they set off for their catch. She is the mother of bees, the queen bee, and she helps beekeepers. The charms to entice bees are thought most effective when repeated on the day of her annunciation.[73]

Attributed all the characteristics of the animal mother,

Mary is related to if not fully identified with the cult of earth. But while the icons of the "Lady of Tender Mercies" and the "Virgin *Orans*" or "Mary *Rusalka*" merely suggested her assimilation to the most archaic pagan deities, her link with Mother Moist Earth was clearly emphasized by the church through the juxtaposition of Mary's holy days with key agrarian festivals.

Mary and Mother Moist Earth

While the peasantry accepted the church's inclusion of Mary's, Christ's, and the saints' holidays in the rituals of the year, they insisted on tying the maternity of the Mother of God to the fertility of the soil and likened her Christian law of brotherly love to the veneration of the *rod* under the aegis of Mother Moist Earth. Like the telluric mother, Mary told her children to love and respect one another as brothers. And like earth, she too insisted on the sanctity of the mother's order in the family and household: "And don't disobey your mother's word: For a mother's word damns. / Whoever disobeys it, / Will turn heaven and earth upside down, / And the sun will fade, / And the moon will die out, / And the stars will dim."[74] Mary reinforced the archaic belief that the law of the mother was the law of the whole cosmic order.

Nonetheless, Mary herself was shown to recognize the powers of Mother Earth as separate from hers and in some respects superseding them. She invoked the earth in her mourning over her son: "Take me, Moist Mother Earth / Take me to you," she cries in the "Lament" cycle of the *Duknovnye stikhi*.[75] The wanderings of the Mother of God over the earth, like Isis in search of Osiris, were represented in the cycle of her feasts, which corresponded to the fertility rituals of the peasantry.[76] Mary, like Mother Moist Earth, was the giver of wealth. The cult of her icons corresponded to the chief periods of planting and harvesting. Koliada, the first of the feast days which celebrated the Mother of God, referred to her maternity in connection with the revival of the powers of the sun. The feast of the Annunciation in March corresponded to the "Greeting of Spring" or the "Entry of the Cuckoo," when the life of the forest enters the fields and the village. Trinity Day, often identified with Mary alone, crowned the festival of the Rusalia and made the assimilation of the Holy Virgin to the pagan maidens most explicit. When in late summer the harvest had been gathered for the feast of the Birth-Giver's ascension, she was represented in prayer as the goddess who was buried only to be immediately resurrected.[77] The first of the new crop was brought into the church as a gift to her, and icons of Mary as the bread-giver abound.[78] The Mother of Christ and the Mother of Bread were worshipped side by side.

The most sacred holiday of the Mother of God in Russia concluded the agrarian calendar with the promise of marriage. Pokrov, celebrated in October, had countless churches named after it. The Russian holiday of Mary the Protectress was first established in the twelfth century. In the fourteenth-century liturgy, she was solicited to intercede before God for all sinners and to protect the Russian land. The icon of Mary "Pokrov" shows her in the center of a group of men.[79] She hovers between earth and heaven with Christ as the sun above her head; but she herself binds the two spheres of being as she will bind woman and man.

The *Pokrov* ("Protection" or "Intercession") of Mary is her veil or dress, which according to legend was brought from Jerusalem to Byzantium in the fifth century and placed in a church dedicated to it.[80] Marriageable Russian peasant girls, on Pokrov Day, which was linked to the pagan worship of fertility, were granted special favors by the Mother of God while she wandered through the countryside. Indeed, Mary's assimilation to the goddess of the embroideries is clear in Vologodka Province, where girls gathered on Pokrov Day for the sole intent of spinning a veil to adorn the icon of the Holy Mother—a veil which resembled the votive towels bearing the figure of the pagan divinity and covered the head of the bride. "Mother Pokrov," they appealed to her, "cover the earth with snow and cover me, young one, with a husband!" But Mary was not just the matchmaker; her "cover" would also protect the future wife in the patriarchal household of her husband.[81] She provided a bond between the generations of women in the paternal family. Mothers, too, invoked her aid for their daughters: "Mother Pokrov, protect my daughter with your cloak when she goes away," pleads one mother; or "Mother Pokrov, cover the earth with snow and my child with a towel" (the pagan headdress of the bride). Women asked for children and abundant harvests at the same time: "Mother Pokrov, decorate the Moist Mother Earth and give me children."[82]

The protection of the Mother of God was solicited on her day in much the same manner as the goodwill of the *rusalki* was sought in spring for the fields and human fertility. The cult of Mary reaffirmed the rule of the mothers and the girls in the life of the peasantry despite the patriarchal faith which had produced her image. In the *Dukhovnye stikhi*, she is addressed as the ruler of all society: "She comes to the church as its ruler, / And is the heavenly tsaritsa of all / In heaven and on earth, / She protects her people with her holy pall."[83]

The worship of Mary as intercessor and protector emerged in its emotional intensity from the deeply ingrained veneration of mother and family. The laws of the maternal order were invoked to disarm those of the patriarchal Father God and tsar. Only through the adoration of Mary, the good mother, could the nation officially demonstrate its adherence to the family cults of a pagan past reviled by the authorities. But between the Christian Mary and the derogated wife (who Mary also represents) in the paternal family, there stands another figure, one who is closer by far to the ancient female divinities and who bridges the gap which the church had attempted to create between them and the denigrated Mary dependent upon father and son for her effectiveness. Although in a distinct form, the most popular saint, the "Holy Mother" Paraskeva-Piatnitsa, "Saint Friday," is often evoked interchangeably with the Mother of God. Paraskeva, however, is a widow and an independent deity.[84]

"Our Little Mother, Paraskeva-Piatnitsa, Protect Us!"

Mary is the goddess of both men and women; both implore her grace and protection. But the cult of Paraskeva-Piatnitsa was dominated by women. Unlike the Mother of God, she was not simply a mother figure but resembled in her "widowhood" the pagan Yaga, with no male restrictions upon her power. Her cult among the peasantry was remarkably resistant to disruption by the church (or indeed, after the Revolution, by the state).

Mary the lovely maiden and beloved (unaging) mother ruled from the skies. Paraskeva the elderly and unsightly goddess ruled from the earth, and she was invoked above all for her gift of fertility in field and community. She was the "Dirty One" as Mary was the "Most Pure." While Mary was the patron of the state as well as the family, Paraskeva protected the *rod* and the natural order above all. Her temple was the home; she had no place in the political world of the state linked with the distant and omnipotent heavens of the Lord Most High. Like the Yaga and the *rusalki*, she carried a spindle; like them she was in contact with the ancestral spirits and communicated between field, forest, and village. While she could control the skies, she was more closely attuned to the chthonian depths of the earth, expressing the homology between woman and nature.

The origins of the curious figure are obscure. Though she was officially adopted by the church as a saint, little is known about her; there is, in fact, considerable doubt about her historical existence. What is clear is that Paraskeva was a pagan deity accommodated by the populace to the demands of the church, which was obliged to adopt her. She was venerated in Greece and the Balkans as well as in Russia; her legend is linked with that of a Sarmatian woman called Saint Phoeina, martyred under the reign of Nero, and with Saint Anastasia of the Greeks. Most likely, the Slavs attributed to the daughter of Prince Boris of Polotsk, who fled from the Mongols to become a nun and died in Rome in the thirteenth century, the qualities of the Greek saint.[85]

Paraskeva is one of the few Russian female saints—and a pagan one, at that.[86] Her epithet, "Friday" (or the fifth day of the week), seems to have come from the translation of the Greek *Paraskeva*, which meant the day preceding the Sabbath or Friday. In pagan worship, however, Friday was sacred to the goddess Zhiva of the Western Slavs, as well as the Romans' Venus (hence *Vendredi* in French, *Venerdi* in Italian) and the Scandinavians' Freya (Freitag in German—"Friday"). The last two goddesses, like Paraskeva, were spinners. This pagan holy day found its way into the Byzantine church in the thirteenth century. Stories of the twelve Fridays were common and exhorted the faithful not to work on those days. Texts in Latin, Greek, Spanish, French, and Italian show the Fridays (Paraskevas) as twelve goddesses who regulate human destiny like the planets in astrology. On each sacred Friday, a significant Biblical event was said to have occurred. Among the Slavs, the twelve sacred days were spread throughout the year, and their strict observance was thought to guarantee wealth and prosperity for their worshippers. Each day provided protection from some specific evil—fire, sickness, flood, and so forth.[87]

In 1589, the Patriarch of Constantinople banned the cult of Fridays. In the same period, the Stoglav Council, set up by Ivan the Terrible to weed out pagan elements in the rituals of the populace, thundered against the festivities around Paraskeva. The Stoglav clergy called the holidays orgies rather than religious rites. Men and women, girls and and old women, naked and with loosened hair, would jump and shake, saying that they had seen Saint Piatnitsa and Saint Anastasia and had been ordered to honor their feast days by dancing. No work was to be done from Wednesday to Friday; women could not spin, wash, or throw stones into rivers. Indeed, so tenacious was Paraskeva's cult that until the eighteenth century in the Ukraine, Friday rather than Sunday was regarded as a holiday.[88]

The feminine fertility nature of these orgiastic rites is underscored in a fifteenth-century Latin sermon delivered to the Poles which refers to girls and women playing and dancing "as the pagans did for Persephone and Venus. We hear that they do not allow the relatives—only females in the family—to take part ... and much evil takes place."[89] But the Stoglav Council not only denounced these rituals invoking fertility, they also condemned "false prophets" who acted in the name of the saint. Paraskeva was a goddess of fate. In the Stoglav document she is accompanied by two other women, Saint Sreda, meaning Wednesday, and Saint Nedelia, or Sunday, linked also to Saint Anastasia. These three old women, spinners, were invoked interchangeably: "Honor Piatnitsa (Friday) on Sreda (Wednesday)," exhorts a religious verse.[90] Indeed, in Bulgaria their role as Fates and mistresses of the cosmic order was underscored by the belief that they labored together in laying down family law and in reviving nature: When one slept, the others worked.[91]

Paraskeva-Piatnitsa, the saint-goddess whose holidays appear in conflict with Christ's, is represented in Russian lore as well as iconic figuration as a tall, thin woman with long flowing hair, not covered like that of the old *baba* or the wife, or braided like that of the girl. She is shown as a *rusalka* or Baba Yaga; like them she is attributed the power of making rain and spinning all creation from her locks as well as her spindle.

In imitation of Christ, Paraskeva has twelve days or twelve handmaidens who surround her as "apostles." For in popular thought, the maids were not merely days but like the *rusalki* appeared at specific periods of the year. On occasion, particularly in the Ukraine, a woman was chosen to play the part of the saint. Driven in a cart to the walls of the church, she was regaled with gifts from the entire congregation. Through this ceremony, the villagers, women predominantly, challenged the official liturgy taking place inside.[92]

Paraskeva, assimilated to the various earth deities of the agrarian cycle and to the ancient witches untamed by the doctrines of the Orthodox clergy, appeared in her iconic representations to mock other Christian saints. On occasion she would even challenge the Mother of God. Paraskeva's icons were claimed to have been discovered in trees, by springs, and over water, as well as on elevations. The wooden carvings of the saint stressed her identification with the pagan goddess of the Tree of Life more explicitly than the images of Mary. The carvings were often found in churches and at crossroads where the spirits of the dead were thought to dwell. Paraskeva was an underworld deity as well as the giver of life; her effigy was placed on top of posts and by springs especially sacred to her. The cult of this dubious saint was so well integrated into the church that even the heart of the Russian Empire, the Red Square in Moscow, was at one time a spot sacred to Paraskeva and marked by a chapel in her name where women came to worship—on Fridays.[93]

The worship of Paraskeva-Piatnitsa was linked with the cultivation and spinning of flax, with women's work. The taboo against spinning on Fridays was observed rigorously not only among the Russians but also among the Southern Greeks and the Balkan Slavs. The Greeks often surrounded the icons of Paraskeva with a row of eyes in deference to the punishment which she was thought to mete out to those who disobeyed her law and spun on her sacred day.[94] The eye symbol may relate her to the all-powerful early Neolithic Eye Goddess. In Russia, she was as feared as the *rusalki* or Baba Yaga. "Piatnitsa is angered by those who don't observe her day, and she takes strong action against them," states the eighteenth-century Pétrine document called the *Spiritual Instructions* on the religious customs of the populace.[95]

Why was there a taboo against spinning, specifically in regard to Paraskeva? The saint's conjectured derivation from the Neolithic Eye Goddess may suggest one clue: She was the one who created and oversaw all things—like the eye-egg divinity of Tripol'e. Spinning was an analogy for the creation of life. It was assimilated to the harvesting and "taming" of the flax, through which field and human fertility were connected. Just as there were taboos against the poking of sticks into the soil while the earth was pregnant in spring, so too the cessation of spinning on Fridays gave rest to the saint and to those whom she guarded, the ancestral spirits immanent in her own body: "Whoever spins on Friday, she tears out the eyes of her sainted relatives with her spindle," goes a proverb expressing the fear of infringing upon family law and thus harming the protective ancestors.[96] For indeed in Greek myth, the acts which are punished with blinding—Oedipus's incest, Tiresias's angering of Hera by his defense of Zeus's infidelities—are clearly related to the violation of a familial and maternal order. By dishonoring Friday and disobeying the saint, a woman betrayed the cult which stressed feminine hegemony over all life. She thereby abandoned the pagan tradition of female centricity in family and nature.

There are two names for Paraskeva in Russian folklore: Paraskeva *Griaznaia*, "Muddy" or "Dirty," and Paraskeva *L'nianitsa*, or "Flaxen." Under these names she becomes mother and daughter, earth and crop: black as the soil and white like spun cloth. The goddess-saint in Ukrainian legend tells the peasants that when they spin they use her unruly hair. But in other proverbs she is the soil worked by men, as well: "On Piatnitsa Day, men must not do field work, and women must not spin."[97] Nor must they braid bast shoes, or twine cord, or sew and weave, or handle flax or linen, thus making dust fall into the eyes of Mother Paraskeva and in blinding her temporarily separate her from her own creation. For though the saint punished her wayward worshippers, she, like the ancestors, was herself tortured by the hand of man. On Friday, like Christ, she was thought to suffer his pains, pricked with needles and spindles like the tortured plant, the flax to which she was likened."[98] Paraskeva was both Demeter and Kore, Mother Goddess and, in the Christian context, Christ, the Dying and Reviving Fertility God. In response, perhaps, to the church's absorption of all female power, the saint denied all notions of masculine hegemony.

Saint Paraskeva was both the tortured plant and the earth which produced it; she was the Mistress of Animals who granted humanity its prey, but she was also identified with her creation. On Paraskeva Day men could not hunt, fish, or go to the forest to gather berries. Women could not cook or wash. On Fridays, only things which revitalized were allowed: The sexual rites denounced by the church were central in "rejuvenating" the family and stimulating nature in her period of rest. Consequently, marriages were lucky if they were celebrated on that day, and those who gave birth would be blessed. Fridays were favorable for healing (performed by women), and milk and eggs produced on that day would protect the house from fire. The chief priestesses who honored Paraskeva were the old women; they enforced the laws of the saint on all members of the household.[99]

Mother Paraskeva-Piatnitsa was the patroness of marriage and birth-giving. In that as well as in her spinning, she was similar to the Finnish-Slavic Mokosh. In fact, the cult of Paraskeva was strongest in the north of Russia, where the pagan goddess was thought to originate. Like Mokosh, whom she resembled in appearance, she protected women.[100] Just as Mokosh appeared integrated to the aboriginal rites of the ancient *bereginy* and *rozhanitsy* of the early Slavic populations, so too "Saint" Paraskeva paganized the religion of the Christianized upper classes by the stress on the autonomy of the goddess. Her college of priestesses—the "God-cursed *baby*" who had once worshipped Mokosh, the *bereginy*, the *rozhanitsy*, and Mother Moist Earth—challenged the all-male priesthood of the Christian church. Just as in earlier times Mokosh was attributed power over women and the family while the male gods assumed the functions of ruling the state, so too in the Christian period Paraskeva was the power of the maternal family, asserting her demands for obedience in the face of the state and its religious order. For unlike the patriarchal Mary, whose holy days were all related to her role as the Mother of God and were shared with her husband, father, or son, Paraskeva's days were her own. Her Fridays punctuated the church calendar as though to assert the dominance of the ancient feminine cycle linked to the rhythm of nature and family life; they reminded those who controlled the social order that they too were contained within it.

The worship of the icon of Paraskeva along with that of Mary reflected the rule of *dvoeverie*, "two faiths." Like Mother Moist Earth, Paraskeva confirmed the need to keep the laws of the family and *rod* sacred. Like Mary, she upheld the law of brotherhood and sisterhood. The sins which she punished were sins against fertility. She railed against those who separated married couples, aborted their offspring, removed the spurs from the rye blooms, or sold *Matushka* (Mother) Rye for exorbitant prices.[101]

She was related to the Mother of God in three instances: In the *Dukhovnye stikhi* she bemoans Christ's death together with Mary. On Pokrov Day, girls requested husbands from her as well as from the Holy Virgin, and Paraskeva's own holiday, October 28, was marked by the making of votive towels to adorn the bride's head. Finally, like the icon of Mary, Paraskeva's guarded against disease and helped women in childbirth: "Whoever worships Paraskeva will never have a fever," states a proverb referring to the beribboned and beflowered image of the saint resembling the *rusalka* or Semik tree in its ornamentation.[102]

Mary, the "official" goddess, was never fully assimilated to the pagan female divinities in all their aspects. Her "underground" powers were merely evoked in her cult to render it acceptable to her female worshippers. Paraskeva, on the other hand, on the margin between official sanction and denunciation, was allowed to assume fully the identities of Mother Moist Earth, Baba Yaga, and the *rusalki* rather than being merely ornamentally "covered" with their functions. Paraskeva was "Flax"; she was "Dirty" earth; she was both mother and daughter despite her lack of specific offspring, and in contrast to the pure Holy Virgin, who mothered only one child, God the Father's. The full identification of the saint with the pagan divinity was particularly explicit in her association with the long-haired *rusalka* as rainmaker and bringer of fertility from forest to community.

In addition to the rules against spinning, farming, and hunting, there was a taboo regarding women's washing their hair on Friday.[103] This prohibition appears to have been identified with the *rusalki*, who were thought to produce rain by combing the moisture out of their wet locks. Nor could women wash clothes. Just as the earth had to rest in order to regenerate itself, so too the forces of untamed nature had to be left to replenish their stock of moisture in order to produce the needed rain. Like the *rusalki*, Paraskeva wandered from water to land and from field and forest and into the community—a journey the Mother of God made only in the service of her son-father-husband. While Mary's element was the starry sky, Paraskeva's was the earth and water.

The chapels dedicated to the saint were called Piatnitsa *rodniki* to connect her with the *rod*, and were most often built by water. Her icon was placed in water, as well, so that it might have the most potent of medicinal powers. Towels embroidered on her day with the image of the fish were thought to be particularly effective in the maintenance of health; and fish caught in her sacred springs or watering places were considered to have special healing properties. Her icons, as we have seen, often appeared in the water—like *rusalki*. The sacred votive towels offered to the wood nymphs were also given to her: "Mother Piatnitsa," she was addressed in prayer for protection, "here is an apron!"[104]

Rain was assured if the believer watered a tree on Friday evening. For finally, like the *rusalki*, Paraskeva was a tree goddess. Her wooden statues, as we have seen, were talismans of her cult. She was the patron of the sacred birch, more specifically linked with it than Mary. In fact, up to the seventeenth century, images to honor Paraskeva were taken outside the village and to a river or into the forest to be placed on a tree. In her role as mistress of the Tree of Life, she was also the initiator of the young and the protector of children. Rituals which consisted of leading children and young men through tree branches in order to confer good health upon them were connected with her worship.[105]

But unlike the *rusalki*, Paraskeva did not lure men to their deaths or show vindictiveness of a capricious nature. In her wanderings she seemed to connect untamed and cultivated nature, ensuring that human beings kept her laws so that they might be spared the harmful effects of infringing upon that wild domain. Her miraculous powers associated with the veneration of the tree, particularly the birch in its iconic as well as its natural form, brought the young health and well-being rather than premature death. In the erotic rites banned by the church, Paraskeva betrayed her link with the dangerous dancing *rusalki*, but again she did so at the service of the regeneration of the community and nature rather than as a prelude to destruction.[106]

Paraskeva was the patron of women—as girls, mothers, and elders. In mediating between the chthonian divinities and the village, she represented the archetypal model upon whose actions the women of the peasantry could mold their own, asserting feminine power and autonomy in a social world which denied them political expression. In short, Paraskeva appears also to have personified the embroidery goddess with whose image we began our attempt to "reconstruct" the figure of the Russian Great Goddess. All creation was subordinated to her laws. Even "mounted warriors," the rulers of the social sphere, had to bow before this mistress of life who proclaimed the primacy of the feminine and maternal order—as the *natural* one.

Against the background of this ancient belief in the pagan and Christianized goddess whose forms and names were many, whose attributes and actions embraced the growth, decay, and rebirth of all nature and thereby embodied cosmic *and* social laws, we can better understand the development of Russian political and cultural institutions. For the gravitational pull of the myth of the feminine divinity—buried in the rites of the peasantry and in the tales told to children—exerts itself, in ways up to now unexplored, over the whole historical enterprise created by the sons of Mother Russia: *bogatyri* (knights), princes, tsars, nobles, intellectuals, artists, and revolutionaries.

1. A modern Matrioshka doll.

2. A nineteenth-century Matrioshka doll. A. and B. Pronin, *Russian Folk Arts*, New York, 1975.

3. An *izba* from Zavarino, decorated with a schematized Tree of Life and with a carved figurine of a horse on the roof. The Prokudin-Gorskii Archives, Library of Congress, Washington, D.C. Courtesy of the Library of Congress.

4. A Ukrainian *pech'* from the early twentieth century. *Folk Art of the Ukraine*, Leningrad, 1982.

5. A girl embroidering, Vladimir Province, 1914. *Narodnoe iskusstvo Rossiiskoi Federatsii iz sobraniia Gosudarstvennogo muzeia etnografii narodov SSSR*, Leningrad, 1981.

6. A peasant woman brings her icon to Pechory Monastery to be blessed. V. Sichov, *The Russians*, New York, 1980.

7. A snake-and-bird-shaped female
figurine decorated with lozenges
and meanders. Cucuteni (Tripol'e),
northern Moldavia, late fifth millennium. National Archeological Museum, Bucharest. M. Gimbutas, *The
Gods and Goddesses of Old Europe,
7000–3500: Myths, Legends, and Cult
Images*, London and Berkeley, 1974.

127

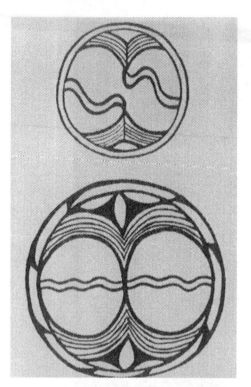

8. The Eye Goddess in schematic form painted on two ceramic dishes. A snake winds across a double-egg motif enveloped in flowing water and decorated with lozenges. Cucuteni (Tripol'e), western Ukraine, fourth millennium. Gimbutas, *Gods and Goddesses*.

9. The Goddess *Orans*: Goddess with upraised arms. Çatal Hüyük, seventh to sixth millennium. J. Mellaart, "Çatal Hüyük, A Neolithic City in Anatolia," *Proceedings of the British Academy*, vol. 51, 1965–1966.

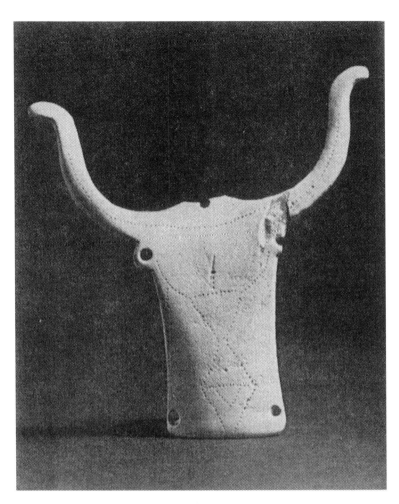

10. The Goddess *Orans*: A bull-horned goddess in the form of a bee. Cucuteni (Tripol'e), northwestern Ukraine, fourth millennium. Archeological Museum, Cracow. Gimbutas, *Gods and Goddesses*.

11. The Goddess *Orans*: "The Mother of God *Orans*," Cathedral of Saint Sophia, Kiev, 1043–1046. D. Obolensky, ed., *Art Treasures in Russia*, New York, 1970.

12. The Goddess *Orans*: The icon of "Our Lady of the Sign," twelfth century. Tret'iakov Gallery, Moscow. T. T. Rice, *A Concise History of Russian Art*, New York, 1967.

130

13. The Goddess as the Tree of Life: A Sarmatian diadem from Novocher-kassk, first to third century A.D. State Hermitage Museum, Leningrad. A. Voyce, *Art and Architecture of Medieval Russia*, Norman, Oklahoma, 1967.

14. The Goddess as the Tree of Life: A bracelet from Kiev, twelfth century. The Historical Museum, Moscow. Pronin, *Russian Folk Arts*.

15. The Goddess as the Tree of Life: The icon of "The Vladimir Mother of God," Simon Ushakov, 1668. Tret'iakov Gallery, Moscow. Obolensky, *Art Treasures*.

16. The Goddess as the Tree of Life: A spinning bench from Nizhnii Novgorod, nineteenth century. *Narodnoe iskusstvo*.

17. The Goddess approached by supplicants: Detail from a Pazyryk felt hanging, fifth century B.C. State Hermitage Museum, Leningrad. T. T. Rice, *The Ancient Arts of Central Asia*, New York, 1965.

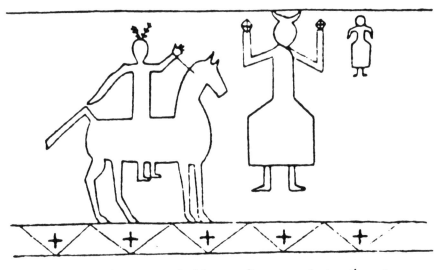

18. The Goddess approached by supplicants: a nineteenth-century embroidery motif from north Russia. B. A. Rybakov, "Drevnie elementy v russkom narodmon tvorchestve," *Sovetskaia etnografiia*, no. 1, 1948.

19. The Goddess approached by
supplicants: The icon of "The Appearance of the Holy Virgin and
Saint Nicholas to the Sexton Iur-
ysh," north Russia, eighteenth
century. Pronin, *Russian Folk
Arts*.

20. The Goddess surrounded by
worshippers: A gold plaque from
a Scythian headdress, Karago-
deuashkh, fourth century B.C.
State Hermitage Museum, Leningrad. E. H. Minns, *Scythians and
Greeks*, Cambridge, 1913.

21. The Goddess surrounded by worshippers: A miniature from the fifteenth century *Radziwill Chronicle* showing soldiers and clergy worshipping the icon of Mary. The British Museum. O. Hoetzsch, *The Evolution of Russia*, New York, 1936.

22. The Goddess surrounded by worshippers: An embroidered towel from Vologodsk, nineteenth century. *Narodnoe iskusstvo*.

23. *Ptitsa-sirin* painted on a chest, Olonets, 1710. *Sokrovishcha russkogo narodnogo iskusstva: Rez'ba i rospis' po derevu*, Moscow, 1967.

24. *Sirin*. Detail from the wall of a nineteenth-century Ukrainian *izba*. *Narodnoe isskusstvo*.

136

25. A "Beautiful Girl" painted on an eighteenth-century cupboard. The Goddess appears as a *deva/divitsa* with animals, birds, and plants. Pronin, *Russian Folk Arts*.

26. Saint Paraskeva-Piatnitsa, a seventeenth-century woodcarving. Perm Museum. A. L. Kaganovich, *Arts of Russia*, New York, 1968.

27. The icon of "The Vladimir Mother of God," twelfth century. Tret'iakov Gallery, Moscow. Obolensky, *Art Treasures in Russia.*

28. An icon of the saints Boris and Gleb, fourteenth century. State Russian Museum, Leningrad.

29. An icon of Saint Basil as a Holy Fool, fifteenth to sixteenth century. State Russian Museum, Leningrad. D. S. Likhachev and A. M. Panchenko, *"Smekhovoi mir" drevnei Rusi*, Leningrad, 1976.

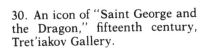

30. An icon of "Saint George and the Dragon," fifteenth century, Tret'iakov Gallery.

31. The monument to Peter the Great by
Falconnet, 1782, Leningrad. Photo-
graph: J. Goetelen. Kaganovich, *Arts of
Russia.*

32. An eighteenth-century *lubok* showing Peter in the form of a
"crocodile" fighting Baba Yaga. From Rovinski, *Atlas*, 1881. P. L.
Duchartre, *L'Imagerie pòpulaire russe,* © Gründ, Paris, 1961.

PART TWO

Mothers' Sons

CHAPTER FIVE

Epic Heroes and Disobedient Sons

"But Dobrynia did not listen to his mother."

—A. P. GIL'FERDING,
"Dobrynia and Marinka,"
Onezhskie byliny[1]

The Russian epic tradition is distinguished from the Western form in that the hero must obey the laws of his mother or wife and perishes when he does not. The Russian hero's powerful guide and yet most feared antagonist is his own mother or mother figure, who appears as an enchantress, temptress, witch, or bride. Only in the goddesses' patronage of Greek and Roman heroes do we find a parallel to the Russian epos. Indeed, the mother of the Russian *bogatyr'*, like the ancient female divinities, is the source of his power and wisdom, the architect of his victories, and the Fate which decrees his defeats.[2] The epic tradition not only reflects the historical process of patriarchalization by the ruling class, it also reveals, in the combined persona of the mother and the obedient son, the peasantry's resistance to it.

In the first section, we examined Russian folklore in the light of the feminine tradition. Now we turn to its expression of masculine values: "The *muzhik* (male peasant) pulls one way; the *baba*, the other," is an often-repeated proverb which underscores the *dvoeverie* in the heart of the family. The feminine faith serves the values of fertility, and prophecy is perceived as woman's particular gift. The masculine system stresses aggression: trial, war, and the hunt.[3] In the lore grounded in the feminine, the individual—whether hunter, fisher, or farmer—is obliged to cooperate with the forces of nature to receive its benefits and is thereby subsumed to the generations of the family and the round of the seasons. Individual self-assertion is antithetical to the laws of the *rod* and nature: The mother, at the center of the family, holds the youth back; the maiden tempts him to remain in its sphere through marriage.

The feminine world, identified with nature, the maternal family, and community, is thus the realm which the epic hero strives first to evade and then to control. In the epos, the sphere of human activity is social: The male individual is a fighter who attempts to remove himself from the ever-renewing cycle of nature in order to master it through his deeds. The masculine ethos, depicted only in the most restrained and controlled manner in the folktale, is vividly expressed in the epic. While feminine lore stresses the cyclical nature of myth and ritual repetition reflecting seasonal changes and their symbolic relationship to human generation, the masculine moves through the epic toward history as the record of individual actions.

From Folktale to Epic

In the first chapter, we saw how the laws of the male gods gradually began to impinge upon those of the Great Goddess. We suggested that this struggle was related to the rise of nomadic and warrior societies coming into conflict with agrarian peoples in their quest for territories. The Russian epic tradition seems indeed to echo this conflict, but in an indirect manner: Transmitted through the centuries not by the warrior class whose values it expressed, but rather by the peasantry it conquered, the epos reflects the demand of this underclass (which fed its masters) to subsume the cult of male divinities and male values into the order of the autochthonous goddesses; that is, to subordinate the militaristic social order to the defense and service of the agrarian one.

In bowing to the myths and ethos of the patriarchal and warrior ruling classes, the peasantry attempted to temper these with their own concerns and values. But over centuries, the gradual process of patriarchalization also affected the themes of folklore and rite. Masculine rituals and supernatural figures became assimilated to feminine prototypes. As elements of the archaic folktale tradition were incorporated into the newer epic one, the ancient divinities of the pagan Slavs and their predecessors, the *bereginy*, the *rozhanitsy*, and the earth mothers, were doubled by masculine counterparts. Christianity, as we have seen, played a vital role in this process by imposing, as had the pagan Varangian rulers before it, the cult of male gods and a priesthood over the indigenous population. In the chronicles written by monks, female deities were given "ruling" husbands or partners.[4] Male figures gradually began to proliferate in Russian lore, reaffirming the importance of preexisting male divinities but challenging and duplicating female ones, as well. The pagan nomadic and warrior ethos asserted itself against the bonds of the maternal and feminine in the ancient mother-centered tradition. There could, however, be no question of dominating or of overshadowing the worship of autochthonous goddesses. As we have seen, Mother Moist Earth had no consort to challenge her authority. The peasantry saw little in its daily experience to confirm patriarchal values at odds with the masculine role in the cycle of farming or with the function of the father in family life and community rituals.

The epic, then, represents the strong affirmation of male power in conflict with feminine forces. But the process whereby the hero attempts to make himself the measure of all things could be initiated only by taking the measure of woman herself through the imitation of her magical strength. In Russian folklore, this usurpation was accomplished by the creation of masculine figures as doubles of pagan goddesses. The *rusalka* has a male counterpart called a *vodianoi* (from *voda*, "water") or a *leshii*, master of the woods (from *les*, "wood"). The *rozhanitsa* of the bathhouse is shadowed by a mischievous male spirit called a *bannik* (from *bania*, "bath"); and the *pech'* of the Yaga is also inhabited by the despotic and quarrelsome *domovoi* or *domovik* (from *dom*, "house"), who lives in the granary and is linked with the ancestral spirits now called *dedy* ("grandfathers"). In Belorussia he is called a snake (*tsmok*) and depends upon the mistress of the house for nurture. Ded Moroz was "Grandfather Frost." Each of these characters expresses through its generic name (*water* sprite, master or *tsar* of the *woods*, *bath* spirit, *house* spirit) his restricted nature.

This duplication by specially created spirits of more archaic ones was continued by the church: Saint Elias presides over the harvest festival of Mother Moist Earth; Saint George fights the serpentlike goddess or Yaga to free the Russians from her grasp; Nicholas, the successor of Artemis, grants fertility to his worshippers. These saints, in turn, mask an even earlier masculine assumption of female functions by the official Slavic gods, Perun and Volos. The wise Baba Yaga of folktale is sometimes replaced by one wise old man or sorcerer; the virgin-mother aspect of the fertility goddess is attributed instead to twin male gods and saints called Kosma and Demian; the *rusalki* or *vily* are said to be the daughters of a sea tsar and live under his rule; wood nymphs are doubled by *leshie*, male and female creatures who inhabit the forest in the form of a tsar and his family, ruling that realm with the despotic might of the lords of Russia.

The assertion of a patriarchal order is of course evident in the folktale itself, where tsars rule and princes seek out magical brides in order to assume the throne. But when we look closely at the folklore hero, we find that his behavior is at odds with an apparently father-centered society: The youth in many tales is remarkable for his passivity, or acts only through the help of magical agents. In his quest, almost always associated with finding a bride, he enters the domain of the female spirits to undergo an initiatory struggle. The youth must come into contact with the animistic world of the forest and meet its mistress before he can fulfill his destiny. Folktales are called *volshebnye skazki*, or magical tales "told from the stove" by old *baby*. We have seen the central role played by women in the cycle concerning Baba Yaga, Vasilisa the Wise, or the maiden-*rusalki*. In short, although the folktale uses the patriarchal social and political order as the context of the quest, it is the family rather than the state which is invoked, and the realm of nature rather than the tsar which shapes the fate of the hero.[5]

The folktale often begins with the violation of family taboo. This may occur through the actions of a stepmother or a step-daughter, never those of a son, father, or stepfather. The hero of the folktale is frequently the youngest son, who is also the mother's favorite. His passivity is well illustrated in the figure of Ivan the Fool or Ivan the Lazy, who sees his strong older brothers leave on their various quests and tells his mother that he'd rather remain with her forever. This hero, lowly by birth and humble in demeanor, triumphs over his brothers through his dependency on the mother. More often than not he is found lying on the *pech'*: Ivan the Fool lives with his widowed mother and stays on the *pech'* while others around him work; or he sits in the ashes or in a pile of millet without his britches on as though to suggest his infancy and his utter subordination to maternal demands. He is, suggests one writer, the "matrilocal groom."[6]

Ivan the Fool is not stupid; he is unsocialized and rebelliously clings to the maternal realm or to archaic matrilocal custom as though championing his mother. Unlike his older brothers, he is kind and generous. He shares his bread with the poor and shows concern for family, both the living and the deceased. Like Cinderella, he sits in the ashes of the *pech'*, where the ancestors dwell, and waits for his magical helper from that realm. The source of the gifts of wealth or of a bride bestowed upon the patient lad is often a tree—the Tree of Life.[7] Living close to the mother-dominated family and natural world, the Fool, like the male shaman, is the recipient of transformational powers which allow him to move through all the realms of nature. Most often these capabilities are conferred upon him by Yaga in his journey to the forest.

In contrast to the passive youth, the women of the folktale are active. As though in conscious opposition to the Christian vision of woman, they are not the devil's helpers but are morally and spiritually superior to the male. Thus, the folktale sets the social order on its head: The youngest and most dependent male is a hero; the weak and morally debased women are the wise ones. Vasilisa the Wise, Helena the Beautiful, and the good Baba Yaga (whose evil can be transformed into good by the hero's show of proper respect) represent ideals of feminine courage and independence and active participation in all aspects of social and "supernatural" life.[8]

But within the context of feminine power, a struggle nonetheless occurs. Ivan the Fool, armed and hence protected with the magical aid he has earned by his motherly behavior, must fight the evil or infertile aspects of the feminine represented by the underworld Yaga, who appears, as we have seen, in a number of forms. He wins because he has been aided by her benign protective and productive nature. This is also true of another central male folklore character called Prince Ivan or Dmitrii, or Aliosha, a youth from the upper classes in quest of a bride who expresses the warrior ethos. But like the Fool, he must pass through the oven or hut of the Yaga to get help in his conflict with various monsters.

The introduction of princes into the folklore tradition and the stress upon conflict with Yaga contrast with the compliance shown to her by female protagonists. For despite the fact that the prince as hero is still the passive recipient of gifts which can be traced to female helpers, and that he wages his struggle in the context of the maternal law, the urge to break through constraint is quite clearly apparent, more evident than even in the Ivan the Fool cycle. The Russian folktale prince appears to perform the feats of Hindu, Iranian, Greek, and Germanic heroes who fight off the umbilical serpents binding them (the family) and in so doing become identified with the sun or its deliverers (heads of divine pantheons and rulers of the state). Saving the sun from the depths to which the forces of the feminine have dragged it daily, the heroes challenge nature's law, which demands the death of the individual and denies him everlasting glory.[9]

The impulse toward freedom from nature's constraints, associated with the restraints of the family, is at the center of the patriarchal epic tradition. While the folktale denies altogether the possibilities of human prowess without supernatural assistance, the epic glorifies a form of superanthropomorphism. The folktale hero is a youth setting out into the forest; the epic hero is a man going forth into the open steppe. The former is plunged into the animistic and timeless world of family and nature; the latter prepares to win wars in the name of the state. The epic is called a *bylina* or *starina*, indicating a specific past. Its characters are identifiably historical: The Mongol invaders and their predecessors are the enemy; the grand princes of Kiev or Novgorod are the hero's patrons. The hero himself generally springs from the people; but even when he is a nobleman, he never attains the status of a ruler.[10] The state forms the context of the epic; the conflict with the feminine is assimilated to the battle with the invading enemy.

Most scholars date the earliest *byliny* from the tenth or eleventh century, but their content may refer back to the concerns of an Indo-European warrior elite. The locus of action in Kiev, Novgorod, and central Russia suggests Varangian variations upon more archaic themes. The *byliny* were most probably disseminated from court to court by traveling entertainers who sang them for the pleasure of their aristocratic audience. While initially, they reflected the interests and world view of the elite alone, when they reached the peasantry through the medium of the wandering *skoromokhi* (pagan players and entertainers), the epics were perhaps modified to appeal to their new audience. Certainly by the eighteenth and nineteenth centuries, when the first folklorists began to gather the *byliny* (ironically, for an upper-class readership), they found them among the peasants of the remote north, where colonization had propelled numbers of rural inhabitants from south and central Russia. There, isolated from foreign influence and modification, the epos was "frozen" in its relatively archaic form.[11]

Through many centuries, an oral tradition intended for the ruling classes was nurtured by those over whom they ruled. The peasantry's adaptation of the heroic epos perhaps explains the peculiar attachment of the male protagonist to the mother or bride and his unsuccessful struggle to assert autonomy and individual glory outside the context of collective well-being. Whereas in the Western epic cycles, the claim to immortality of the individual rests upon a challenging of the order of the cosmos, the Russian hero perishes only when he asserts his individuality over the laws of nature embodied in the cult of earth. Boasting for him is a fatal flaw.[12]

Russian epics have been divided into two categories. The first is the *un*heroic cycle, close to the folktale, with its dominant theme being the quest for a bride; the second is the heroic epos, which exalts the male in his defense of the motherland. The latter is related to the gradually evolving notion of Russia as a *rodina* (birthland) common to all her children. Both the epic cycles have as their protagonists *bogatyri*, a term derived from the Turkish word for "knight." In the Russian—as opposed to the Western—tradition, there is a female knight or heroine, called a *polianitsa* (from *pole*, "field"). She is more powerful than her male counterpart, who must challenge and tame her still-magical force but does not condemn her for her strength. The *polianitsa* resembles the folktale enchantress called the *bogatyria*, who chooses her own husband and through whose persona we can see the interpenetration of epos and fairytale. In both genres she appears as the all-powerful goddess to whom the hero must come in order to confirm his own identity. But in the context of the epic, dating, perhaps, from the Scythian period, she may also be an echo of the Amazon myth.[13]

The assumption that the *polianitsa* represents a vestige of a woman-centered social order assimilated to a patriarchal one is supported by the fact that this figure is represented in her most forceful incarnation in the oldest of the epic cycles, called by scholars the mythological cycle. There the acts of protagonists seem to evolve in the timeless atmosphere of the folktale. Though the city of Kiev is mentioned, the action may refer to a more remote period. The second of the cycles, called the Kievan-Vladimir, moves from the inchoate temporal sphere into the historical realm. All activity is focused on the city of Kiev. The third cycle of the epos reflects the history of Novgorod; but given the simultaneous settlement of the two regions by the Varangians, it may be linked in time with Kiev. Both deal with events from the twelfth to the fourteenth centuries. The Galician-Volynian cycle is the fourth; it includes the Muscovite epos, which dates well into the seventeenth century.[14]

The Cycles of the Epos

The Mythological

Four heroes dominate the first epic cycle. Their names indicate a pre-Varangian origin. Dunai and Volga are river names. Volga is sometimes referred to as Volkh, the name of the Slavic and Varangian priesthood. The others are Mikula (the plowman) and Sviatogor ("Holy Mountain"). All four appear in an embryonic form of characterization, as though they had just been created. The mythological cycle reflects tribal nomadic movements and shamanic rites. Magic still infuses these first epics, and people and animals live in a state of promiscuity that is found in the folktale.[15] And here we find the same conflict between matrifocal and patrifocal cultures that was outlined in our first chapter. The presence of the *polianitsa* in the full glory of her supernatural power not only indicates the introduction of this persona from the folktale tradition, but also refers symbolically to the matristic social structure which the hero must overcome.[16]

The tale of Dunai and Nastasiia-*Polianitsa* is one of the most widespread and most popular of all the *byliny*.[17] It is also the most violent depiction of conflict between a man and a woman of equal power. The heroine is established as the enemy of the Varangian princes and, no doubt, of their nomadic-warrior predecessors, as well. The story begins at a feast, where the Grand Prince of Kiev tells his *bogatyri* that he is seeking a wife. In some versions this wife is identified with the daughter of the Tatar Khan, enemy of Kiev; in others she is one of two sisters. The oldest of the sisters is called Nastasiia-*Polianitsa*, famed for her skill as an archer and huntress; the younger, Apraksiia, is a spinner and Wise Maiden. Together, the two young women clearly possess the attributes of Artemis as huntress and Fate, and of the Amazons, her priestesses.

Dunai, the grand prince's chief *bogatyr'*, volunteers to bring the young woman to his overlord. Marriage is here assimilated to the victory over the enemy, and Dunai must wrest the girl from her father. But the father never appears in the course of the story, and it is apparent that the princesses are the sole rulers of this mysterious realm. Dunai wishes to present the docile and wise spinner Apraksiia to his lord and marry the warrior Nastasiia himself. In one version, his bride capture suggests a rape: Dunai is said to arrive at Apraksiia's *terem* and tear it down, sending the frightened young woman to his ruler in Kiev. But while the younger girl seems to go without a struggle,

Nastasiia disguises herself as a Tatar and attacks Dunai, hissing like a serpent and thereby resembling the archaic Scythian serpent goddess. In another version, Dunai, like the hunter-herder Herakles, goes in quest of prey and comes upon a tent in which the warrior princess Nastasiia is said to live. Unlike Herakles, he does not approach it respectfully but immediately shoots at the young woman. Missing, he hits an oak tree, making Mother Earth shake. He has committed the first of his evil deeds in attacking the Tree of Life and the tent of the Amazon, who is also the Wise Maiden; for this proscribed act alone, he would deserve to die. Nastasiia attacks him in a rage, like a serpent, but Dunai is saved (like Scythian warriors) by his horse.[18]

The Atalanta-like challenge of the *polianitsa* angers Dunai, but he cannot refuse the young woman. After a considerable struggle, he gets the better of her and carries her off to the palace of the grand prince. There he marries Nastasiia; but she won't be so easily tamed. She begins to boast that she is the best archer of the realm. Dunai, his honor sullied by her claim, cannot bear the thought of defeat at her hands. As he raises his sword to kill Nastasiia, she tells him that she is pregnant and, prescient, like the heroine of folktale, will give birth to a son whose legs are silver to the knees, his arms golden to the elbows; in his hair the stars will shine, and he will illuminate the darkness like the "Red Sun" himself.[19] When she reveals herself to be the goddess of the skies, Dunai only fears her power more intensely, and kills her without pity. But when he recognizes the gravity of his crime as the destruction of life itself, personified in the figure of the pregnant mother giving birth to the cosmic order, he knows that he must die, and he kills himself.

Two rivers arise over the bodies. Over Dunai flows the mighty Danube, over Nastasiia the smaller tributary, the Nastasiia River. Even in death the hero marks his victory over the goddess of life; for indeed the river Danube was once considered by the population of the area to be a female divinity. The clash of social and cosmological systems is clearly evoked: Nastasiia-*Polianitsa* was "defeated" through marriage, but she resisted the patrilocal and patriarchal bond, and her subordination and vengeance resulted in the destructive act which brought tragedy and infertility to the land. The epic suggests the power of the husband over his wife and her tributary status to his central role in family and realm. At the same time, it warns about the dangers to life which the patriarchal order embodies.[20]

Whereas the struggle of Dunai and Nastasiia results in infertility linked to masculine aggressiveness, the story of Volga or

Volkh, who bears the sacred name of "Mother Volga" as well as that of the ancient Slavic shamans, shows how the power of the feminine must be *absorbed* rather than contested. The epic of Volga/Volkh illustrates a successful male initiation into a shamanic priesthood under the aegis of the mother; it also depicts the manner by which the family bond is replaced by the law of ruler and state.

The story begins with the prince's mother walking through her garden alone: "She leapt from a stone onto a fiery serpent," who proceeds to wind itself around her leg, giving her the appearance of the Scythian serpent-tailed maiden. But this serpent is male, and the princess conceives a son: "In the sky the moon shone brightly / And in Kiev a powerful *bogatyr'* was born / Young Volkh Vseslavich. / Mother Moist Earth shook and trembled . . . / To have given birth to a *bogatyr'*." Here the once-powerful goddess in her garden is now identified only with the earth, who bears (though her son is still the shining moon) the son of a sky god. Volkh behaves like the infant Herakles: "When Volkh was a quarter of an hour old / He spoke in a voice like thunder: / 'My Lady, My Mother, do not swaddle me, / Don't bind me with sashes. / But swathe me in strong steel armor / And on my head place a golden helmet.'" At the age of seven, his mother begins to instruct him in reading and writing to augment his already considerable power. At the age of ten, he acquires shamanic magic from her: "The first wisdom he was taught / To a bright falcon to turn. / The second wisdom he acquired / Into a grey wolf to turn. / The third wisdom he learned / Into an auroch's golden horns to turn."[21] By the age of twelve, he begins to assemble a band of youths who will be his military retinue, or *druzhina*; and by fifteen the process is complete, and Volkh leaves his mother's side.

From the very start, the "unnatural" relationship of mother and son and the absence of a father are underscored. The serpent arrives from the skies rather than from the earth to dominate the mother; the baby immediately evades the confines of the maternal sphere and loosens the bond with her in order to forge another and closer one with his company of youths. The family order is superseded by the male band. With her wisdom, he aspires to conquer the universe. With his *druzhina*, he goes out into the steppes to fight.

One can see that the figure and story of Dunai reflect the ethos of the partiarchal warrior-invaders, and the story of Volkh, son of "Mother Volga" or clever student of the *volkhv* (shaman) teacher, suggests the process whereby the autochthonous population empowered their own men to defend and rule over them. Indeed, the third story of this mythological cycle, that of Mikula, indicates the values of a native farming people reminding their rulers of the true source of their power. Mikula is a giant tied to Mother Moist Earth, the source of his strength. Unlike the noble Dunai and Volkh—warrior and shaman—Mikula is a farmer. The earth rather than the state dominates his activities.

Mikula, traced by scholars to the Varangian fertility god Volos, is also related to Volkh-Volga. In one version of the epic cycle dealing with this figure, Volga's uncle gives him three cities, with the peasants of the surrounding countryside thrown in.[22] As Volga goes out to inspect his holdings followed by his retinue, he comes upon a giant plowman who walks so fast behind his plow that the hero cannot catch up to him. Nor can he meet Mikula's challenge to pull the plow out of the soil. Whereas Volga is presented in the epic as the son of a sorceress-goddess, a warrior, a hunter, and now a merchant prince who owns cities, Mikula represents the peasantry who feed their overlord, first by plowing the land, then by making it flourish, and finally by baking *pirogi*.[23] Consequently, the earth in union with her son, Mikula, who is both the servant to and carrier of her power, is represented as the source of all wealth in the state, greater by far than the might of the soldier or the cleverness of the merchant-shaman.

Mikula's strength, drawn from Mother Moist Earth, is opposed by the brutality of another Titan called Sviatogor, whom Mother Earth refuses to carry and has exiled to the hills. Like Dunai, Sviatogor is a warrior doomed for his aggressive nature. Indeed, when he breaks out of his exile, he goes to Russia as though on a rampage and challenges the peasant Mikula.[24] Mikula's strength, earned in the service of his demanding Mother Moist Earth, is invincible. But Sviatogor does not perish at the hands of Mikula; rather, he cedes his power to the most famous Russian *bogatyr'*, Ilya of the pagan city of Murom, the boldest peasant defender of the Russian land.

Ilya Muromets meets Sviatogor in a scene linking the mythological to the "historical" second cycle. For Ilya is the hero of the Kievan epic and the popular champion of *Matushka Rus'* herself. When Sviatogor, already an old man, sees the new champion, Ilya, on the road, he picks him up and places him in his pocket or bag—his male heroic womb. After three days of such an initiation, Ilya is taken out, and the two men pledge brotherhood and ride into the "green meadow where a great marvel appears." This marvel is a tomb. Sviatogor knows that it is for him, and he lies down in an oaken coffin, infusing the new hero with his ebbing powers. One version ends with a kiss of death through which the men pledge kinship. But in another, the meeting of the two heroes is mediated by a sorceress. In that version, Sviatogor is married to a beautiful *deva*, once perhaps a *rusalka* or Tree of Life goddess. He had "freed" her from her covering of bark to imprison her in a crystal casket, thereby trapping her dangerous powers. While the husband is asleep, the perfidious wife escapes, sees Ilya, and puts him into the titan's bag or pocket. Sviatogor discovers his wife's treachery and, like Dunai, kills her in a fit of rage. The murder precedes the giant's own death and succession by Ilya. The meeting of the two men through the intermediary of the feminine thus results in the death of the old consort and the adoption of the new. Sviatogor, the predator and invader, expires, exhausted, for the earth cannot carry him, nor can he imprison woman's power and compete with nature's forces.[25]

The Kievan-Vladimir Cycle

The most archaic of the *stariny* or *byliny* seem to illustrate quite clearly the manner through which the hero must acquire feminine power in order to assert his own in the service of the community and state. The cycle suggests a historical paradigm for the gradual compact made between the rulers of foreign origin and the native population of Kievan *Rus'*. It also contains the voice of the peasantry, reminding their tsars of their demands for protection rather than pillage. In the Kievan cycle, the male protagonists also draw their strength from land and from woman. The natural mothers or Mother Moist Earth herself infuses the three most prominent figures of the cycle, Ilya of Murom, the peasant; Dobrynia, the Kievan boyar; and Aliosha, the son of the clergy, with their power. But each reflects a different attitude toward women: Ilya, the Christianized peasant and champion of the Russian land, ascetically rejects marriage and is ultimately punished for hubris by being absorbed into the womb of Mother Moist Earth; Dobrynia, the boyar widow's son, obeys his mother and marries a powerful *polianitsa*; and Aliosha, the priest's son, fights the evil Kievan *baba*, only to be beguiled by her.

The theme of the conflict with the inimical and feminine challenger as the independent maid and wife continues as *polianitsy* or sorceresses assert their autonomy and hegemony over the male and become identified by the heroes with the enemies of

Kiev. Although the church and the ruling classes saw the feminine as potentially evil and rebellious, nonetheless, mothers and benign brides remain the source of the heroes' strength, while the figure of Mother Earth broods over their destiny. Just as the tales of the first cycle were cautionary, so too are these Kievan epics. The three heroes, Ilya, Dobrynia, and Aliosha, will enter a contest with woman as seducing enchantress; each will fight the enemies of Russia, often depicted as monsters and serpents of folktale who disclose her evil nature; and each will, in the end, when boasting of his great powers, meet his death in a Russian *Götterdammerung* which drags the sinful champions to the depths of Mother Moist Earth's womb.

The most popular of Russian epic heroes, Ilya of Murom (the city of the Wise Maiden Fevroniia and the sun-moon widows, Mary and Martha), embodies, in the view of some scholars, the values of the native Kievan Slavic aristocracy, which shared the peasantry's view of the role of family and the cult of soil, and resisted patriarchal Varangian beliefs and customs.[26] Through time he came to embody the male ethos of the Russian peasantry, with its fear of and yet respect for women. Born "from the *pech'*" and dwelling in its warmth, he is led by his fate back to the depths of the maternal soil when he shows himself behaving like one who contests the natural order. But the central period of Ilya's life is devoted to the service of Mother Russia, just as Mikula the peasant's had been focused on Mother Moist Earth. He is therefore represented as the peasant champion who articulates the first stirrings of national unity.

Like the Fool of folklore, Ilya begins his adventures only after he has drawn power from the mother's "peasant throne." "He sat on the *pech'*, on the *muravlen'e* [glazed stove]," the story begins. Furthermore, like the swaddled babe, he has "no arms, no legs." For thirty years he remains passive, until one day a group of men appears, *kaleki* or itinerant pilgrims, who wean him from his maternal home. The male band greets him with the words that welcome Christ at Easter, as if to identify him with both the Son of God and the sun freed from the constraints of earth, *pech'*, and the maternal bond, the source of his immobility.[27]

When the pilgrims have left, Ilya immediately gets down from his place on the *pech'*. In some versions his mother resists his leavetaking like the pagan women who had resisted the removal of their sons by the Kievan Prince Vladimir. "Do not ride to Kiev City," his mother warns him, "I will not give you my blessing." Ilya, thirty years old, cries and pleads like a child. She relents only when he promises to protect the peasantry.[28] In other versions his mother gives him a magical horse called Borushka Matushka ("Little Mother") or Kosmatushka, which will carry the peasant-turned-warrior in safety as long as he stands behind his promise.

Ilya leaves home carrying a clod of maternal soil with him in traditional peasant manner and proceeds to cross another feminine threshold, the river Oka: "Thank you, Mother Oka, for giving me food and drink," he tells her, in much the same manner as the folklore hero greets Baba Yaga with his request. Ilya Muromets crosses the river only because he is armed with his mother's blessing and mounted on his magic horse. No sooner is this threshold left behind than he meets the giant Sviatogor and, more important, his "evil" *polianitsa* wife. The enchantress as harlot who seduces the hero or harbors his enemy is present not only in the epic of Ilya but in that of Aliosha and Dobrynia, as well. She is the *rusalka* whose powers they must absorb before conquering her. She is often identified with the forces of the enemy who attack Kiev (the Tatars), but she also embodies the temptations of the pagan religion and the mother-centered family.[29] Ilya's conflict with the pagan order is vividly depicted in the story of "Solovei the Nightingale."

The story begins with Ilya crossing a forest-swamp where Solovei lives. In some versions Solovei sits at the crossroad like the spirits of the ancestors and the *rusalki*. He is the guardian of all the living and the dead, like Baba Yaga, whose persona he shares. Ilya must fight with Solovei and his family in this underworld realm to complete his initiation into knighthood. He shoots at Solovei, and the bird, as in folktales, pleads for his life. He asks that Ilya take him back to his family, where Solovei's Yaga-like wife and three daughters—who live with their husbands under their parents' roof in matrilocal custom—greet him. Ilya is obliged to defeat the daughters and their husbands in conflict and to refuse the wife's promises of ransom. Instead he takes the caged Solovei to Kiev.[30]

In conquering Solovei and his matrilocal family, Ilya passes through the third of his initiations in the realm of the feminine: his deliverance from the *pech'* with the aid of the church; his absorption of heroic prowess from Sviatogor, helped by his *polianitsa* wife; and now the "harrowing of hell" and the capture of the powers of Solovei-Baba Yaga. Solovei is killed before the prince and his boyars to indicate that his order has been brought to bay and woman, its source and priestess, tamed. Only then is Ilya declared the defender of the Russian land.

The further struggles facing Ilya and his brother *bogatyri* continue to involve *polianitsy*. The dragon mothers have been evaded, the Yagas and *rusalki* have been defeated; now the adversary of the liberated youth makes her appearance again in the form of a seductive or threatening girl (*deva*) who would pull the hero back to the maternal realm through marriage. Ilya's first battle after being named champion of Kiev and servant of Prince Vladimir, the "Red Sun," is with a powerful maiden who comes to besiege the city. She is the size of a mountain, like Sviatogor himself. On her wrist she holds a hawk, a bird of prey. She whistles and roars like Solovei, and, challenging the *bogatyri* of Kiev, she threatens to destroy the whole city, the Christian citadel of the "Red Sun."

Ilya will not confront her directly. Frightened despite his bragging, he hides behind an oak tree, where he watches the giantess fling a huge mace up into the air and catch it when it lands. The *polianitsa* seeks to drag the sun, Vladimir and his court, back to her realm—to knock him out of the sky. Finally, Ilya emerges to face the maid. Only through his support by "tamed" Mother Earth, who seeks defenders to protect her against invasion, does Ilya manage to win. But before killing her, he discovers that she is his daughter by Sviatogor's wife, come to avenge her mother.[31] Again Ilya, peasant champion of the state and the church, has overcome the power of the maternal family and wrested himself from its spell by killing his own daughter, a crime which is preceded by his boasting. He is not immediately punished for his infraction; first he must defend the Russian land.

Ilya's independence from family bonds is counterpointed by the adventures of Dobrynia (whose name is derived from *dobryi*, "good"), paradoxically closer than the peasant Ilya to his aristocratic mother, who, assuming paternal functions, is both nurturer and lawgiver. Dobrynia depends upon her magic to save him from disaster.[32] In the story of "Dobrynia and Marinka," the young boyar does not go out to fight the enemy like Ilya; his first venture had resulted in failure, and now the enemy is inside the walls of Kiev in the person of the sorceress Marinka, who resembles Prince Vladimir's troublesome wife, the pagan Apraksiia. The widow warns her son about the powers of the young witch: "She has poisoned many princely boyars / And she has made many youths ill. / She has poisoned nine *bogatyri* / And she will poison you as the tenth," his mother warns him. "But Dobrynia did not listen to his mother."[33] He falls under Marinka's spell and returns to his mother for permission to wed her.

The widow, addressed as "Ruler of the World," does not give

her permission, and again Dobrynia disobeys her and suffers. He goes back to the enchantress, who like Circe turns him into a golden auroch, the bull sacred to the Great Mother Goddess. This transformation initiates the battle of sorceresses over the fate of man. Dobrynia's mother overcomes Marinka, the perfidious *rusalka* and Yaga bride, in order to rescue her son. In some versions Dobrynia then takes revenge, like Saint Nicholas by tearing Marinka in half.[34]

Dobrynia learns not to act alone or to dismiss his mother's wisdom. When he asks her to let him marry, she gives him a bride, a *polianitsa* called Nastasiia, whom he must first challenge and fight like an Amazon. Dunai's independent bride appears resurrected, at least in name and attributes, through the powers of Dobrynia's mother. The story of Ilya and Sviatogor is reversed. Nastasiia is now linked to the all-powerful mother who conquers her male challenger. Placing Dobrynia in her bag, she exclaims, "If there is a young lad in my bag, he will become my brother; if there is an old man in my bag, I will cut off his head; but if he is equal to me, I will marry him."[35]

Nastasiia, the free *polianitsa*, chooses her own husband in conformity with the matrilineal and matrilocal order characterized by Dobrynia's mother, the widow. Unlike the Christianized Ilya Muromets, who defeats and kills his daughter *polianitsa* (whose mother had also placed him in a "pocket") and by this action breaks with the bonds of the matrilineal family, Dobrynia conversely finds himself conquered by his bride and obliged to marry her with his mother's consent. Paradoxically, Nastasiia loses her magical powers and freedom when she is brought to Kiev (patrilocally) to become a wife, dwelling in the house of her mother-in-law while Dobrynia ventures out, finally free, to defend the city against its enemies. The epic indicates an accommodation—or a wished-for one—with the peasant mothers regarding patrilocal custom in which the bride is made to sacrifice her power while the mother's remains intact. At the same time, Nastasiia, deprived of her independence in order to allow her husband to protect the Russian land, is not without wile. In Dobrynia's absence, encouraged by the pagan wife of the Kievan ruler, Apraksiia, she takes up with his *bogatyr'* "brother," the chaste Aliosha. No longer an Amazon and fighter, Nastasiia will express her untamed nature in the continued choice of lovers and mates; and in so doing she challenges the patriarchal order.[36]

The defeat of the Kievan *bogatyri* comes at the end of the Kievan cycle and implies that the order which they represent is antithetical to the peasantry who had kept the epic tradition alive.

In the final battle of Ilya, Dobrynia, and Aliosha with the enemies of Kiev, called the "Slaughter of the Kams," the struggle between pagan women as *rusalki*, Yagas, *polianitsy*, and monsters
is assimilated to that with the Tatar armies. Echoing the ancient
battle of the Kievan clergy with the women, the epic also articulates a warning against the cult of male heroism which attempts
to transcend the realm of Mother Moist Earth.

In the course of his battle with the Kams, Ilya Muromets
boasts that his power comes directly from the Russian land.
This popular story has a number of variants. Most begin with an
assembly of the knights at the court of Vladimir. The *bogatyri* include not only those of the Kievan cycle but also Mikula and
Dunai. Headed by the grand prince, they all set out to church to
ask the Mother of God for victory in the coming battle. Others
go to ask their own mothers to bless them. At the campsite they
must first wash in the spring water and wipe themselves with
clean white towels. Then the battle with the Tatars begins. The
enemy forces appear to multiply like the many-headed serpents
of the folktale, and the heroes soon tire of the conflict. Only one remains to pursue the enemy, Dobrynia or sometimes Ilya.[37]

Dobrynia sleeps in his white tent, where next morning there
appears an old hag, whose name in the epic is Baba Latingorka
or Goryninka. She is related by name to the holy mountain
(Sviatogor, from *gora*, "mountain") and to the dragon Gorysh-
che, who had kidnapped Dobrynia in the first tale about this
bogatyr'. She appears like a *polianitsa* as well as a Yaga and serpent, carrying a sword and lance reaching to the skies. This
Tatar scourge, now fully identified with the pagan *baba*, throws
her challenge at the *bogatyr'*: "Who will be the strongest; for I
will defeat all the *bogatyri* together."[38]

Dobrynia fights, is wounded, and falls to the ground. In one
version, this is described in deliberately coarse fashion: "She
puts her ass on his white face. / And she says: / 'Kiss my white
ass!' " In other versions of this scene she is a great *polianitsa* who
defeats all the heroes together until Ilya declares: "We cannot
fight, brothers, with the dead!" She is clearly the mistress of the
underworld, Baba Yaga. When Baba fells Dobrynia, Ilya presents
himself as Dobrynia's ineffectual savior. He gives him advice to
contend with the coarseness of the *polianitsa*-hag. But Dobrynia
dies of shame. In other variations, the *bogatyr'* is not allowed to
die vanquished in this manner, and Ilya arrives to fight Baba, defeating her so that he can boast proudly: "We will come to the
city of Kiev / And I will tell my story at the great feast. / I will relate what I did to the most brave *polianitsa*."[39] But in the most dra-

matic of versions, dealing with the fight of the heroes with Baba, Aliosha comes to the aid of Dobrynia, who has been killed near the river Safat by two "Tatars" represented respectively as a *polianitsa* and a dragon-*baba*. Resurrected by the Christian Aliosha (who had himself been subjected earlier in his career to death by the river Safat), they are joined by Ilya.

The three champions, each strengthened by immersion in the river and the use of the ritual towel, set out to defeat their enemy the Tatars and are joined by the whole corps of *bogatyri*. Boasting that they are invincible, they break the protective spell of the river and reveal their excessive pride: Immediately there appears before them an army like a many-headed dragon. As each enemy is slaughtered, another stands in his place. Routed by invisible forces, they retreat toward the "stone mountains." There they see a cave, and the whole band of Kievan *bogatyri*, entering it to seek protection from the enemy hordes, is turned into stone. Earth takes back the proud. Like the Gorgon-serpent, she freezes them into her womb.[40]

The defeat of the Kievan heroes can be interpreted as an echo of the demise of the Kievan princes at the hands of the Mongol hordes resulting from their internecine feuding. The consequence of this warfare was perceived by the clerical chroniclers of the period as the abandonment of the rulers' defensive functions in regard to the church as well as the maternal soil. But translated into the peasant folk traditions, this historical theme accumulates, as we have seen, much broader symbolic meanings. The *bogatyri* die because they challenge the cyclical order of nature in asserting the importance of their individual actions. In defeating the forces of death, they fight to a Pyrrhic victory and are punished for their hubris. The peasantry, fatherless sons and daughters of Mother Earth, transmute the epic tradition of their rulers into cautionary tales: Only those who protect the community and are close to Mother Moist Earth can hope to win her favor, and in so doing accept their ephemeral role in the cycle of life.

The Novgorod Epos

The heroes of Novgorod are merchants as well as warriors. In the city which called itself initially "Mother" Novgorod and, as it grew in size, importance, and wealth, assumed the title of "Lord" Novgorod, the epic clash of matristic and patristic traditions is apparent. The Varangians first settled in that city before descending to Kiev on their trading route to Byzantium. In Novgorod, as in Kiev, they encountered a population whose customs reflected the great freedom of its women. The Novgorodian epos expresses deep respect for the *baba* and worship of the *rusalki* or magical maidens inhabiting the lakes and rivers and inaccessible swamps protecting the city from its enemies. This is apparent in the two most famous Novgorodian epics, those of Vasilii Buslaev and Sadko the merchant.

The city of Novgorod was governed by elected rulers, boyars, whose principal role was to defend its inhabitants and their riches. The epic of Vasilii Buslaev, dating from the twelfth century, emphasized the function of the governor as a servant of the populace. At the same time, the presence of a powerful mother who restrains her warrior son indicates the general outlines of the veneration of the feminine: Buslaev is presented as the spoiled and willful child of a powerful and wealthy sorceress, the widow Amelfiia Timofeevna.[41] Like the mother of Volga, she teaches him. As he grows, he begins to rage over the city like a wild bull rather than a boyar-defender. The townsfolk ask the widow to control her high-spirited son, and she sends her servant, the "Black Maiden," to drag the youth home. But the same "Black Maiden" releases him from the dungeon in which his angry mother had placed him, and again he plunders the city. The widow with her servant girl recalls stories about Baba Yaga; the mother's and the girl's control over the rampaging male suggests the figures of a religious cult—like those of Demeter-Kore. This is underscored when the citizens of Novgorod appear before the widow Amelfiia, bringing her presents to appease her ire: "Oh our mistress, Little Mother," they address her as though she were a goddess whose laws they may have violated or ignored, "accept these gifts from us, but take away your terrible treasure of a son. . . ."[42] The widow, satisfied with this show of contrition and tribute, forbids her son from warring against the town.

In the second part of the epic, however, the pagan widow is seen in a Christian context, and her son seems to be in the perilous process of assuming the new faith. In "Vasilii Buslaev's Pilgrimage," the boyar youth decides to set off to Jerusalem and goes to his mother for her blessing. His mother replies that he may go but must "do only good things," and warns him: "If you go to war / I will not give you my blessing / And even Moist Mother Earth will not carry you or receive you."[43] However, when Buslaev violates a pagan taboo (regarding the honoring of the dead) by kicking a skull and appears to "go over" to the Christian creed in Jerusalem, she punishes him with death.

While Buslaev died in disobeying his mother's commands, his retinue has learned the lesson well. They respect and honor the widow goddess, and for that she rewards them with treasure brought from the vaults of her palace by the "Black Maiden." For Amelfiia and her "Kore" incarnation rule over the wealth of the citizens of Novgorod and protect them with her warrior votaries. "Thank you, Mother Amelfiia, for feeding and providing for us, young men," they salute her.[44]

The popular epic of the merchant Sadko further underscores the battle between the pagan divinities and their votaries and the church. Sadko manages, however, to appease each sufficiently to emerge successful from his ordeal. Based on the story of a rich Novgorod merchant of the twelfth century, the epic of Sadko begins in the city, where the youth is a *gusli* player. The townsfolk no longer listen to his pagan music. As he sits by "Mother Lake Ilmen," like the rejected priest of a forbidden creed, the sounds of his *gusli* are heard by the *rusalki* (in some versions together with their father the Sea Tsar). Enchanted, they give him a magical fish, with which he becomes a rich merchant. But Sadko forgets the source of his power, and he is punished for his pride by being thrown into the sea, in the course of a violent storm, as a sacrifice to the Sea Tsar. The daughters of the ruler of the deep save him from drowning and take him to their father's dwelling, a house made of wood, like the peasant *izba*. In some versions, the Sea Tsar shares his power with a tsarina. Like Baba Yaga, he will not let Sadko go; the tsarina, his benign aspect, frees him instead. Nonetheless, Sadko is obliged to remain in this underworld for thirty years—like Ilya of Murom on his *pech'*. And like Ilya he is rescued, in a number of versions, by the church in the figure of Saint Nicholas.[45]

The Sea Tsar forces Sadko, the pagan musician, to marry one of his daughters. Saint Nicholas or the tsarina advises the youth to choose the plainest and least alluring. The pagan mother thus saves him from the enticing *rusalka* nature of her daughters; and when Saint Nicholas is Sadko's deliverer, the choice of a plain bride serves as a Christian penance. Sadko follows the advice of his guides, and the spell under which he had played his *gusli* for the tsar of the underworld is broken. Back in the city of Novgorod, Sadko prospers. In those versions where the saint appears, his wealth suggests the benefits of conversion to the merchant class. But the source of Sadko's fortune is still the river and the lake where the *rusalki* dwell. Together with the church, they continue to be regarded as the guardians of Novgorod's well-being.

The Muscovite Epos

In the *starina, bylina,* or epos of the early period, the male's strivings for complete autonomy from the feminine realm and desire for self-assertion through battle are not successful. The peasant tradition tempers male pride with the reminder of nature's inexorable cycle; and although warriors and merchants may exploit the resources of earth, the epos seems to say, they depend upon their Mother Moist Earth and her peasant children for nurture and wealth. While this is true of the more archaic epics, those of the Muscovite period reveal an antagonism between men and women which leads to disastrous confrontation and the complete disintegration of family life. Indicating that the subjection of woman results in infertility, the Muscovite cycle appears to reflect popular resistance in the form of feminine rage and the pain caused by the increasing patriarchalization of society on the part of the aggressive and despotic rulers of the Muscovite state during the fifteenth and sixteenth centuries.

The most violent and widespread of the Muscovite epics is the tale of "Prince Roman and His Wife." There the ruler's battle for control over his wife—associated with the pagan populace—assumes murderous proportions. The tale begins with the plaintive voice of Prince Roman's little daughter, who goes to her father in search of her mother: "Oh my lord, little Father, / Prince Roman Vasilevich, / What is my mother doing?" she asks him fearfully. The despot Roman will not tell his daughter. Running into the garden, the girl sees an eagle in the sky. It brings the child her mother's hand with a golden ring upon it. The young princess goes to the river, where she comes upon the remains of her beloved mother guarded by animals and birds as though they still revered a Mistress of Animals. The girl gathers up the body in this curious inversion of the myth of Isis and Osiris, Kore and Demeter. Then she buries her mother like the *baba* must, and there the tragic story ends. Other versions of this curiously unsatisfactory ending identify the mother with the witch and enchantress Maria, who evades death only by accepting the Christian faith.[46]

The response to the wife-killing or wife-taming Roman in the Muscovite cycle is found in the *bylina* of "Prince Mikhailo." The conflict between a passive bride and a vengeful mother who resists the usurpation of her powers by a "tamed" and "foreign" woman begins with the departure of the husband. The mother, like Baba Yaga, assumes the role of the grudge. Denigrated in her own home, she will punish the woman whom her son has brought in to contest her restricted powers. In so doing, the mother expresses her anger with the social order debasing her. She murders her son's wife by boiling her to death in the bath-house temple of the *rozhanitsy*, the one remaining symbol of her birth-giving powers as *rod* mother. Mikhailo returns, and like the daughter of Prince Roman looking for her mother, he goes in quest of his bride. Finally his mother tells him, "Your bride is in a well-lighted chamber— / in an oaken coffin." The shock kills the youth. The mother, who, through her anger, has destroyed the whole family and hence the hope for new life, as well, begins to wail: "Alas my friends, I have sinned. / I have caused three souls to perish. / I have destroyed my son, my daughter-in-law / And her little unborn child."[47]

Roman's apparently unmotivated murder of his wife as Maria the White Swan is "balanced" in the killing of the whole family by Mikhailo's angry mother. Through these two epics, the brutal prince and the resisting and furious pagan *baba* continue to confront each other with increased hostility, producing death and infertility. This raging battle leading to disaster is encapsulated in a Muscovite *bylina* which is also a popular ballad concerning a ruler of Galicia, son of Prince Roman. In the epic of Prince Danilo, the warrior and despot is challenged for his autocratic self-assertion by an army of girls, who, like brave Amazons, appear to champion the popular will. When Danilo invites them to sing about Ilya of Murom, they refuse:

> "But we will sing you a song
> About the scoundrel Danilo,
> The robber, the pagan,
> The villain, the heathen."
> Then Danilo grew pale,
> And he ordered them all to be executed,
> All their white heads to be struck off.
> But all the people rose up,
> And sent the guards packing,
> They drove all the guards away
> And came at Danilo himself,
> And forthwith slew him.[48]

Like brides resisting their grooms' "invasion" in the patriarchal wedding rites, the girls thwart the tyrannical will of the ruler, the "groom," and the seducer. The threat of punishment for their anger instigates the revolt of the populace against the prince and the heroic ideal he expresses, which serves only to oppress the children of Mother Moist Earth and dishonor her priestesses rather than defend them.

The Russian epos reflects the presence of strong mothers and brides, of strong daughters and mighty sons. But the image of a powerful father is either absent or dimly perceived in the elusive figure of the Grand Prince Vladimir of Kiev, the "Red Sun" dishonored by his perfidious and uncontrollable wife, or in the aging but unmarried Ilya Muromets, beholden to earth for his power. The father's absence even in the heart of a tradition associated with masculine self-assertion testifies to the peasantry's transmutation of the epic to correspond to the realities of agrarian life.

The folktale places the listener in a world of nature and teaches the proper attitude toward its laws and manifestations. Predicated upon the demand for fertility, the folktale remains in the timeless realm of the seasonal cycle and family life and in the rituals accompanying them. The epic, on the other hand, reflects the emergence of another order challenging the obsession with fertility by taking the listener into the arena of war and thus history. The epic hero, then, leads us into the social and political world of men, where the protective power of the state, served by its warrior champions, impinges upon the world of nature and the maternal family. The hero, paradigmatically, asserts his own break from and control over the realm of mothers and brides in the form of a battle against the feminine. The shift of focus from nature and ritual in the folktale to war, state, and history brings with it the necessary denigration of woman. She is the enemy in the epic, the fifth column within the walls of the patriarchally ruled city; yet while she is a formidable foe, she is still regarded as an indispensable source of power. Her gift is conditional: She grants might to her sons but demands that it be exerted only in the service of the collectivity she champions, and she thwarts attempts at arrogant self-aggrandizement.

The absence of fathers in the Russian epos and the presence of tortured and often ineffectual heroes dominated by mothers and wives and challenged by powerful Amazons, winning only when they resist the snares of the feminine but dying when they boast of their victory, expresses a clearly limited view of male autonomy. The epic, changing from its aristocratic origins through retelling in the peasant community, teaches the male individual his proper role; at the same time, it becomes an outlet for popular political expression to remind the rulers of Russia of their "mandated" function as defenders rather than oppressors.

An examination of the epic tradition affords us a glimpse into the historical process of patriarchalization of Russian culture and society from earliest times and betrays at the same time the resistance which this political process engendered in the *narod* (populace), particularly in its peasant masses. For the epic accompanies the gradual and brutal evolution of state power and the emergence of an autocrat or tsar (Caesar) who imposes himself by the seventeenth century as the father-owner of the land, *Matushka Rus'*. The appearance of a father figure is therefore a late phenomenon in Russian history and corresponds to the gradual establishment of a despotic state allied to a servile patriarchal church. But even in the seventeenth century, the title of "father" popularly accorded to the tsar was seen in different ways by the ruler, his servants, and those over whom he asserted his paternity. The peasantry continued to consider the tsar as the protective son and champion defending Mother Earth as Mother Russia and her children and laying down his life to that service. He was regarded in many ways as the historical expression of the paradigmatic Dying and Reviving Son-Consort of the Great Mother. Like the peasantry, he was obliged to serve her in order to receive the benefits of her fertility.

The ruling classes, insomuch as they deferred to the will of the autocrat, saw in the role of the father the need for domination and self-assertion over the land, the peasantry, and a family structure marked by the need for feminine "magic."[49] In the next chapter, we will follow the further divergence of the opposing ideologies outlined in the epic tradition by looking at the myths of kingship and sainthood through which the rulers justified their assumption of despotic power, and we will see how the church rationalized these claims. At the same time, we will explore the peasant response to the assertion of omnipotent fatherhood on the part of the tsar as expressed in popular movements as well as in epos and apocryphal tale.

CHAPTER SIX

From Saintly Son to Autocratic Father: The Myth of the Ruler

> Did not Suzdal and Moscow too
> Gather together the land for you?
> Tightly the bags were packed with gold
> In coffers for a dowry stored.
> And raised in a frescoed narrow room [*terem*]
> A bride were you, the Tsar your groom. . . .
>
> But you refused the Tsar's embrace. . . .
>
> —M. VOLOSHIN, "Holy Russia"[1]

The development of an autocratic ideology elevating the figure of a God-like Father Tsar (*Batiushka Tsar'*) over the motherland (*Matushka Rus'*) and resulting in the emergence of the epithet "Holy Russia" (*Svetlaia Rus'*) accompanied the ascendancy of a paternal family order linked to the missionary activity of the church. The early Slavs, as we have seen, did not worship strong father gods; neither were they inclined to accept despotic rule. The official Varangian pantheon of gods reflected only the interests and ambitions of the ruling orders and not the predilections of the ruled. With the introduction of Byzantine Christianity came the possibility of assimilating the cult of a paternal god to that of a mighty secular ruler. But the character of Jehovah was too impersonal. Christ's image as a stern judge whose severity was tempered by his close union with his mother corresponded more closely to the agrarian worship of a Mother Goddess and her Son-Consort. Initially, then, the cult of the father was to be evoked only through the cult of the son; the transformation of the saintly filial to the stern and despotic paternal image marked the growth and consolidation of Muscovite tsardom.[2]

In tracing the notion of rule among the early Slavs and their Varangian overlords, we turn to the literary and ecclesiastical works from the period of Kievan *Rus'* (the ninth to the thirteenth centuries). The influence of the church in creating images of princely power was of considerable importance; yet even here we find a base in older mythological sources associated with fertility: the twin motif and the tradition of sacral kingship. When we look at the transformations in the "official" vision of the ruler from the thirteenth to the early eighteenth centuries, at the rites and rituals surrounding kingship, and at popular movements and legends revolving around the figure of the autocrat, we begin to discern the outlines of a popular ideology at odds with the proprietary and increasingly bureaucratic administration of the tsars. Out of this ideology emerges the image of a suffering and enserfed motherland, a "widow" awaiting her rightful husband.

Varangian Genesis: Prince and People

Writing in the sixth century, the Byzantine historian Procopius, who reported on the Slavs' worship of rivers and female divinities, also asserted that they "are not ruled by one man but they live from old under a democracy, and consequently everything which involves their welfare, whether for good or ill, is referred to the people."[3] In the same century, the Byzantine Emperor Mauricius wrote that "the Slavs like liberty; they cannot bear unlimited rulers and are not easily brought to submission." The Emperor Leo agreed: "The Slavs are a free people, strongly opposed to any subjection."[4]

The central institution of government was an assembly called the *veche*, reported first among the Western Slavs. The historian Thietmar of Merseberg noted that at Stettin (where the statue of the idol Svantovit was venerated), the popular assembly governed through unanimous vote. It is not clear to what extent women participated in the councils, but in the light of the matrilineal and matrilocal features of kinship among such Slavic tribes as the Derevliane and the Poliane, we can speculate that women participated in government in some form.[5]

By the eleventh century in Kiev, the institution of the *veche*, now composed only of the male heads of families, had already been challenged by the Varangian rulers.[6] But the continuing struggle with the early princes suggests the native population's resistance to their attempts to assume more than a contractual role as defenders. The *veche*, rooted in an archaic family and clan tradition, tried to control the Varangian warrior class as it would a mercenary force. And initially the political ambitions of the aggressive Riurik princes were restrained by native custom. In order to maintain their claims to rule over the autochthonous population of *Rus'*, the Varangian princes were obliged to observe the cult of the *rod* and of Mother Moist Earth.[7] But their predatory social organization was ill-suited to the establishment of a solid and peaceful state, and the Varangian protectors gradually came to dominate the land they had been called to defend. Creating a principality without the principle of primogeniture, the Riurik clan soon found their lands partitioned among their descendants. As a result, the source of wealth continually diminished. By the twelfth century, internecine warfare was widespread.

For millennia, as we have seen, the fertile steppes of the Ukraine had been overrun by nomadic tribes. Attacks on the Kievan principality continued through the thirteenth century. The Kievan state was poorly defended; the *veche* had been weakened and the land despoiled by the continuous fratricidal wars. The Mongol hordes led by Batu Khan, took the Ukraine and central Russia with shamefully little resistance from her feuding defenders.

The collapse of a state created for the express purpose of protecting its inhabitants is decried in Russia's first national epic, the twelfth-century *Lay of Igor's Campaign*, in which the predecessors of the Mongols, the Turkic Polovtsy or Kumans, attack and defeat the Riurik princes. In the epic we hear the cry of the native population demanding that their rulers check their own political ambitions and place themselves at the service of the motherland as her self-sacrificing *bogatyri*. The notion of Russia as a common mother whose family, living and dead, is torn asunder by her battling and disobedient champions is first invoked in this twelfth-century epic. It warns them of death and the ensuing sterility of the land. Here Mother Earth and *Rus'* are identical as the genetrix of the great extended family.

Like the epics which passed through and were modified by the peasant tradition, the poem was composed for the Kievan nobility. Its heroes are not supernatural beings but (with the exception of Vseslav, the shamanic werewolf) men and women whose connection with nature appears far stronger and more intense than with any social order. Was the poet a member of the native Kievan populace rather than of Varangian stock, and his "song" written to remind foreign rulers of their obligations? Certainly the conflicts and concerns of the Riurik princes are placed against the background of a natural law evoked in feminine form.

The poem unfolds on three different levels. The first, which provides the narrative thread, tells the story of Prince Igor's fight and defeat at the hands of the Polovtsy and of his escape. The second concerns the notion of fate and the function of prophecy. The chief protagonist here is Igor's wife, Iaroslavna, who is connected with the forces of nature and protects her husband through her magical powers. The third level represents an admonition to the princes to unite against their common enemy. This relates to an underlying structure of the epic in which the clash of armies and the singing of mythical maidens evoke the rites of a peasant wedding.[8] The poet expresses his anger at the feuding of the princes, which results in their defeat and suggests instead the need for fertility through "marriage" rather than death through warring.

The *Lay of Igor's Campaign* opens with the evocation of the shamanic bard (*volkhv*) who calls himself the grandson of the fertility god Volos. Only then do we see Igor setting out against the invaders. But like an arrogant bridegroom, he begins his campaign without thought for the bride and the motherland he must defend. He goes without maternal blessing, and nature, in the form of a magical bird called Div (like *deva* or *rusalka*), appears to bar his route and signal disaster while luring him toward his enemies.[9]

The self-assertive boldness of Igor and his fellow princes is not the only cause of their impending eclipse in darkness (earth). The other has to do with their family feuds and the disintegration of the princely *rod*, leading to the conquest of the motherland. In violating family law by internecine warring, they also violate the order of nature. The ancestral spirits are disturbed, and the maternal earth weeps at her sons' destruction, though it is she who punishes them with storm and death: "Human lives become shortened through the princes' discord. / In those days the plowman spoke but rarely, / and the ravens cawed, dividing corpses among themselves."[10]

The plowman is the hidden "center" of the warrior epos. He clings to Mother Earth, and she to him; he is both her groom and her son. The political ambition of the princes brings a quite different harvest: "The black earth under the hooves / was strewn with bones, / was covered with blood. / Grief overwhelmed the Russian land."[11]

Igor had ignored all the auguries of nature and paid no heed to the prophetic fears of his wife. The dissension among the princely clan appears in some way related to the men's dismissal of feminine wisdom and the need to unite as in marriage. Grief, Div, the prophetic bird, and the swan maiden Obida appear like Fates or Harpies condemning the land to suffering and barrenness. Injured nature, seething with fury at the pride of the warriors, can be placated only by a sorceress. Like the good mothers and the gentle *polianitsa* wives of the epic heroes, Iaroslavna, the wife of Igor, comes to the aid of her husband. As the women's hymn of mourning for those killed in battle spreads through the land, Igor, thought to be among the dead, is depicted as the sun and fertility god who has disappeared, a prisoner of malevolent nature, here in the shape of the invading forces. His liberation represents the liberation of the sun; his return to the land will result in the renewal of vitality. Iaroslavna will save him, restoring life by collaborating with the forces of nature like a peasant woman bringing back spring in the seasonal rites. Her voice, that of the faithful wife, protects like a balm against the pain and destruction of war: "Like a seagull I will fly along the river Danube. / I will dip my beaver-trimmed sleeve into the river Kaiala. / I will cleanse the bloody wounds of my prince, / on his mighty body."[12] Iaroslavna's words are not a lament (as they have been called); they are a conjuration. She speaks like a goddess reviving her consort, captive of the forces of the underworld. At the same time, she reprimands the winds, the river, and the sun for their hostility toward him.

The sorceress's magic works.[13] The elements appear to respond to her power and turn in favor of her husband. She has invoked fire, water, and air to restore Igor to life and bring fertility back to the devastated land. But she has not appealed to earth, which still turns against the prince. Groaning, like a mistreated, ignored, and yet all-powerful mother, earth awakens the enemy. The mother who bears all her children without distinction is angered by Igor's fighting and feuding. But the elements invoked by Iaroslavna carry Igor to the river Donets, thwarting earth's vindictiveness. The river is the genetrix Igor had ignored, and now homage is paid to her so he may cross safely and reach his bride: "Oh my river Donets! / There will be no small glory for you, / for you have lulled the prince on your waves. . . ."[14] He speaks directly to nature as his wife had done and thanks her for her maternal care. In the final verses, Igor, chastened, assumes the form of a sun god who is allowed to reemerge from his captivity. As the head who forgets the body he carries—Mother Earth and her children—Igor is like the foolish sun who leaves the world; in order to avoid destruction, he must be her captive. Only after he has learned the bitter lesson—that in detaching himself from the land, he, like Ilya Muromets, loses his power and she loses her defender—can order be restored. In the final verses, Igor, a prodigal son, goes to the Church of the Mother of God, his Christianized Mother Earth.[15]

But the motif of the prince's filial relationship to the earth has been juxtaposed to another: his role as her groom. Indeed, the epic is filled with allusions to folk wedding ritual. The narrator looks at the clashing armies and perceives them as participants in an immense wedding through which the Kievan ruler and the land are united. The Don River provides wedding wine. The "Gothic maidens," who are said to "jingle" Russian gold, and the Germans, Venetians, Greeks, and Moravians, represented as a female chorus, sing songs of praise and reproach.[16] The narrator, the bard who calls himself the son of Volos, reminds his rulers that the farmer is the nurturing source of the realm.

Igor, now a champion of the maternal land, must fight for her as a Christian serving Mary, a groom of Mother Church. For indeed, the church had from the start regarded the ruler's function as a helper in missionary work. Just as the native population saw him as their defender, so the church hoped to make of him the protector of the faith and associated him with Christ. Thus, among pagans and Christians, in different measure, the ruler appeared to assume the mythic persona of the Dying and Reviving God, ensuring the safety and well-being of the land as well as the spiritual salvation of its inhabitants.

Princes and Saints

The first evocation of Russia sheltered from her enemies by a ruler cleansed of pride appears in the *Lay of Igor's Campaign*. This pagan image of self-effacing filial devotion could be assimilated by the church to that of a humble and humiliated son of Mary. The Orthodox emphasis upon the incarnation of Christ, his voluntary role as a scapegoat, and his close association with humanity—his kenosis—affirms the sacredness of matter. In his icons as child-God with Mary, Christ is depicted as absorbed in her maternal embrace or pictured as an infant in her womb. In the sacred image of maternal encompassment and the dogmatic expression of divine immanence in nature, Christ "descends" to share with humanity death and resurrection within the context of the seasonal cycle and the generations of the *rod*.[17]

The persona of Mary had a necessary analogue in Christ as a

fertilizing sun god serving to awaken the earth. The continuing popularity of the twelfth-century sermon by Cyril, Bishop of Turov, "On the First Sunday after Easter," can be attributed not only to the beauty of his language but to the powerful identification of Christ's Resurrection with nature's spring flowering under the heat of the sun. Cyril begins his sermon with the denunciation of pagan worship; but at the same time he promises his listeners that the Resurrection of Christ is also the resurrection of the ancestral dead they continue to venerate. Sunday is the supreme day of prayer and of life, the day of birth and rebirth, and paganism is "melted by wisdom." Inversely, "spring is a beautiful faith in Christ" which regenerates mankind, "and the stormy winds are the evil, sinful thoughts that, having changed to virtue through repentance, generate soul-saving fruits; but the earth of our being, having received the Word of God like a seed, and, passing through an ecstatic labor, through the fear of him, brings forth a spirit of salvation." Christ is "the giver of fruits," and the church is presented as giving her converts "suck" from "the milk of its teachings."[18]

The covert identification of Christ with the functions of a sacrificed fertility god dying for his fellows occurs also in the hagiography of the first ruler-saints of Russia. They protect the population from sin by their *imitatio Christi*, their imitation of the Son of God and their devotion to the unity of the family, as well. Princes Boris and Gleb are Russia's oldest saints. The brothers' saintliness was expressed in their nonresistance to evil. Standing against the tide of fratricidal Riurik conflict, they expressed a pagan ideal sanctified by the church—that of self-abnegation called a *podvig* (burden).

The Russian Orthodox emphasis on humility and the denial of individualism and self-assertion is strikingly close to the pagan cult of ancestors. That connection is evident in the story of the two brother princes, sons of Vladimir the "Red Sun." The account of their martyrdom in the *Primary Chronicle* dates from the twelfth century. The tale begins when Boris, fighting the invading Pecheng armies, hears of his father's death. Returning to Kiev, he learns that his brother Sviatopolk had planned to kill him in order to take over his lands. Boris displays his utter meekness and submission to the murderous desires of his older brother by doing nothing to avoid his death.[19]

Boris is the first of the *strastoterptsy* (passion sufferers). He is martyred by his own *rod*, and yet he is the saint of family cohesion, who demonstrates the ethos of cooperation and brotherly love. His passivity in the face of the older brother's violence suggests that he will not violate the law of the family as his older brother has done. The story suggests that fratricide can be counteracted only through the selflessness of the most moral and obedient members of the family.

The death of Gleb, his brother, is no less brutal. Learning that Sviatopolk will murder him next, Gleb cries out to Christ: "It were better for me to die with my brother than to live in this world. . . . Pray for me that I may endure the same Passion." Their joint graves became the site of miracles. Shortly after their deaths, in 1015, the church canonized them as "Protectors of the land of *Rus.'* "[20] The triumph of fraternal love and family unity is juxtaposed to the fratricidal strife of the princes, linked to their desire for ownership of the land and its wealth. The brothers receive the title of "protectors" or "intercessors." Their "feminine" self-denial thus identifies them with the Mother of God, the most potent of all intercessors.

But the cult of Boris and Gleb was not Christian in its origin; the church simply gave it its blessing in order to satisfy the new converts. For while the worship of Mary incorporated that of the pagan Great Mother Goddess, and the figure of Christ evoked the pagan Dying and Reviving Fertilty God, the brothers Boris and Gleb suggested the veneration of the ancestors absorbed by the missionary clergy into Christian rite. In making the brothers guardians over the Russian land, the church merely recognized the central role of the *roditeli* (ancestors) in the Kievan household.[21]

While the author of the *Primary Chronicle* wrote for the upper classes and admonished the rulers of the state to share their power with the church by using it in the service of missionary work, the popular *Dukhovnye stikhi*, circulating among the *narod*, present the story of Boris and Gleb in a different form. In the "Spiritual Verses," the heroes must answer to the demands of the mother like the *bogatyri* of the epics. The widow pleads with them not to visit their perfidious older brother, but they disobey her, and like all who transgress maternal orders, they perish.[22] Hers is the voice of the *narod*, that great family perceived as a nation. The brother saints sin because they violate their mother's prophetic warning; but the older brother, Sviatopolk, identifying himself with the paternal state, transgresses altogether the laws of the maternal *rod* and ignores the pain of the "birthgiving" mother who binds them all.

In the popular version of the legend, not only are the brothers placed under the authority of their mother, but they are also associated with plant life. When they implore their tormentors to spare them, they say: "Do not reap unripe wheat ... / Do not tear up the garden roots from the moist earth. / Do not kill us in our youthful years."[23] The *strastoterptsy* (from *strast'*, meaning "sexual passion" as well as "suffering") are analogues for the "agony" of the harvested plant, and in certain icons, where they appear in the midst of a field of sprouting grain, their function as fertility or plant gods links them to the ancestral spirits dwelling under the earth.

The official version of the legend stresses the need for the princes to submit to the authority of the church. Their sacrifice is presented in the light of that submission. In the popular "Verses," the self-denial recalls the rites of fertility in which youths may have been immolated for the health and vitality of the land inseminated with their blood. In the official version, a church is built over their remains; in the popular one, a Tree of Life, a "white *stolb*," grows directly from their bodies and suggests their phallic "service" to the earth, as well as their reabsorption as sons within her womb.[24] But the complex image of the brothers as fertility gods derives from a number of mythological paradigms. First, the tradition of the twin or brother motif is tied to the archaic cult of Mother Goddesses in Greece and the Near East; second, it draws on the worship of the family in the pre-Varangian period; finally, it can be traced to the kingship rituals of the Riurik princes.

The Twin Motif and Sacral Kingship

The Greek Dioscuri, who die and rise from the dead, are heavenly brothers who help mankind as protectors and fertility deities. Unlike their disruptive sisters Helen and Clytemnestra, the brothers are peacemakers. Astral divinities, they resemble Artemis and Apollo, another set of twins born of Leto or Latona (daughter of Phoebe-Artemis, the moon and sun goddess). Connected to bird and water nymphs, the Dioscuri displace them as rainmakers. The Dioscuri are also horsemen. Their link with the horse comes from their mother, Leda, a mare who could also become a swan and whose transformational powers were usurped by Zeus.[25]

The twins are sometimes seen with their sister Helen as a divine trinity. In Sparta, where the Dioscuri were worshipped with particular fervor, Helen is often shown as their mother. A swan maiden, she is pictured flanked by the twins. Sometimes she assumes human form; at other times her analogue is the tree. Indeed, the girls of Sparta practiced a rite of placing crowns of garlands on a plane tree called a Helen Tree, just as Russian peasant girls decorated and named the birch *rusalka* or Semik. In fact, Helen-Leda appear as the mother-daughter pair, like Phoebe-Leto/Latona, connected to and replaced by their male twins, warrior gods.[26] The sons are clearly of later origin, and the omnipotent goddess who accompanies the Dioscuri suggests the separation of the mother-daughter dyad by the interposition of a male or a male duo.

The cult of the Greek twins came to Russia from Greece via the worship of the "baptized" Dioscuri, Kosma and Demian. The brothers were patrons of medicine and metallurgy. In popular Slavic lore, they appear as smiths and plowmen. Like the Dioscuri, Saints Kosma and Demian are the guardians of the land and the bringers of fertility. Their cult, grafted onto that of the warrior princes, the saints Boris and Gleb, assumes the full panoply of attributes given to the twin gods, thereby appealing both to the peasantry and to the upper classes. Boris and Gleb unite the land from above, as rulers wish to do, through an ideology of state invoking a heavenly father; Kosma and Demian unite it from below, through the land and the family under the aegis of the agrarian goddess.[27]

The link of the princes Boris and Gleb with the Dioscuri via the saints Kosma and Demian is one element in their cult; another may refer to the rites of sacral kingship. According to Sir James Frazer's theory of the origin of kingship, the ruler must assume the symbolic role of the Dying and Reviving Fertility God for his people and be replaced by a young and vigorous male when his vitality wanes. Since the early Slavs had no tradition of kingship, they may have associated the life and death of Boris and Gleb with the cult of their ancestors, whom they held responsible for the sprouting of new crops. Indeed, in pre-Kievan calendars, the months when the brothers were invoked, from May to July, marked the growth and harvest of the grain, helped, as we have seen in folklore and ritual, by the spirits of the deceased members of the *rod*. In popular sayings, the names for barley and wheat grown in the Kievan region since the Tripol'e era are "Boris and Gleb." The murder or sacrifice of the two youths occurred at harvest time, the "time of suffering," and could be directly assimilated to the fate of the grain. After their deaths, the princes were thought to descend to the world of ancestors before moving to the Christian heavens as administrators of the patriarchal god.[28]

But the cult of the saints may also trace to a tradition of Varangian rather than Slavic origin. Finding no mythos to justify the institution of sacral kingship (though there was clearly an attempt to assimilate the Scandinavian ruler god Thor, king of a warrior elite, with the Slavic Perun, a god of fertility) and no hierarchical base upon which to construct a religious and social rationale for their rule, Varangian rulers turned to the myth of another Norse god, Odin, as a way to link the ethos of the state to the agrarian one based upon the family.[29]

Odin was a fertility god who hanged himself voluntarily from the World Tree Yggdrasill in order that he might provide salvation—harvest—for his people. In times of famine or plague, the Nordic kings sacrificed victim substitutes to Odin by hanging them on a tree. The Nordic god was easily assimilated to the sacrificed Christ and the Christian ruler, his earthly counterpart. The murders of Boris and Gleb assume, then, the expression of a ritual performance. As avatars of fraternal love and family unity, they take the place of their older brother and senior aspirant to the throne. The possibility that the death of the brothers reflects Scandinavian rites to Odin, accommodated to the customs and beliefs of the Slavic tribes, is further corroborated by the semiofficial legend of the bodies found on the sacred birch.[30]

The kenosis and martyrdom of the first Russian saints are therefore not *ab origine* simply the expression of Christian virtues; they also bear the residues of the Dioscuri myth, the agrarian cult of ancestors of the Slavic tribes, and the practices of sacral kingship among the Norsemen. The paradigmatically heroic nature ascribed to the ruling princes of Kiev by the missionary church concealed the clergy's collaboration with the ruler in persuading his subjects to obey a kingship they may have resisted, as well as a faith they certainly abhorred.[31] The Russian saints Boris and Gleb are distinguished by their ethos of nonresistance to evil through their behavior as willing victims rather than proud rulers. This insistence on the transcendence of aggression for the sake of the *rod* suggests that kingship introduced so late into Slavic tribal life was acceptable only insofar as it helped preserve family unity. It expressed the importance of the subordination of individual members to the needs of the collectivity, whether *rod* to *narod*, family, clan, or nation.

Saint George

Under the aegis of Mary, the ideal of kenosis as humility and self-abnegation also formed the basis for the canonization of individuals from the ranks of the clergy. The Mother of God played a significant role in the creation of saints from the monastic orders. Saint Theodosius, the eleventh-century founder of the Kievan spiritual center the Pecherskaia Lavra, dedicated the Monastery of the Caves to Mary. His teachings on the sacredness of matter can best be understood as a Christianized expression of the fruitfulness of the maternal soil and the veneration of ancestors dwelling within it. The national hero Saint Sergius of Radonezh, whose fourteenth-century monastery, the Troitsa Sergeevna, was the center of Muscovite religious life, was also devoted to the Holy Mother of God, who had "chosen" him to be among the elect.[32] Subsequent saints continued to evoke Mary as the mainspring of their faith. But in the case of the ruler, there was a shift in the church's emphasis from princely kenosis to princely aggression in defense of orthodoxy. This change was most apparent in the cult of the legendary Saint George, the patron saint of Russia. As with Boris and Gleb, his cult had its source in the veneration and subsequent masculinization of feminine power.

While Saint Nicholas shared with Mary the patronage of the land as wealth- and health-giver and was associated with the Varangian fertility god Volos, George, the warrior saint who bore traces of the cult of Perun, emerged by the sixteenth century as the dragon-slaying hero who humbled the earth and its inhabitants under the hooves of his white horse.[33] Whereas Boris and Gleb expressed the notion of princely self-denial for the welfare of the *rod* and *narod*, and the monk-saints displayed a passive and "feminine" ideal of holiness under the aegis of the Mother of God, Saint George, whose cult was related to the consolidation of Muscovite sovereignty, suggested a change in the image of saint and ruler from sacrificial victim to aggressive and self-assertive defender of the land.

The "Moscow Horseman," later identified with the warrior saint, first appeared as the patron of the Russian rulers under the Muscovite Grand Prince Vasilii II in 1415.[34] The identification of saint and prince under his successor, Ivan III, the first Russian tsar, marked the transformation of the Kievan ideal of service into overlordship. When we look at the origins and development of the myth of Saint George through the official and popular images of this soldier-saint, we discover two opposing conceptions of the role of the ruler: One derives from the official view of this patron of the tsars, the other from the peasantry's vision of his relationship with *Matushka Rus'*. One suggests authority and control, the other defense and nurture.

The Greeks, the English, and the Georgians also adopted Saint George as their protector. In Greece and Russia he was associated with Saint Demetrius of Salonica. The two saints were sometimes placed together iconographically, like Boris and Gleb, the sacred "twins." Both derive their names or functions from ancient goddesses. Saint Demetrius Church in Eleusis, called the Church of Saint Demetrius or Saint George, was erected over the sanctuary of Demeter, whose name he bears. For that reason he is also sometimes referred to as "Saint Agriculture."[35] But in Christian legend, Demetrius is a warrior saint converted to the new faith and in no way tied to the land. A similar origin is imputed to Saint George, believed to have lived as a Roman soldier in Cappadocia in the third or fourth century. The church seemed to have adapted his cult from the patron god of the Roman forces, the Persian god Mithra. Like the archaic sky god who replaced the Great Goddess at the end of the first millennium on the Black Sea, George rides upon a white charger; but like Demetrius, soldier of Demeter, George is also linked to the land. He resembles the pillar god Svantovit worshipped by the Western Slavs, a warrior and fertility divinity. But George is also the patron of the flocks in Russia and Greece.

Both Demetrius and George are saints represented on horseback, and like the sun god Mithra are dragonslayers who fight a telluric opponent. In adopting Saint George, who combined both military and agricultural roles, as their patron, the Byzantine emperors were motivated, perhaps, by a desire to unite the Roman armies' worship of Mithra with the popular veneration of Demeter as a way to illustrate the nature of their imperial authority. For the church, the unification of these opposing religious conceptions in the persona of the saint was a way to appeal to both groups of worshippers by associating its missionary work with the power of the Byzantine Empire while at the same time asserting its own claims of hegemony over it. Furthermore, the iconographic image and legend of Saint George, patron of the new Caesars, suggested to the population of the empire that their security depended upon the strength of the Byzantine armies under the banner of the new and powerful faith. In short, the veneration of Saint George marked the absorption of the archaic mother cult into an ideology justifying church and state dominance.

The Christianization and masculinization of Demeter into Demetrius had a considerable number of analogues as the missionary church spread its nets over pagan peoples. One such "sex change" occurred in the substitution of Saint Nicholas for Artemis among the inhabitants of the Black Sea region. Nicholas, so closely associated with Mary that he often appeared as her consort, was the most revered of the Russian mythical saints (in Moscow alone there are forty-one churches dedicated to him). In contrast to Saint George, who, like the Varangian Perun, embodied princely power and military might, Nicholas, like his prototype, Volos, represented the egalitarian ideals implicit in agrarian fertility beliefs: Linked to the worship of Mother Moist Earth, his cult also suggested that the peasantry saw themselves as children of the Great Mother, all equal in that respect. Nicholas was, above all, an intercessor and miracle worker, the holy man of the peasantry. It was widely believed that he would succeed God Himself when that divinity grew old, as though he filled the functions of the aging and reborn fertility deity. In Siberia, the identification of the saint with a god of produce was unequivocable: Saint Nicholas was the patron of agriculture.[36] His duties were as varied as those of Mary, and he too was seen as the shelter of mankind. Like the archaic Artemis, he was the patron of children, sailors, merchants, pilgrims, and travelers, and the bringer of wealth.

The popularity of the saint certainly derived from his closeness to Mary in his feminine qualities of compassion and protection. But while Mary was the guardian of marriageable girls, Nicholas was the patron of boys, to whom he preached the virtues of peace rather than war, familial accord rather than self-assertive pride. Nicholas personified the male ideal in the mother-centered family of a farming populace rather than a warring one. That he was so perceived by the Russian people and assimilated to another and more ancient personification of male (and female) initiation is strikingly illustrated in the existence of a peculiar church in Moscow called "Saint Nicholas on Chicken's Feet."[37]

George shared with Nicholas the functions of initiating youths and protecting the soil; but while the companion and helper of Mary expressed to the youth a vision of obedience to the family and pacific pursuits, George was the dragon fighter who taught the boy how to break with the umbilical coils of the maternal *rod*. He was a phallic, aggressive sun god, piercing the earth-bound serpent with his spear, a fitting symbol of sainthood for the power-hungry Muscovite tsars proclaiming their hegemony over their princely Riurik *rod* and their peasant subjects. But the legend and icon of Saint George, passed on to the populace by church and tsar like a form of catechism teaching them the nature of the relationship between ruled and subject, was not received in the spirit intended by their masters. The saint was reabsorbed into the agrarian calendar (from whose rites he had originally emerged) and into folklore as a fertility daemon and the defender of earth like other *bogatyri* and princes of the Kievan epos.[38] The peasantry projected upon this didactic figure of patriarchal authority the ethic of filial piety.

April 23 was the day sacred to Saint George in the farming calendar, where he was attributed the patronage of stockbreeders and plowmen. As we have seen, the linkage of the two marked the attempt to impose the ethos of the sun god as the dominant deity of warrior and herder onto that of the farmers' earth goddess. In peasant lore, his defensive function was translated into that of protecting cattle from wolves. He was the savior who defended domesticated nature, Mother Earth, from her wild and evil aspects, the Yaga who ate her own progeny; he was the solar hero who protected life from extinction in the abyss of the night and controlled the might of the winds; he was the master of domestic herds on whose day their fate was predicted. George protected, predictably, against witches. At the same time, his persona betrayed underworld attributes clearly derived from pagan agrarian divinities and shamanic practices.[39]

In the farming calendar, Saint George's Day marked the beginning of the working year. On that day George appeared in his fertility aspect. In April in Belorussia, as well as in other areas, a young man called George was dressed in greenery and flowers. He carried a burning torch in one hand and a *pirog* in the other. He was accompanied into the fields by girls singing: "George has unlocked the moist earth / and scattered dew / over all *Rus'*." Then they proceeded to divide up the *pirog* for a ritual feast to ensure fertility.[40] In the Ukraine on Saint George's Day, a curious symbiosis of Christian and pagan rites occurred. The priest and his acolytes went out into the fields to bless the new crops; afterwards young couples lay down and rolled around in the sown field. Elsewhere it was the priest himself who was identified with the saint and submitted to the indignity of being rolled by women over the sprouting grain.[41]

Saint George incorporated the role of the plant god and the guardian of cattle, but he was above all the solar deity. Popular legends show him languishing in a dungeon. He escapes through the intervention of the Mother of God, who sends the winds to free him, and sets out across the Russian land to revive nature, which had died while he lay underground. The peasantry adopted the saint as a son who served the mother as both fertility god and warrior to protect and revive the land for the benefit of its inhabitants. The *Dukhovnye stikhi* contains a number of legends devoted to his exploits. He is often accompanied by three "serpent" sisters, representing the malignant aspects of the triune goddess as well as pagan resistance to conversion. George's mother, who guides his actions, is Sophia the Wise, akin to Vasilisa in folklore.[42] The youth George can save the land and his perfidious sisters from the enemy serpent-tsar only through the authority of two mothers who guide him—Mary and Sophia. His victory is hedged in by the women's compliance and his assertion of autonomy dependent upon the observance of the mothers' commands. In the context of peasant belief expressed in the *Dukhovnye stikhi*, even the fact of conversion is regarded as an act of filial devotion rather than paternal oppression—made evident in the iconographic image of George adopted by the tsars.[43]

The legends concerning the dragonslaying horseman and the rites associated with him in the course of the seasonal cycle express the desire of the peasantry for the restriction of the ruler's authority. They also call for a "maternal" church. All power appears to derive from the consent of the feminine. Saint George's missionary activity is assimilated to the life-producing fertility of the earth.

The Muscovite grand princes, however, beginning with Vasilii II, saw in the persona of Saint George the evocation of the power of Byzantine emperors. Urged by the Russian Orthodox church to act as defenders of the faith and propagators of its institutions, the self-created tsars of the fifteenth and sixteenth centuries regarded their role as one of eradicating the serpent of disbelief while simultaneously defeating the remnants of the Tatar hordes encamped on Russian soil. These functions appeared to be merely the pretext for the assertion of despotic power. The Muscovite tsars challenged and vanquished all resistance to their increasingly tyrannical appetites. The icon of Saint George crushing the serpent would soon become the symbol of the enserfment of the population by an autocrat bent on expanding his estate.

From Prince to Tsar

The evolution of an ideology justifying autocratic rule on the part of the Muscovite grand princes was marked by historical accident and exigency as much as by theoretical links with Byzantine and Mongol forms of governance.[44] The transformation of the image of the saintly prince and son into the figure of paternal authority emerged in response to the catastrophic Mongol invasion. Predicated upon the absorption of the princely *rod* and the general population as the *narod* into the single sheltering figure of the mighty tsar, the process was abetted by the church, which, like the populace, sought a powerful protector, but one who could be used to consolidate the gains of missionary work among a still-recalcitrant people. The ideology of tsardom was developed from the fourteenth to the sixteenth centuries among the Muscovite princes.

The Byzantine *basileus* (ruler) was perceived by the Greek church as a pious leader, a stern judge in the image of Christ *Pankrator* helping his people attain salvation. The Russian church's adoption of this view, together with the belief in the immanence of the prince in the *narod* or people, reflected the immersion of the Son-God in his own creation. But the impact of the Mongols' conquest resulted in the demand for a strong leader to stand over the nation. Such a ruler was personified in the figure of the Mongol Khan, a distant overlord, above the law, a conquerer ruling a subdued populace.[45] For his Russian subjects, the infidel Khan represented the absolute values of the state. He was quite distinct from his captive peoples, wishing only to extract their wealth, and finally giving the duties of tax collection to the eager and ambitious Muscovite princes. They, in turn, found their role quite compatible with the proprietary values of their Riurik merchant-warrior ancestors and used their privileged position to strengthen their claims over their princely brothers and rivals.

Out of the protracted process of collusion between prince and Mongol overlord, there emerged in the fifteenth century an enriched and powerful grand principality of Moscow, whose rulers could indeed call themselves the protectors of the church and the administrators of the Russian land. As the Mongol Empire dissolved, they extorted wealth for their own benefit. By the fifteenth century, three elements had entered into the consolidation of autocratic ideology: liberation from the Mongol yoke; the gradual unification of the lands under the leadership of the wealthy Muscovite princes, who challenged and defeated their own extended *rod*; and the fall of the Byzantine Empire to the Turks in 1453, with the subsequent need to establish another headquarters for the Orthodox church.

By marrying Sophia Paleologue, the daughter of the Byzantine ruler, the first tsar, Ivan III, cleared the path for his assumption of the mantle of the Defender of Orthodoxy, which had fallen from the shoulders of the defeated emperor. Adopting the seal of the Byzantine *basileus*, the Roman double-headed eagle representing the Janus-like guardianship of imperial borders, Ivan proceeded to establish his superiority over the entire Riurik family and the lands they governed. Moscow became the center of *Rus'*. The legend of its foundation bears the imprint of imperial ambitions expressed in the imagery of folklore: It refers to the appearance of a two-headed bird of prey before a boyar who was hunting with his men in the forest. The Byzantine seal of imperial power, attributed a Russian source, also recalls the ancient motifs of hunters empowered by magical birds. But the new locus of princely authority needed additional legitimization: On the spot where the double-headed bird had appeared, the boyar proceeded to build a church called Paraskeva, around which the city was said to grow.[46] From the fifteenth to the seventeenth centuries, Italian architects were brought in to design and build the Moscow Kremlin, uniting Renaissance forms to traditional Russian ones. The self-assertion of the grand princes as builders mirrored the assumption of the title of Caesar, translated as *tsar'*, successor to the Roman and Byzantine rulers.[47]

In 1480, the "Mongol Yoke" had officially been cast aside with the Tatar Khan's acknowledgment of the superior might of the Muscovite forces. Ivan had taken the title *tsar'*, and his successors would adopt the image of "The Dragonslayer," defender of the church and protector of their people.[48] But the arrogation of imperial might needed the blessing of the church. Only under Ivan's successor, Vasilii III, did the clergy officially consecrate the Muscovite rulers as successors to the Western and Eastern empires through a doctrine called "Moscow the Third Rome." The church self-interestedly accorded the autocracy the role of protecting the Orthodox faith. "Two Romes have fallen," the doctrine proclaimed, referring to the demise of Rome and Byzantium, "and a third stands." The third was Moscow.[49]

While Ivan, called "the Great," is regarded by historians as the centralizer of the Russian lands, his illustrious descendant, Ivan the Terrible (*Groznyi*, "awesome" or "severe"), further consolidated autocratic power. The image of the dreaded *paterfamilias* of the church, the Lord-God Jehovah, was incarnated in the figure of Tsar Ivan. Ivan the Great conquered or confiscated the territories of his *rod*, but his relatives did not complete the subjection of the princely clan. Ivan the Terrible, however, was the very embodiment of the tsar's conflict with the *rod*, with the peasantry, and with women—who represented a "fifth column" of resistance to the patriarchal order of the autocrat. By the seventeenth century, the position of women among the upper classes, enclosed in a *terem*, had reached its nadir, and during Ivan's reign the ethos of the Kievan saintly princes would be turned on its head: Now the *narod* was to serve the prince and ruler; it died for his salvation.[50]

The Father Tsar

In Muscovite juridical language, the word for "family," *sem'ia* (smaller than the generic *rod* or clan), signified a conspiratorial band or a conspiratorial agreement. The source of this new meaning refers first to the battle waged between the tsar and his princely relatives in his attempt to assert proprietary demands over them. But the attack upon the family was broader in context. The autocrat looked upon the *narod*, his subjects and the *sem'ia* or *rod* in which they lived, as an overlord who possessed both the land and the families living from it. Indeed, Ivan not only turned against his relatives, killing his oldest son in a murderous rage, but he also struck at the church, ordering the death of the saintly Patriarch Philip, who opposed his will on moral grounds.[51] In his double murder, Ivan rejected the traditional role of the saintly son and kenotic savior and assumed the persona of the terrible father-judge punishing the sins of his people.

The tsar was thus the paradigm of the father of a patriarchal family. It is no accident that Ivan's "taming" of his own *rod* should coincide with his effort to transform the families of his subjects. In the first part of his reign, before the terror that succeeded the death of his first wife, Ivan collaborated with the church in the creation of the *Domostroi* (Law of the Household), in which the father assumed the role of the abbot. His wife and children were souls to be saved. It is surely in large part due to his "instruction" for the upper classes that proverbs regarding the necessary subordination of women (so long emphasized by the Kievan church) made their way into popular parlance: "The husband is the law unto his wife," or "The husband is the father of his wife." Above all, he was regarded as a divine figure: "As God is to the people, so is the father to his children."[52]

Ivan the Terrible's subjection of the family and the church was accompanied by the tethering of the entire ruling class, the *boiarstvo*, to the needs of an expanding state. The Muscovite kingdom, assuming the configuration of a military barracks through Ivan's creation of a proprietary state-within-a-state (the *oprichnina*), was readied to crush internal enemies from among the princely relatives, as well as external foes.[53] In a famous exchange of correspondence (1564–1579) between Ivan and his former favorite, Prince Kurbskii, the latter, who had fled Russia in fear of his life, accused Ivan of abrogating the Christ-like role assigned him by the *narod* and becoming instead its enemy, an Anti-Christ, tormenting his people and staining Holy Russia with blood. Kurbskii, champion of the *boiarstvo*, suggested that persecution by the tsar had made *them* the new Christ figures. Ivan accused Kurbskii of hubris: "You have risen against God." But Kurbskii in his *History* answered the autocrat and his favorites by calling them destroyers of Russia: "They have torn the belly of their mother, that is, of the Holy Russian land who has borne and raised them." Kurbskii was the first to suggest an antithesis between Holy *Rus'* and her ruler.[54]

Indeed, by tearing away the coils of family bonds, Ivan struck a blow at the source of his power, the peasantry, as well. For the logic of remunerating the servants of the autocracy with territorial possession, a custom begun by Ivan's predecessors, demanded that the peasantry be prevented from evading their overlords to colonize the lands vacated by the Tatars or the vast and empty expanses of Siberia. Unable to restrain the flight of peasants from the center of the Muscovite state, Ivan and his successors began to limit the periods when they could legally abandon their masters' estates. The process of gradual restrictions on movement culminated in the 1649 Legal Code, which officially introduced serfdom. The peasant *narod* labored for the glory of the autocrat by serving whose who served him.

The result of Ivan IV's brutal reign was the creation of a centralized state supported by a bureaucracy beholden to the ruler. The warrior ideal of the paternal state had replaced the peasants' ideal of the maternal *rod* and land. That transformation, which occurred under the conditions of foreign wars, domestic massacres, and the mass flight of peasantry coerced into labor for the tsar's retainers, resulted in the devastation of the land. Ivan's murder of his eldest son brought on the tragedy of the period of Polish invasion called the "Time of Troubles." The mysterious death of Dmitrii, his youngest, marked the extinction of the Riurik clan. In striking against the family, Ivan succeeded in destroying his own dynasty and brought the nation, the *narod*, to the brink of disaster.

But despite the change of the Christ-like prince into a tyrant, the idea of a saintly tsar did not disappear.[55] Instead it retreated into popular legends like those associated with Saint George, on whose name day serfs were legally allowed to move from place to place. In fact, rather than blaming the tsar for his betrayal, the peasantry denounced the newly established service aristocracy for whom it was forced to labor. They were thought to be the culprits responsible for distancing the ruler from his people and misleading him in regard to the *narod*. At the end of Ivan's reign, there emerged a new (or newly reformulated) myth expressing the ancient wishes of the populace for a self-sacrificial son and husband to protect the land: The popular image of "Holy Russia" as Mother Russia was juxtaposed to that of the all-powerful tsar whose sovereignty rested upon her well-being.

In the course of the seventeenth century, the myth of "Holy Russia," found in Kurbskii's writings, emerged in popular discourse as an epithet defining the land and its inhabitants as a feminine and antistate force. Holy Russia, the common motherland of the twelfth-century *Lay of Igor's Campaign*, meant the earth upon which Christ trod. Its identification with the person of Mary, its guardian, who carried Christ in her body, was implicit. In contrast to the historical or temporal Muscovite tsardom, the term "Holy Russia" meant the nonhistorical and hence transcendent land. "Holy Russia" lay beyond the grasp of the tsars who ruled it; she would remain the holy motherland whether she was governed by a tsar or not. All this was clearly articulated in the popular songs and legends of the period.[56] In short, in adopting this epithet, the *narod* answered the self-assertive claims of the tsars, who wished to encompass the land in their own persons, with the counterclaim that only service to the protection of the earth and devotion to the family would confer power upon the ruler; that Russia contained tsars like the mother; and that, like the peasant hero Ilya of Murom, tsars drew their own strength directly from her.

By identifying the land with an image of divine maternal containment, the epithet "Holy Russia" also referred to the myth of the Great Mother Goddess who yearly married her consort-son in order to bring fertility to the soil. The saintly princes of Kiev had, in the imagination of the *narod*, been defined by their filial and protective duties toward the maternal earth. But after the Mongol occupation revealed the inability of such sons to withstand either fratricidal conflict or external conquest, the populace recognized the need for a more powerful figure of a husband-father who would shelter his holy "bride," Mother Russia, and her innumerable children under his defensive banner. This notion of the wedding of the tsar, called *Batiushka* (Little Father), to *Matushka* (Little Mother) *Rus'*, was expressed in the rituals of coronation and marriage imposed upon the tsar by popular custom, as well as the demands of the church.

Father Tsar and Mother Russia:
Rites of Marriage and Increase

Only through marriage did the groom in the patriarchal family become truly a man, and only after a symbolic wedding to the motherland did the autocrat receive power over her. Thus, the union with the feminine continued to be, as from time immemorial in the consecration of kings, the prerequisite for the assumption of masculine authority. In the coronation rites of the Muscovite tsars from the fifteenth to the seventeenth centuries, the sacred *hieros gamos* (the uniting of the god and goddess, resulting in fertility) was reinvoked to induce the future well-being of the land. The coronation was identical to a wedding and thus suggested both matrilocal and patrilineal custom: The tsar assumed the throne only through his union with Mother Russia and ruled his land from her very center. He lived in "Mother" Moscow, the mother of all cities in the popular imagination, the "humpbacked old woman" of proverbs.[57] He was crowned in Holy Mother Church, specifically the Cathedral of the Assumption of the Mother of God, the most celebrated of the Kremlin churches. Emerging from his palace in the Kremlin to the sacred Red Square to salute the populace, he was greeted as the embodiment of the rising sun. When they left the Church of Mary, the tsar and tsarina, like the groom and bride of peasant weddings, were showered with gold and silver, rather than grain and coins. Furthermore, the autocrat was arrayed with a sacred embroidered towel, as though the feminine *narod* had expressed consent to his assumption of power. Then he walked from the Church of the Assumption to the Cathedral of the Archangel Michael, where his predecessors lay—moving from the "house of the mother" to the tombs of the ancestors. In the course of the coronation ceremonies, the tsars promised to defend the Russian motherland like Christ and to be her husband, as well.[58]

The rituals of consecration were filled with pagan customs through which the *narod*, "Holy *Rus'*," accepted her mate. The wedding of the tsar was an appeal for abundance under his reign. The rites of the agrarian calendar further expressed the popular demand that the ruler incarnate the forces of increase: Beginning in the seventeenth century, when the tsar came out of the church on Christmas Eve accompanied by a procession of people carrying rams, he and his family were placed in a sled as the embodiment of Koliada. The sled would stop at a number of houses, where the tsar would bestow his blessing on the inhabitants, wishing them a "good year." The host then showered the tsar with presents, a Koliada tradition, and entertained him in his house. In Christmas songs praising the tsar, his connection with the sun divinity is quite clearly enunciated.[59]

The winter rites were followed by those of Easter, when the ruler acknowledged the power of the fertility goddess worshipped at Rusalia by peasant girls. In 1539, the traveler Olearius described the ceremonies of "Pussy Willow Saturday," preceding Palm Sunday. The tsar, surrounded by his servants and the inhabitants of Moscow, walked out onto Red Square, carrying branches of pussy willows in their arms. Then from the Church of the Assumption of the Virgin, "was brought out a huge tree with fruit and placed upon a sled. Under the tree stood five boys in white singing hymns and followed by youths carrying candles."[60] The source of this image of spring flowering and fertility was, unequivocally, the Mother of God, from whose domain the fruit-bearing Tree of Life emerged: The tsar, carrier of her gifts to the *narod*, was hailed as the palm-carrying Christ, the groom who met her in the Red Square.

In the fall, the tsar would again go out into the people, but now in the guise of the spent and ailing sun god bringing them the harvest. On the first of September (Bab'e Leto), the ruler presented himself to the *narod* to be showered with gifts. Blessed by the patriarch, he would be questioned about his health. Then the populace would call to the tsar to "be healthy, be healthy for many years, our ruler."[61]

On these three occasions—in winter, spring, and fall—the tsar became "immanent" in his people, going among them as the god who promised wealth in winter (was "born"), who united with the Mother of God in spring, and whose powers waned in the fall. But there was yet another occasion when the tsar unmistakenly embodied the sun god and consort of a Great Goddess: During the wedding ceremonies of the autocrats, the sacred *hieros gamos* was again performed as the union between the tsar and his wife, who impersonated the *narod*. When Michael Romanov, the first of the new dynasty, met his bride, her head was adorned with a garland of gold and jewels inscribed with the name of each Russian city. She was *Matushka Rus'*, and the wedding, much like that described for the Riurik Tsar Vasilii III, was a sumptuous imitation of peasant customs.[62] In accepting the peasant wedding rite and identifying his bride with the land, the tsar agreed to serve his people and Mother Moist Earth, who produced grain to feed her children.

The autocratic rite of the sacred marriage between tsar and

motherland, whom he promised to serve and protect, defined the role of the ruler as son dependent on earth for his power. The church placed considerable stress upon these dual functions of the prince and tsar: The one asserted his Christ-like kenotic nature, the other his role as the patriarchal husband in the Christian family. But in both relationships, the rituals of the peasantry appear to have "corrected" the dogma of the church by emphasis upon the motherland according the "gift" of power to her champions.[63]

Mother Russia's Champions: Immolated Tsarevich and Holy Fool

"If all the laws perished, the people would live in truth [*pravda*] and justice [*spravedlivost'* or *pravda*]," proclaims a popular proverb suggesting the illegality of the autocratic state and the concomitant desire to live under an order characterized by one word, *pravda*.[64] The legends and rites through which the *narod* reminded the ruler (or his "false servants") of his duties were effective only in keeping alive the peasantry's sense of betrayal. By the second half of the seventeenth century, precisely when the epithet of "Holy Russia" appeared as the popular expression of a divine motherland facing the power of the autocrat, almost two-thirds of the enserfed labor in the countryside was being used to feed the huge military and bureaucratic machinery needed by the tsar to enlarge his own sphere of authority.[65] The relationship of autocrat as a son to the maternal *narod* was succinctly illustrated in the custom of paying the bureaucratic class through direct extortion from the populace: The activity of administering lands was called *kormlenie*, or "feeding." Like greedy children, the tsar and his minions sucked the "breast" of the *narod* dry.

In the process of asserting his rights over the land and abandoning the obligations of filial piety and humility, the autocrat Ivan the Terrible had propagated another myth. By the murder of his first son and the mysterious death of his youngest, the *narod* saw him abandon the sacrificial persona of the early rulers and assign this princely function to the son-surrogate, the tsarevich.[66] The manner in which the *narod* understood the actions of their cruel tsar in the legends they created around him suggests that the peasantry was not unaware of the transformation through which their ruler had divested himself of his ancient kenotic obligations, as well as his role in bringing fertility to the land.

The cycle of *byliny* centered on the reign of Ivan *Groznyi* is dominated by one called "The Tsar Resolves to Kill His Son." It opens during a feast held in "Mother Moscow" at which "powerful and mighty heroes" are assembled together with "bold women warriors." The paradoxical appearance of such strong women precisely at a time when the female population of the upper classes had been divested of much legal power, enclosed in *teremy* and subjected to the will of their husbands serving the tsar, suggests the continued resistance of strong women among the *boiarstvo* now associated (in the epic) with the *narod*'s sense of injustice. These women take the part of Ivan the Tsarevich when in the course of a feast Ivan the Terrible hears that his son has conspired against him; immediately he takes the youth to the Moskva River, where the executioner's block is set up.

The mother intervenes: "It is not the red sun rolling along the earth / It is the Orthodox tsarina who has passed through / On her way to her dear brother." The mother, here associated with the red sun as the Kievan princes had been, goes to the house of her brother to announce the approaching death of her son and to seek revenge.[67] The son is represented as the light of the earth, no longer its sun like his ancient predecessors. The mother has assumed the role in order to ask for vengeance against the action of an unnatural father usurping power and violating the taboos of the *rod*.

In the epic, the brother, Nikita Romanov, goes to the river to stay the execution of the tsarevich by substituting himself for the tsar. Then proceeding to avenge his sister and nephew, Romanov goes to kill the informer—the tsar surrogate here—who had alerted Ivan to a plot against him. Ivan the Tsarevich is saved by his uncle. But when Tsar Ivan learns the truth, he acknowledges his mistake and rewards the uncle who had prevented the evil deed.[68] Thus, through the intervention of the tsarina, the brother-in-law reminds the tsar of his duties and the limits of his power. By killing his son, Ivan is seen to destroy the principle of light, fertility, and family upon which the wealth and prosperity of his kingdom and its inhabitants rest. The righteous force of the mother's *rod* is contrasted to the patriarchal brutality of the father's. The representation of the feast at which strong *bogatyri* and bold women sit together is illustrative of the continuing power of the maternal family in the ethos of the peasantry elaborating the epic tradition with its own values.

The myth of the Immolated Tsarevich is closely linked to the phenomenon of the Pretender (*samozvanstvo*, "self-calling"); both emerged from the reign of Ivan the Terrible and were attached to the deaths of his two sons. While the murder of the eldest, his namesake, provided the theme for the first, the mysterious disappearance of the second, Dmitrii, provided the source for the second and more tenacious legend. Stories abounded describing a Pretender who would lead an injured and impoverished peasantry before the tsar to express their grievance about his corrupt officials. The legends tell of a "Deliverer Tsar," a Christ-like savior marked with the sign of the cross come to defend the *narod* as its son and champion.[69] He frees his suffering motherland from the serfdom instituted by evil boyars and landowners, stops all unjust taxation, and punishes the greedy. He is assimilated to the folkloric "Ivan the Tsarevich" or "Prince Dmitrii." As such he is close to the *narod*, its creation.

But in these popular stories, corrupt officials get wind of the plans of the Savior; they kidnap the good tsar and throw him into a dungeon, from which he is liberated by the son of the *narod*, the peasant. The tsar then wanders through the land like a pilgrim, sharing the suffering of his people. Eventually returning to Moscow, he is recognized as the true ruler, punishes the unjust, and lavishes honor and wealth upon the populace. Sometimes the Tsar-Deliverer is a child, the Tsarevich Dmitrii, and his freedom from imprisonment appears even more suggestive of the birth of the fertility god.

The legends emerged during the Time of Troubles in the seventeenth century and continued to be told to the twentieth. Their span corresponded with the rise and fall of serfdom, and represented the peasantry's "revolutionary ideology." The triumph of the ideal ruler divorced from his people by the evil forces of officialdom would mean the utter destruction of the whole social system and the substitution of another in which the tsar's chief preoccupation would be the well-being of his *narod*. In fact, the myth of the Tsar-Deliverer also concerned the tsar as an inauthentic Pretender occupying the throne.[70] This demand for a ruler united with his subjects, a member of the *rod*, its son and illuminating sun, was only one form of protest. Another, linked with the Christian tradition of sainthood, was the institution of *Iurodstvo*, or "Holy Foolishness," closely tied to *Matushka Rus'* in the popular imagination. While Ivan the Tsarevich represented the first "immolated son," and Dmitrii, the sacrificed child, was the prototype for the Pretender phenomenon, Ivan the Terrible's second son, the half-wit Fiodor, who briefly succeeded his father, was associated with Holy Fools.

Iurodstvo is older than the two previous myths—though they in turn echo the archaic rituals of male sacrifice. It has its roots in the Byzantine and subsequently Kievan period and parallels the myth of the saintly prince. "Holy Foolishness" originated in north and northeast Russia, where the *volkhvy* once held power with Varangian rulers. The Fools assumed the kenotic role once occupied by the princes. Just as the myth of the Pretender "corrected" the actual image of the tsar, so too the *narod* through its Holy Fools reminded both church and state of their lapsed duties. The *Iurodivye* first appeared among the monks of the Kievan Pecherskaia Lavra. By the reign of Ivan the Terrible, they constituted a genuine popular moral force in opposition to the actions of those in power. Thereafter they were condemned by the state-directed church, which had previously accommodated them into the ranks of sainted clergy.[71]

The origins of the *Iurodivye* may be found in the Greek *saloi*, or holy men, but their appearance and behavior, as well as the areas where they were generally to be found, suggest a Christianized continuation of pagan shamanic practices. The Russian Holy Fool distinguished himself from the *saloi* by his emphasis upon deeds rather than exhortation. His power lay in the strength of his will, his resistance to evil, and his prophetic gifts. The Holy Fool picked up the *podvig* cast aside by the holy prince—that is, he took upon himself the task of serving the collectivity abandoned by the power-hungry rulers who would build the state of Muscovy. The Russian *Iurodivyi* served the *narod*, slept upon Mother Moist Earth, and braved the elements without fear.[72]

Whereas the Greek *saloi* had been particularly devoted to the poor, and among them to prostitutes (thereby echoing his more archaic origins in the cult of Kybele worshipped by eunuch priests), the Russian Fool was tied to the Mother of God, his particular protector. Pokrov, or the Feast of the Intercession, was also the day sacred to the *Iurodivyi*, who shared his attributes with the folktale simpleton, the favorite youngest son of the mother. Since the folktale fool, like his counterpart in the world, had no pride, he could perform actions contrary to those considered "manly," and in so doing help the community as well as himself; his, too, was a permanent injunction against patriarchal vanity.[73]

The *Iurodivye* associated themselves with the Church of the Mother of God, as well as sought her protection. Procopius, a fourteenth-century *Iurodivyi* from Novgorod, slept either in the streets or on dunghills, and later took refuge on the porch of the cathedral dedicated to Our Lady of Ustiug—thus connecting Mother Earth and Mother Mary. His prophecies related to matters over which both Mother Earth and the Mother of God officiated, namely, family concerns and bad weather; he also interceded with Mary on behalf of the citizens of Ustiug to protect them from disaster. But his relationship to the pagan Mother Earth and the *volkhvy* or shamanic prototypes was best illustrated in his habit of carrying three poles or pokers in his left, "feminine," hand. The direction which these pokers assumed predicted whether or not the coming harvest would be plentiful.[74]

The most famous of the *Iurodivye* was Saint Basil, whose life provides the most complete account of the Holy Fool in the Muscovite period and whose image was long preserved in popular legend. He is said to have begun his life as a holy man by wandering the earth, walking naked into the city, and punishing dishonest food merchants. Most important, he served to remind the Tsar Ivan of his atrocities, and of his betrayal of the motherland. In contrast to Ivan, who had been a profligate widower "beating Mother Russia," Basil lived with a widow to protect her. The brave and defiant *Iurodivyi* denounced the tsar for his bloody reprisals against real and imagined enemies, and though he died in 1550 without witnessing the worst excesses of Ivan's reign, he was thought in the popular imagination to have reproached the tsar for his massacres.[75] He was buried in the church Ivan had built to honor his victory over the Kazan Tatars: Our Lady of Kazan (which housed the icon of the Mother of God, the famed "Lady of Merciful Sorrows"). In the seventeenth century, the *narod* renamed the building Saint Basil's, a name which it still bears.

Not surprisingly, the church, firmly attached to the secular power after Ivan's reign, refused to canonize succeeding Holy Fools, whose championing of the populace in opposition to the wealthy church and proprietary state was too plainly effective to be tolerated. Indeed, despite the highly individualistic form of moral protest against the excesses of the rich and powerful, the implicitly political role of the *Iurodivye* began in the sixteenth century with Saint Basil. Their "Foolishness" provided protection against the fury of the men in power. They soon became so numerous that they seemed to form a class apart in Moscow. Their disheveled hair gave them a resemblance to the worshippers of Paraskeva. Their dirtiness went together with the use of obscenities—also a prominent feature in the rites of the Goddess-

Saint. The word *pokhab* used to designate the *Iurodivye* referred to their obscene gestures and to their nakedness. All aspects of their appearance and behavior, as well as their "debasesment," reveal a covert link with the fertility cults of the *narod*.[76]

The *Iurodivye*, assuming the attributes of scapegoats, were beloved by the people and feared by the tsars. As the ever-visible servants and reminders of the suffering motherland awaiting her savior, they arose from the ranks of the *narod* (and sometimes from the upper class, as well) to challenge the rulers over their obligation to make the land fertile through a just and peaceful administration rather than sucking it dry like any predatory military force. The Holy Fool "husbanded" Holy *Rus'* as her brave and yet self-abnegating son.

The Great Schism: The Tsar as Anti-Christ

By the seventeenth century, Russia was rent by a number of religious, cultural, and political discontinuities—fissures already created in the Kievan period and further aggravated under the Muscovite tsars. Christianization had led to *dvoeverie*: the Muscovite tsardom had created two political entities, one calling itself Holy *Rus'*, the other its paternal ruler. The chaos characterizing the Time of Troubles announced the beginning of a period which would close with a dramatic religious as well as political schism dividing the nation into two opposing groups, the persecuted and the persecutors. The *Raskol* (Break or Schism) occurred officially in 1666–1667, when the church council met to agree on changes in religious practice and expelled those who refused to comply.

The popularly elected Michael Romanov, in whom the *narod* hoped to find its healing savior was succeeded by Alexis, who proceeded, like his Muscovite predecessors, to enlarge the base for the creation of a secular and totalitarian state which used its subjects rather than served them. The gradual divestment of their saintly persona over the period of two centuries would culminate in the eighteenth century with the tsars' assumption of the title of "emperor," the leader of a political entity rather than a holy motherland. But even the patron of the *Raskol*, Tsar Alexis, continued to accept the epithet of "Pious and Gentle" despite his signing of the 1649 code of law which legalized serfdom, and his admiration, in xenophobic Muscovy, of all things Western. During his reign, the image of Saint George, the defender of the Holy Motherland, was replaced by the portrait of the tsar himself, a secular ruler rather than a mythical paradigm of sanctity and filial devotion.[77]

Tsar Alexis had appointed the Kievan-trained and Catholic-influenced Nikon as patriarch of the Russian church. Nikon sought unsuccessfully to use his position to strengthen the church vis-à-vis the crown. His first task, however, had been to make changes in church rites, which through time had become excessively idiosyncratic, paganized, and out of touch with the mainstream of Greek Orthodox and Western theology.

The changes instituted by the patriarch appear to have been minor, but they precipitated a dramatic split in Russian religious culture and magnified the fissures of *dvoeverie* into a chasm dividing believers. Among the reforms ordered by Nikon was the proclamation that priests should thenceforth make the sign of the cross by raising three fingers rather than two, that hymns and ritual responses be ended by three rather than two alleluias, and that Christ's name be spelled differently. Nikon also sought out icons which did not correspond to Byzantine models and burned those he found. But even Alexis protested the sacrilege of destroying icons and ordered that they be buried in the earth instead.

Alexis did not oppose Nikon's reforms; indeed, Nikon's efforts to centralize the ecclesiastical power concurred with the tsar's desire to gain greater control over the nation and paralleled the edict of enserfment he had signed. Through his patronage of Nikon, Alexis now controlled the religious life of the *narod*. The decision to change the nature of ritual, even in its slightest detail, appeared to the populace and the village clergy as a rejection of the past and an abrogation on the part of the autocrat of his role as the defender and servant of the church. In tampering with accepted rites and dogma, the patriarch and his master appeared to modify the Christian religion itself. The ritual invocation of the dual nature of Christ signified in the priest's holding up of two fingers and the singing of two alleluias was radically changed when the number three was substituted. The *narod* and the provincial clergy saw in this and other such changes a transformation of the nature of the divinity.[78]

By colluding with Nikon's reforms, the tsar in the eyes of the populace appeared in the guise of an Anti-Christ. The destruction of the "totemic" icons proved irrevocably that the reformer and those who supported him were epigones of the devil. And indeed, the year of the reform, associated with the "evil" number 666, was one of plague, famine, and solar eclipse, for which the patriarch was blamed. When disaster succeeded disaster, Tsar

Alexis was constrained by public anger to exile Nikon, though he kept his reforms intact. But the damage to the nation's faith in tsar and church was irreversible and would result in the turning away of a substantial segment of the population from all official authority.

When Avvakum, the archpriest and leader of the revolt, called to Nikon and the tsar to "give us back our Christ," he was expressing a demand for just rule and saintly rulers so long articulated in the *narod*. At the church council of 1667 which sat in judgment on his insubordination, he likened himself to other resisters to state and church, the *Iurodivye*: "We are fools for Christ's sake. You are honorable, but we are hated; we are weak, but you are strong."[79] The Christ he sought had been "shown" to him in the religion learned from his mother. The Savior was not the figure of theological debate but the Suffering One, a Holy Fool. For Avvakum and his followers, the new Christ represented by three fingers was an Anti-Christ created by the satanic officials to corrupt the people. Avvakum saw both the patriarch and the tsar as traitors to Holy *Rus'*; the evidence for their treason lay in their espousal of Western innovations which corrupted a sacred tradition and estranged them from the pious *narod*. The archpriest's resistance cost him exile to Siberia and intense hardship, culminating in death. Among the people, his figure became an iconographic manifestation of saintly resistance to evil, for which the princes Boris and Gleb had long been venerated.

The archpriest's rebellion was taken up in the ranks of the lower clergy. In the period prior to the *Raskol*, priests had officiated in the village communities without the intervention of the patriarch in Moscow. Nikon's reforms touched upon their close relationship with the peasantry, through which the pagan practices of the *narod* had made their way into church ritual and dogma. The village, or *mir*, had selected their priests and obliged them to respect their ancient customs and rituals.[80] Nikon threatened to disrupt this delicate balance linking the *dvoeverie*.

Avvakum's most earnest and devoted followers were women. Like the Kievan *baby* who had resisted the ruler's attempt to change the religious beliefs of his people, they again rebelled against the tampering with a faith they had tried to accommodate to more ancient beliefs. But the women's championship of the "Old Believers," as those who stayed true to the old faith came to be called, coincided with the nadir of their power and, like the uprising of the peasantry against serfdom, was linked to the increased restrictions on freedom. Avvakum had promised his followers a real equality in the relationship of men and women, as well as in all aspects of social life. In his famous *Autobiography*, he had made his wife a heroine, presenting her in the form of a *polianitsa*, brave, hardy, and faithful, accompanying her husband in his wanderings through Siberia and sharing fully in his suffering. In praising his wife's courage, Avvakum also credited his mother for the intensity of his faith. By recognizing the power of woman, Avvakum championed the unheard revolt of those still attached to egalitarian agrarian customs.[81]

But the persecuted martyr and heroine of the Schism, its feminine icon, sharing Avvakum's torments in the eyes of the *narod*, was a relative of the Tsarina Maria who had also opposed Nikon's reforms. The *boiarina* Morozova, together with another high-born woman, Princess Urusov, would not bend to the dictates of the church despite pressure from relatives and dignitaries, including the tsar himself. Her stalwart refusal, despite incarceration and torture, to bow to the will of church and state resembled that of the "God-cursed hags" of Kiev many centuries earlier. This heroic woman who became a popular saint, working against the church rather than for it, is described in her biography as linking her fate closely to that of Mother Earth, like a peasant woman. As she neared death in her prison cell, she asked her guardians to allow her to wear clean clothing when she expired so that her body would not "dirty" the "Most Clean Mother Earth."[82] Her pious example helped to draw legions of other women into the ranks of the Old Believers.

The movement ignited by Avvakum began to take on its most explosive aspects after the Council of 1666 validated Nikon's reforms and in 1667 expelled those who would not accept them. A mass hysteria spread over the north and northeast of Russia, causing whole communities to immolate themselves; they preferred to die like martyrs rather than submit to the tyranny of the Anti-Christ's state.

Death represented the most radical form of escape from the tentacles of the state; another was flight from its center. Villagers abandoned their lands and retreated into the forests of the north and Siberia or descended into the Don and Dnieper regions to join the free Cossack communities formed by peasants who had escaped during Ivan the Terrible's reign. The Old Believers, numbering up to one-third of the nation, established settlements out of the reach of the state. The Orthodox church lay in the grasp of the Anti-Christ and no longer guaranteed the true sacraments. Consequently, the only manner through which the *narod* might commune with the divine was through prayer and those rites which could be performed by the community as a whole without the offices of the clergy. A radical wing of the Old Believers, called the "Priestless," dispensed with the clergy altogether, but the majority continued to accept the nominal intervention of priests in their lives and hoped for an eventual conciliation with the state after the departure of the Anti-Christ. This group called itself the "Priestly" (*Popovtsy*, as opposed to the *Bespopovtsy*, or "Priestless").[83]

The rejection of the church led to the resurgence of pagan beliefs. Among the Priestless sect, the Confession to Earth assumed a central place. The *Raskol'niki* (Schismatics) had settled the territories of the far north and founded countless communities. Freed from the repressive authority of the state, they combined the rigor of monastic life with the democratic freedom and egalitarianism which may have characterized the ancient Slavic communities. Marriage, no longer consecrated, led to the practice of concubinage. With no priests to absolve them of guilt, they turned to the pagan Mother Earth to tell her their sins; she became the mediatrix between the human and divine worlds.[84]

As could be expected, the position of women in the Old Believer communities was a respected one. In rejecting the sacraments of marriage, the Old Believers, particularly in the radical priestless sects, rejected also the patriarchal and hierarchical order of the family, reverting instead to anarchic free unions, including marriage by a tree or a lake, and to pagan burials in woods or gardens.[85]

The wholesale desertion of the state by the Old Believers was a prelude to the flowering of Orthodox sectarian groups in the eighteenth century. Whether or not influenced by similar movements in the West or developed through an evolution of the Schismatic tradition, they continued to emphasize the importance of women, the sacredness of matter, and egalitarian and democratic forms of rule. The most radical of these sects was called the *Khlysty* (Flagellants), who in turn generated another group called *Skoptsy* (Eunuchs). The *khlysty* appeared in the north in the seventeenth century, where the most fervent of the Old Believer sects had established themselves. Their cult was served by women "prophetesses" and men called "prophets," whose vigils for forecasting the crops, the weather, and the catch of fish ended with orgies. Women were also called "Mothers of God" and were regarded as the mothers of the future male *Khlysty* members who might become its "Christs"—a role they assumed after intense suffering and through a ritual "resurrection." Governed by its prophetesses and prophets, each community was called a ship, seen as floating on Mother Moist Earth. Like the Quakers and the Shakers, anyone moved by the divine spirit—which descended on the group during its trance dances—could become a leader.[86]

The *Khlysty*, ruled by the son Christ and his mother, were initiated into the mysteries of birth, death, and resurrection through ritual dances presided over by a prophetess or a Mother of God present to induce trance states among the worshippers. These Mothers of God, generally widows or women separated from their husbands, rather than being elected like Christs, were "discovered" in the course of the dances as particularly adept prophetesses. Generally the *Khlysty* preferred robust younger women as leaders and invoked them in their hymns in language to suggest their identification with Mother Moist Earth as well as Mary. To emphasize the assimilation of these priestesses to pagan divinities, such women were given the title of *boginia* (goddess). The secret dancing rites were open only to initiates and consisted of the *radeniia* of "joyful whirling," during which the participants would flagellate themselves while running in circular processions. The orgiastic "games" resembled the pagan Rusalia and Kupalo festivities. They were accompanied by hymns in which Mother Earth, who nurtured each soul, was frequently evoked.[87]

The orgiastic rites of the *Khlysty* did not appeal to all members, and one group broke away. Calling themselves the *Skoptsy* (Self-Castrators), like the eunuch priests of Kybele, the men of the sect submitted themselves to the ritual "sacrifice," often performed on them by women. The leader of the *Skoptsy*, Ivan Selivanov, calling himself Peter III, needed to obtain the benediction of the famous *Khlysty* Mother of God Anna Romanova in order to assume the title of God and claim to be a true tsar or a pretender to the throne. Like the *Khlysty*, who came to call themselves the "People of God," the *Skoptsy* based their worship entirely upon inspiration and prophesy, whirling like dervishes to induce trance states. Women were particularly important in the invention and diffusion of the popular cult; and the chief priestess, Anna Ivanovna, was called "Empress."[88]

Tsar Peter Fights the Witch Baba Yaga

The divisions between tsar and *narod* created in the course of the seventeenth century were deepened in the first decades of the eighteenth century by the son of Tsar Alexis, Peter. In his reign, the schism between *Batiushka Tsar* and *Matushka Rus'*, caused by serfdom, religious strife, and increased centralization and secularization, would be further widened by the autocrat's

turn to the West and divestment of his role as a religious paternal figure in favor of that of imperator over a secular state. No
longer the *rodina* (motherland), Russia would henceforth in official language assume the name of *otechestvo* (fatherland, from
otets, "father"). In changing the sex of his nation, the tsar responsible for Russia's westernization ushered in a break with the mythological and religious aspirations rooted in the agrarian world
view of his subjects, and in so doing he came to incarnate, even
more than his father, the very image of the devil.[89]

One of the most famous of the popular *lubki* (satirical draw-
ings) circulating in Russia in opposition to Peter's reformation of
the motherland to fit a Western mold shows the tsar in the guise
of a bearded crocodile. (Illustration no. 32.) Seated on a pig or
boar, facing him, as though about to charge the raised paws of
the monster, is the witch Baba Yaga with mortar and pestle, axe
and rake.[90] She sticks her tongue out at him while her mount
bares its sharp teeth. Between the two figures and dividing them
stands a tiny tree or bush with a branch sticking out of the witch's
rear. Here is the angry Grudge, the resistant Muscovite and Kievan
Mother Russia, the mistress of this vastly reduced Tree of Life
which separates her from the crocodilian or all-devouring tsar.
She opposes his hunger with her own: Her phallic tongue and
the toothed opening of the pig-boar's mouth suggest her image
as the container as well as destroyer of all life.

Peter, the crocodile, represents the beast of the Apocalypse,
the Anti-Christ, with the face of a cat rather than a lion, an enor-
mously long beard which descends to his feet, and an equally
long tail rising to his waist. The phallic tsar (responsible for the
symbolic castration of his male subjects by ordering the cutting
of beards as a necessary condition for westernization) attacks
the feminine *narod*, angered at his arrogance. His battle recalls
that of the epic *bogatyri*, Ilya and Dobrynia against the Baba
Latingorska. The *lubok* is also a satirical and distorted image of
Saint George's battle with the dragon; the tsar is the monster,
and Yaga on her pig appears as the saint.

This virulent hatred on the part of the populace toward a
tsar accorded the epithet of "Great" by courtiers and historians resulted from his strengthening of the state and his rejection of the
customs of both his *rod* and his *narod*. Like his famous predecessor, Ivan the Terrible, Peter had been left fatherless among a
princely clan who reasserted their ancient prerogatives at the
death of each autocrat. Both tsars thus began their conflict with
the motherland as fatherless sons left unprotected by their powerless mothers; both regarded their battle for autonomy as one

which involved their very existence; and both saw the threat to their lives from their own *rod*. Both killed their oldest sons, suspected of collusion with their mothers, and thereby deprived themselves of direct male heirs.

In his youth, Peter had turned to the European community in Moscow to escape the struggles of court life. His journey to western Europe further accentuated his fascination with Western technology and manners. But Peter's abandonment of *Matushka Rus'* and his successful efforts to westernize her confirmed, in the eyes of the Old Believers and the peasantry, as well, that he was indeed the Anti-Christ. For when he returned from abroad, Peter not only set about to change the administrative structure of Russian government, depersonalizing the relations between sovereign and officials by creating a more efficient machine to respond to his will, but he also determined to change the physical appearance of his people. Abolishing the Byzantine patriarchate, he placed the governance of the church, now called the Holy Synod, under the thumb of a lay procurator general. The *Dukhovnyi reglament* (Spiritual Code) of 1721 required all parish priests to report on those who did not confess and to record all crimes to which they had been privy, under threat of punishment. The religious life of the population became an affair of state.[91]

Peter worsened the situation of the serfs through the institution of a poll tax levied against each "soul," as he sardonically called the male heads of the family. This tax increased their financial difficulties and extended the yoke of serfdom to groups hitherto free of it. Like cattle, serfs could now be sold as families rather than individuals. Furthermore, the burden of military conscription carried by the peasantry was made more onerous through Peter's wars and industrial schemes, for which he employed serf labor. Rebellions flared up as they had under the religious reforms of his father, and peasants and soldiers fled to escape a tsar they considered damned. But the long arm of the autocracy reached them all eventually, helped as it was by the dreaded *Preobrazhenskii prikaz* (Secret Police).[92]

What had been done to constrain the peasantry to perform the ruler's will was also done to the *boiarstvo*. To tame the unruly aristocracy, whom even Ivan the Terrible had failed to suppress, Peter replaced the right to serve with a "Table of Ranks" which gave priority to official rank over hereditary nobility and obliged the *boiarstvo* to perform assigned duties. With government service necessary, the nobility were forced away from their estates, breaking the personal bonds between themselves and their serfs.

Peter's reforms were intended to turn Russia into a Western nation and make its ruler a secular sovereign. Russia, the *otechestvo*, represented the abstracted will of the autocrat freed from all familial bonds and allegiance to the *narod*. Like a god usurping the maternal attributes of a goddess, Peter had changed its sex from female (mother) to male (father) by transforming its administration; now he set about changing its appearance to reflect his own. He ordered all members of the aristocracy to shave their beards (a traditional symbol of male potency) and all townspeople to wear "Hungarian clothing." He founded schools where Western subjects—particularly of a technological nature—were taught, and obliged his *dvorianstvo* (courtiers) to attend them. He freed upper-class women from the *terem*, had them dress in the European manner, and ordered them to mix freely with men.[93] He encountered considerable resistance to all these reforms. Changes in religious ritual had split the nation in the period of the *Raskol*; changes in the gentry's education and outward appearance now set them apart from the peasantry, who maintained their traditional dress and customs.

Modifying the internal organization of his nation and the physical aspect of its inhabitants, Peter then set out to transform the shape of Holy Mother Russia herself. She was no longer called Holy *Rus'* but *Rossiia*, like the secular (though still feminine) partner of the *otechestvo* ruler; Peter moved her capital from Mother Moscow, with her many-domed churches, to the bleak borders of the land deep in the northern marshes. As though wishing to master her "from above" and evade her stifling embrace by assuming a foreign name, Peter called his city by the Dutch "Sankt Pietersburgh," Peter's city, and bowed to custom only in attributing the epithet "Saint" to it. This "Window to the West," a defiantly secular domain built by fiat on the treacherous Neva River close to the ports of the Baltic, received a masculine epithet in popular tradition, "Piter." The "Father City" was constructed on pylons sunk deep into the swampy ground and was supplied with food by the Muscovite countryside.

The transference of the capital from the heart of Russia to the head was strikingly symbolic of the epic hero Peter's need to detach himself from his motherland and rule over her with a power drawn from a political, cultural, and social tie to the markedly patriarchal West. He housed his new bureaucracy in "Sankt Pietersburgh," where they could not plot against him as they

had in Moscow.[94] Here too he began to train a new class of techni-
cians and engineers to help him drag his backward nation into
the "concert of Europe" and make Peter, indeed, "Great."

Thus, Peter created a new Russia; of this he was quite aware
when he assumed the title of "Father of the Fatherland" and
dropped that of "Most Gentle Tsar"—and with it any connection
to sainthood and familial traditionalism. The senate he had
brought into being accorded him the new title, and in their eager-
ness to please the all-powerful ruler, his Orthodox as well as lay
apologists declared: "Our Father, Peter the Great, You have
taken us from nonexistence to existence." Likened to Jehovah, a
"Father of the country," he is said to have "given Russia a new
birth."[95]

This eulogy to male parthenogenesis, modeled upon that of
Genesis, in which the land was represented as both fathered and
mothered by the autocrat, did not impress the peasantry. In the
Time of Troubles, they had called for a *Batiushka tsar'* to defend
"Holy Mother *Rus'*." He was seen to be not independent of her
but rather her groom, the husband of the family to which the
whole populace belonged. Peter's divorce from his familial status
and obligations and his assertion of autonomy from the motherland could not be understood. In countless proverbs, the peasantry
attempted to restore the proper balance which the pride of the
ruler had destroyed: "Moscow is the mother of all towns," they
asserted, as though to put Petersburg in its proper perspective
as her "son." "Peter feeds, Moscow is the food," and "Peter is
the head; Moscow is the heart," the peasantry proclaimed, attempting to come to terms with a ruler called Anti-Christ by many
of his rebellious subjects.[96] And they attempted to correct the tsar's
overweening pride with a quite different vision of his achieve-
ments in the *byliny* they composed about him. There he was again
reunited with his mother, who was the source of his power, as
is the mother of any epic hero.

The legends about Peter's exploits make much of his giant-
like stature. He appears like a true *bogatyr'*; his childhood is likened to that of Vseslav or Volga in the most ancient of the Kievan cycles. He receives his great wisdom from his all-powerful
mother; his sister and regent, Sophia, is represented as a witch,
like the sister of the folklore Prince Ivan, the enchantress who
would swallow the sun. All these aspects of his life and appearance are worked into the vocabulary of folklore and epic; but his
trip to the West is represented as a truly novel and monstrous oc-
currence, a mythic voyage associated with the crossing of the

river Puchai in earlier epics, and one which he undertakes without the consent of his mother.[97]

In the *byliny* influenced by the *Raskol'niki* (Old Believers), when Peter leaves *Matushka Rus'*, he meets on the "other shore" an enchantress in the form of a queen of Sweden who is cast in the role of the destructive river Puchai herself and attempts to drown him. Failing to do so, she tries, like Baba Yaga, to roast him alive.[98] While in some versions Peter is saved by a peasant or an Old Believer and returned to his motherland—his proper place as tsar—in other versions he is represented as an Anti-Christ not by his own nature but through the machinations of the Swedish enchantress. In the epic, his city of Saint Petersburg is called damned, barren, and it is devastated by the angry river Neva. When he goes to the West, Peter is kidnapped by the foreign witch who rules over the lands across the sea, and she substitutes a changeling in his place. When the *Strel'tsy*, his retinue infiltrated by Old Believers, rebel against the False Tsar, they are presented as martyrs rather than traitors.

In the *byliny*, the *narod* remembered Peter's family ties. He had repudiated his first wife, the daughter of Muscovite boyars Tsarina Iudoksiia, seeing in her the incarnation of the ancient customs of the *rod* he wished to break. Instead, he married a Lithuanian woman of low origin, the future Empress Catherine I. In the epic it is the false tsar who marries Catherine, while the true tsar, in prison, is devoted to his Muscovite bride. Peter's divorce and remarriage had flouted custom, but the murder of his oldest son, Alexis, accused, like the son of Ivan the Terrible, of plotting with his mother and the Muscovite *boiarstvo*, is portrayed in the epic cycle as the act of a changeling tsar, an Anti-Christ who destroys all natural bonds.

Of his deeds as husband and father, the peasantry had little good to say, vindicating his actions as simply those of an imposter; but in his relationship to his mother, Peter is represented as the dutiful son of a Muscovite tsarina who listens to her prophetic advice. In the *bylina* about Peter's victory over the Swedes, she foretells his success and appears to be the source of it: "I have seen, Mother, in a dream, a Great Mountain. / On this mountain is a white rock, / on this rock is a bush, / on this bush sits an eagle, / in his claws he holds a crow." She answers him: "My child, I will explain your dream: / The Great Mountain is Holy Moscow, / the white rock is our Kremlin, / the bush is the tsar's palace, / the eagle is the tsar. / The crow is the king of Sweden. / Our ruler will win the earth of Sweden."[99]

The image of Peter in popular legends and *byliny* is not, understandably, a consistent one. When he is not being decried as an Anti-Christ, by the Old Believers in particular, his actions, too brutal and foreign to rationalize, are assigned to those of a changeling. Sometimes his mother is said to have given birth to a daughter and, fearful of her husband's reactions, exchanged her for the son of a German woman.[100] Thus it appeared as though a foreign ruler, Peter, had created a foreign city, detached from the center of Holy *Rus'*. Alienating himself from his subjects physically and psychologically, the tsar, like the devil, dragged the nation with him in his "Fall." Indeed, the policy of the self-created "Father of the Fatherland" was that of binding and starving the motherland. No longer in the image of Christ, he could not guarantee salvation to his subjects; no longer immanent in his *narod* as its groom and son, he could not provide wealth like a fertility daemon.

Tsar Peter completes the process begun by the Muscovite grand princes: Having gained supremacy over his *rod* and arrogated ownership over Holy Mother Russia, he and his successors would then proceed to turn the nation into a military stronghold. Peter was the first of a long series of autocrats who through marriage alliances would by the end of the nineteenth century be strangers in their own land. The many centuries of struggle between the merchant-warriors who were first invited to share the rule of Kiev with a populace they in turn exploited was ended by the Westernizing autocrat. In his introduction of Western culture and technology, Peter effectively split the nation into two camps: the bitter, enserfed, and impoverished Mother Russia, expressing the union of peasant and soil; and a bureaucratic upper class—created by the tsar to implement his vision of the motherland—divorced from its traditions by education, manners, and language. By the eighteenth century, the division between the ruler and the nation, which originated in the Kievan period as a religious split separating the pagan worshippers of Mother Earth from her Christianized and insufficiently saintly or devoted ruler-sons, had been exacerbated by the *Raskol*, dissolving the uneasy Muscovite marriage of Mother Russia to Father Tsar. By the nineteenth century, the schism had developed into a gulf separating the official *otechestvo* from the unofficial *rodina*: In this "Dual Russia," the government and upper classes became a foreign military invading force keeping *Matushka Rus'* in its thrall.[101] But the pride of the autocrats estranged from the land which gave them birth would not long remain unchallenged; new champions emerged to assume the discarded kenotic mantle of Mother Russia's protectors.

CHAPTER SEVEN

Pushkin and Other Champions
from the Intelligentsia

Russia and I, must we suffer one destiny? . . .

—A. Blok, "Russia and I"[1]

The epithet "Holy Russia," found in popular discourse from the seventeenth century and linked to the archaic notion of earth as a common mother, *Matushka Rus'*, would, in the course of the nineteenth century, be taken up by a Western-educated class—the intelligentsia.[2] Whereas the seventeenth-century "Holy Russia" was associated with the aggrieved *rodina* severed from its head, the rightful or Christ-like tsar, the nineteenth-century version represented the intelligentsia's response to its own sense of severance from the motherland. Both the epithet and the myth behind it suggested a mission based upon the kenotic (and symbiotic) ideal of service and self-sacrifice which had been cast aside by the ruler. While "Holy Russia" represented the Christian Orthodox nature of the motherland, "Mother Russia," expressing for intellectuals the needs of the *narod*, evoked the suffering peasantry awaiting a savior to deliver it from the grip of a cruel autocratic order. Yet behind that representation and the implicit desire for championship lay the demand of an educated class for identity, which could be gained only by wresting power from the autocrat.[3]

The first of Russia's great writers, Alexander Pushkin, was also the first to elaborate on the terms of the myth and on the yearnings and dilemmas which lay barely concealed beneath its surface.

Pushkin: Facing Mother Russia and Father Tsar

By creating an educated elite to serve as the instrument for westernizing and tightening his grip over the land, Peter behaved like the Christianizing Varangian Grand Prince Vladimir of Kiev, who had taken youths from their families and estates to send them to his newly established schools. Those who resisted the emperor's will suffered harassment, banishment, or death. Westernization of the upper classes, which proceeded through the eighteenth century and resulted in a forcible divorce from their traditional culture, was repeated with each generation through the customs of child-rearing: The higher ranks of the nobility continued to place their infant offspring at the breasts of peasant nurses, while the gentry mothers often remained a shadowy presence. The peasant woman came to represent, for her charges, the bountiful and ever-nurturing avatar of Mother Earth. It is perhaps for this reason that the idyllic memory of childhood floats over the writings of a number of nineteenth-century gentry intellectuals. It expresses their deep emotional attachment to those nurses and the ever-remembered stories and customs of the *narod* with which the nurses surrounded their masters' infants. Childhood, in the accounts of these writers, belonged in the land of the mothers, of *Matushka Rus'*, where devotion and anarchic freedom were indistinguishable and linked to the sense of communion which they attempted to rediscover in their adult years.[4]

The break with the natural mother and peasant nurse quite often occurred simultaneously in the life of the male child, while his sister remained in the feminine realm. Sometimes the youth went to a regimental or boarding school. Sometimes a foreign tutor would be brought in to wean him from mother and peasantry. Western (technical) education, the sine qua non of nobility since Peter, was humanized in the course of the eighteenth century by the stress on the acquisition of a general and specifically "moral" knowledge.[5]

The early "exile" of the child (sometimes no older than seven) to a distant institution created a keen feeling of rootlessness and isolation. Most schools were established in urban areas, while their pupils had generally been raised on their parents' rural estates. Consequently, the child's departure from home appeared to him as a banishment from the countryside and the *narod*, or Russia as a maternal nurturing force, where he had been allowed to roam freely and from whom he had gained his first "wisdom" in the form of folktale and rite.[6] The military regimentation of the state school reflected the distant father himself and, obliquely, the autocrat who had indirectly torn the child from the mother, the country estate, and the peasantry attached to the soil.

The feelings of anguish and fear evoked by the sudden isolation imposed upon the "banished" children were recorded in countless nineteenth-century memoirs. A number of boys and youths responded by joining together, united in their common alienation and loneliness, into study groups, which in the eighteenth century became the prototypes for Masonic and philosophic circles. Indeed, for many rootless gentry, the world of ideas, of utopian dreams, replaced the emotional warmth of the lost paradise of childhood. But if the young "intelligents" of the early nineteenth century set out in search of the union of the isolated self with the community through the study of philosophy and theosophy, that path frequently led to art and literature. The role promised to the artist—above all the writer—was that of a prophet. He would, in time, become the spokesman and champion for his motherland, *Matushka Rus'*.[7]

Literature played a central role in Russian culture through the nineteenth and twentieth centuries. On the one hand, its evolution intensified the schism between the peasantry and the educated classes, creating two separate traditions, written and oral. That division not only was expressed in the form of two languages (folk and "refined"), but it was also based upon clear distinctions in subject matter. While the heroes and heroines of folklore and epic represented generalized traits, archetypal forms, aggregates of collective identity, Western literary genres of the period emphasized a concern with the individual.[8] On the other hand, literary production became increasingly an attempt on the part of the educated class to bridge the chasm between itself and the *narod*. But while literature was the principal political outlet through which the intelligentsia could galvanize public opinion for its programs, it also served as a vehicle for the creation of identity through a radical questioning of the very foundations of the self in its relationship to the collectivity—most particularly seen as a maternal force.

Literary themes revolved, not surprisingly, around the question of "how to live" *(kak zhit')*. The so-called "Hamlet Question," which haunted the tiny minority of educated Russians through the first half of the nineteenth century, was discussed in the context of the limitations which family, nature, and *rodina* placed upon the individual's quest for freedom from constraint; and it always came up against the problem of autocratic self-assertion. The question of the self was a "family problem," in which Mother Russia and Father Tsar fought over the loyalties of their intellectual children. It is precisely this issue which Alexander Pushkin outlined for future generations.

Pushkin's literary landscape is pastoral, a lived-in vista of villages and their inhabitants, of estates and their families. If self-knowledge comes to the individual, it usually originates in the community and is conceived in communal terms. But if the relation with nature is filial and harmonious, conflict arises elsewhere. Beginning with Pushkin, literature is charged with two opposing myths and images: The first one depicts the city, Saint Petersburg, associated with the impulse for state and individual self-aggrandizement; the second is that of the countryside, linked to the feeling of communion with the round of nature, with the warmth of family life, and with folklore, poetry, and the traditions of the *narod*.[9] Art is seen to emerge out of this latter domain, and its agent is woman.

It is therefore no accident that Pushkin gave his heroines the strength their masculine counterparts lacked. Pushkin was the first great writer to depict the nineteenth-century "intelligent" as the weak and divided son pursuing his self-interest or attempting to gain power over his fellows in order to confront the image of the death-dealing father-tsar: Only by returning to the motherland, Pushkin shows, could he be made whole again.

Pushkin himself made the journey from Saint Petersburg to Moscow and its countryside both metaphorically and physically. He bridged the gap between *rodina* and intellectual life by infusing a derivative literature based on Western models with the vitality of folklore and epic, popular language, and ritual, and by using the mythological paradigms contained in Russian folk culture to make his own work resonate with the myriad sounds emanating from that "Mother Lode." He fashioned a literary language from the foreign terms and stilted expressions of court life and infused it with the sounds of native speech.

Pushkin was born in 1799 into an aristocratic family. His upbringing was thoroughly in the French mold. Later, at Tsarskoe Selo, the school for the youth of the highest nobility, he continued to receive the education of a Western gentleman and began his brilliant career as a poet. His muse was a Sophianic one, erotic and melancholy. Tsarskoe Selo (which he named his *"rodina"* or "homeland") was haunted for him by the shade of a beautiful woman dressed in rags who appeared to give the boys and young men there "difficult advice." In his recollections of those days, he wrote about his attempts to evade her by escaping into the garden. But that garden was dominated by two statues: The male one was filled with pride and anger, like a tsar; the female one was beautiful and sensual, but also magical and perfidious, like a *rusalka*. The beautiful woman was also mistress of the garden; and her name was Fate.[10] Pushkin's later work would be permeated by the image of this demanding muse Mother Russia, wearing tattered clothing like a mistreated peasant woman.

Pushkin's production was prodigious, and the first major poem (begun in 1817), a mock fairytale, *Ruslan and Liudmila*, was already the work of a consummate poet. Written in the urbane and ironic tone of Aristo, it was intended to make fun of the eighteenth-century classical tradition by juxtaposing the earthly metaphors of peasant lore with those of a foreign literary convention. Already Pushkin was grappling with the hubris implicit in the Western tradition. The poem met with an uproar on the part of the court literati for its disrespectful mockery and barnyard imagery. The critics responded by denigrating his work as the product of a despised and abandoned folklore.[11]

If Pushkin's first major undertaking created a free and colloquial way of writing in opposition to the borrowed Western classical stiffness of Russian imitators, it represented the condition of his noble countrymen, as well—Russians in foreign dress. His next scandalous production, in 1819, also met with official displeasure. In his famous "Ode to Freedom," Pushkin was not simply mocking his compatriots' westernized sensibilities and unmasking their native roots in the process of displaying his own exuberant and playful poetic genius; he was taking on the autocrat. The poem announced that Russia was a land of whips and tyrants. Fraternizing with the young officers who had accompanied Tsar Alexander I to Paris after Napoleon's final defeat and who had absorbed during their stay there the liberal ideas of the French Revolution, Pushkin was being drawn into the growing storm of an aristocratic revolt.

The increasingly reactionary despotism of the once-liberal Alexander had dashed the hopes for reform, in the shape of a constitution, among the educated officer corps. The lively and iconoclastic poet, himself striving for creative freedom, shared their concerns. He warned the autocrat that he and his ilk would challenge the ruler to champion the motherland: "Despotic thief," he wrote, "upon your brow I read the curse of the *narod*."[12] In another poem, entitled "Noel" (1818), he again attacks the misuses of the autocracy, underscoring the Christological myth which it has discarded; in "The Village" (1819) he deplores his motherland's misery.[13] These works were circulated among his liberal friends but soon came to the attention of Alexander, who promptly exiled him. From that moment on, Pushkin would live under constant surveillance of the tsar.

Pushkin's enforced stay in the Caucasus resulted in a number of stories and poems, but his talents flourished after the return from the south and a protracted stay on his country estate at Mikhailovskoe. There Pushkin began a new life, and a new literature in which he would evoke the realities of Russian life. There he found his muse of Tsarskoe Selo in the guise of his aged nurse, Arina.

Arina Rodionova was the ruler of the estate, managing Pushkin's affairs as his careless mother had not. The relationship of the poet to the peasant woman was that of a son toward his own mother. In the long winter evenings when he chafed at his enforced exile, she was his sole companion. And like the mothers depicted in the epics, she seemed to take the part of the kindly teacher instructing her wayward and rebellious charge in the old wisdom of folklore. His days as the rampaging *bogatyr'* were over; chastened, he returned to the mother. It is through Pushkin's genius that the folktale was brought to the attention of the reading public as a respectable poetic form. "We have," he wrote, "a language of our own" expressing Russia's true features.[14]

During the long days at Mikhailovskoe, Pushkin not only listened to Arina's stories, which haunted him all his life, but he roved the countryside and attended fairs and festivals, making himself familiar with all forms of folk poetry: lyric, epic, "Spiritual Verse," dirge, riddle, proverb, charm, and marriage rite. He decided to use them as he would use his observations of village customs to construct the framework of his future literary production.[15]

In Mikhailovskoe between 1824 and 1826, Pushkin wrote the draft of his long "epic" masterpiece *Eugene Onegin*, and outlined his historical drama *Boris Godunov*. In *Eugene Onegin* we are introduced to the westernized nobleman, a *bogatyr'* without a cause, the individual later called "the Superfluous Man," who, like Godonov, the first "false tsar" in popular imagination, is not organically rooted in the *narod* and consequently cannot serve or render it fertile. Indeed, when he rediscovered the motherland on the estate ruled by his old nurse, Pushkin coined a new word: *prostonarodnost'*, to express his feelings about the sense of community and virtue embodied in the land and the peasantry living upon it. But his is not a literature about the life of the serfs; rather, his concern was to show how far their masters had strayed from a filial and defensive task to become an oppressive force. In *Eugene Onegin*, Pushkin presents his reader with the idle and alienated aristocrat; the *narod* he will not "save" is embodied in the persona of a gentry girl, to whom the poet gives the name of Tatiana, a synonym for Mother Earth in peasant lore and related to Shakespeare's queen of the fairies.

"Perhaps Pushkin would even have done better to call his poem *Tatiana* and not *Onyegin*, for she is indubitably the chief character," observes Dostoevsky in a eulogy to his venerated literary predecessor.[16] The story, which begins in Saint Petersburg, is a journey to the countryside: The westernized aristocrat Onegin is not raised, he is constructed in a foreign mold. His life of debauchery is like that of a puppet whose strings are pulled by autocratic fiat. He serves his maker as a courtier would; he is a Western decoration. But the tale begins with his sense of anomie and a concomitant desire to leave the city to claim an estate left to him by a recently deceased relative. In the country Onegin stands apart, a bored observer—a parasite as he had been in the capital.[17]

Soon, however, Onegin meets a neighbor, the youth Lenskii, fresh from his studies in Germany and filled with Romantic yearning. Unlike the egotistical and calculating rake Onegin, Lenskii expresses spontaneity and passion; but these too are filtered through Western categories of feeling and thought. Onegin does not take to the effusive candor and ardor of his neighbor. Lenskii's quest for fusion with nature and with woman, intellectualized though it be and limited by his claim to poetic genius, threatens the cold detachment of the hero, who is no more able to befriend than he is to love: "But friendship, as between our heroes, / can't really be; for we've outgrown / old prejudice; all men are zeros, / *the units are ours alone. / Napoleon's our sole inspiration.*"[18] Power and self-assertion through conquest are the dark shadows which are cast by the "icon" of Napoleon, whose persona Pushkin uses to illustrate the evils of Russian despotism as well as the Western ideology of the self.

Lenskii will act as the go-between to unite the Saint Petersburg aristocrat, created to resemble the tsar, with the all-sensitive and all-merciful Tatiana. It is as though Pushkin were obliquely suggesting the way in which the Russian intelligentsia moved from the cold rationalism of the Enlightenment, taught to them by the autocrat, Catherine II, to the nature philosophy of the Mystics and the Romantics, which in turn guided them to the rediscovery of the *narod* and showed them their role in "fusing" with it.

The soul of the *rod* and the *narod* is Tatiana. She is like Isis awaiting her mate. Tatiana, named for the earth, is made to embody all that is spontaneous and close to the rhythms of the soil. She is "whole," *tsel'naia*, depicted by Pushkin as a zoomorphic goddess.

Lenskii takes Onegin to visit the family, the Larins. There Tatiana, the muse, waits like life itself, fusing imagination, feeling, and sincerity undeformed by social convention and foreign culture: "She fell in love—the hour was fated ... / so fires of spring will bring to birth / a seedling fallen in the earth." But her groom is no match for this incarnation of the peasant goddess: "Lord Byron, with his shrewd caprices, / dressed up a desperate egoism / to look like sad romanticism."[19] It is early summer and the time for union, but nothing will come of it. Onegin's tyrannical egoism, like the tsar's oppressive city, produces wintery isolation and death, the tragedy of infertility rather than the renewal of life in nature's cycle. Pushkin commiserates with his heroine: "Tatiana dear, with you I'm weeping: / for you have, at this early date, / into a modish tyrant's keeping / resigned disposal of your fate. / Dear Tania you're condemned to perish."[20] Her mate is the invading Napoleon; he is the Western reflection of the despotic tsar who has conquered his own land rather than serving her in marriage.

Tatiana decides to declare her love to Onegin in a letter. But Onegin coldly demurs. His Romantic alter ego, on the other hand, the naive Lenskii, falls prey to the luring sister Olga. She is Tatiana's other self: her underworld aspect, the cruel *rusalka* who kills her suitors as Tatiana welcomes hers. The climax of the action occurs on Tatiana's name day, January second, the period of Koliada, of the death and rebirth of the sun. On her name day, Tatiana as represented by Pushkin is earth herself, the expression of the peasant world and of nature, the seeress who will predict the barren future. First Pushkin carefully underscores her close link with nature and *narod:* "Tatiana (profoundly Russian being, / herself not knowing how or why) / in Russian winters thrilled at seeing / the cold perfection of the sky."[21] She goes out with the peasant girls to tell fortunes in the bathhouse.

The peasant girls' prophecies are only a prelude to Tatiana's greater clairvoyance, which comes to her in a dream. She dreams of wandering in the woods through the winter "deathscape" of snowdrifts. Pursued by a bear, she is carried into a hut, where Onegin rules over a company of misshapen and hideous creatures. Onegin, who distorts nature, is also a freak; he reverses the natural order. He is Hades kidnapping Kore. While Tatiana yearns for marriage and union, Onegin seeks power, conquest. Lenskii enters to save the girl, and Onegin kills him. Not even the carrier of the Romantics' *Naturfilosofie* can melt the cold egocentricity and rationalistic desire for domination which inform Onegin's actions.

Tatiana's dream becomes reality on her name day, where Onegin appears only as an intruder, the messenger of winter and of death. First he breaks his friendship with Lenskii by spitefully flirting with the cold-hearted *rusalka* Olga. Lenskii responds by challenging him to a duel; Onegin has ruptured the union between man and woman, man and man. He deliberately ignores the unhappy Tatiana, and she recognizes the monstrous and hollow rapist of her dream. On the following day, Lenskii is killed by Onegin. The "great poet," worshipper of the goddess of love, is dead. He is a sacrificed Son-Consort, the Adonis who dies for the love of his perfidious and changeable mistress. His tomb is adorned by two intertwined trees through which a brook runs: The ploughman there delights to doze, / girl reapers as the streamlet flows / dip in their jugs."[22] Nature has placed him into her own pastoral mode! And this is precisely the fate Onegin wishes to avoid. Aspiring to mastery through standing over nature rather than yielding to her design, his murder of Lenskii is paradigmatic of the murder of the tsarevich by the tsar. Lenskii dies because he reminds Onegin too clearly of a fate he will not accept—a fate which tyrants attempt to deny through creating a monument to their deeds and thus detaching themselves from nature's cycle. But Onegin's defeat is announced by his housekeeper, who shows the girl around the now-empty place: "I pray God grant his soul salvation . . . down in our damp earth-mother's womb."[23]

With Onegin's departure, Tatiana, the country girl, Kore herself, nature's promise, is sent to the city to marry. In leaving the countryside, she enters the realm of Hades, leaving the land of the living, to rediscover her nightmare vision of artificially constructed beings inhabiting Onegin's hut. In Saint Petersburg she will become a "petrified" moon goddess: ". . . like the majestic moon she drives / among the maidens and the wives."[24] The artless maiden has now become the sovereign of an artful society, thus frozen into an unnatural posture. Now Pushkin identifies Tatiana with his own muse: She is Russia, and she is the eternal feminine debased by the tsars and their court; she is the goddess of love and life, the embodiment of art and all creation "westernized" beyond recognition and tormented in her chains.

While Tatiana assumes the sad role of ruling over a freakish society, Onegin is traveling abroad, ever evading the rootedness he fears. But when he returns to Saint Petersburg, he is in turn smitten by this divinity who rules over the Hades on the Neva. Though he arrives in spring, there is no rebirth in the underworld. His cold Tatiana is now married and a dutiful wife. Onegin, with "corpse-like feature," goes to find her through a hall "without a living creature." She sits there enthroned like a sorrowful Kore: "the princess, sitting peaked and wan / alone, with no ornament on / she holds a letter up, and leaning / cheek upon hand she softly cries. . . ."[25] The letter is from Onegin; he now declares his love, and she rejects him in turn. Eugene is "thunder-struck," destroyed and petrified by this female ruler of the underworld who (in sorrow) takes her revenge on those who did not respect her benign and life-affirming attributes.

In *Eugene Onegin*, then, Pushkin illuminates the conflict of city and country, tsar and *narod*, through the relationship which his "superfluous" hero develops with these respective poles of his existence. Western individualism reflected in the blend of rationalism and self-interest of the Enlightenment and the narcissism of Romantic longings for a spiritual homeland attained through art and philosophy are allied, in the persona of Pushkin's hero, with the autocratic impulse. Individualism, whether in Western or tsarist guise, means discontinuity with tradition and alienation from the life-giving forces of nature and community. Despotic rule over life can only result in death; for such tyranny on the part of man is merely hubris. Tatiana embodies the suffering of the *narod* rejected by her lover-ruler and yet mate. She is the muse of the poet and the life force which gives birth to and nourishes the collectivity. Exiled to the autocratic prison of Saint Petersburg, she can only perish and wreak her vengeance on her captors.

Tatiana became the model for countless heroines of Russian literature—from Tolstoi's Natasha in *War and Peace* and Dostoevsky's women-Amazons-victims to Chekhov's hopeful protagonists seeking deliverance from those unable to provide it. As the avatar of the *narod* awaiting her deliverer, Tatiana is a counterpoint to and context within which the weak and "superfluous" men of Russian literature play out their destinies. Superfluous noblemen not merely by their undefined social position between tsar and *narod*, but in the expression of an individualism at odds with Russian traditional collectivity, they bring to their women the burden of an egotism which serves only to prevent their necessary reunion.

The undertow of the novel is political. Disguised by the play of gentry protagonists, it is the tsar's power over his countrymen and -women which Pushkin contests. *Eugene Onegin* is concerned with the limits of individual self-assertion within the context of nature and *rodina*. In such later works as the play *Rusalka* (1832), Pushkin again underscores the danger of the individual's despotic disregard for women and nature—and for the *rodina* she represents. But the story in which that theme receives its most dramatic expression is called "The Queen of Spades" (1833). There the feminine assumes the guise of Yaga rather than the benign earth or Tatiana, the kind Vasilisa of folktale. And the hero worships no longer at the literary shrine of Byron, but at the more sinister military one of Napoleon. The man of letters cedes to the man of calculation and action.

The hero of this brilliant novella is not the "French" Eugene, but the German Hermann, a uniformed middle-class engineer. His ambitions are more clearly directed than those of Onegin, who chafed against the restraints of family and tsar. Hermann's would-be bride is not the kindly and "whole" *(tsel'-naia)* Tatiana but the withholding and chthonian Yaga, the old countess. While Onegin sought mastery through rape, Hermann contemplates murder. His escape in "The Queen of Spades" is not from the lure of the *rusalka* and the trap of marriage but from the ties to the mother and the death to which she condemns all her progeny.

The story begins with a winter gathering around a card table in Saint Petersburg. The presence of fate is immediately announced by one young aristocratic officer: His aged grandmother, the countess Anna Feodorovna, is said to hold the secret to the cards. The young men gathered together are playing a game she seems to rule; they are reckless and ready to succumb to their destiny. But Hermann, the calculating German, wants to rule fate rather than remain her pawn. He holds back and will not play. The grandson of the mysterious countess, amused at Hermann's reluctance, tells the curious story of the old woman's secret. In telegraphic fashion, Pushkin informs us about the countess's life: Now eighty years old, she had once lived at the court of Versailles, where she was accorded the epithet of the "Venus of Moscow." Her husband was by all accounts her servant and feared her. One day the beautiful countess lost heavily at cards and turned to the services of the famous magician the Comte de Saint Germain, who gave her the secret of three cards. "A fairy tale," observes Hermann.[26]

Pushkin has taken the reader into the land of the *skazka*

(fairytale) as well as into the period of the ancien régime. The countess is both the Empress Catherine illuminated by the city of light called Versailles and the archaic Yaga of folktale. She is, in short, the "Vénus Moscouvite" in Western dress. She dispenses her luck to those who play her game; like the Sophia of the Masonic lodges—with whose teachings Pushkin was quite familiar—she initiates men into her wisdom. But as the underworld Yaga of the *narod*, she does so only to seduce and kill or hold men in her thrall. She embodies the cycle of life. And Hermann, rashly approaching her in winter, the season of death, is her overproud victim.

"The old Countess*** was seated before the looking glass in her dressing room. Three lady's maids stood by her."[27] She is presented like a goddess surrounded by attendants—or three "Fates." She is also, like Baba Yaga, waited upon by her youthful aspect, a girl, here her ward Lizaveta, who sits at an embroidery frame, like the fairytale Vasilisa awaiting her mate. Into this "holy of holies" of female mysteries enters the grandson Tomskii ready to serve her. Tomskii approaches the old woman with a gift of Western novels. The countess asks for "something new." Her grandson responds with an offer of a Russian novel, to which she replies sardonically: "Are there such things?"[28]

The engineer is introduced to the countess-Yaga as a "novel" human being before the discussion about the literary genre. The foreign youth and the old *baba* will become the actors in the truly Russian "novel" which Pushkin is now writing: a folktale with a Romantic twist, the story of an epic quest but in a Western mode in which the hero kills the mother and breaks all sacred bonds of love to wrest from her the secret of life and power. In the countess's labyrinthine and old-fashioned mansion, Hermann enters to perform the "Western" act of brutal self-assertion.

While Tomskii brought together the engineer and countess in an initiatory manner like a Mason proposing another for entrance into a higher order, the function of the real go-between is assumed by the countess's ward, Vasilisa-Lizaveta. Like Tatiana, she waits for love. And like Tatiana, she is duped and rejected. Lizaveta, like Vasilisa of the Yaga tales, is obliged to perform the old woman's chores, but her martyrdom and obedience will in the end be rewarded with the hoped-for marriage. She is nonetheless the first to catch the spying Hermann, who comes to look at the house where his good fortune may lie. He arrives, like a folklore hero, at the door of the house of the Yaga-countess. No longer in the forest but just as dangerous, it is located in the wintery heart of Peter's city: "Some unknown power seemed to have at-tracted him to it. He stopped and began to look at the windows. At one he saw a head with long black hair, probably bent down over a book or a piece of work. The head was raised. Hermann saw a small, fresh face and pair of dark eyes. That moment decided his fate."[29]

Lizaveta is both Vasilisa and *rusalka* who acts in the service of Yaga to entice the youth inside. She is the principle of love as the old woman is the embodiment of death. The avaricious Hermann uses the girl to introduce himself into the house by feigning love, writing letters to her copied from German Romantic novels. Like both Lenskii and Onegin, he is all artifice. Successful in persuading the lovelorn Lizaveta to accord him a rendezvous in her room, located above that of her mistress, Hermann gains entry into the mysterious mansion. But Hermann schemes badly. It is winter when he sets out on his quest, a time which insures the defeat of the hero lured in by his greed.[30]

"Hermann passed through into the bedroom. Before an iconcase, filled with old-fashioned images, glowed a gold sanctuary lamp."[31] Two portraits in this shrine disclose the countess's double face: She is the young westernized "Venus," the dangerous beauty; and she is the icon-worshipping old Russian *baba*. She is alone; yet her husband is present, as though to decorate her chapel. Hermann must cross this sacred space in order to reach Lizaveta's room, where his proper initiation would involve love and eventual marriage. But Hermann seeks another kind of treasure and acts in bad faith. Rather than pass through this Yaga's hut in order to receive his bride, he remains hiding in the countess's chamber to challenge the old woman on her own ground by "marrying" her instead.

Pushkin parodies the Pentheus-like lover and his desire to see his beloved unveiled: "Looking quite yellow, the countess sat rocking to and fro in her chair, her flabby lips moving. Her dim eyes reflected a complete absence of thought and looking at her one would have thought that the awful woman's rocking came not from her own volition but by the action of some hidden galvanism." Suddenly she sees her visitor, and "an indescribable change came over her death-like face. Her lips ceased to move, her eyes came to life; before the countess stood an unknown man."[32]

The old lady, like a goddess of the waning moon (dressed in gold and silver), has no wealth to offer. But Hermann's perverted pride blinds him to the danger he courts. He falls at her feet as though she were a goddess and he a suppliant: "I entreat you by the feelings of a wife, a lover, a mother, by everything that is sacred in life, do not deny my request! Reveal your secret to me!"[33] Hermann, the Saint Petersburg construction himself, the engineer, asks to exchange the secret of life which the countess possesses as a woman, lover, wife, mother, for that of wealth, success, male autonomy. The old woman remains silent. Hermann, driven to despair, pulls out his pistol and screams: "You old witch . . . ! I'll force you to answer. . . ."[34] But the countess evades him, dying without uttering a word.

It appears that Hermann has failed. At the ball, Lizaveta, whom he betrays, had been warned by Tomskii: "This Hermann . . . is a truly romantic figure: he has the profile of a Napoleon, and the soul of a Mephistopheles. I should think that he has at least three crimes on his conscience."[35] The magical number three of folklore is used by Pushkin as a numerical framework for the action. The story is told in six sections: There are three main characters, the countess, Hermann, and Lizaveta; three maids surround her; three cards yield her secret. Hermann is armed with "three virtues"—thrift, moderation, and industry—and is made to carry three crimes on his head. It is three days before he encounters the countess after hearing about her secret. But while the number three suggests the spheres and attributes of the Great Goddess in folklore—of birth, maturity, and death, or the cycle of life—in this tale it arches out to entrap the egotistical youth: The division of the plot into six parts places Hermann's life under the number of ambivalence and trial.[36]

When Hermann finds that the countess has died, he runs to Lizaveta's room in a panic to tell her about his ambitions and the truth of his duplicious letters, rather than declaring the love he does not feel. "You are a monster," Lizaveta retorts, and notices at that moment that "he bore an astonishing resemblance to a portrait of Napoleon."[37] He too has invaded Muscovite and Holy Russia—the house of the countess—and Russia has receded before his armies just as the countess evades his lethal embrace in death. But the good maiden Lizaveta lets him escape.

Three days after the murder (it is, after all, the countess who rules the trinity with her cards), Hermann is mysteriously drawn to her funeral. He is rumored to be her natural son. Approaching the body, he sees the countess wink at him. She has broken her silence and now openly mocks the young man's vulgar designs, driving him to madness. Three old women appear at the side of the coffin. Hermann will be pursued by the fury of the countess. He is a matricide.

That night she appears to the half-delirious Hermann as a

woman in a white dress. Significantly, he mistakes her for his old wet nurse. The countess now materializes in a maternal form—the role to which he had alluded in his suppliant's prayer: Dressed in white, she comes as a bride, as well. She is merciful (unlike the youth) and agrees to fulfill his request on one condition—that he marry her ward, Lizaveta Ivanovna. He must espouse the feminine cycle of mother, wife, and lover and reject his demand for independence before he can benefit from the wealth the cards will bring. The three cards—a three, an ace, and a seven—assume feminine forms in Hermann's fevered mind: "At the sight of a young girl he would say: 'How shapely she is! Just like the three of hearts.'" The three "bloomed before him in the shape of some luxuriant flower, the seven took the appearance of a Gothic gateway, the ace—of an enormous spider."[38] But the ace is also a "pot-bellied man." The girl is both flower and gateway; the hag is both enveloping spider and its maternal or wealth-giving aspect containing the feminized or rich (pot-bellied) male.

Pushkin's trinitarian framework widens to include these other numbers, whose significance he draws from the science of numerology familiar to Masonic initiates. In that system, the number three represents the process of generation—the attributes of the fertility goddess. The number one, or ace, represents God and man's attempts to gain divinity. Seven is associated with the course of time and the movement from life to death, as well as the phases of the moon (before becoming the number of days of the Creation in Hebrew myth). As the Gothic gateway in Hermann's imagination, it represents the door to life and death. Indeed, the three and the seven are presented as the first and last cards of the sequence, suggesting the movement from generation or the realm of the goddess to the attempt at conquest over time, passing through God, the ace or one.[39]

For three nights in a row, Hermann shows up at the gambling tables. While he wins on the first two, on the third he bets his ace (the "spider")—and is conquered by the Queen of Spades, who seems to wink at him: "He was struck by an unusual likeness. . . . 'The old woman!' he shouted with terror."[40] The game continues as though Hermann had never played; the round of life proceeds without him, and he is destroyed by it: The individual who asserts himself over nature and woman provokes the very thing which he evades—the annihilation of the self.

Pushkin concludes this dramatic story in one short paragraph which reads like the last stanza of a *bylina* rather than the ending of a novel. The good (Lizaveta, Tomskii) are rewarded for their obedience, with marriage. Hermann, the rebel, the sinner, loses his reason, the very faculty he used to evade the countess's order. In Room 17 of Obukhov Hospital, he is condemned to repeat the names of the cards which led to his doom. The number three is missing. He is alone. The sequence has been reversed from one to seven. The cycle of the goddess interrupted by Hermann traps him, like a spider's web.[41] The spider is known to consume her mate after coupling with him, like the Great Mother Goddesses of archaic times.

The Napoleonic individual, like his literary and narcissistic predecessor in *Eugene Onegin*, is doomed by his pride. His self-assertion is at odds with nature's order and the *rodina's* collective and familial customs. In the face of Mother Russia, Pushkin shows the westernized individual perishing. But if the motherland will not tolerate such egotism, what of the tsar, the autocrat? Can he afford to break out of her sphere? In his great epic poem "The Bronze Horseman," Pushkin shows the individual facing the "Father," whose laws are as restrictive as those of *Matushka Rus'*.[42]

In 1825, the small group of officers whose company Pushkin had left when he was sent into exile decided to challenge the autocrat directly by calling for a constitution and, parenthetically, for the emancipation of the serfs. Alexander I had died suddenly and was succeeded by his brother Nicholas, known for his Prussian and reactionary leanings. The Decembrist revolt was the first Russian revolution. But it was a gentry revolt, and though the rebels called for freedom from autocracy, they did so with their own interests in mind.[43]

Pushkin was not involved in the uprising, but later he announced that had he been allowed to return to Saint Petersburg, he too would have participated. He continued to correspond with the exiled leaders, who were all his friends or acquaintances. Since political action was denied to him, Pushkin contented himself with the role of chronicler of the age. Not surprisingly, in two of his major works, *The Captain's Daughter* and "The Bronze Horseman," he meditates upon the relationship of the individual to the autocrat.[44]

Pushkin wrote "The Bronze Horseman" at a time when he felt the greatest need to dissemble in order to get his work past his censor, Nicholas. Married to the beautiful Natalia Goncharova, whom he called his "Madonna," he soon discovered that she was closer to a malevolent *rusalka*, dragging him into the life of the imperial court. When writing about his existence in the capital during this period (1831–1836), he observed that his life was "nothing at all"—words he used to describe the unhappy hero of his mock epic poem, the clerk Eugene.[45] Riddled with debts from the ever-growing expenses of court life, Pushkin, who now wrote for a living, could not have felt more like a bureaucrat, a courtier, a clerk at the service of the state constructed at the cost of incredible suffering and slavery by the great Peter.

"The Bronze Horseman" turns the traditional themes of the *bylina* on their head: The *bogatyr'*-ruler, Peter, whom Pushkin claims to admire as the father of a glorious Russian empire, is nonetheless represented as attacking his land and its inhabitants rather than defending them. His antagonist is the angry river Neva; but in attempting to swallow up the creation of the proud tsar, she punishes his people and leaves him unscathed. The story centers on the confrontation of a poor clerk, Eugene, with the statue of the tsar on his rearing bronze steed trampling the serpent of ancient tradition. In *Eugene Onegin* and "The Queen of Spades," Pushkin showed how the self-assertive and egotistic hero who challenges the feminine order of nature perishes tragically. In "The Bronze Horseman," the personal tragedy of the educated and alienated nobleman, the superfluous one, assumes the form of an apocalypse.[46] Onegin's and Hermann's defeat resulted in isolation and madness, for they broke the vital and life-giving ties of communion with woman. In the poem, Peter's victory over the Neva River and her child, the suffering and tormented clerk who carries the burden of the tsar's reforms, ends in the cataclysmic revenge of nature. Doomed to perish as a martyr to the autocrat's order, Eugene anticipates the rise of a revolutionary intelligentsia drawn from classes closer to the soil. He is the first of the breed whose successors will flourish in the universities.

The statue of Peter stands like an idol over Saint Petersburg. His is a pagan image—for the Orthodox church had stigmatized the making of statues, which it associated with pagan cults. Certainly Pushkin was well aware of the injunction and of the irony: the Anti-Christ tsar of the Old Believers, rearing over his "foreign" city, his likeness commissioned by Catherine II, a German tsarina. In the Old Believer tradition, as well as in popular lore, Peter the heretic was linked with the vampire.[47] The vampire tsar draws the blood of all living things and grows each day more powerful from his victims. If the Yaga image of the countess in "The Queen of Spades" reveals the hoarding nature of the angry chthonian goddess, Peter, in "The Bronze Horseman," completed in the same year, reflects that of the warrior as a predatory feeder.

Pushkin begins the poem with an (ironic) ode to the pride of the warrior tsar:

> There, by the billows desolate,
> He stood, with mighty thoughts elate, . . .
> And thus He mused: 'From here, indeed
> Shall we strike terror in the Swede;
> And here a city by our labor
> Founded, shall gall our haughty neighbor'
> 'Here cut'—so Nature gives command—
> Your window through on Europe. . . .[48]

The tone is Biblical. Peter creates ex nihilo, like Jehovah. His cutting of a window to the West is dictated not by nature but by the tsar's will; in building his city, Peter imprisons her in granite: Pylons are sunk into the swampy ground to support his artificial production. The city is torn from the belly of nature.

When the story is told, Peter is long dead. Cast in bronze, he rides through the motherland with the sheer force of his demonic will. The Neva, on the other hand, continues to flow and will soon surge out of the embankment which surrounds her power over life and death. But before Pushkin begins to describe her assault, he introduces the reader to a new antihero. We first meet Eugene against the background of the river's anger and restlessness. The Neva is depicted as the *rusalka*, a deadly enchantress. Indeed, Pushkin begins Part One of the poem with the russification of his city's name: Against the background of the Neva, it is no longer a Germanic Saint Petersburg but the Slavic Petrograd, "City of Peter." In this section, the river and Eugene emerge to challenge the mighty autocrat. The poet gives him the same name as his condemned aristocrat, but this clerk is also the product of the tsar's reforms: alienated, isolated, a prisoner of the vampiric ruler. He is, in fact, a mock hero. Pushkin now lays the blame for the anomie of his two Eugenes directly on the monstrous pride of their creator: "Our hero—somewhere— served the State; / He shunned the presence of the great . . . / Cared not of forebears dead and rotten, / Or antique matters long forgotten."[49]

The clerk Eugene has been forcibly wrested from his *narod* and from the *rod* which gave him birth. With no past and no future, he appears to be as artificial a creature as the mock city in which he lives. But, unlike his noble and Romantic prototype, the young bureaucrat is a child of the Neva more than of the tsar. Like a peasant or folktale hero, he is on his way to visit his fiancée, Parasha, who lives in the middle of the river on one of the Green Islands. Like the hero of the ballad and epic, he must cross the river to reach her. But the Neva has been distorted and maddened by the tsar's pride, and Eugene is made to suffer for the sins of the father like the unhappy tsarevich of history and legend. She will not give life, will not unite the lovers. To spite the tsar, she will separate them. Like the *rusalka*, or Yaga, the river drowns the artificial city and its inhabitants. The girl Parasha will be the victim of her rage as life itself seems to fall into the grasp of a deadly impotence, a witch's revenge on those who deny her power. For although Peter has died, his legacy haunts the city with death and sterility. Parasha the maid is a folktale character, too. Closer to the *narod* than Tatiana, she lives in a hut with her widowed mother, surrounded by the greenery of the island. She embodies the life-affirming countryside carried in the waves of the maternal Neva but overshadowed by the threatening and martial statue of the tsar.

Peter, whose omnipotent image is that of the defender, Saint George, is ironically powerless before the fury of nature he has aroused. So too are his royal successors. For the Neva is not just nature tethered to the will of the dead autocrat; she is quite clearly the symbol of the *rodina* who took her revenge during the reign of Catherine II in the peasant rebellion of Pugachev, a Pretender tsar. During the apocalyptic flood through which nature casts judgment on the work of rulers, Eugene finds refuge in the square where the statue of the emperor stands. The clerk sits astride one of the stone lions standing like sentries, and faces the tsar; and while he clings to the wild beast—nature untamed—he thinks: "Alas, too close to the wild water, / A paintless fence, a willow tree, / and there a frail old house should be / Where dwelt a widow, with a daughter / Parasha—and his dream was she!"[50]

But it is not nature that the clerk blames for his misfortune; rather, he defies the bronze idol who is the source of this tragedy. Seated astride his wild mount, Eugene is the rebel carried by the roaring river to avenge her. The all-powerful but commonly hidden force of the river teaches him rebellion, like the *rodina*, her champions. Finally she recedes, sated, and: "Stole back, and left her booty stranded / And unregarded. So a bandit / Bursts with his horde upon a village / To smash and slay, destroy and pillage. . . ."[51] Pugachev, the Pretender, is the bandit; the river is the *narod*, and Eugene learns fury from her.

When the waters calm down, he goes to cross the river to find his fiancée. But all is gone, just as he had feared, and he goes mad, returning to the river which had claimed his bride like an inconsolable child to his mother. He sleeps upon her embankment like a Holy Fool. Only through insanity and rebellion, through suffering and death, can he evade the cold spell of the City of Peter and return to nature, his mother. She has reclaimed him from service to the autocrat to serve her ends. His torment transforms him into another being. Servant of the Neva who carries his bride, the lowly clerk now goes to the statue of the tsar as a revolutionary challenging his power with his own pitiful weakness: He shakes his fist at the autocrat. But the threat of this maddened and miserable underling must be a serious one, for it causes the bronze tsar to come to life and pursue him on his fiery steed. Peter, the rationalizing despot, the bringer of Western technology and habits, is transformed by Pushkin into a figure of folklore—that very element which the tsar had attempted to eradicate in his newly reconstructed secular state. The geometricized city of the tsar-innovator now appears to be dominated by the fantastic, awesome, and yet ridiculous character from a *bylina* or mock epic who terrorizes its most apparently insignificant and demented of inhabitants:

> With arm outflung, behind him riding
> See, the bronze horseman comes, bestriding
> The charger, clanging in his flight.
> All night the madman flees; no matter
> Where he may wander at his will,
> Hard on his track with heavy clatter
> There the bronze horseman gallops still.[52]

The phantom tsar must hound the poet-clerk, turned Holy Fool; his revolt is allied with and analogous to that of the river. But he does not catch him! And it is to the Green Islands—like the magical island of folklore—that the terrified and broken youth runs to escape the statue's wrath. The maternal river carrying the hut inhabited by Parasha and her mother takes him to his final resting place—in Mother Moist Earth. Eugene has returned home. As in *Eugene Onegin*, spring brings death rather than renewal. The tsar's will has been done. But nature's revolutionary cycle spares no one; out of the martyred body of the poor poet mocked by Pushkin as a clerk will emerge others better prepared than he to chase, in turn, the marauding tsar from his stone pedestal.

The theme of masculine pride is explored quite pointedly in *Eugene Onegin* and "The Queen of Spades" in the context of Western cultural and intellectual challenges to a Muscovite and peasant tradition shaped by an archaic familial order. In "The

Bronze Horseman," this clash between the individualistic ethos of the West and the collectivist one of an agrarian society is explicitly politicized in the form of an opposition between tsar and *narod*. The poem was rejected by the censors, and though it was published posthumously in 1837, it became accessible in its complete form only in the twentieth century. In it Pushkin illustrates that at the heart of all distortion in the psyche of his fellow countrymen lies the demand for power over nature and domination over fate embodied in the persona of the autocrat, whose militaristic rule breeds psychic and social sterility or impotence and courts revolt from the peasant as well as the enlightened children of Mother Russia. The infertility and isolation engendered by Onegin and Hermann in their conflict with woman and family and their refusal to adopt a filial piety or humility before the force of life are a sin placed at the feet of their creator, who best exemplifies it: Idle and westernized noblemen, Germanicized engineers, depersonalized clerks, debased and rejected maidens, "murdered" *baby*—these are the inhabitants of Peter's kingship over a bridled nature. But this patriarchal bondage is consistently challenged through its internal psychic dynamic— the Oedipal struggle. The Muscovite murder of the tsarevich will be avenged: The son will wrest power from the father and embrace the *rodina* himself.[53] The debates of the 1840s and 1850s among the educated gentry will lay the psychological, moral, and social groundwork for the creation of an active and rebellious intelligentsia. But *Matushka Rus'*, the land and its people, will determine the identity and the direction of the creative impulses and intellectual discourse of its artists and thinkers.

CONCLUSION

The Mother as Russia

> I know why it is you weep, mother mine.
>
> —N. A. NEKRASOV, *"Rodina"*[1]

In *Eugene Onegin*, Tatiana, sentenced like Kore to dwell in a Hades called Saint Petersburg, predicts her sad fate:

> " . . . I am doomed to perish, yet to die
> through him is sweetness' self. In grumbling
> I find no sense; the truth is this,
> it's not in him to bring me bliss."[2]

Tatiana's prophecy of abandonment is Pushkin's warning that the rootless westernism of Mother Russia's educated sons will betray all that is best in the motherland, a theme taken up and developed by Fyodor Dostoevsky in the last half of the nineteenth century. In his "Pushkin Speech" (1880), Dostoevsky points out that Onegin lives as an exile and a wanderer in the very heart of his native land. Tatiana, on the other hand, is the embodiment of Russia. As Kore, the daughter, she has the power to reunite him with Mother Russia through marriage: "Here is contact with her own . . . people, with their sanctities." The tragedy of Onegin and Tatiana is that "she passed through his life unrecognized by him and unappreciated."[3] Yet Russian woman, Dostoevsky tells us, the guardian of life-affirming and altruistic values, was a "great power" leading to the "principal and most salutary regeneration of Russian society," because she drew her strength from the "sacramental" soil, the source of rebirth. But her qualities of gentleness were spurned and ignored; she was a "martyr for the

Russian man"—like Tatiana and like the motherland, her analogue.[4]

In his prophetic novel of revolution *The Possessed* (1872), Dostoevsky presents us with another Tatiana. No sweet and romantic maiden from the gentry, his Maria Lebiadkin is deformed, wounded, beaten. Like Tatiana she is clairvoyant; like her she predicts her own ruin. The "simple-minded" cripple whose name, Lebiadkin, refers to the swan, is the abandoned and reviled wife of the intellectual Nicholas Stavrogin (whose name means "cross" and "horn," suggesting images of Christ and the devil). Like Onegin, he suffers from an anomie which has its source in the "disease" of westernization, with its stress on individualism. Maria, on the other hand, is a "traditional" Russian woman. We see her sitting at a table with a candlestick, a song book, a mirror, and a crust of bread. As she lays out the worn cards, she begins to tell her fortune: "It all comes out the same . . . a journey, a villain, someone's perfidy, a deathbed. . . ." She goes on to recall a meeting in a convent with a woman atoning for making prophecies who asks her the meaning of the Mother of God. Maria replies, "She's the great Mother, the hope of the human race." By her answer, Maria reveals her own nature as Kore, who, like Tatiana, can lead the alienated back to the maternal land they had forsaken. The prophetess drives that point home: "The Mother of God is our great mother earth and there's great happiness from man in that. . . . And once you've soaked the earth a foot deep with your tears, you'll rejoice right away. . . . There's such a prophecy."[5]

Maria, called an "extraordinary dreamer" who perishes at the hands of the corrupt and westernized revolutionaries, is, Dostoevsky suggests, the soul of Russia—a Holy Fool whose enigmatic pronouncements puncture the logic of the talkative and autocratic intellectuals around her husband. She unmasks Nicholas as an Anti-Christ, a Grishka Otrepiev, the Polish-backed false tsar of Russia's Time of Troubles. But she is also an expression of Mary, the Mother of Christ ("the Swan"), who waits in vain for her savior and whose child—real or imaginary, but the fruit of a "damned" union—dies at birth. Maria embodies Russia's *dvoeverie:* She is Vasilisa the Wise Maiden, the swan-*rusalka* who tells fortunes. She is Kore, but she is also Demeter, Mother Moist Earth of the peasantry, searching for her true tsar to deliver her from barrenness and oppression. She is, in short, the icon of Mother Russia abandoned and matryred by those self-willed intellectuals who claim to be her champions and yet, like petty autocrats, despise her. Burned by the ardor of the revolutionary intelligentsia, Maria Lebiadkin shares a fate not dissimilar to that of Tatiana, frozen into an unnatural pose in icy Saint Petersburg. Both embody Russia's rejected and yet life-giving soul. In *The Possessed*, Dostoevsky warns the educated class that as self-professed defenders of *Matushka Rus'* they must, like Ilya Muromets, return to Mother Earth to regain a meaningful identity and invincible strength, else they will lead her to a cataclysm, which will engulf them, as well. Theirs must be a kenotic devotion expressed in the assumption of Christ's burden *(podvig)*. Only then can they avoid a false and pernicious pride.[6]

In the decade after Pushkin's death, the educated gentry, seeking to revise the role of the ruler and make room for their own political ambitions, rallied around the *rodina* and, while attempting to define her nature, presented themselves as her filial champions. Those who stood on the side of European reform, the Westernizers, hoped to wrest her from the grip of the tsars through the philosophical and social theories of the West. Conversely, the traditionalists or Slavophiles saw Russia's greatness in the revival of her native institutions and pointed to the peculiar notion of collectivity *(sobornost')* through which "Holy Russia" united her children and rescued them from a sterile individualism. By the latter part of the nineteenth century, the image of Russia as a mother suffering under the yoke of the autocrat, deserted and maimed but kind and self-sacrificial, appeared widely in the writings of the intelligentsia. The turn to the land as mother emerged against a background of social and psychological dislocation produced by the tsar-mandated modernization of an agrarian society. Both Westernizers and Slavophiles, like their successors the Populists, saw in Russia's cultural and social backwardness the promise of a great and "fertile" truth delivering humanity at large from the evils of history and uniting the individual and the collectivity—as in the image of the Matrioshka—in a harmonious whole. The intelligentsia assumed the role of the "Humiliated Christ," sacrificing their personal ambitions for the salvation of their motherland. But the guide to that reunion with the *rodina* and its promise of an "earthly paradise" would be woman, peasant woman, in particular.

The persona of woman as priestess and redeemer, the chief repository of virtue in the form of agape, is central to Russian literature of the nineteenth and twentieth centuries, a literature which served as the principal outlet for the political, social, and religious aspirations of the educated classes. The desire for a woman savior is expressed in a constant adulation of the ethical strengths of the good woman and the refusal to consider the virtues of male heroism. Male identity is perceived as precarious, contingent, existing only in the ethereal world of ideas rather than rooted in the "real" world. Woman, on the other hand, is regarded as the essence of stability, of life, of growth, of *lichnost'* (individuality) itself. She is "whole" *(tsel'naia)*, while man is neurotic, torn.[7]

Russian literature to the present day repeats the theme of the prodigal son's return to the motherland for absolution, empowerment, and rebirth. The mythic pattern—explored in the preceding chapters—behind this gravitational pull is vividly expressed by three of Russia's most prominent writers, whose work, conveying the concerns of individuals in a society in turmoil, spans the sixty-year period before and after the 1917 Revolution. Leo Tolstoi, Maxim Gorky, and Alexander Solzhenitsyn, like Dostoevsky before them, speak in the voice of the prophet. Each calls for a return to the mother as the symbol of the *rodina* in order to find a new moral and social order and challenge the old one. Each points to the figure of the poor or peasant mother's qualities of self-sacrifice as the source or the repository of all values. And each attempts to evade—or cover—the pride against which Pushkin and Dostoevsky had warned by invoking the kenotic ethos.

Tolstoi's short story "Father Sergius" (1911), written toward the end of his long life, invokes the mother-son relationship with special clarity.[8] With the story of a journey from Saint Petersburg into the depths of the countryside, Tolstoi takes up the Onegin theme of the "superfluous man." His hero, Kasatskii, a brilliant young Imperial Guards officer unable to find sufficient outlet for his overbearing ambition and thwarted by the autocrat in his private life, as well, leaves Saint Petersburg society to enter a monastery. Assuming the name of Father Sergius, but still unable to tame his pride, he decides to retreat to a cave hermitage. Having become known as a miracle worker, he is seduced by one of his suppliants. Humiliated, he leaves the hermitage to turn to his lonely childhood friend, now a poor but kindly widow, who instructs him in the true nature of humility. He leaves her to end his life in Siberia, cultivating a garden, looking after the sick, and teaching children.

The undisguised didacticism of the story highlights the mythic pattern we have observed. Kasatskii's initial attempts to unite himself to what he calls the "high deal" of masculine power embodied in the autocrat are dashed by Tsar Nicholas's tyranny, expressed in his sexual possessiveness—here over Kasatskii's fiancée. But like Pushkin's Onegin, Kasatskii is infected with the disease of autocracy and responds by leaving the hierarchical order of the state, the "military band" of the Imperial Guards, in order to challenge *Batiushka Tsar'* in the monastery as "Father" Sergius—removed and aloof but, unlike the ruler, saintly, as well. The church, however, is tainted with the autocrat's shadow (Tolstoi himself was excommunicated for his heretical ideas). In descending to the cave hermitage, Sergius leaves the world of men in a still false and egotistical attempt to defy the power of the autocrat by isolation from others.

The cave, the locus for the holy father's temptations, leads to his rebirth. Just as the world of the autocrat challenged him sexually in order to denigrate him, so in the world of the mothers two *rusalki* or seductresses threaten his hard-won aloofness with their demands for a "Dionysian" self-obliteration. He propitiates the first with a symbolic castration, chopping off his finger to prevent himself from succumbing to her. But he fails in his second temptation. His pride is tamed, and his isolation is broken. To expiate his sin, which is itself a sign of impending grace, he cuts his hair, dons peasant clothing, and leaves the hermitage to descend again—this time beyond the cave and into the countryside, to Mother Earth. Only after this final fall, the acknowledgment of his humanity, is he prepared to be reborn from the male world of aggressive power and individualism into the sphere of the *rodina*, where the peasantry appear to merge in an affective collectivity under the aegis of the mothers. As he contemplates suicide by a river bank, he sees, in reverie, his own mother's house in the country and his childhood companion Pasha, sad and rejected like Tatiana for her simplicity. "They were all boys together," he recalls, "and she was being brought to join them. And they had to play with her, and it was boring. She was silly." He remembers how this "male band" teased and tormented her and "made her show them how she could swim. She lay on the floor and went through the motions and they laughed and made fun of her." The gentle Pasha, who shows the boys how to swim, will teach Sergius how to ford the river—like the Puchai of the epics—which threatens to swallow up those who approach her with excessive pride. "He dreamt that an angel came to him and said: 'Go to Pashenka and learn from her what you must do, how you have sinned and how you can be saved.' "[9]

Old and close to poverty, Pashenka resembles the good Yaga in her cramped quarters, where she will initiate Sergius into her cult of generosity, self-sacrifice, maternal solicitude, and abhorrence of aggression. It is a gospel of unstinting love and appears in stark relief against the male world of the tsar and the monastic fraternity. Pashenka, who asks for nothing in return for her kindness, has no pride. "I know nothing and I would like you to teach me," Sergius implores her. When she takes him in he muses: "Pashenka is all that I should have been and was not. I lived for people pretending it was for God, while she lives for God and thinks she is living for people. . . ."[10] Reborn in Pashenka's house and armed with her gospel of non-resistance to evil, Sergius is free to wander through the motherland in communion with her peasant children rather than rising over them like an autocrat. Through his descent into the life and ethos of the mothers, Sergius gains the power he has so long sought: Taking up the tsar's rejected kenotic burden, he becomes morally superior to the ruler.

In his descent from the masculine world of the state and society into the victimized and humbled one of the motherland, Sergius gains a superiority of his own in the name of the mother who creates rather than the father who merely disposes. Tolstoi's protégé, Alexis Peshkov, alias Maxim Gorky, consecrated as the father of Socialist Realism, was closer to the *rodina* by birth, taking up his pseudonym, meaning "bitter," to vindicate the destiny of his beloved grandmother, who died a homeless beggar. Whereas Father Sergius, like his creator, an aristocrat, finds self-affirmation through a turn to the nurturing motherland, Gorky, who came directly from that realm, appeared, through his own veneration of mothers, to express the ethos of the peasantry and to transform their suffering into a revolutionary force which could, more effectively than Father Sergius's, overturn the autocrat. What Tolstoi's hero does for the sake of personal salvation, Gorky's characters perform for the collectivity.

In *Childhood* (1913), dedicated to his grandmother, Gorky presents us with a description of life among the lower classes. His grandparents are urbanized peasants. Gorky contrasts his kindly, meek, and generous grandmother to his cruel, self-willed, and greedy grandfather. Like an autocrat in his domestic realm, the peasant-turned-tradesman is subject to tantrums during which he beats and abuses his old wife. Their relationship repeats that between the tsar and the *rodina*. Like Russia, the family is divided by a *dvoeverie*. The grandmother prays to her goddess Mary to protect her from abuse. She addresses her as though she were a pagan Great Mother, mistress of the Tree of Life ("Fount of all joy, beauty inexpressible, like an apple tree in full bloom . . ."), or a divinity of the domestic fires and of the skies ("Light of my soul, guardian of my hearth, sun of my heaven, so bright, so gentle . . ."). The whole world appears alive and interconnected to her, and everything in it is sacred.[11] The grandmother, whose endurance and humility are sustained by the underground cult of female divinities, is described by Gorky as a wise priestess who tells the child fairytales.

The grandfather, on the other hand, calls this woman a "witch" and rages against her as though trying to tame a force far more powerful than he. His God is a despot, and his stories are "true accounts," not fables. Like the tsar, the grandfather's God lives far away. Like a warrior, He is terrible to those who sin against Him: "For him God was a raised sword, a lash over the heads of the wicked."[12] Clearly Gorky's grandparents recapitulate the imposition of conquering and predatory male divinities upon ancient fertility cults dominated by women. Grandmothers' mythology reflects the image of the Matrioshka. It stresses nurturing and encompasses the diversity of life. It protects and also seeks protection from assailants. There is no room here for a strong father, only a son willing to sacrifice his life in the cause of her continuous creation and recreation.

But if Gorky saw himself as a son, defending his grandmother against her husband by arousing Mother Russia against the autocrat, he did so by redefining the relationship of son to mother in his most influential novel, *Mother* (1906). In this work, which was adopted soon after its publication as an official Soviet tract and later was pronounced a model for all Soviet Realism, the icon of the mother is given over to the service of the son. He teaches her rather than following her guidance. Like the votive towels embroidered with the image of the Great Goddess, *Mother* "covers" a political program with its ancient "numinous" powers. For the pastoral myth expressing Russia's nature as a collectivity rooted in the soil was challenged and betrayed— that is, used for the sons' purposes—by her Soviet champions seeking to restructure an agrarian society. Although no woman appears among the fathers—Marx, Engels, Lenin—as in *Mother* the maternal myth was appropriated by the Soviet regime to connect the nation on an affective level, and the party itself assumed a maternal guise.[13] Not surprisingly, among the first successes of the Soviet cinema, so effectively used as a means to raise popular consciousness, are two films whose titles and content invoke archaic ties: Pudovkin's *Mother* (1926), a dramatization of Gorky's ponderously didactic novel, served to consolidate the gains of the 1917 Revolution; and Dovzhenko's *Earth* (1930), evoking the cult of the soil through its lyrical imagery, was aimed to lead the peasantry into collectivization.

Maria Lebiadkin's prophecy of death and betrayal in *The Possessed* was fulfilled. Already in the late 1920s writers such as

Zamyatin, Pilnyak, and Bulgakov, among others, were issuing dramatic warnings against the perfidy of the new rulers and depicting the destruction of the human soul and, analogously, that of the motherland. They were silenced under Stalin, but their concerns were repeated with courageous forcefulness in the 1960s by the most famous of contemporary Russian dissidents, Alexander Solzhenitsyn, a leader among the sizeable group of "Russophiles" or nationalists echoing nineteenth-century Slavophile and Populist beliefs.[14]

Solzhenitsyn's short story "Matriona's Home" (1963) is the best-known example of a "revolutionary traditionalism" to emerge during that decade in response to the massive and heartless industrialization of the Soviet Union and the shift of its population from the black earth of the countryside to the concrete-block cities.[15] Like his predecessor Tolstoi, Solzhenitsyn the intellectual descends into the depths of the sacrosanct soil in order to denounce Russia's rulers. He does so by evoking the moral superiority of that guardian of the Russian soul, the peasant mother. Indeed, the Soviet regime, having first vigorously denounced the *baby* ("God-cursed" by Christian missionaries in Kievan *Rus'*), gave up on them and permitted older women to continue traditional religious practices. The village, almost untouched as a microcosm of prerevolutionary Russian life, is still inhabited by an aging peasantry tending their gardens and looking after grandchildren.[16] By depicting individuals in the context of ancient myth and modern reality rather than the rationalized and progressive future of Socialist Realism, Solzhenitsyn attacks the very basis of Soviet literary convention, through which the regime aspires to mold the social life and psychological outlook of the population.[17] In contrast to Gorky's *Mother*, Matriona is the male protagonist's mentor.

The hero, like Solzhenitsyn himself, is a mathematician. Like the author, he returns from a labor camp to teach in a remote village in the "innards" of the motherland. Like Tolstoi's Father Sergius, the "Social Man" betrayed by the political order, he wants to efface himself, to lose himself "in deepest Russia . . . if it is still anywhere to be found."[18] The train, a symbol in nineteenth-century literature of the crushing impact of modernization on traditional values, brings him to the station of Torfoprodukt (Peat Product). This, Solzhenitsyn suggests, is the end of the road for Russia as a humane community. It is a fabricated name, referring to products rather than human beings. In his search for lodgings, the protagonist turns to a woman, who offers him milk. The mathematician's descent from the heights of intellect to the state's labor camps, and from the train to the station Torfoprodukt, is, like that of Father Sergius, an escape from a male world of oppression to the female one of nurture. The "milk-giver," like the female helper in the fairytale, leads him into the countryside to a village, where a destitute widow, Matriona, lives alone. Her house is dilapidated, but it is the antithesis of Torfoprodukt, for it expresses her humanity and genuine warmth. The house sits within the fenced confines of garden and yard, Matrioshka-like, large enough to contain an entire *rod* or extended family. Like the ailing land, she too is ill, condemned and close to perishing. Solzhenitsyn presents her as Russia's soul and restorative moral force. The mathematician comes to her for regeneration. He finds her, like Yaga in the fairytale, lying on the *pech'* in a room overgrown with plants. Her sole companion is a stray cat taken in out of pity. The house, which, like Yaga's hut, contains all life commingled, is also alive with the rustling of mice and cockroaches.

Matriona greets her prospective boarder as she does all those who enter her house with "some good-natured words. . . . They begin with a warm throaty gurgle, the sort of sound grandmothers make in fairy tales."[19] She agrees to share her home with the mathematician. He, in turn, learns about her misfortunes: Widowed during the war, her children dying in infancy, she fell ill and was dismissed without a pension from the collective farm where she worked for twenty-five years. Betrayed by the state, she has spent her time grappling with an indifferent bureaucracy to receive her dead husband's pension. Yet despite her physical weakness, suffering, and financial hardship, she is unfailingly generous to others more fortunate than she. Her lack of greed is set against the men and women who take and hoard in imitation of the state dominated by the phase of "socialist primary accumulation." She is an outcast. The villagers, particularly the old peasant Faddei, take advantage of her good nature. With his axe, Faddei appears to incarnate the brutality and rapacity of the Soviet regime and of Russian men.

Despite his own faith in Orthodoxy, Solzhenitsyn insists on describing Matriona's charity and goodness as emerging from a religion older than Christianity: "Her strongest beliefs were superstitions," says the mathematician. And yet, her guest observes, "she had fewer sins on her conscience than her gammy-legged cat." Like the peasants' Mother Earth, she allows her children to exploit her, and like her she dies for the well-being of others. Forced by Faddei to provide lumber for his daughter, Matriona's ward, she watches the mutilation of her home: "It was plain to

see that they were wreckers, not builders, and that they did not expect Matriona to be living there very long."[20] The disfigurement of Matriona's *dvor* (household and yard) by the male band is a prelude to the tragic accident which will claim her life. As though sensing disaster, the mathematician asks his landlady to pose for a photograph sitting at the loom. The camera reproduces an icon: the epiphany of Matriona as the Great Mother Goddess illuminated by the rays of the "red" sun. It is her final appearance. In helping the men transport the wood to another site, Matriona is killed by a train. The accident, Solzhenitsyn implies, is a metaphor for the catastrophe of Russian history. Matriona's mutilated body is Russia maimed. Her tragic destiny is determined by men driven by the crudest of material impulses. But the martyred Matriona's ethos continues to challenge that of the state. In her selfless devotion to her fellows, in her lack of desire for material gain, she is, Solzhenitsyn concludes, the only true Communist. He ends with a proverb: "We had lived side by side with her and never understood that she was the righteous one without whom . . . no village can stand
Nor any city
Nor our whole land.[21]

Like the maligned and martyred Matriona, the Matrioshka doll, too, is debased, a souvenir of the motherland sold to tourists and given to children as a plaything, her archaic significance forgotten. And yet in Soviet literature, art, and life, her iconographic presence continues, unobserved, to express a mythology of maternity in which the relationship of mother to child is regarded as a primordial and gravitational force. It suggests a notion of brother- and sisterhood as the form of all social community and the basis for individual existence. Like the ancient Great Mother Goddess, the Matrioshka spills all creation out of her body; like the protective and nurturing individual mother, she gathers her children "under her skirts," where they must find identity through nature's cyclical rhythms of confinement and release. The religion of the mothers and the myth of Russia as a common mother have been largely disregarded, yet together they embody what is perhaps the central mystery of the Russian people.

Notes

INTRODUCTION: RUSSIA AS MOTHER

1. S. Graham, *Undiscovered Russia* (London and New York, 1914), 327. Historians drawn to exploring the peculiarities of the Russian temperament also suggest, if only in passing, that it is connected with the feminine. See J. Billington, *The Icon and the Axe: An Interpretive History of Russian Culture* (New York, 1966), 20; and G. P. Fedotov, *The Russian Religious Mind*, vol. 1 (New York, 1960), 9–15, 344–362. Y. Yevtushenko, "A Russian Toy—Roly-Poly," *Yevtushenko Poems*, H. Marshall, trans. (New York, 1966), 33. All but commonly accepted names and surnames will be transliterated according to the Library of Congress style unless the source to which I refer has used another system.

2. On the cult of Jumala, see I. S. Trubetskoi, "K voprosu o 'Zolotoi Babe,'" *Etnograficheskoe obozrenie*, vols. 68–69, nos. 1–2, 1906, 52–62. For an overview of the Matrioshka's history in English, see A. and B. Pronin, *Russian Folk Arts*, (New York and London, 1975), 115–119: and S. Massie's summary of the Pronin passsage in *Land of the Firebird: The Beauty of Old Russia* (New York, 1980), 189–190.

3. See H. Smith, *The Russians* (New York, 1976), 307, 430, for the peculiar forms of Russian nationalism.

4. V. Weidlé, *Russia: Absent and Present*, A. Gordon Smith, trans. (New York, 1961), 19–20, refers to the nostalgia for the "free space," associated with the majestic monotony of the Russian landscape in Russian folksongs.

5. K. Kuznetsov, "Iz muzykal'nogo proshlogo Moskvy," *Sovetskaia muzyka*, no. 5, 1947, 39, trans. mine.

6. D. Vernet, "La Volga: Dans le coeur de chaque russe," *Le Monde*, July 22–23, 1979, 7.

7. The nineteenth-century German scholar who emphasized this point is A. von Haxthausen, *Studies in the Interior of Russia*, S. F. Starr, ed., E. L. Schmidt, trans. (Chicago, 1974), 285.

8. S. Levin, *Forward from Exile: The Autobiography of Shmarya Levin*, M. Samuel, trans. (Philadelphia, 1967), 5.

9. Fedotov, 20.

10. See W. W. Miller, *Russians as People* (New York, 1961), 29; F. A. Stepun (S. Kravchinsky), *The Russian Soul and Revolution*, E. Huntress, trans. (New York, 1935), 19.

11. Cited in E. Elnett, *Historic Origins and Social Development of Family Life in Russia* (New York, 1926), 129. "Piter is the head—Moscow is the heart," and "Moscow is the mother of all towns," occur in other proverbs. See V. I. Dal', *Poslovitsy russkogo naroda* (Moscow, 1957), 329, trans. mine.

12. N. Berdiaev, *The Russian Idea*, R. M. French, trans. (Boston, 1962), 6. Recent feminist theory has raised the issue of the very meaning of motherhood, specifically in the Western context. See the pioneering work of N. Chodorow, *The Reproduction of Mothering* (Los Angeles,

1978). This study will show that in an agrarian society such as Russia's, the archetype of the mother as a "fertile" container emphasized the positive value of relatedness—an orientation which, Chodorow argues, cripples Western women in a world which stresses "individuation" over communion. However, in Russia as elsewhere, a generalized expression of this conflict is evident in the historical opposition of warrior ruling class and peasant mentalities. Not until the emergence of the intelligentsia in the nineteenth century was the issue of individuality fully addressed.

13. F. I. Tiutchev, *Polnoe sobranie sochinenii* (St. Petersburg, 1913), 202, trans. mine.

14. Berdiaev, 6.

15. One difficulty in tracing a myth in the context of Russian culture involves defining the country geographically. The present Russian Soviet Federated Socialist Republic is the largest of the fifteen republics which together constitute the USSR and stretch six thousand miles from west to east. Within this territory are a vast number of nationalities and tribal groups. But its extent dates only from the eighteenth century. Earlier the Russian state consisted of the area around Moscow; from the fifteenth to the eighteenth centuries, it expanded to recover the Tatar-dominated lands of ancient Kiev in the Ukraine and to absorb territory to the north. This study will concentrate upon the religious beliefs and customs of the Slavic peoples of the USSR, mainly those of the Great Russians and the Ukrainians; it will also refer to Belorussian source materials.

16. For a seminal analysis of these differing conceptions of power, see M. Cherniavsky, *Tsar and People: Studies in Russian Myths* (New York, 1969).

CHAPTER ONE: THE FIRST MOTHERS

1. Fedotov, 362.

2. A. N. Afanas'ev, *Narodnye russkie skazki A. N. Afanas'eva* (Moscow, 1957), vol. 2, 134–160.

3. I. Lissner, *Man, God, and Magic*, J. M. Brownjohn, trans. (New York, 1961), 286, argues for a link between these earliest-known figurative representations and the "auxiliary dolls" in the rites of Nordic hunters. Soviet archeologists, intent on finding a matriarchal stage of development, see the figurines as clan mothers in a matrilineal social order. See Z. A. Abramova, "Paleolithic Art in the USSR," *Arctic Anthropology*, vol. 4, 1967, 83–84; A. D. Stoliar, "K voprosu o sotsial'no-istoricheskoi deshifrovke zhenskikh znakov verkhnogo paleolita," Akademia nauk SSSR, *Institut istorii i arkheologii*, vol. 7, 1975, no. 185, 202–219; and S. A. Tokarev, "K voprosu o znachenii zhenskikh izobrazhenii epokhi paleolita," *Sovetskaia arkheologiia*, no. 2, 1961, 12–20. D. Zelenine, *Le Culte des idoles en Sibérie*, G. Welter, trans. (Paris, 1952), 29–30 and 174–176, and C. Schuster, "Pendants in the Form of Inverted Human Figures from Paleolithic to Modern Times," *Report to the Seventh International Congress of Anthropological and Ethnographic Sciences*, Moscow, 1964, vol. 7, 105–117, regard the female figurines as amuletic or curative. Debate

about the functions of the Venus figurines continues among archeologists and historians. It is summarized in S. B. Pomeroy, *Goddesses, Whores, Wives, and Slaves: Women in Classical Antiquity* (New York, 1975), 13–15.

4. See E. O. James, *The Cult of the Mother Goddess* (New York, 1959), 257; and A. Marshack, *The Roots of Civilization* (New York, 1972), 111, 302, 314.

5. G. R. Levy, *The Gate of Horn* (New York 1946), 3–70.

6. S. Giedion, *The Eternal Present: The Beginnings of Art* (New York, 1962), 211; A. Laming-Emperaire, *La Signification de l'art rupestre paléolithique* (Paris, 1962), 227-228; J. Hawkes, *Prehistory* (New York, 1965), 295–296. The suggestion of male contingency—the phalli engulfed *in utero*—is quite possibly related to the active denial (if not actual ignorance) of paternity among Paleolithic peoples. What appears as androgynous imagery, phallic stands in the caves, may instead describe the parthenogenetic nature of a mother divinity. A. D. Stoliar (208) argues for the notion of the human collectivity contained in the body of the Great Mother.

7. Marshack, 335–336.

8. On the beliefs in a primordial and omnipotent Mistress of Animals among Nordic tribes, see O. Nahodil, "The Mother Cult in Siberia," in V. Dioszegi, ed., *Popular Beliefs and Folklore Traditions in Siberia* (The Hague, 1968), 459–477; A. F. Anisimov, *Kosmologicheskie predstavleniia narodov-severa* (Moscow-Leningrad, 1959), 20–30, 45–46, 53–54; A. A. Popov, "Tavgiitsy: Materialy po etnografii Avamskikh i Vedeiveskikh Tavgiitsev," *Trudy Instituta antropologii i etnografii Akademii nauk SSSR*, vol. 1, no. 5, 1936, 84–109; G. N. Prokofiev, "Tseremoniia ozhivleniia bubna u Ostakosamoyedov," *Izvestiia Leningradskogo gosudarstvennogo universiteta*, vol. 2, 1930, 370; I. M. Cazanowicz, "Shamanism of the Natives of Siberia," *The Smithsonian Institution: Annual Report of the Board of Regents*, 1924, 415–434; and M. Eliade, *Shamanism: Archaic Techniques of Ecstasy*, W. R. Trask, trans. (Princeton, 1972), 81, stresses the centricity of a male divinity among the peoples devoted to shamanic practices but does observe a strong residue of belief in all-powerful goddesses or female spirits, which he associates with an ancient matriarchy.

9. Çatal Hüyük's excavator, J. Mellaart, in *Çatal Hüyük* (London-New York, 1967), 23–24, argues for the existence of a fertility cult dating from the Paleolithic. See also J. Mellaart, "'Çatal Hüyük, A Neolithic City in Anatolia," *Proceedings of the British Academy*, vol. 51, 1965–1966, 206–208; and B. Goldman, "Typology of the Mother-Goddess Figurines," *Jahrbuch für Prähistorische und Ethnographische Kunst*, vol. 20, 1963, 8–12. On the decoration of the shrines and for a description of the figurines as well as the divine pantheon, see Mellaart, *Çatal Hüyük*, 178–202. The maternity of the goddess is underscored. In hunting frescoes, women and children stand vigil over the hunt while men in animal skins dance before them. This image of maternal watchfulness may explain why only women and children were buried in the shrines and smeared with ocher from the nearby caves of the Taurus Mountains: Anointed with the symbol of blood—and rebirth—the mothers appear to guard the living from the land of the dead. Like the Russian *rusalki* of later times, they seem to channel the power of the ancestors to the community. On the matrifocal aspects of Çatal Hüyük, see R. Rohrlich-Leavitt, "Women in Transition: Crete and Sumer," in R. Bridenthal and C. Koonz, eds., *Becoming Visible: Women in European History* (New York, 1977), 39–40; and E. Boissevain, "A Tentative

Typology, Chronology, and Distribution Study of the Human Figurines of Eastern Europe and the Near East in Early Farming Levels," *Actes du 7e congrès international des sciences préhistoriques et protohistoriques*, vol. 1, 1966, 385–387.

10. Mellaart, *Çatal Hüyük*, 106–107, 115–117, 161–168, 180–202, 207– 209.

11. For the extent of the goddess's cult, see O. G. S. Crawford, *The Eye Goddess* (New York, 1957), 27–28. On Tripol'e, see the brilliant analysis of M. Gimbutas, *Gods and Goddesses of Old Europe, 7000–3500 B.C.: Myths, Legends, and Cult Images* (London, 1974). R. E. F. Smith, *The Origins of Farming in Russia* (Paris, 1959), 10, sees Tripol'e culture as an extension of Mediterranean cultures. Gimbutas regards the "Old European" complex as autonomous. For another analysis, see R. Tringham, *Hunters, Fishers, and Farmers of Eastern Europe, 6000–3000 B.C.* (London, 1975), 166–180; and S. N. Bibikov, "Rannetripol'skoe poselenie Luka-Vrublevetskaia na Dnestre," *Materialy i issledovaniia po arkheologii SSSR*, no. 38, 1952, 191–274. Bibikov reviews the Soviet literature on Tripol'e.

12. Gimbutas, *Gods and Goddesses*, 112–195, and B. A. Rybakov, "Cosmology and Mythology of the Agriculturalists of the Neolithic," pts. 1 and 2, *Soviet Anthropology and Archeology*, vol. 4, nos. 2–3, 1965–1966, 16–33, 33–52.

13. Gimbutas, *Gods and Goddesses*, 201–205; Rybakov, "Cosmology and Mythology," pt. 2, 39–42. On the gradual process of patriarchalization associated at Tripol'e with plow agriculture, see S. N. Bibikov, "Khoziaistvenno-ekonomicheskii kompleks razvitogo Tripoliia," *Sovetskaia arkheologiia*, no. 1, 1965, 59-60.

14. T. G. Movsha, "Sviatilishcha Tripol'skoi kul'tury," *Sovetskaia arkheologiia*, no. 1, 1971, 201–205; idem, "Ob antropomorfnoi plastike tripol'skoi kul'tury," *Sovetskaia arkheologiia*, no. 2, 1969, 32–34; and idem, "Goncharnyi tsentr tripol'skoi kul'tury na Dnestre," *Sovetskaia arkheologiia*, no. 3, 1971, 228–234. Movsha suggests that the female figurines represented priestesses of a Great Mother Goddess in a still-matrifocal society. Rybakov, "Cosmology and Mythology," pt. 1, 18–20, also regards the figurines as priestesses. T. C. Passek, "Ostianye amulety iz Floresht," *Novoe v sovetskoi arkheologii*, 1965, 83, regards them as amulets, but in "Itogi rabot v Moldavii v oblasti pervobytnoi arkheologii," *Kratkie soobshcheniia o dokladakh i polevykh issledovaniiakh instituta materialnoi kul'tury*, vol. 106, 1954, 84–97, he argues for the presence of a Great Goddess and a funerary cult dominated by women. N. E. Makarenko, "Sculpture de la civilization tripolienne en Ukraine," *Jahrbuch für Prähistorische und Ethnographische Kunst*, vol. 3, 1927, 126, regards the figurines as toys resembling those found among Ukrainian children. T. A. Popova, "Zoomorfnaia plastika tripol'skogo poseleniia Polivanov Yar," *Kratkie soobshcheniia Instituta arkheologii SSSR*, vol. 123, 1970, 13, indicates their association with bull figures around the hearth. And G. P. Sergeev, "Rannetripol'skii klad u S. Karbuna," *Sovetskaia arkheologiia*, no. 1, 1962, 143–144, also argues for a male-female fertility cult and the indication of sun worship. Bibikov, "Rannetripol'skoe," draws clear analogies between the fertility rites of Russian peasants and Tripol'e artifacts. See 204-205, 252, 258, 274. So does Rybakov.

15. See Gimbutas, *Gods and Goddesses*, 238; and Rybakov, "Cosmology and Mythology," pt. 2, 48–50.

16. For a striking example of the masculine arrogation of feminine

divine power, see the Sumerian creation myth in which the son of the Great Goddess Tiamat, the god Marduk, carves the world out of her conquered body.

17. The "Royal Scythians" who appear to administer the territories are thought to be of Indo-European origin. G. Vernadsky, *Ancient Russia* (New Haven, 1943), 51, summarizes the controversy regarding the racial origins of the Scythians as a "horde." They are perhaps of Altaic or Slavic as well as Indo-European racial stock and constitute a confederation of tribes called Scythia, he concludes. T. T. Rice, *The Scythians* (New York, 1957), 39–42, sees them as Indo-European peoples of Iranian and Ugro-Altaic stock and suggests that the difficulty of attributing one origin to them is related to their nomadism and intermarriage. S. P. Tolstov, "The central Asian Scythians in the Light of the Most Recent Archeological Discoveries," *Soviet Anthropology and Archeology*, vol. 2, no. 4, 1964, 16, indicates an Indo-European and Letto-Lithuanian origin.

18. For an account of the relationship of Herakles with the Mother Goddesses of Greece, see R. Graves, *The Greek Myths*, vol. 2 (Baltimore, Maryland, 1955), 100.

19. Herodotus, *The History of Herodotus*, G. Rawlinson, trans. (New York, 1956), 207–208. On another origin myth from the royal or ruling Scythians in which Zeus mates with a river goddess, see Herodotus, 206; and L. A. Elnitskii, "Skifskie legendy kak kul'turno-istoricheskie materialy," *Sovetskaia arkheologiia*, no. 2, 1970, 65, traces the name of the first ruler, Targitaus, to a half-fish, half-woman divinity. P. Chalus, *L'Homme et la religion* (Paris, 1963), 357–374, points to the widespread custom among the Indo-European warriors of uniting their male and celestial divinities to the goddesses of farming populations through marriage or a sexual union. J. Fontenrose, *Python: A Study of Delphic Myth and Its Origins* (Berkeley, 1959), 94–96, discuss the nature of the cave-dwelling and snake-tailed goddesses in Greek mythology.

20. Z. R. Dittrich, "Zur Religiosen Ur and Frühgeschichte der Slaven," *Jahrbuch für Geschichte Osteuropas*, vol. 9, 1961, 486–508; and M. Rostovtzeff, *Iranians and Greeks in South Russia* (Oxford, 1922), 34; also "Le Culte de la Grande Déesse dans la Russie méridionale," *Revue des études grecques*, vol. 32, 1919, 462–464. For Soviet theories linking the woodland goddess to Tripol'e prototypes and on a movement toward patriarchy illustrated in the myth, see V. P. Petrov and M. R. Makarevich, "Skifskaia genealogicheskaia legenda," *Sovetskaia arkheologiia*, no. 1, 1963, 30–31; and D. S. Raevskii, "Skifskii mifologicheskii siuzhet viskusstve i ideologii tsarstva Ateia," *Sovetskaia arkheologiia*, no. 3, 1970, 90–101.

21. Rostovtzeff, "Le Culte," 466; E. H. Minns, *Scythians and Greeks: A Survey of Ancient History and Archeology on the North Coast of the Euxine from the Danube to the Caucasus* (Cambridge, 1913), 542–545; and Rice, *The Scythians*, 85. In the Greek myths, the area inhabited by the Taurians, Sindians, Sauromatians, and Meotians is linked with Jason's quest for the Golden Fleece, with the vengeful Circe, and with Iphigenia, high priestess of Artemis's cult in the Taurus, a cult which involved male sacrifice.

22. The literature on the Amazon myth is as polemical as it is proc. M. O. Kosven, "Amazonki: Istoriia legendy," *Sovetskaia etnografiia*, nos. 2 and 3, 1947, 33–59, 3–33, gives an overview of the myth reflecting matriclan origins as it appears in various cultures and at various periods.

The American scholar S. Pomeroy, 24–25, argues that the myth is a reflection of masculine guilt. W. K. C. Guthrie, an English classical scholar, in his *The Greeks and Their Gods* (Boston, 1954), 59, suggests a pattern of matriarchal-patriarchal conflict between the autochthonous population and the Greek invaders. G. Vernadsky, the Russian historian, in *Kievan Russia* (London, 1943), 155, argues for the prevalence of matriarchal forms of social organization among the Scythians, Sarmatians, and proto-Slavs reflected in the Amazon myth. On Amazons as "Moon Maidens," see Graves, vol. 1, 355; vol. 2, 125.

 23. Herodotus, 238–239; Rostovtzeff, "Le Culte," 468–469; T. Sulimirski, *The Sarmatians*, (New York, 1970), 34–48; M. I. Khazanov, "Materinskii rod u Sarmatov," *Akademiia nauk SSSR, Institut veseobshchei istorii, Vestnik drevenei istorii*, no. 2 (112), 1937, 141–142.

 24. On the matrifocal nature of the Prokhorovka culture, its armed clan mothers, and its connection with the Sarmatians, see Khazanov, 144; and B. N. Grakov, "TYNAIKOKPATOYMENOI: Perezhitki matriarkhata u Sarmatov," *Vestnik drevnei istorii*, no. 3, 1947, 100–121; and M. G. Moshkova, *Proiskhozhdenie rannesarmatskoi (prokhorovskoi) kul'tury* (Moscow, 1974), 4–10.

 25. See Petrov and Makarevich, 23–28, and T. T. Rice, *The Ancient Arts of Central Asia* (New York, 1965), 39. For a discussion of the carpet, see S. I. Rudenko, *Frozen Tombs of Siberia: The Pazyryk Burials of Iron Age Horsemen*, M. W. Thompson, trans. (Berkeley, 1970), 289. Tolstov, 25, argues that the Messagetae and Sacae tribes of this area were indeed, as Herodotus suggested, matriclans. So does Rudenko, 212. The Finno-Ugric tribes of the Siberian Andronovian culture, from whom the Scythians adopted the horse, venerated a Mother Goddess. The many stone figures, called *kammenye baby* and spread through the steppes of east and central Russia, are thought to have originated with this culture, as well. The *baby*, shaped like Matrioshka dolls, are found over tombstones and upon pillars. They are sometimes flanked by horsemen and frequently are decorated with carved serpentine ribbons, sun disks, or ram or bull horns. See M. P. Griaznov, "Minusinskie kamennye baby v sviazi s nekotorymi novymi materialami," *Sovetskaia arkheologiia*, no. 12, 1950, 128–156; T. Sulimirski, *Prehistoric Russia* (New York, 1970), 266; and Minns, 239–240.

 26. Herodotus, 221 (the translator anachronistically used the Roman names for Greek gods). See also I. M. Linforth, "Greek Gods and Foreign Gods in Herodotus," *University of California Publications in Classical Philology*, vol. 9, no. 1, 1926, 1–25. See G. Dumézil, *Mythe et épopée: L'Idéologie des trois fonctions dans les épopées des peuples indo-européens* (Paris, 1968), 104. For an analysis of Great Goddesses as genetrices of their nations, see his *Déesses latines et mythes védiques* (Brussels, 1956). On the ritual mating of the king and the mare goddess, see J. Puhvel, *Myth and Law among the Indo-Europeans* (Berkeley, 1970), 168–172; and W. D. O'Flaherty, *Women, Androgynes, and Other Mythical Beasts* (Chicago, 1980), 147–282.

 27. Herodotus, 224–225. On the shamanic nature of the Enarees, see G. Dumézil, "Les 'Enarées' scythiques et la grossesse du Narte Hamyc," *Latomus*, vol. 5, 249–255; and K. Meuli, "Scythica," *Hermes*, 70, 1935, 123–132.

 28. Grakov, 119; and Sulimirski, *The Sarmatians*, 33–34.

29. Khazanov, 141; Grakov, 106–110; Sulimirski, *The Sarmatians*, 34. An intricately fashioned headdress found in the first-century B.C. tomb of a queen or priestess at Novocherkassk, on the lower Don, shows the supreme female divinity in the form of her ideogram as Tree of Life, double-egg, and bird of prey. See Minns, 218, and A. Voyce, *The Art and Architecture of Medieval Russia* (Norman, Oklahoma, 1967), 55–56. On the link of the Dacians and the Sarmatians, see V. A. Gorodtsov, "Dakosarmatskie religioznye elementy v russkom narodnom tvorchestve," *Trudy Gosudarstvennogo istoricheskogo muzeia*, pt. 1, 1926, 7–36.

30. On the arrogation of the fire cult (practiced by Sauromatian women) by a priesthood, see Khazanov, 142–143. Rostovtzeff, "Le Culte," 478–481, and *Iranians and Greeks*, 159, writes that the image of the Great Goddess on the coins of the Bosphoran kingdom in the second century is "shadowed" by that of a male figure of a king on the reverse side. See also Minns, 629ff. For the influence of the Meotians and Sauromatians on the Bosphoran kingdom from the seventh century B.C., see M. Rostovtzeff, "Queen Dynamis of Bosphorus," *Journal of Hellenic Studies*, 39, 1919, 88–109.

31. Rostovtzeff, *Iranians and Greeks*, 179–180.

32. M. J. Dresden, "Mythology of Ancient Iran," in S. N. Kramer, ed., *Mythologies of the Ancient World* (Garden City, New York, 1961), 352–353. For a summary of the connections between the Sarmatians, the Slavs, and the Iranians, see M. Gimbutas, *The Slavs* (New York, 1971), 64. B. A. Rybakov, "Iskusstvoe drevnikh slavian," *Istoriia russkogo iskusstva* (Moscow, 1953), 60, 66, describes the discovery of a Slavic buckle. On the connections between Scythians, Sarmatians, Dacians, Antes, and Slavs and the motifs of later Slavic peasant embroideries, see Gorodtsov, 7–36; B. A. Rybakov, "Drevnie elementy v russkom narodnom tvorchestve," *Sovetskaia etnografiia*, no. 1, 1948, 94–99. For another linkage of the Scythian-Sarmatian-Dacian goddesses with Russian peasant art, see L. A. Dintses, "Drevnie cherty v russkom narodnom iskusstve," in B. A. Rybakov, ed., *Istoriia kul'tury drevnei Rusi: Domongol'skii period*, vol. 2, 1951, 465–491; A. K. Ambroz, "On the Symbolism of Russian Peasant Embroidery," *Soviet Anthropology and Archeology*, vol. 6, no. 2, Fall, 1967, 22–35; and I. Ia. Boguslavskaia, "O transformatsii ornamental'nykh motivov zviazannykh s drevnei mifologiei v russkoi narodnoi vyshivke," *Report of the Seventh Congress of Anthropological and Ethnographic Sciences*, vol. 7 (Moscow, 1964), 74–82.

33. Procopius, *History of the Wars*, H. B. Dewing, trans. (Cambridge, 1924), vol. 4, 270–271; and Tacitus, "Tacitus on Germany," T. Gordon, trans., *Harvard Classics*, vol. 33 (New York, 1910), 100, 118, 121–122. See also P. S. Leicht, "Tracce di paganesimo fra gli slavi dell' Isonzo nel sec. XIV," *Studi e materiali di storia della religione*, vol. 1, 1925, 247–250.

34. Saxo Grammaticus, *Gesta Danorum* (Strasbourg, 1886), 564ff. On the mare cult among the Indo-Europeans, see note 26 above. J. Bystron, "Les Rites agraires chez les peuples slaves et l'origine du culte agraire," *Actes du congrès international d'histoire des religions*, vol. 2 (Paris, 1925), 206, associates the rites for Svantovit with modern customs. See also S. M. Solov'ev, "Ocherk nravov, obychaev i religii slavian, preimushchestvenno vostochnikh, vo vremena iazycheskie," *Arkhiv istoriko-iuridicheskikh svedenii*, vol. 1, 1876, 42; and A. A. Potebnia, "O

mificheskom znachenii nekotorykh obriadov i poverii," *Chteniia obshchestva istorii i drevnostei rossiiskikh*, nos. 2, 3, 4, 1865, 46. On Svantovit as a god who absorbs the Great Goddess, see Rybakov, "Drevnie elementy," 100. For an illustration of the idol, see J. Machal, "Slavic Mythology," in *Mythology of All Races*, vol. 3 (New York, 1964), plate 31.

35. For the mention of the worship of the goddess Zhiva, see Helmhold, *Chronica Slavorum*, ed. in *Monumenta Germaniae Historica: Scriptores (Rerum Germanicum)*, vol. 1 (Hanover, 1868), 52. The coexistence of the two cults is suggested by the twelfth-century German historian Herbord in connection with the worship of another polycephalous pillar god, Triglav, in the military fortress of Stettin. The temple was located near a holy tree and spring where the common people came to make offerings. See Herbord, *Dialogus de vita Ottonis episcopi Babenbergensis*, ed. in *Monumenta Germaniae*, vol. 2, 32. On polycephalous gods, see V. V. Ivanov and V. N. Toporov, *Slavianskie iazykovye modelirushchie semioticheskie sistemy* (Moscow, 1965), 30–52. The authors' semiological analysis underscores the binary aspects of religious worship and points to the existence of two separate systems, male and female respectively (175–178). Among the Western Slavs, they argue, Zhiva, the goddess, opposes the male gods (51). On Zhiva, see A. N. Afanas'ev, *Poeticheskie vozzreniia slavian na prirodu*, vol. 3 (Moscow, 1869), 686–688.

36. Herodotus, 235–236; Jordanes, *The Gothic History*, C. C. Mierow, trans. and ed. (Cambridge, 1960), 59; Dittrich, 488, links the Slavs to the descendants of the Tripol'e culture. E. Gasparini, *Il matriarcato slavo* (Florence, 1973), 2–12, 489, sees a matriarchal native population gradually overcome by an Indo-European one. On matrilineal customs among the Finno-Ugric peoples, see O. Loorits, "The Development of the Uralian Culture-Area," *Slavonic and East European Review*, vol. 31, 1957, 2–8. For an overview of Soviet and East European theories regarding the origin of the Slavs, see J. Eisner, "Les Origines des Slaves d'après les préhistoriens tcheques," *Revue des études slaves*, vol. 24 (Paris, 1948), 129–142. Soviet scholars suggest that the Slavs emerged from a number of civilizations, including those of Tripol'e, the Ural cultures, the agrarian Scythians, and Carpathian settlers (see 140). This view concurs with the pioneering studies by the Czech historian L. Niederle, *Slavianskie drevnosti*, T. Kovaleva and M. Khazanova, trans. (Moscow, 1956), who argues for the complex origins of the Slavs. For a summary of archeological and linguistic evidence, see Gimbutas, *The Slavs*, 17–26; and F. Dvornik, *The Slavs: Their Early History and Civilization* (Boston, 1959), 3–45.

37. See, for example, Gimbutas, *The Slavs*, 23–26.

38. See Gasparini's massive study, especially 2–11. Earlier pioneering works indicating a matriarchal basis for Russian culture have not been widely acknowledged. See M. Kovalevsky, *Modern Customs and Ancient Laws of Russia* (London, 1891); E. Elnett, *Historic Origins*; and L. Seifert, *Die Weltrevoluzionäre, von Bogumil, über Hus zu Lenin* (Vienna, 1931). On Slavic women's power and freedom before the advent of Christianity, see S. S. Shashkov, *Istoriia russkoi zhenshchiny* (St. Petersburg, 1879), 1–52.

39. S. H. Cross and O. P. Sherbowitz-Wetzor, eds. and trans., *The Russian Primary Chronicle, Laurentian Text* (Cambridge, Massachusetts, 1953), 14–15. Among the Bohemian Slavs, chroniclers also noted that girls

not only chose their husbands but even went hunting and took part in warfare—like Amazons. See Cosmas Pragensis, *Chronica Bohemorum*, cited in Kovalevsky, 15, and Shashkov, 5.

40. On the rulers of the Poliane, three brothers and a sister, Lebed ("Swan"), see Cross and Sherbowitz-Wetzor, 54–55. See I. Boba, *Nomads, Northmen, and Slavs: Eastern Europe in the Ninth Century* (The Hague, 1967), 49, who argues that the ancient and democratic clan rule of the *veche*, or assembly of family heads, was challenged by three rulers of Khazar or Altaic descent. For a discussion of matrilineal customs among the ancient Slavs, see D. Tomasic, *The Impact of Russian Culture on Soviet Communism*, (Glencoe, Illinois, 1953), 31–39; and P. Bushkovitch, "Rus' in the Ethnic Nomenclature of the Povest' vremennykh let," *Cahiers du monde russe et soviétique*, vol. 12, no. 3, 1971, 304. For an overview of debate on the origin of Rus', see Cross and Sherbowitz-Wetzor, 35–50.

41. Gasparini, *Il matriarcato slavo*, 11, 61, 221.

42. See L. Sadnik, "Ancient Slav Religion in the Light of Recent Research," *Eastern Review*, 1948, vol. 1, no. 1, 36–43, and E. V. Anchikov, "Old Russian Pagan Cults," in *Transactions of the Third International Congress for the History of Religions*, vol. 2, 1908, 244–259. For other forms of accommodation between male and female divinities, see R. Lannoy, *The Speaking Tree: A Study of Indian Culture and Society* (London, 1971), 10–11.

43. Rybakov, "Drevnie elementy," 104–105.

44. A. Kalmykov, "Iranians and Greeks in South Russia," *Journal of the American-Oriental Society*, vol. 45, no. 1, 1925, 70, shows the connection between the Scythian serpent maiden and the *sirin* or *rusalka* of Russian folk culture.

45. On the centricity of the bathhouse as a temple among the Eastern Slavs, see P. S. Efimenko, "Materialy po etnografii russkogo naseleniia Arkhangel'skoi gubernii," *Izvestiia obshchestva liubitelei estestvoznaniia, antropologii i etnografii pri imp. Moskovskom universitete*, vol. 30, *Trudy etnograficheskogo otd.*, bk. 5, pt. 1 (Moscow 1877), 104; and I. Vahros, "Zur Geschichte und Folklore der grossrussischen Sauna," *Folklore Fellows Communications*, vol. 82, no. 197 (Helsinki, 1966), 199–200. In the Balkans up to this century, the cult of the *rozhanitsy* involved a ceremony in which the worshippers, sometimes three old women, drank out of a horn or rhyton and predicted the child's fate. See Iu. Arbatskii, *Etiudy po istorii russkoi muzyki* (New York, 1956), 68; and K. Moszynski, *Kultura ludowo slowian*, vol. 2 (Warsaw, 1967), 696–701, on the figure of the Dolia as a *rozhanitsa* or fate-giver among the Poles, Belorussians, and Ukrainians.

46. See "Slovo sv. Grigoriia, izobreteno v toltsev' v tom, kako pervoe pogani sushche iazytsi klanialsia idolom' i treby im klali," in N. Gal'kovskii, *Bor'ba khristianstva s ostatkami iazychestva v drevnei Rusi*, vol. 2 (Moscow-Kharkov, 1916), 18. Ivanov and Toporov, 172, link Rod with protective household spirits. Since such spirits were often associated with the ancestors, the assimilation of Rod to them seems quite plausible.

47. On the word for "vampire" derived from the Russian *upir*, see J. Perkowski, *Vampires of the Slavs* (Cambridge, Massachusetts, 1976), 185; M. Summers, *The Vampire in Europe* (London, 1929), 288–301, shows that the vampire is linked to a wise woman, and in *The Werewolf*, (London, 1933), 15, argues that among the Slavs, a werewolf generally became a vampire after death. H. Dontenville, *Histoire et géographie mythiques de*

la France (Paris, 1973), 140, shows the association of wolves, werewolves, swans, and women serpents with a Mother Goddess.

48. M. Szeftel, "The Vseslav Epos," in *Roman Jakobson: Selected Writings*, vol. 4 (The Hague, 1966), 341–348, on the werewolf and the caul. See also S. Baring-Gould, *The Book of Werewolves* (New York, 1973), 117.

49. E. V. Pomerantseva, *Mifologicheskie personazhi v russkom fol'klore* (Moscow, 1975) 80–82. For a more complete discussion of male divinities both pagan and Christian, see chapter 5 below. On the anomalous case of the deity called Div by medieval chroniclers and seen sometimes as masculine, sometimes as feminine, and linked to the *leshii* in Russian folklore, see Ivanov and Toporov, 173, 176.

50. For a summary of conflicting theories regarding the nationality of the Varangians, see Boba, 5.

51. Soviet historians stress the polarity of beliefs and customs between the rulers and the ruled. See B. D. Grekov, *Kiev Rus'* (Moscow, 1959), 517. But some Western historians are in agreement with this assessment. See Vernadsky, *Ancient Russia*, 326–327, who associates it with differing tribal traditions.

52. See V. N. Perets, "Drevnerusskie kniazheskie zhitiia," *Issledovaniia i materialy po istorii starinnoi ukrainskoi literatury XVI-XVIII vekov* (Moscow, 1962), 36, 77. See also A. Gieysztor, "The Slavic Pantheon and the New Comparative Mythology," *Minutes of the Seminar on Ukrainian Studies Held at Harvard University*, no. 5, 1974–1975, 82–84.

53. For an overview, see Gimbutas, *The Slavs*, 162; and Ivanov and Toporov, 24, 100–101, on their link with Mokosh.

54. R. Jakobson, "Slavic Mythology," in *Funk and Wagnalls Standard Dictionary of Folklore, Mythology, and Legend* (New York, 1949), 1026–1027. On the link with the hearth fire, see Machal, 298.

55. Machal, 256-260; Gimbutas, *The Slavs*, 162–164.

56. For Finnish beliefs, see Machal, 323–324. On vestiges of the worship of the sun as mother among the Ukrainians, see V. M. Vasilenko, *Russkaia narodnaia rez'ba i rospis' po derevu XVIII-XX vv.* (Moscow, 1960), 51. For a discussion of the cult of the sun as a goddess in Russia, see Potebnia, 223-232, and Gasparini, *Il matriarcato slavo*, 584–585.

57. M. Gimbutas, "Ancient Slavic Religion: A Synopsis," in *Essays in Honor of Roman Jakobson*, vol. 1 (The Hague, 1967), 747; G. Alexinsky, 'Slavonic Mythology," in *The New Larousse Encyclopedia of Mythology*, R. Aldington and D. Ames, trans., (Harmondsworth, Middlesex, 1972), 285. On the all-powerful female sun deity among the Hittites, see James, 184. Stribog, god of the winds and son of Dazhbog, does not appear in later folklore. On his association with the Iranian goddess of fate, Çri Deva, see G. Vernadsky, *Kievan Russia* (New Haven, 1973), 51–52. The sun god Khors is linked to the Persian Khursid; Div originates in the Persian goddess Deva, from whom the word *devushka* (girl) may be drawn. See V. J. Mansikka, *Die Religion der Ostslaven* (Helsinki, 1922), 201; and Gimbutas, "Ancient Slavic Religion," 51–52. On the relationship of Div, Deva, and Mokosh to the *vily* and *rusalki*, see Dittrich, 495–496.

58. Kalmykov, 69–70; C. Huart, "The Mythology of Persia," in J. Hackin, ed., *Asiatic Mythology*, F. M. Atkinson, trans. (New York, n.d.), 45. See also Ivanov and Toporov, 25–28, 175, on the link with Mokosh.

59. B. A. Rybakov, "Rusalii i bog Simargl-Pereplut," *Sovetskaia*

arkheologiia, 1967, no. 2, 91–116; and K. Trever, *The Dog-Bird Senmurv Paskudj: The Dog-Bird of Persian Mythology* (Leningrad, 1938), 11–63.

60. Afanas'ev, *Narodnye russkie skazki*, vol. 1, 415–430, 436–438, vol. 2, 227–230.

61. Grekov, 515–517; and E. S. Reisman, "The Cult of Boris and Gleb: A Remnant of Varangian Tradition?" *Russian Review*, vol. 37, 145–147.

62. F. Haase, *Volksglaube und Brauchtum der Ostslaven* (Breslau, 1939), 155–156.

63. J. G. Frazer, *The New Golden Bough*, T. H. Gaster, ed. (New York, 1964), 75; and Jakobson, "Slavic Mythology," 1026, on the virgin who invokes rain, called Perperuna among the South Slavs.

64. On the conflict of Perun and Volos and Volos with Mokosh, see V. V. Ivanov and V. N. Toporov, *Issledovaniia v oblasti slavianskikh drevnostei* (Moscow, 1974), 164. B. A. Uspenskii, "Kul't Nikoly na Rusi v istoriko-kul'turnom osveshchenii," *Trudy po znakovym sistemam*, no. 10 (Tartu, 1978), 127, shows Volos Christianized as Saint Blasius and also apparent in the figures of Saint Nicholas (whose cult was in turn grafted onto that of Artemis on the Black Sea) and Saint George.

65. For one such clerical condemnation, see "Slovo nekoego Khristoliubitsa i revnitelia po pravoi vere," in Gal'kovskii, 38–39. Ivanov and Toporov, *Slavianskie iazykovye*, 25, 175–178, argue that Mokosh's adversarial role toward the gods suggests the existence of separate male and female religious systems.

66. Haase, 42-44; Trubetskoi, 52–62. On Mokosh's link with the *bereginy*, see Vernadsky, *Origins of Russia*, 123.

67. Trubetskoi, 58–59. There is a functional relationship between Artemis and the Vogul goddess linked with Mokosh, as well as a similar history: Both are ousted by male gods. (See 60–62.)

68. Vernadsky, *Origins of Russia*, 123, assimilates Mokosh with the Scythian Tabiti and the Iranian Anahita. A. Brückner, *Mitologia slava*, J. Dicksteinowna, trans. (Bologna, 1823), 143, derives Mokosh's name from the stem *osha*, associated with Russian and Slavic words relating to sovereignty, virginity, universal power, and love.

69. Cited in I. Kologrivof, *Essai sur la sainteté en Russie* (Bruges-Paris, 1953), 167, trans. mine. On the cult of earth and attempts by the clergy to disassociate it from Mary, see S. Smirnov, "Drevnerusskii dukhovnik," *Chteniia obshchestva istorii i drevnostei Moskovskogo universiteta*, April-June, 1914, 274.

70. V. Komarovich, "Kul't roda i zemli v kniazheskoi srede, XI-XIII vv.," *Akademiia nauk SSSR: Trudy otdela drevnerusskoi literatury*, vol. 16, 94–98.

71. Ibid., 93–103; and E. E. Golubinskii, *Istoriia russkoi tserkvi*, vol. 1, pt. 1 (Moscow, 1901), 177, 211–214; Fedotov, 344–347; Vernadsky, *Origins of Russia*, 124–125; R. Zguta, "The Pagan Priests of Early Russia: Some New Insights," *Slavic Review*, vol. 33, no. 2, 1974, 259–266.

72. Cross and Sherbowitz-Wetzor, 150–151.

73.On the usurpation of rainmaking functions associated with the *volkhvy* bringing serpents from the sky, see Komarovich, 102.

74. Cross and Sherbowitz-Wetzor, 69.

75. See Komarovich, 93. For parallels between the Kievan legend

and a Czech myth of a denigrated female priesthood, see L. Léger, *Les Anciennes civilization slaves* (Paris, 1921), 86. Léger stresses the lack of a developed priesthood among the Slavs.

76. M. O. Howey, *The Horse in Magic and Myth* (London, 1923), 193, 205.

77. That process of distillation of feminine power is well illustrated in the description of a sacrificial custom among the Varangians by a tenth-century Arab traveler, Ibn Rustan. See A. Ia. Harkavi, ed., *Skazaniia musulmanskikh pisatelei o slavianakh i russkikh (s poloviny VII do kontsa X veka* (St. Petersburg, 1870), 93–102. N. K. Chadwick, *The Beginning of Russian History* (Cambridge, 1946), 80–81, argues for the Swedish origin of the female sacrifice.

CHAPTER TWO: RECONSTRUCTING THE RUSSIAN GREAT
GODDESS: RUSALKI AND BABA YAGA

1. A. Pushkin, *"Rusalka,"* in A. S. Pushkin, *Sochineniia*, vol. 1 (Moscow, 1964), 107, trans. mine.

2. I. I. Zemtsovskii, ed., *Poezii krest'ianskikh prazdnikov* (Leningrad, 1970), 97, trans. mine.

3. On the abstract representation of the goddess as an amuletic "fertility" lozenge (symbol of the female sex organ), see Gorodtsov, 8–10, and Boguslavskaia, 74–82. On the symbolism of the ritual towels, see E. Gasparini, "Studies in Old Slavic Religion: *Ubrus*," *History of Religions*, vol. 2, no. 1, 1962, 115–121; and A. N. Svirin, *Drevnerusskoe shit'e* (Moscow, 1963), 5–13.

4. On the rich store of embroidery and the dominant role of the goddess motif, see Voyce, 70–72; and Vernadsky, *Origins of Russia*, 143. See also E. Warner, "Work and Play: Some Aspects of Folk Drama in Russia," *Comparative Drama*, vol. 12, no. 2, 157–158.

5. Gorodtsov, 8. Girls were traditionally obliged to spin, weave, and sew sacks for storing the produce of the harvest. This activity was assimilated to their powers over fertility and birth. The religious symbolism of the embroidered towels dedicated to the goddess of fertility was also found in peasant dances. Dancing and weaving were predominantly women's activities, on which the well-being of the community was thought to depend. The *khorovod* (round dance), the most characteristic of peasant dances, reflected the mandalic image of the sun (Khor), but also, more archaically, that of the womb, which "spins out" life. Indeed, the *khorovod* was also a female initiation rite involving a spinning dance in which a male child was used as a shuttle. The very pattern of the *khorovod* reveals the image of dots and lozenges, of swirls and meanders found on Tripol'e vessels to schematize the womb of the goddess. For an illustration of that pattern, see P. Shein, *Velikorusy v svoikh pesniakh, obriadakh, obychaiakh, verovaniakh, skazkakh, legendakh*, vol. 1 (St. Petersburg, 1900–1902), 348.

6. See Gorodtsov, 9–16; Dintses, 61–76; Rybakov, "Drevnie elementy," 99–106. For an overview of the motifs of peasant art with a strong emphasis on a male sun cult, see A. Netting, "Images and Ideas in Russian Peasant Art," *Slavic Review*, vol. 35, no. 1, 1976, 48–68.

7. Ambroz, 29.

8. Afanas'ev, *Narodnye russkie skazki*, vol. 2, 389–394. For a discussion of those images of the goddess, see Boguslavskaia, 74–77.

9. On early Slavic images, see Gorodtsov, 19; and Rybakov, "Drevnie elementy," 102.

10. Rybakov, "Drevnie elementy," 103, ignores the female sexual symbolism of the lozenge here.

11. Ibid., 104–105; and Gorodtsov, 18–20.

12. N. Matorin, *Zhenskoe bozhestvo v pravoslavnom kul'te* (Moscow, 1931), 46. The goddess in her triune form has masculine counterparts who are modeled, in later times, upon her functions. See chapter 5 below.

13. Among the Ossetians of the Black Sea region, who are thought to be the descendants of the Scythians and the Sarmatians, there are still legends of women who have the power to change into serpents. In south Russia, there is a belief that witches have tails, vestiges of the serpents they once were. See Kalmykov, 69–70.

14. Vasilenko, 42–98.

15. D. K. Zelenin, "Istolkovanie perezhitochnykh obriadov," *Sovetskaia etnografiia*, no. 5, 1935, 11.

16. Moszynski, 601–602.

17. Pomerantseva, 77–78.

18. I. M. Snegirev, *Russkie protonarodnye prazdniki i obriady*, vol. 1 (Moscow, 1837), 131.

19. Ibid. For a synthesis of Russian folklore in English, see W. R. S. Ralston, *Russian Folktales* (New York, 1880), which is based largely on Afanas'ev's work. On the *vily* and *rusalki*, see 119–120.

20. B. Branston, *Gods of the North* (New York, 1980), 190–191.

21. Gimbutas, *Gods and Goddesses*, 136–150.

22. Rybakov, "Rusalii i bog," 37–49, on the role of the bracelets in the rain ritual associated with the girls acting as *rusalki*.

23. See chapter 1, note 57, and W. D. O'Flaherty, ed., *Hindu Myths* (Harmondsworth, Middlesex, 1976), 238; W. N. Brown, "Mythology of India," in S. N. Kramer, ed., *Mythologies of the Ancient World* (Garden City, N.Y., 1961), 312–313. On the primordial Indian Great Mother Goddess, see H. Zimmer, "The Indian World Mother," in J. Campbell, ed., *The Mystic Vision: Papers from the Eranos Yearbooks*, R. Mannheim trans. (Princeton, 1982), 70–102.

24. Dittrich, 495–496; H. Masse, *Persian Beliefs and Customs* (New Haven, 1954), 344–356. For Afanas'ev's views on the word *deva*, see his *Poeticheskie vozzreniia*, vol. 1, 225.

25. Machal, 257. This theme of the nymphs' isolation in inaccessible regions is found in a number of Eastern as well as Western folk traditions. Among the Albanians, the *vily* were called "those without" to indicate that they lived without men. They were patronesses of horses, but when they appeared with Medusa-like locks, they brought disease. See L. M. J. Garnett, *Balkan Home Life* (New York), 63–66; and F. Copeland, "The Golden-Horned Hind (Zlatorog), A Slovenian Legend," *Slavonic and East European Review*, vol. 11, 1933, 654.

26. Solov'ev, 36; G. K. Zavoiko, "Verovaniia, obraidy, i obychai velikorussov Vladimirskoi gubernii," *Etnograficheskoe obozrenie*, nos. 3–4, 1914, 86, 101.

27. Mansikka, 96–97, argues that the ancient name of the *rusalki*

was that of Radunitsa, a holiday closely linked to the Rusalia, the festival of the *rusalki*. On the assimilation of the female ancestor with the *rusalka*, see A. V. Tereshchenko, *Byt' russkogo naroda* (St. Petersburg, 1848), vol. 6, 134.

28. See Haase, 153. On the *rusalka* portrayed as a sphinx who asks three questions of those who seek her out, see Afanas'ev, *Poeticheskie vozzreniia*, vol. 3, 151–152.

29. Solov'ev, 38, trans. mine.

30. Vasilenko, 43, 46; I. I. Shangina, "Izobrazhenie konia i ptitsei v russkoi krest'ianskoi vyshivke XIX-nachala XX veka," *Sovetskaia etnografiia*, no. 3, 1972, 116–118; and Matorin, 59–60, 62–64.

31. Haase, 153; Moszynski, 686; Pomerantseva, 731; Vasilenko, 78–79; W. R. S. Ralston, *The Songs of the Russian People* (London, 1873), 142–143; O'Flaherty, *Women, Androgynes*, 211–212, summarizes the goddess-bird-horse motif in proto-Indo-European and Indo-European cultural complexes.

32. In Estonia, *rusalki* or forest maidens, protectresses of trees and animals, were thought to be immanent in the forest itself, which became an animate being through them. See I. Paulson, *The Old Estonian Folk Religion* (Bloomington, Indiana, 1971), 62–69. On modern birch festivals, see V. L. Brudnyi, *Obriady vchera i segodnia* (Moscow, 1968), 97–98. On folk traditions and rituals surrounding the birch tree, see D. K. Zelenin, "Totemicheskii kul't derev'ev u russkikh i u belorussov," *Izvestiia Akademii nauk SSSR, otdelenie obshchestvennykh nauk*, no. 6, 1933, 611, who insists on the girls' ritual as totemic.

33. Vasilenko, 44; and F. J. Oinas, *Studies in Finnic-Slavic Folklore Relations* (Helsinki, 1969), 170.

34. See Snegirev, vol. 2, 1; Afanas'ev, *Poeticheskie vozzreniia*, vol. 3, 117–194; Vasilenko, 52. When peasant girls became "rainmakers" like the *rusalki*, they braided boughs into their hair to resemble them. See Frazer, 74–75, for Balkan customs. Washboards were often embossed with the image of the *rusalka-sirin* to stimulate rain through the actions of the women washing and to ensure the durability of the spun garments.

35. R. Caillois, "Les Spectres du midi dans la mythologie slave," *Revue des études slaves*, vol. 16, nos. 1–2, 1936, 24–25; and Moszynski, 692, on the *poludnitsy*. On the Ukrainian charms in which the sun is feminine, see Vasilenko, 51, trans. mine. For stories about the Firebirds, see Afanas'ev, *Narodnye russkie skazki*, vol. 1, 424–430.

36. Rybakov, "Rusalii i bog," 41–42.

37. Solov'ev, 39; and Ralston, *Russian Folktales*, 143. Among the Belorussians, for example, the custom was to make a plow only out of birchwood where the *rusalki* were thought to dwell. The plow thus became an instrument for the transference of generative power from forest to field and did not "wound" the earth with a "foreign" object.

38. The cult of the *rusalki* is clearly close to that of the *rozhanitsy* so hated by Christian missionaries.

39. Vasilenko, 42; and Pomerantseva, 79–80.

40. The sexual role of the *rusalki* was akin to that of the Greek Bacchantes. The symbolism attached to the *rusalki* as initiators into sexuality was most graphically expressed in the Serbian *poludnitsy*, depicted as hairy women who enticed young men and then placed them in their mouths! See Caillois, 35–36.

41. M. G. Wosien, *The Russian Folktale* (Munich, 1969), 134. On the Kore-Demeter motif, see C. Kerenyi, *Eleusis: Archetypal Image of Mother and Daughter*, R. Mannheim, trans. (New York, 1967).

42. R. Bleichsteiner, "Iranische Entsprechungen zu Frau Hölle and Baba Yaga," *Mitra*, no. 3, 1914, 68. On the fowl culture as a feminine domain, see A. Serner, *On 'Dyss' Burial and Belief about the Dead during the Stone Age with Special Regard to South Scandinavia* (Lund, 1938), 116.

43. V. I. Dal', *Poslovitsy russkogo naroda* (Moscow, 1957), 590, trans. mine.

44. Potebnia, 91–94; Afanas'ev, *Poeticheskie vozzreniia*, vol. 3, 587595.

45. Zavoiko, 110–111.

46. For an analysis of male fears, see W. Lederer, *Fear of Woman* (New York, 1968), 192–211; and H. R. Hayes, *The Dangerous Sex: The Myth of Feminine Evil* (New York, 1972).

47. R. Briffault, *The Mothers: A Study of the Origins of Sentiments and Institutions* (New York, 1927), vol. 2, 557. On witch cults in general, see H. C. Lea, *Materials toward a History of Witchcraft*, A. C. Howland, ed. (Philadelphia, 1939); J. C. Baroja, *The World of the Witches*, N. Glendinning, trans. (London, 1964); and M. Marwick, ed., *Witchcraft and Sorcery* (Harmondsworth, Middlesex, 1970). On Russian witches, see Potebnia, 130–131; Wosien, 136–139; P. I. Efimenko, "Sud' nad ved'mani," *Kievskaia starina*, vol. 7, 1883, 337. All three scholars regard Baba Yaga as a chthonian goddess. Afanas'ev, *Poeticheskie vozzreniia*, vol. 3, 586–595, tends to see her as a witch only.

48. S. A. Tokarev, *Religioznye verovaniia vostochno-slavianskikh narodov XIX-nachala XX veka* (Moscow, 1957), 22–29. On the monopoly that women in medieval Russia maintained over the healing arts, see R. Zguta, "Witchcraft and Medicine in Pre-Petrine Russia," *Russian Review*, vol. 37, no. 4, 440. Only later were sorcerers given the name of *znakhar*, and under this name they could belong to both sexes.

49. See Afanas'ev, *Poeticheskie vozzreniia*, vol. 3, 596–658, on witch trials in Russia. It should be noted that in Afanas'ev's collection of stories in which Yaga appears, her evil nature is stressed—it is less apparent in the Ukraine. It is also quite possible that the emphasis on her evil aspects may refer to the fact that male ethnologists collected the tales and that women, out of hostility to the outsider, might have underscored the ominous aspects of the witch. In so doing they evoked the sense of dishonor and oppression which the figure of Yaga suggests for her own sex, which she appears to avenge. She declares her independence from the world of men and thus affronts the social order. On linguistic sources of her name, see R. Jakobson, "On Russian Fairy Tales," in A. N. Afanas'ev, *Russian Fairy Tales*, N. Guterman, trans. and ed. (New York, 1974), 649; I. Bobula, "The Symbol of the Magna Mater," *American Journal of Archeology*, vol. 62, no. 2, 1958, 221–222; and E. Laroche, "Koubaba, déesse anatolienne et le problème des origines de Cybèle," *Elements orientaux dans la réligion grecque ancienne* (Paris, 1960), 122.

50. Antagonism toward witches was directed most particularly to their withholding food and causing natural disasters. In medieval Russia, the church spoke out against witches. In one case, that of the bishop Serapion, the appeal was against the drowning of witches be-

cause such vengeance affirmed their power over the natural world. See E. V. Petukhov, "Serapion Vladimirskii russkii propovednik XIII veka," in *Zapiski istoriko-filologicheskogo fakul'teta Imperatorskogo S.-Petersburgskogo universiteta*, vol. 17, 1888, 11–12.

51. The belief in witch goddesses who appeared in monstrous form, particularly to men, was widespread. See Bleichsteiner, 68; A. Ross, "The Divine Hag of the Pagan Celts," in V. Newall, ed., *The Witch Figure* (London, 1973).

52. See Afanas'ev, *Narodnye russkie skazki*, vol. 2, 171–210.

53. For links with the Indo-European mare cult, see O'Flaherty, *Women, Androgynes*, 149–280.

54. For a version in English of "The Chestnut Grey," see A. E. Alexander, *Russian Folklore: An Anthology* (Belmont, Massachusetts), 1975, 133–140. For Baba Yaga and Zamoryshchek, see Afanas'ev, *Narodnye russkie skazki*, vol. 1, 166–168.

55. See Afanas'ev, 376–382.

56. In folk tradition, the frog suggested the image of the wandering uterus. See Gimbutas, *Gods and Goddesses*, 178–179, and Potebnia, 201–206. On the bear cult, see Ivanov and Toporov, *Slavianskie iazykovye*, 160–165, who associate the bear with Volos and Saint George. But there was a Muscovite belief that under his skin the bear was in fact a witch. See M. Zabylin (Zabelin), *Russkii narod: Ego obychai, obriady, predaniia, sueveriia i poeziia* (Moscow, 1880), 242–243. In the Urals, it was thought that a bear was a woman cursed by the Christian god. For stories in which the bear appears as the caretaker of the forest, assuming Yaga's role, see Afanas'ev, "King Bear," in *Narodnye russkie skazki*, vol. 2, 90–93.

57. In the Ukraine, witches were also called "snakes." See Afanas'ev, *Poeticheskie vozzreniia*, vol. 3, 588. The word *zmeia* (snake) is drawn from the word *zemlia* (earth) in the Slavic pagan tradition. See Ivanov and Toporov, *Slavianskie iazykovye*, 104.

58. Afanas'ev, *Poeticheskie vozzreniia*, vol. 3, 455–456. On witch trials by water designed to release rain held by the witch, see R. Zguta, "The Ordeal by Water (Swimming Witches) in the East Slavic World," *Slavic Review*, vol. 36, no. 2, 1977, 219–230; and P. Efimenko, 383.

59. Gasparini, *Il matriarcato slavo*, 640.

60. Ibid., 649–652; and N. A. Ivanitskii, *Pesni, skazki, poslovitsy, pogovorki i zagadki* (Vologda, 1960), 201, trans. mine.

61. For lunar mythology, see Briffault, vol. 2, 600–640.

62. M. Eliade, *Patterns in Comparative Religion*, R. Sheed, trans. (New York, 1970), 170; and Afanas'ev, *Narodnye russkie skazki*, vol. 1, 136–138. The figure of the cannibal witch or divinity who devours the sun may well be drawn from Eastern mythology and is echoed in that of the West, as well.

63. Afanas'ev, *Poeticheskie vozzreniia*, vol. 2, 540. See also T. Stratilesco, *From Carpathians to Pindus* (Boston, 1967), 178.

64. V. N. Toporov, "Khettskaia Salsugi i slavianskaia Baba-Yaga," *Akademiia nauk SSSR, Institut slavianovedeniia, kratkie soobshcheniia*, vol. 38, 1963, 32–36; and H. Gaster, "The Child Stealing Witch among the Hittites," *Studi i materiali di storia delle religioni*, vol. 23, 1951–1952, 134–135.

65. For one such description, see Tereshchenko, vol. 4, 41.

66. For a Jungian analysis of the nature of maternal possessiveness—not a view sympathetic to women as mothers—see E. Neumann, *The Great Mother: An Analysis of the Archetype*, R. Mannheim, trans. (Princeton, 1970).

67. Potebnia, 131.

68. Gasparini, *Il matriarcato slavo*, 634, suggests that tales about Baba Yaga were told at ritually preestablished times, regulated by women and coinciding with spinning. On Baba Yaga's link with the Hittite Salgusi as initiator into rites of death and rebirth, see Toporov, 28–37.

69. Afanas'ev, *Narodnye russkie skazki*, vol. 1, 173–182.

70. On the fear of maternal and, by extension, female violence in the form of castration, through which the male child feels absorbed back into the body of the mother, see Neumann. The literary critic R. Girard, *Violence and the Sacred*, O. Gregory, trans. (Baltimore, 1977), 36, takes a historical-anthropological approach to the relationship between sexuality or emerging sexuality and the violence for which women are blamed.

71. On male initiation, see Gasparini, *Il matriarcato slavo*, 650–652. On male rituals in which meals were eaten in a witch-medium's house, see R. Reinach, "Le Souper chez la sorcière," *Actes du congrès international d'histoire des religions* (Paris, 1925), vol. 1, 498. On shamanic initiation rites, see M. Eliade, *Myths, Dreams, and Mysteries*, P. Mairet, trans. (New York, 1967), 81–84. On the relationship of the cult of earth with male and female initiations, see Wosien, 45; and on the power of women in the folktale, see M. L. von Franz, *Problems of the Feminine in Fairy Tales* (Irving, Texas, 1977), for a Jungian perspective.

72. Wosien, 69–70, 111–115, 130. For examples of female helpers, see the story of the "Bogatyria Sineglazka" in M. K. Azadovskii, *Russkaia skazka* (Leningrad, 1931–1932), vol. 1, 186–199.

73. Gasparini, *Il matriarcato slavo*, 635–637.

74. Afanas'ev, *Narodnye russkie skazki*, vol. 1, 159–165. In this story, the themes reflecting vestiges of matrilinity and matrilocality are not apparent. But in others, the motif of brother-sister incest, such as that of "Prince Danila Govrila," "Sister Alionushka, Brother Ivanushka," "The Milk of Wild Beasts," and "Masha Soplivka" (in V. G. Bazanov, ed., *Velikorusskie skazki v zapisiakh I. A. Khudiakova* [Moscow-Leningrad, 1964], 84–85; and Afanas'ev, *Narodnye russkie skazki*, vol. 1, 187–190, and vol. 2, 94–108), suggest that although the church and the patriarchal social order did not accept the archaic expression of matrilinity indicated by the incest taboo, the peasants continued to affirm it.

CHAPTER THREE: RECONSTRUCTING THE RUSSIAN
GREAT GODDESS: MOTHER EARTH

1. B. Pilnyak, *Mother Earth and Other Stories*, V. T. Reck and M. Green, trans. (Garden City, New York), 1968, 51.

2. Fedotov, vol. 1, 12.

3. B. A. Rybakov, "Kalendar' IV veka iz zemli Polian," *Sovetskaia arkheologiia*, no. 4, 1962, 66–89, traces the annual agrarian festivals of the Slavs to the fourth century A.D. Matorin, 136–137, argues for the later emergence of the Mother Earth cult based on the advent of agriculture.

4. See Frazer, 339–461, and James, 237–238. On the twin motif, see chapter 6 above.

5. Fedotov, 19. Demeter is derived from the Doric *da* for "earth" and *mater* for "mother." Graves, vol. 1, 43, 92, associates her name with "Barley Mother." Kore-Persephone-Hekate, who are linked with her, mean respectively "green corn," "ripe corn," and "harvested corn."

6. Fedotov, 18–19. The proverbs are from P. Bezsonov, ed., *Kalieki perekhozhie* (Moscow, 1861), vol. 4, 145; vol. 5, 480; vol. 2, 356, trans. mine; and S. Smirnov, "Drevnerusskii dukhovnik," 272.

7. On connections between plants and animals, see Haase, 175; and Zavoiko, 119, 126, on animals and earth. Proverbs are from Dal', 802, 912, trans. mine.

8. Afanas'ev, *Poeticheskie vozzreniia*, vol. 1, 114–150, tries to find consorts for Mother Earth. Her parthenogenesis is quite apparent in the rites performed by women who appear to "milk" the maternal skies like their predecessors at Tripol'e: Among the Belorussians as well as among peasants in the area of Moscow, during a drought, women harnessed the strongest among them to a plow and went to the river, where they began to work up the dry river bed in the hope that this would stimulate rain from the skies. Often the ritual was led by a pregnant woman, whose full belly was considered analogous to the rain cloud. See Zelenin, "Istolkovanie," 5–9.

9. Haase, 138–139; Tokarev, 73; V. Stepanov, "Svedeniia o rodil'nykh i krest'ianskikh obriadakh v Klinskom uezde Moskovskoi gubernii," *Etnograficheskoe obozrenie*, vol. 70–71, nos. 3–4, 1906, 230–231; V. N. Kharuzina, "Neskol'ko slov o rodil'nykh krest'ianskikh obriadakh i ob ukhode za det'mi v Pydozhskom uezde," *Etnograficheskoe obozrenie*, vol. 68–69, nos. 1–2, 1906, 90. In many creation myths, life merges from a watery chaos.

10. See, for example, a Koliada song in Zemtsovskii, 56. For representations of the sun and moon as feminine in the Ukraine, see Dal', 950; and Afanas'ev, *Poeticheskie vozzreniia*, vol. 1, 223–224.

11. S. Smirnov, 268–275; Tokarev, 76; Haase, 170; and D. K. Zelenin, *Ocherki russkoi mifologii* (Petrograd, 1916), 84–85.

12. Haase, 169–171; S. Smirnov, 276.

13. Women solicited the fruitfulness of the soil by offerings of food and drink. The famous Ukrainian Easter eggs were placed at graves and upon the earth itself in memory of those whom it contained. See Haase, 172–173; Paulson, 102; Moszynski, 512–513. For Tripol'e antecedents, see Gimbutas, *Gods and Goddesses*, 168. On legends concerning the origin of the plow which suggest that it represents a male victory against a serpentlike Baba Yaga, see Potebnia, 10. For a notion of earth devouring her children, see S. Smirnov, 267, 272–273.

14. Cited in S. Smirnov, 281–282, from unpublished materials. For other plowing taboos, see Moszynski, 510–511, trans. mine; and Tokarev, 74–75. Mother Earth is sometimes associated with the thunder god Perun; but even he can "mate" with her only at specific times. He is linked with the sun as the male principle and hence is born and dies each day out of her "womb."

15. Dal', 372, 388, 594, trans. mine.

16. Ibid., trans. mine. On the fire cult, see V. N. Kharuzina, "K voprosu o pochitanii ognia," *Etnograficheskoe obozrenie*, vol. 70–71, nos. 3–4, 1906, 68–205. On the role of the female elder transporting fire from an old to a new *izba*, see M. Matossian, "The Peasant Way of Life," in W.

S. Vucinich, ed., *The Peasant in Nineteenth Century Russia* (Stanford, 1968), 20.

17. Gasparini, "Studies in Old Slavic Religion," 112–139, and *Il matriarcato slavo*, 601–620, shows the role of the towel in the Slavic rites of exhumation. For similar customs among the Dravidians in India, see Serner, 187.

18. Stepanov, 225–233; Zabylin, 535. For proverbs stressing the mother-child bond, see Dal', 387.

19. On lullabies, see A. Martynova, "Life in the Pre-Revolutionary Village as Reflected in Popular Lullabies," in D. L. Ransel, ed., *The Family in Imperial Russia* (Urbana, Illinois, 1978), 171–185. The mother directs the growth of the child: "Every time a mother pulls a child by the hair, it shrinks—that is why the stubborn don't grow much," we hear in one proverb. See Dal', 383, trans. mine. On the mother's protective spells, see Sakharov, *Skazanie russkogo naroda*, vol. 1, 19, cited in Zabylin, 295, trans. mine.

20. Haase, 157–158; Tokarev, 75, 101; Afanas'ev, *Poeticheskie vozzreniia*, vol. 1, 144; and S. Smirnov, 269.

21. See Ralston, *Songs*, 317–322. For the invocation to earth, see Zavoiko, 88, trans. mine.

22. The ancestors protected the home from their position in the *pech'* and the icon corner. In a child's game of tag, when the girls and boys touched home they yelled out, *"Chur menia"* or "Ancestor protect me." See H. Troyat, *Daily Life in Russia under the Last Tsar*, M. Barnes, trans. (Stanford, 1979), 211. On the relationship of *chur* and *rod*, see V. V. Ivanov and V. N. Toporov, *Slavianskie iazykovye modelirushchie semioticheskie sistemy* (Moscow, 1965), 187–188. The sacrifices of food to the ancestors are described in Snegirev, vol. 2, 117.

23. The past tense is used in the description of agrarian rites, since in our day they represent aberrant, if often persistent, exceptions to the Soviet rule. See Brudnyi, 99–100.

24. On Lada, see M. F. Mur'ianov, "Mif o Lade," *Russkii fol'klor*, vol. 12, 1974, 220–225; Afanas'ev, *Poeticheskie vozzreniia*, vol. 1, 227–229. For Lada's link with the mare-bird cult, see O'Flaherty, *Women, Androgynes*, 211–212. On Lada's link with Finnish or Latvian as well as Carian and Lydian goddesses, see Snegirev, vol. 1, 111; Haase, 120; Nichols, 242; and Graves, vol. 1, 207.

25. See M. T. Znayenko, *The Gods of the Ancient Slavs* (Columbus, Ohio, 1980), 21, 82–83, 140; and Afanas'ev, *Poeticheskie vozzreniia*, vol. 1, 228–229.

26. Afanas'ev, *Poeticheskie vozzreniia*, vol. 1, 229; and W. Tooke, *View of the Russian Empire*, (London, 1800), vol. 2, 68.

27. Mur'ianov, 221–222; Snegirev, vol. 2, 20; M. Nichols, *Man, Myth, and Monument* (New York, 1975), 243.

28. R. Reeder, *Down along the Mother Volga* (Philadelphia, 1975), 125; Zemtsovskii, 389, trans mine.

29. V. I. Propp, *Russkie agrarnie prazdniki* (Leningrad, 1963), 14–15.

30. Afanas'ev, *Poeticheskie vozzreniia*, vol. 3, 747–748, 730–731; and Potebnia, 223.

31. For a typical Koliada song evoking the image of a birth aided

by the peasantry, who stimulate the warming powers of the sun by lighting bonfires, see Shein, 309.

32. "An old woman walks around," the song begins. "She wears a *sarafan* with a hundred patches. / On each patch there is a hundred rubles. / On the last patch there are no estimates." Zemtsovskii, 148, 161, trans. mine.

33. Ibid., 125, 76–77, trans. mine.

34. See Zavoiko, 133; S. Benet, ed. and trans., *The Village at Viriatino* (New York, 1970), 140; and Zemtsovskii, 99, trans. mine.

35. Zemtsovskii, 131–132, trans. mine.

36. See Zabylin, 13–26; and Propp, 107. Keys and locks, windows and doors, and bread covered with the votive towels were invoked in this ritual. The Soviet scholar V. I. Chicherov, in his seminal study of winter agrarian rites, shows the custom of fortunetelling involving the whole family. But it would appear that the church could accept this pagan ritual more readily if a male peasant was in charge. See Chicherov, *Zimnii period russkogo narodnogo zemledel'cheskogo kalendaria XVI-XIX vekov* (Moscow, 1957), 94.

37. Chicherov, 115ff. See also E. V. Pomerantseva and S. I. Mints, *Russkoe narodnoe poeticheskoe tvorchestvo, Khrestomatiia* (Moscow, 1963), 119; and Zemtsovskii, 138–139. Maskers are called "swans" and "geese" in verses collected in Pomerantseva and Mints, 119. On the image of the "winter *rusalka*," see V. N. Vsevolodskii-Gerngross, *Istoriia russkogo teatra* (Moscow-Leningrad, 1929), 159. For Bulgarian customs, Garnett, 73.

38. Propp, 52; I. I. Veletskaia, "O novgorodnykh rusaliiakh," in B. A. Rybakov, ed., *Slavianie i Rus'* (Moscow, 1968), 394–396; and G. Megas, *Greek Calendar Customs* (Athens, 1963), 47.

39. Propp, 112–113. Propp associates the rites of comedy and tragedy with Demeter and Beaubo (the old woman who succeeded in making the grieving mother laugh, causing nature to bloom) rather than Dionysus. See 120. For the rite of "raising the dead," see 69, 114–115. For a description of a Belorussian custom, see Vernadsky, *Origins of Russia*, 153.

40. The yule log ceremony is found in many parts of Europe, as well as among the Slavs. See Megas, 36; Solov'ev, 28; Veletskaia, 395, trans. mine; and Afanas'ev, *Poeticheskie vozzreniia*, vol. 3, 734–735.

41. Iu. Sokolov, *Le Folklore russe*, G. Welter, trans. (Paris, 1945), 88; Propp, 16–17.

42. See L. S. Nosova, "Mapping the Russian Shrovetide Ritual," *Soviet Anthropology and Archeology*, vol. 14, nos. 1–2, 1975, 50–70; Afanas'ev, *Poeticheskie vozzreniia*, vol. 3, 696–697; Vsevolodskii-Gerngross, 162; Solov'ev, 30; Propp, 71. Laughter, like comedy, was intended to stimulate the earth.

43. Zemtsovskii, 239, 240, 246, 260, for songs welcoming Maslenitsa with food. For other rituals, see Propp, 123–127; Benet, 131. On the relationship of *bliny*, ancestor worship, and the moon, see Solov'ev, 35; Propp, 17; Tereshchenko, vol. 2, 329.

44. See Sokolov, 91; Solov'ev, 30; Gasparini, *Il matriarcato slavo*, 666–667, on the *khorovod* as a moon dance.

45. Nosova, "Mapping," 56–58; Vsevolodskii-Gerngross, 164; Frazer, 313–316.

46. Verses from Shein, 338, trans. mine. See also Propp, 31–34; Ralston, *Songs*, 213–218; and Garnett, 209–210.

47. On life as the goddess Zhiva and death as the goddess Morena or Mara, see Afanas'ev, *Poeticheskie vozzreniia*, vol. 1, 100–101; vol. 3, 693–696. In the Ukraine, a doll called Mara/Marena is burned, and out of her ashes emerges Zhiva, or Life. See also Haase. For verses, see Zemtsovskii, 289, trans. mine.

48. Snegirev, vol. 1, 6–46.

49. Ibid., 13–16; and Afanas'ev, *Poeticheskie vozzreniia*, vol. 3, 703–704.

50. Snegirev, vol. 1, 47–54, 49, trans. mine.

51. Megas, 129.

52. Gasparini, *Il matriarcato slavo*, 502; Sokolov, 94–95; Vsevolodskii-Gerngross, 168–170.

53. Snegirev, vol. 2, 809; Zabylin, 63; Zemtsovskii, 446, trans. mine.

54. Propp, 61. See the *rusalka's* song in Zemtsovskii, 446. In some areas, a girl disguised as a hunchback went into the forest and was identified as Semik. She was accompanied by a youth dressed as a woman. Only females, or males associated with women by dressing like them, could enter the forest, the domain of the souls of the dead as well as the *rusalki* who embodied them.

55. For *kumstvo* songs, see N. A. Rimsky-Korsakov, *Sto russkikh narodnykh pesen* (Moscow-Leningrad, 1951), no. 50: and Zemtsovskii, 398. The word *kuma* is related to the English word *gossip*, which originally meant common godmothership. See Ralston, *Songs*, 215, note 6.

56. Zelenin, "Totemicheskii kul't," 607–620.

57. Propp, 130–131; Afanas'ev, *Poeticheskie vozzreniia*, vol. 3, 705; Zavoiko, 154. On the initiation rites of the Southern Slavs involving the assimilation of girls with the earth and the clan including the ancestors, see A. Koleva, "Vesenie devich'i obychai u nekotorykh iuzhnoslavianskikh narodov," *Sovetskaia etnografiia*, no. 5, 1974, 74–85.

58. See Zemtsovskii, 398, trans. mine; Zelenin, "Totemicheskii kul't," 617–618.

59. Snegirev, vol. 1, 147–150. Snegirev observes a ceremony in certain areas in which women and girls fought over the Semik or *rusalka* tree, taking it into the fields like the Maslenitsa doll and spreading the remains over the ground. Indeed, in the mysteries of Eleusis, the chief priestesses played the roles of Kore and Demeter both. This was particularly true of the festival of Thesmorphia, reserved for women alone and designed to ensure the growth of seed grain. The myth of Kore-Demeter appears to have predated that of Adonis and suggests the vestiges of female solidarity. Pomeroy, 77–78, suggests that it referred to the prepatriarchal period of horticulture.

60. Cross and Sherbowitz-Wetzor, 56; Snegirev, vol. 2, 24–25; Zabylin, 72; and Mansikka, 115.

61. On the association of Kupala and Cybele, see W. Stscherbakiwskyj, "The Early Ukrainian Social Order as Reflected in Ukrainian Wedding Customs," *Slavonic and East European Review*, vol. 31, 1952, 345.

62. Snegirev, vol. 2, 59–60; Vernadsky, *Origins of Russia*, 113–114. For songs, see Zemtsovskii, 473, 475, 480.

63. Zemtsovskii, 41, 486, trans. mine.

64. Machal, 313; Vsevolodskii-Gerngross, 171–173. For Kupalo's name, see Afanas'ev, *Poeticheskie vozzreniia*, vol. 3, 712–713; Haase, 103. On the sun cult linked with Iarilo, see Ivanov and Toporov, *Slavianskie iazykovye*, 120–137.

65. Zabylin, 82; Ivanov and Toporov, *Slavianskie iazykovye*, 123124, 132, on his association with the auroch and the auroch's with woman in Slavic folklore and on his Priapic and Dionysian nature. See also Snegirev, vol. 2, 53, 61.

66. Cited in P. I. Mel'nikov, *Polnoe sobranie sochinenii* (Moscow, 1909), vol. 4, 4, trans. mine.

67. Haase, 99–101; Afanas'ev, *Poeticheskie vozzreniia*, vol. 1, 441442.

68. Vsevolodskii-Gerngross, 171.

69. Zemtsovskii, 457, trans. mine; and for other songs, 462. See also Snegirev, vol. 2, 33–38.

70. Zemtsovskii, 450–451, trans. mine; and A. L. Melkov, "Nekotorye detskie igry v Kurskoi gubernii," *Etnograficheskoe obozrenie*, nos. 3–4, 1914, 181–182; E. Warner, 161–162.

71. Snegirev, vol. 2, 60–68; Zabylin, 85; Sokolov, 98.

72. Zemtsovskii, 533, trans. mine. The girl harvesters were called bees, headed by the mistress of the house, the queen bee. In the rites of Demeter and Kore at Eleusis, the priestesses attached to the temple were also called *Melissae* or bees. See Pomeroy, 76.

73. Zabylin, 102; Zemtsovskii, 499, trans. mine; Snegirev, vol. 2, 93–96.

74. Shein, 94, trans. mine.

75. Zavoiko, 161, trans. mine; Dal', 387, 373, trans. mine.

76. Gasparini, *Il matriarcato slavo*, 434. See also Shashkov, 1–52.

77. Gasparini, *Il matriarcato slavo*, 9, 274; and on joint family ownership, 255, 284–285. See also W. T. Shinn, "The Law of the Russian Peasant Household," *Slavic Review*, vol. 20, no. 4, 1961, 603–605. On the son's need for maternal blessing, Gasparini, *Il matriarcato slavo*, 259–260. For vestiges of matriclan custom in the folktale hero, see E. M. Meletinskii, "The 'Low' Hero of the Fairy Tale," in F. J. Oinas and S. Soudakoff, eds., *The Study of Russian Folklore* (The Hague, 1975), 253.

78. S. de Beauplan, *A Description of Ukraine* (London, 1732), cited in Gasparini, *Il matriarcato slavo*, 237, trans. mine.

79. Ibid., 233–237, 299–304, 399–401.

80. On Russian wedding customs in general, see Reeder, 18–25; and on the Ukraine in particular, W. Stscherbakiwskyj, 325–351. For collections of wedding songs, see D. Uspenskii, "Svadebnye velichal'nye pesni," *Etnograficheskoe obozrenie*, vol. 70–71, no. 304, 1906, 234–241; and N. P. Kolpakova, ed., *Lirika russkoi svad'by* (Leningrad, 1962). Shashkov, 102–117, discusses the persistence of pagan wedding rites.

81. Kolpakova, p. 8, trans. mine.

82. On the girl as tree, land, or garden, see Kolpakova, 14–15, 120; and on the groom as warrior or hunter, 69–70. The Ukrainian song is from Ralston, *Songs*, 295, 299.

83. Reeder, 19–20; Stscherbakiwskyj, 330; and for an example of a bride imploring her brother for his help, Kolpakova, 277.

84. Arbatskii, 71–72, trans. mine. The *vila* sometimes carried a serpent in her hand instead. It represented her long and free-flowing mane of hair, the *krasota*. See Matorin, 98.

85. T. Volkov, "Rites et usages nuptiaux en Ukraine," *L'Anthropologie*, vol. 2, 1891, 538, 540. The song is cited in Stscherbakiwskyj, 337–338.

86. Volkov, 550. For the role of the uncle, see Stscherbakiwskyj, 345. The conflict between matrilocal and patrilocal weddings is found in a number of folktales, most vividly in "The Bride in the Bathhouse." See Ivanitskii, 176. The custom of laying down the law is linked perhaps to the Thesmorphia celebrating the establishment of the first laws by women in Attica—laws based on agrarian rituals rather than those of the *polis*, or city.

87. Volkov, 556–557; and Stscherbakiwskyj, 331–334.

88. Cited from unpublished material in Volkov, 565, trans. mine.

89. The pagan Rusalia was evoked in the custom of the couple having garlands placed in their hair and made to carry candles while they walked around the lectern. Brudnyi, 50. For the celebration of a wedding by having the couple walk around a tree, see Shashkov, 116. On the rite of "stepping" on the bride and her obligation to remove the groom's boots, see Alexander, 88–92.

CHAPTER FOUR: THE COMING OF CHRISTIANITY:
MARY AND PARASKEVA-PIATNITSA

1. L. Tolstoi, *War and Peace*, L. and A. Maude, trans. (New York, 1966), 850.

2. On the centricity of Mary in Russian religiosity, see D. Samarin, "Bogoroditsa v russkom narodnom pravoslavii," *Russkaia mysl'*, vol. 39, 1918, 1–38; Berdiaev, 6. Kologrivof, 156–168; and D. Strottman, "Quelques aperçus historiques sur le culte marial en Russie," *Irenikon*, vol. 32, 1959, 134–187, link the cult of Mother Earth and Mary.

3. It is likely that the myth was modeled on that of Constantine's mother, Helena, whose role in the Christianization of the Roman-Byzantine Empire was surely symbolic of the importance of fertility cults overseen by women in the Roman Empire. Olga also took the name of Helen. See Vernadsky, *Kievan Russia*, 40.

4. Cross and Sherbowitz-Wetzor, 78–87.

5. The motif of an evil and pagan Kievan princess burying men is found in the popular *Dukhovnye stikhi*. See "Forty Pilgrims and One" in Alexander, 359. The story reflects on the persistence—and strength—of pagan customs in which women play a central role. Chadwick, 29–30, argues, however, that the ship burial is a Scandinavian tradition which required that the wife perform an actual or ritual form of suttee for her husband.

6. See K. Waliszweski, *La Femme russe* (Paris, 1926), 6.

7. Cross and Sherbowitz-Wetzor, 111.

8. By the sixth century, the Roman and Eastern churches had become accustomed to using the power of rulers in the work of conversion.

See F. Lot, *The End of the Ancient World and the Beginnings of the Middle Ages*, P. and M. Leon., trans. (New York, 1962), 50.

9. Elnett, 21; Fedotov, 375.

10. Vernadsky, *Kievan Russia*, 154–157. See also Ia. N. S. Shchapov, "Vliianie obshchestvennogo mirosozertsaniia na sotsial'noe polozhenie zhenshchiny v Rossii," *Sochineniia*, vol. 2 (St. Petersburg, 1906), 80–104; and Shashkov, 21–23.

11. S. Smirnov, "Baby bogomerzkiia," *Sbornik statei posvulshchennykh Vasiliu Kliuchevskomy* (Moscow, 1909), 219–221; and Cross and Sherbowitz-Wetzor, 117.

12. See Dal', 386, 370, trans. mine; S. Smirnov, 223; and A. P. Shchapov, 108–110, who discusses the stress on feminine sinfulness in Kievan and Muscovite Russia.

13. On the misogyny in Roman Catholicism, see M. Warner, *Alone of All Her Sex: The Myth and Cult of the Virgin Mary* (New York, 1976). Even Vladimir was surprised at the denigration of woman and nature. See N. K. Nikol'skii, "O drevnerusskom Khristianstve," *Russkaia mysl'*, no. 6, 1913, 1820. On the notion of feminine evil, see N. Aristov, "Sud'ba russkoi zhenshchiny v dopetrovskoe vremia," *Zaria*, 1871, no. 3, 191–192; and Shashkov, 71–101. On the patriarchalization of the feminine image, see J. D. Grossman, "Feminine Images in Old Russian Literature and Art," *California Slavic Studies*, vol. II, 1980, 33–70.

14. Tertullian, *Disciplinary, Moral, and Ascetical Works* (New York, 1959), cited in M. Warner, 58. See also G. Ashe, *The Virgin* (London, 1976), 10–11. For a Jungian perspective, see F. Heiler, "The Madonna as a Religious Symbol," in *The Mystic Vision: Papers from the Eranos Yearbooks*, R. Mannheim, trans. (Princeton, 1968), 348–374.

15. M. Warner, 51–52. The Gnostics attempted to integrate the teachings of the great fertility religions into Christianity. See E. Pagels, *The Gnostic Gospels* (New York, 1981), 57–83.

16. *Izmaragd*, vol. 1, chap. 54, and vol. 2, chap. 52, cited in Fedotov, vol. 2, 76–77; and A. P. Shchapov, 108–110.

17. On the overwhelming power of woman as sinner, see proverbs in Dal', 352, 388. For example: "When a husband sins, it's a human mistake; when a wife does, she carries the whole house with her." 368, trans. mine. On the Kievan princes' fear of their wives' influence, see A. P. Shchapov, 112–113.

18. This is M. Warner's thesis.

19. Cited in S. Smirnov, "Baby," 223–224, trans. mine.

20. Cross and Sherbowitz-Wetzor, 94–95; S. Smirnov, "Baby," 225; and A. I. Almazov, *Tainaia ispoved'*, vol. 3, cited in S. Smirnov, "Baby," 229, trans. mine. The echoes of this centuries-long resistance on the part of women to the teachings of the church can be found, for example, in the belief (in east central Russia) that *eretiki*, or heretics, in the majority women, would become vampires. See F. J. Oinas, "Heretics as Vampires and Demons in Russia," *Slavic and East European Journal*, vol. 22, no. 4, 1978, 433–441.

21. The *Dukhovnye stikhi* were sung by wandering cripples, beggars, and blind men and women traveling through north and central Russia and singing in return for food and shelter. Called *liudi bozhie* (people of God), they were devoted most particularly to the Mother of God. In south

Russia, like troubadours, they accompanied their songs with a musical instrument—the *bandura*. They adapted apocryphal legends from the Old and New Testaments which had filtered into Russia through Byzantium and the West. The most famous of these, "The Wanderings of the Mother of God in Hell," like many others, was interwoven with pagan themes. A considerable number of songs center on the life and laments of Mary, who appears as an all-knowing goddess. There is also an important cycle of songs dealing with the lament of Adam and Eve expelled from Paradise. For the version showing Eve as a goddess in her own right, see "Ispovedanie Evyne," Tischendorf, *Apocalyses apocryphae* (Leipzig, 1866), 1–32, cited in M. Gaster, *Greeko-Slavonic Literature and Its Relation to the Folklore of Europe during the Middle Ages* (London, 1887). On the Hebrew reversal of the creation of woman by man, see T. H. Gastor, *Myth, Legend, and Custom in the Old Testament*, vol. 1, 21–23. In Sumerian belief, it is the goddess who creates man out of clay.

22. A. D. de Groot, *Saint Nicholas: A Psychoanalytic Study of His History* (The Hague, 1965), 136, 149–151.

23. See N. Gogol's famous short story "Vyi" (in *Mirogorod: Four Tales by Nikolai Gogol*, D. Magarshack, trans. [New York, 1968], 175–219) for another version.

24. M. O. Skripil, *Russkie povesti XV-XVI vekov,* (Moscow, 1958), 108–115, trans. in S. A. Zenkovsky, ed., *Medieval Russia's Epics, Chronicles, and Tales* (New York, 1963), 237–247.

25. The persistence of pagan cults is attested to by the discovery of numerous pre-fourteenth-century sacrificial vessels. See J. V. Haney, "On the 'Tale of Peter and Fevroniia, Wonderworkers of Murom,'" *Canadian-American Slavic Studies*, vol. 13, nos. 1–2, 1979, 143.

26. Zenkovsky, 240.

27. Ibid., 241; and Haney, 150.

28. Zenkovsky, 245.

29. Ibid.

30. Ibid., 246; and Haney, 160–162.

31. Rybakov, "Drevnie elementy," 105.

32. Clement of Alexandria, "The Gospel According to the Egyptians," cited in R. E. Witt, *Isis in the Graeco-Roman World* (Ithaca, New York, 1971), 278. See also Pagels, 57–83. Mary assumed all the aspects of her pagan prototypes: Though mother of Christ and bride of God, she remains a virgin. Like Isis and Ishtar, she mourns her dead consort-son. She protects her children under the cape of heaven and earth. C. Ochs, *Behind the Sex of God* (Boston, 1977), 68–71.

33. M. Warner, 65–66.

34. Mary continued to be represented in triune (parthenogenetic) form as virgin, mother, and elder. At Christ's crucifixion, she was triplicated like the Fates: Mary the Mother, Mary Magdalene, and Mary Cleopas. See Ochs, 78.

35. Saint Anselm, *The Prayers and Meditations of Saint Anselm* (London, 1973), 141, cited in M. Warner, 197.

36. E. Benz, *The Eastern Orthodox Church*, R. and C. Winston, trans. (Garden City, New York, 1963), 37.

37. S. Bulgakov, *L'Orthodoxie* (Paris, 1932), 164–165.

38. The bridge between Isis, Sophia, and Christianity is spanned by

the Hellenistic Jew, Philo of Alexandria. "Holy Wisdom" meant for him the mother of the divine *Logos*. In his writings, she is identified with Isis, the mother of Horus. Gnostics also assimilated Isis to Sophia, thereby fighting the church's extirpation of all aspects of the feminine from the cult. These heretics suggested that Jehovah was merely instrumental to the Great Mother, who had created all things. Only through his hubris could he claim such all-embracing power. He began to believe that he had made everything. In the Gnostic documents recently discovered, Sophia or Wisdom is represented with a daughter, like Demeter and Kore. She becomes angry with God's arrogance and leaves him. Sophia entered the dogma of the church through a sex change—as the *Spiritus Sanctus*! See Witt, 184; E. Pagels, "The Suppressed Gnostic Feminism," *New York Review of Books*, vol. 26, no. 18, 1979, 45; M. Warner, 39, 198.

39. I. E. Grabar, ed., *Istoriia russkogo iskusstva*, vol. 1 (St. Petersburg, 1909), 148. .

40. A. Tertz (A. Sinyavsky), *A Voice from the Chorus*, K. Fitzlyon and M. Hayward, trans. (New York, 1976), 238–239. On the identification of the church with Mary and motherland in both Russia and the West, see N. P. Kondakov, *Ikonografiia Bogomateri*, vol. 1 (St. Petersburg, 1914–1915), 345–349.

41. Bezsonov, vol. 5, 204, trans. mine.

42. Dal', 329, trans. mine.

43. I. Smolitsch, "Die Verehrung der Göttesmutter in der Russischen Frommigkeit und Volksreligiösität, *Kyrios*, vol. 5, 1940–1941, 199–201; and A. Lebedev, *Razlichie v uchenii vostochnoi i zapadnoi tserkvei o Presviatoi Deve Marii* (Moscow, 1881), 152–153; I. Hapgood, *Service Book of the Holy Orthodox Church* (Boston, 1906), 470.

44. Strotmann, 182.

45. Matorin, 128.

46. Samarin, 14.

47. Matorin, 24, 31. See also D. I. Uspenskii, "Narodnye verovaniia v tserkovnoi zhivopisi," *Etnograficheskoe obozrenie*, vol. 68–69, nos. 1–2, 1906, 73–87, for miracles attributed to icons of Mary and Saint Paraskeva.

48. Strotmann, 181.

49. Another renowned *Umilenie*, the fourteenth-century Bogoroditsa of the Don, was said to have been given to Russia's national hero, Prince Dmitrii Donskoi, by his warriors on the eve of their battle against the Tatars. Their victory over the enemy was attributed directly to the icon. M. W. Alpatov, *Art Treasures of Russia*, N. Guterman, trans. (New York, n.d.), 74. See Bezsonov, vol. 3, 681–689, for the popular expression of Mary as peacemaker in the *Dukhovnye stikhi* and for her appearance in a column of fire to save a monastery.

50. Haase, 19; Afanas'ev, *Poeticheskie vozzreniia*, vol. 1, 484.

51. Bezsonov, vol. 4, 117–118, trans. mine.

52. The discovery in Novgorod of an icon placed inside a "holy" *pech'* makes the link with Mary explicit and echoes the Paleolithic and Neolithic practices of locating female figurines near or in the hearth. See Matorin, 119.

53. Bezsonov, vol. 5, 178–179, trans. mine.

54. Christ's answer to his mother's lament is to ask her, " 'Leave me

to Mother Moist Earth.' " Ibid., 177, trans. mine. The cycle of the "Dream of the Mother of God" is represented as amuletic. In reciting the verses, each mother became a fategiver and a lawmaker. Ibid., 178.

55. Ibid., 185, trans. mine.

56. Alpatov, 103. On a similar hymn showing the Sumerian goddess Inanna mourning for her son-lover Tammuz, see M. Warner, 206, 221.

57. E. de Savitsch, "Religious Amulets of Early Russian Christendom," *Gazette des beaux-arts*, vol. 23, 1943, 113; and M. Warner, 321.

58. In a Siberian version of this legend, the tree is represented as the Tree of Life. See I. Novgorod-Severskii, *Skazki sibirskie i legendy o Bozhei Materi* (Munich, n.d.), 146.

59. "Khozhdenie Bogoroditsy po mukam," in N. K. Gudzii, ed., *Khrestomatiia po drevnei russkoi literature* (Moscow, 1962), 98, trans. mine.

60. Matorin, 42–43.

61. Rybakov, "Drevnie elementy," 105–106.

62. Matorin, 75.

63. Ibid., 92; and Garnett, 141. Isis of the Hellenistic period was the astral deity from whom the association of Mary with the skies was undoubtedly borrowed. See M. Warner, 256.

64. "Povest' o Marfe i Marii," in Gudzii, 352–355.

65. Bezsonov, vol. 3, 788–789, trans. mine.

66. Afanas'ev, *Poeticheskie vozzreniia*, vol. 1, 223; vol. 2, 357–360.

67. The white stone may be an echo of the cult of the Scythian *kamennye baby*. Qualities of healing are attributed to it—as they were to the "stone women." Stones in general, venerated by the Slavs, were seen as outcroppings of Mother Earth's "holy bones." See M. Gimbutas, *Ancient Symbolism in Lithuanian Folk Art* (Philadelphia, 1958), 96; and Matorin, 76.

68. Pomerantseva and Mints, 112; charm taken from *Zapiski russkogo geograficheskogo obshchestva etnografiia*, vol. 2, 1871, 442, cited in Haase, 294. For descriptions of Mary sewing with a gold thread, see 276.

69. Afanas'ev, *Poeticheskie vozzreniia*, vol. 1, 483–485 and 354–356. Mary's icon is called "the serpent" in some areas. See Matorin, 73.

70. See T. T. Rice, *A Concise History of Russian Art* (New York, 1967), 39 for the sixteenth-century icon; Bezsonov, vol. 4, 35; and Matorin, 88.

71. For an illustration of the "Ustiug icon," see Alpatov, 43; for an evocation of Mary in charms as a spinner, see Haase, 178.

72. Afanas'ev, *Poeticheskie vozzreniia*, vol. 1, 540–542, on the pigeon. The icon of "Mary the Dove" or "Mary with Pigeons," called the *Golubitskimi*, is discussed in Matorin, 73. In Serbia, the connection between Mary and the *rusalki* is obliquely made in the custom of calling a certain church, the "Holy Trinity," by the name of "Holy Mother Rusalia." Legends of Saint Nicholas planting trees at miraculously appearing springs where the *rusalki* or *vily* had previously been worshipped and then expelling the demons from those places suggest the process of Christianization. See ibid., 81–82.

73. Zabylin, 339, 350, 379–380.

74. Matorin, 105–106, trans. mine.

75. Bezsonov, vol. 4, 216, trans. mine.

76. L. S. Nosova, *Iazychestvo v pravoslavii* (Moscow, 1975), 92–93. On Mary's many feast days associated with pagan fertility rites, see Smolitsch, 198–199.

77. Smolitsch, 212; Strotmann, 186–187.
78. Nosova, *Iazychestvo*, 91.
79. Kondakov, vol. 2, 93.
80. Ibid., vol. 1, 347–348.
81. Afanas'ev, *Poeticheskie vozzreniia*, vol. 1, 239–240, trans. mine.
82. See Potebnia, 75, 80, 81, trans. mine; and Haase, 281.
83. Bezsonov, vol. 5, 63–64, trans. mine.
84. For a depiction of the popular veneration of Mary, see S. Tchetverikoff, "Piété Orthodoxe: De l'esprit religieux russe et de la dévotion du peuple russe pour la Mère de Dieu," *Irenikon*, vol. 3, no. 7, 462. The association of Mary with more archaic divinities occurred naturally in most of the regions where the new creed was introduced. See M. Warner, 275–276.
85. K. Onasch, "Paraskeva Studien," *Ostkirchliche Studien*, vol. 6, nos. 2–3, 1957, 127.
86. The Orthodox church found itself at pains to attribute sainthood to its recalcitrant female "converts." Consequently, the list of female saints is short. It begins with the Varangian Olga and continues with Saint Efrosina of Polotsk (d. 1173), remembered as a builder of convents. Two other saints include the thirteenth-century Lithuanian Kharitida of Novgorod and Glikeriia of Novgorod, canonized in the sixteenth century, about whom scarcely anything is known. Of the five Russian saints, only two are Russian: Efrosina of Murom and Efrosina of Suzdal. The first was a peasant woman who became associated with Fevroniia of Murom; the second was martyred by the Mongols in the thirteenth century and assimilated to Saint Paraskeva. Her chief virtue, according to the *vita* of the sixteenth century, was humility and nonresistance to evil, characteristic of most Russian male saints. See Kologrivof, 275–276. None of the women on this short list are shown as striving after spirituality like their Western counterparts.

The lack of women saints has been attributed to the denigration of women in the Byzantine tradition, as well as to the custom of imprisoning women of the upper classes in *teremy* from the period of the Mongol invasion. But in fact, there appeared to be little incentive for either peasant women or their sisters from the *boiarstvo* to die as martyrs for a faith which deprived them of all power in the family and the community, as well as separated them from the female deities they worshipped. See D. Atkinson, "Society and the Sexes in the Russian Past," in D. Atkinson, A. Dallin, and G. W. Lapidus, eds., *Women in Russia* (Stanford, 1977), 10–14, on the role of the church toward women in Kievan and Muscovite Russia.

One saint, not yet mentioned, is a seventeenth-century "mother," Iuliana Lazarevskaia. Her *vita*, written by her devoted son, was composed in accordance with the church's notion of perfect womanhood. Iuliana was completely self-abnegating and dependent as a wife and mother. She fed the starving and worked for others as an assiduous spinner. When she died, she was buried by her husband; but over her grave stood a *pech'*— the pagan symbol of feminine power! Her body, when exhumed, had turned to *kvass* (a fermented drink made of bread). In short, Iuliana is associated with the elements of the pagan goddess: *pech'*, *kvass*, bread, and spinning. Her nurturing virtues are assimilated to the Christian notion of altruism. Through her story, the virtues of the peasant *baba* were firmly placed under the aegis of the church, the pagan sources of her power thus denied. Clearly, this "saintly" or powerless role was not one many aspired to fulfill. Iuliana and Fevroniia served the church's insistent missionary work among its female parishioners. For Iuliana's *vita*, see K. Druzhina-Osoryin, "Povest' o sviatoi i pravednoi materi Iulianii Lazarevskoi," in M. Skripil, *Russkaia povest' XVII veka* (Moscow, 1954), 39–47.

87. A. N. Afanas'ev, *Narodnye russkie legendy* (Kazan, 1914), vol. 1, 94–95; *Poeticheskie vozzreniia*, vol. 1, 230; and A. N. Veselovskii, "Opyty po istorii razvitiia khristianskoi legendy," *Zhurnal ministerstva narodnogo prosveshcheniia*, vol. 189, 1977, 330–331, 353.

88. Afanas'ev, *Poeticheskie vozzreniia*, vol. 1, 232; and *Narodnye russkie legendy*, 94–95.

89. "Sermones Polonici," in C. H. Meyer, *Fontes historiae religionis slavicae* (Berlin, 1931), 72, cited in Onasch, 138, trans. mine.

90. Bezsonov, vol. 6, 162, trans. mine; and Afanas'ev, *Poeticheskie vozzreniia*, vol. 1, 232–234.

91. Ralston, *Songs*, 204; Haase, 180–182, 185, links her with Baba Yaga.

92. Afanas'ev, *Narodnye russkie legendy*, 98.

93. Onasch, 135; Chicherov, 56–57.

94. Megas, 144–145.

95. Afanas'ev, *Narodnye russkie legendy*, 95.

96. Among the Persians, there is also a taboo against spinning on Wednesdays and Fridays. See Masse, 262, 411–412. Proverb from Dal', 924, trans. mine. See also Chicherov, 40–49.

97. Chicherov, 42; Onasch, 134, 139; Potebnia, 221; Dal', 924, trans. mine.

98. Onasch, 135. There are a number of legends surrounding the "torture of flax" among Slavic and Finnish peoples, linked to the cult of ancestors and to bathhouse rituals conducted by girls, when they predict their future. See Oinas, *Studies in Finnic-Slavic Relations*, 179-192.

99. Veselovskii, 355–362.

100. Chicherov, 42. In the area of Novgorod, there were stories of Mokusha, with long hands, who visited spinners. See Onasch, 139.

101. In the *Dukhovnye stikhi*, for example, she appears to a hermit living in "Holy Mother Desert" and tells him, "Go to Russia / And tell the thodox to love one another." Bezsonov, vol. 6, 160–161, 171, 173–174, trans. mine.

102. Ibid., 122, 170; Onasch, 138; Afanas'ev, *Narodnye russkie legendy*, 98; *Poeticheskie vozzreniia*, vol. 1, 241.

103. Chicherov, 58.

104. Ibid., 57.

105. Matorin, 88; Nosova, *Iazychestvo*, 100–101; Onasch, 136; Haase, 183.

106. On the exhortation to "Make merry on Fridays," see Onasch, 135.

CHAPTER FIVE: EPIC HEROES AND DISOBEDIENT SONS

1. A. P. Gil'ferding, *Onezhskie byliny zapisannye A. P. Gil'ferdingom letom 1871* (Moscow, 1951), 213, trans. mine.

2. W. E. Harkins, "Does Russia Have a Tragic Epos?" in *Slavic and*

East European Journal, vol. 21, no. 3, 1977, 307–312, argues that the Russian epic lacks a tragic hero. A. Barker, *The Mother Syndrome in the Russian Folk Imagination* (Columbus, Ohio, 1986), studies the epic hero in a psychoanalytic context, stressing his conflict with an aggressive, "phallic" mother.

3. Dal', 351, trans. mine. See Ivanov and Toporov, *Slavianskie iazykovye*, 177, for the duality and conflict of masculine and feminine mythologies in Russia.

4. Among the Western Slavs, the legend of the conflict of two gods, Bielobog (the White God) and Chernobog (the Black God), who contend over the fate of the world, suggests two religious systems, earth and sky, fertility and pastoral, respectively. Indeed, certain feminine pilgrimages destined to finish in orgy were called by men "the worship of Chernobog." See Gasparini, *Il matriarcato slavo*, 550–551.

5. S. Dunn, "The Family as Reflected in Russian Folklore," in Ransel, 155–157, argues that in the folktale, both the protagonist and the antagonist are often female.

6. Dunn, 156; Meletinskii, 237, 245–253. See also Gasparini, *Il matriarcato slavo*, 650–651, on initiation rites of the male through the body of a mare in Slavic folklore.

7. Meletinskii, 241–247.

8. A. A. Nechaev and N. Rybakov, eds., *Russkie narodnye skazki* (Moscow, 1959), 4.

9. In Belorussia and among the South Slavs, Perun is sometimes made to assume the fertility functions of the Yaga, flying on a great grindstone supported by mountain spirits subject to him. Afanas'ev, *Poeticheskie vozzreniia*, vol. 1, 291.

10. A. E. Alexander, *Bylina and Fairy Tale: The Origins of Russian Heroic Poetry* (The Hague, 1973), 56, 100; and Barker, 29–30, on the social origins of the hero.

11. For a discussion of the debates over the origins of the epos, see F. J. Oinas, "Russian *Byliny*," in F. J. Oinas, ed., *Heroic Epic and Saga*, (Bloomington, Indiana, 1978), 237–240; idem, "Folklore and Politics in the Soviet Union," *Slavic Review*, vol. 32, no. 1, 1973, 45–49; idem, "The Problem of the Aristocratic Origin of Russian *Byliny*," *Slavic Review*, vol. 30, no. 3, 1971, 521; N. K. Chadwick, *Russian Heroic Poetry* (New York, 1964), 27–28; Sokolov, 175.

12. Harkins, 309–310.

13. Barker, 46.

14. Oinas, "Russian *Byliny*," 240–246; Chadwick, 11–17, sees only two cycles: Kievan and Novgorodian. Oinas concurs with the nineteenth-century scholar A. Rambaud, *La Russie épique* (Paris, 1876), who sees three: Primitive, Kievan, and Novgorodian; 33, 54, 130.

15. Oinas, "Russian *Byliny*," 240; Rambaud, 108.

16. Barker, 43, points to the need for Kievan women to take charge while their husbands were at the wars. However, this is true of other epic traditions where there is less concern with the power of the women left behind.

17. D. M. Valashov, "Dunai," *Russkii fol'klor*, vol. 16, 1976, 95.

18. A. P. Evgen'eva and B. L. Putilov, *Drevnie rossiiskie stikhotvoreniia* (Moscow, 1977), 58–59.

19. Ibid.

20. Valashov, 97. We hear echoes of this tragic story in the folktale of *"Bogatyria* Usonusha" (or Sineglaska). But there the relationship of the youth to the all-powerful maiden is reversed: He marries her in matrilocal custom, even though she finally seeks him out. He acquires power as a king only through her. See I. A. Khudiakov, *Velikorusskie skazki v zapisiakh I. A. Khudiakova*, V. G. Bazanov, ed. (Moscow, 1964), 53–62. The story of Dunai may refer to the historical expansion of the Sarmatian tribes around the Don and the Danube, inhabited by an autochthonous Slavic population of farmers. These peoples may have worshipped a warrior goddess and mother of the sun who was identified in her moon aspects with the spinner, her sister Apraksiia. See Valashov, 101–105.

21. Evgen'eva and Putilov, 32–33, trans. mine. A number of scholars have commented on the similarity of this hero to the brother of Riurik Vseslav of Polotsk, who was renowned as a shaman. There is also a resemblance to Oleg, the father of Olga of Kiev. One writer argues that Volga was in fact the son of Olga, who taught him her magic as sorceress. See Rambaud, 33–34; Sokolov, 181; Chadwick, *Russian Heroic*, 34–35.

22. Chadwick, *Russian Heroic*, 44–45. Mikula has been linked with the god Volos. See B. A. Uspenskii, 99.

23. Nechaev and Rybakov, 210.

24. Chadwick, *Russian Heroic*, 51–52.

25. Ibid., 52–53; D. Ukhov, *Byliny* (Moscow, 1957), 214–219. See the commentary on 477 for the debate over the origins of this figure.

26. Rambaud, 54; Chadwick, *Russian Heroic*, 67. I. A. Khudiakov, *Materialy dlia izucheniia narodnoi slovesnosti* (St. Petersburg, 1863), 5–6, regards Ilya as the personification of Perun—a view shared by later scholars. See Gimbutas, *The Slavs*, 166.

27. A. M. Astakhova, *Byliny severa* (Moscow-Leningrad, 1938–1951), vol. 1, 499–500, trans. mine. See also Rambaud, 110–112. The story of Ilya's "cure" is thought to have been added later by peasant storytellers, while the more archaic versions concern the passing of power from Sviatogor to him. See Astakhova, vol. 2, nos. 28, 47, 80, 93, 95; and M. Speranskii, ed., *Russkaia ustnaia slovesnost' byliny* (Moscow, 1916), 133–134. For a discussion of Ilya, see Chadwick, *Russian Heroic*, 57–58; and Ukhov, 449–463. The later accounts accentuate Ilya's relationship to the peasantry, his championing of their demands for justice and protection.

28. Astakhova, vol. 1, 502, trans. mine.

29. Nechaev and Rybakov, 212. The movement across the magical river which lets the hero pass or hinders him occurs in a number of other epics, most notably that of the son of a sorceress, Dobrynia. See Evgen'eva and Putilov, 98–106; Ukhov, 125; Gil'ferding, 20–21, 51, 89. In a ballad called "The Youth and the River Smorodina," the folktale aspects of maternal power are underscored as though to challenge the masculine ones of the epos. The unnamed hero dies as a result of his rash attempt to outwit the river. See Gil'ferding, 379–380.

30. Chadwick, *Russian Heroic*, 67–70; Nechaev and Rybakov, 213, 216. The link between Solovei and Baba Yaga is explicit in one version, in which his house is surrounded by palings on which the heads of *bogatyri* are fixed. See Evgen'eva and Putilov, 186.

31. In some versions this conflict is with a male falconer who refers to his mother as a *polianitsa*, wishing to be avenged by her son. See Astakhova, nos. 2, 11, 20, 40, 70, 79; Rambaud, 54–56; Gil'ferding, no. 77.

32. Barker, 59.

33. Gil'ferding, 213, trans. mine.

34. Ibid., 215; Evgen'eva and Putilov, 42–45.

35. A. M. Astakhova et al., *Byliny pechory i zimnego berega* (Moscow, 1961), nos. 81, 81a, 98, p. 228, trans. mine.

36. Rambaud, 96; Astakhova, nos. 6, 16, 55, 75, 97. The Kievan cycle is not restricted to these heroes. Others outside the area of Kiev display even more striking characteristics of a matrifocal order. Diuk Stepanovich, the *bogatyr'* from Galicia, has an all-powerful mother who is represented as a goddess. See Astakhova, vol. 2, 296–307; and Rambaud, 95–96. In another epic about the *bogatyr'* Potyk, the conflict between matrifocal and patriarchal orders reflects the process of Christianization and introduces a Russian version of the story of Helen of Troy. See Astakhova, 308; and Rambaud, 419–420. Helen appears under the name of "Maria the White Swan." But she is not the benign Mother of God. Instead she is the perfidious *rusalka*. It is of interest that her name is often given to the bride in wedding rituals. Like the peasant bride and like Apraksiia, wife of Vladimir, she too is kidnapped and expresses her anger in the paternal family by remaining pagan and pitting men against each other. See Ukhov, 289. Maria's vindictiveness is counterbalanced by another *polianitsa*, in the epic of Stavr Godinovich, who has a wife called Vasilisa, daughter of Mikula the plowman. Not only does she save her husband from prison through her wisdom, but she also astonishes the Kievan court by her prowess as a warrior. She is perhaps the embodiment of the ideal of the maternal family. Her magic is used for benign ends and provides both protection and wealth.

37. Nechaev and Rybakov, 239; Ukhov, 103–113, 463; Speranskii, 383, 391, 400; Evgen'eva and Putilov, 189.

38. Speranskii, 401, trans. mine.

39. Ibid., 401, trans. mine; Evgen'eva and Putilov, 185, trans. mine; Astakhova et al., 458, trans. mine.

40. Speranskii, 413–419.

41. Ukhov, 493. Barker, 87–101, focuses on the Oedipal dilemma and compares Buslaev to the mother-dominated Greek hero Achilles.

42. Ukhov, 351, trans. mine. For the historical background of the boyarina Marfa Possadnitsa's conflict with Tsar Ivan in the fifteenth century, see Rambaud, 139.

43. Ukhov, 353, trans. mine.

44. Ibid., 359, trans. mine. This twelfth-century epic appears to refer to the festival of Maslenitsa, with whom the Black Maiden is associated. See Ukhov, 493.

45. Ibid., no. 44; Gil'ferding, no. 70; Barker, 69–85; and K. Blakely, 'Folktales of Ancient Russia: *Byliny* of Lord Novgorod the Great," *Slavonic Review*, vol. 3, no. 7, 1924, 52–62.

46. Ukhov, 430, 431, trans. mine.

47. Chadwick, *Russian Heroic*, 175–177; Dunn, 168–169, points to the clash between the family and the feudal order.

48. Chadwick, *Russian Heroic*, 174.

49. See N. Chodorow, "Family Structure and Feminine Personality," in M. Z. Rosaldo and L. Lamphere, eds., *Woman, Culture, and Society* (Stanford, 1974), 50–51, on the boy's attempts to gain "an elusive masculine identification" through the rejection of the mother. While Chodorow's

analysis represents a feminist critique of psychoanalytic thought, especially in relation to the emphasis upon masculine self-assertion, A. Barker, who also deals with the problem of masculine self-assertion, does so from within a Freudian-Lacanian framework.

CHAPTER SIX: FROM SAINTLY SON TO AUTOCRATIC
FATHER: THE MYTH OF THE RULER

1. M. Voloshin, "Holy Russia," in D. Obolensky, ed., *The Penguin Book of Russian Verse* (Harmondsworth, Middlesex, 1965), 257–258, trans. mine.

2. This is the central argument in Cherniavsky, *Tsar and People*.

3. Procopius, 269. For similar institutions among the Gauls and the Germans, who held women in high esteem, see Kovalevsky, 133.

4. Mauricius, *Strategicum*, chap. 11; and Leo, *Tactica seu de re militari*, chap. 18, 99, cited in Kovalevsky, 121.

5. Thietmar of Merseburg, cited in Kovalevsky, 122. On women's power, see Shashkov, 5–9, 18–28.

6. Kovalevsky, 135. B. D. Grekov follows the Marxist evolutionary theory to account for the development of the Varangian state. See particularly his *Bor'ba Rusi za sozdanie svoego gosudarstva* (Moscow, 1945). A. Vucinich, "The First Russian State," *Speculum*, 28, no. 2, 1953, 324–334, challenges this schema by suggesting that it is not sufficiently grounded in evidence and has been discredited by modern scholars. My own approach has been suggested by the continuing coexistence of matriclan and patriclan world views in Russian culture and the enormous significance accorded to the maternal feminine in particular. The mentality of the peasantry still seems rooted in kin structures based on vestiges of the matriclan; that of the upper classes, in militaristic and nomadic custom.

7. See Komarovich, 84–101. On the institution of the *veche*, see Vernadsky, *Kievan Russia*, 185–187.

8. See R. Mann, *The Song of Prince Igor: A Great Medieval Epic* (Eugene, Oregon, 1979), for a survey of wedding imagery.

9. "The Lay of Igor's Campaign," in Zenkovsky, 142.

10. Ibid., 145–146.

11. Ibid., 146.

12. Ibid., 156.

13. See Rambaud, 217; and R. Jakobson, "La Geste du Prince Igor," in *Selected Writings*, vol. 4 (The Hague, 1966), 287.

14. Zenkovsky, 158.

15. Ibid., 160.

16. R. Mann, "Is There a Passage Missing at the Beginning of the Igor Tale?" *Slavic Review*, vol. 41, no. 4, 1982, 670–671.

17. The noted theologian S. Bulgakov, *The Orthodox Church*, E. S. Cram, trans. (London, 1944), 174, stresses the kenotic ideals adopted by the Russian Orthodox church. But the French cultural historian A. Besançon, *Le Tsarévitch immolé* (Paris, 1967), arguing from a psychoanalytic perspective, suggests that kenosis, in the context of tsarist rule, expresses an unresolved Oedipal conflict, deep in the Russian psyche, and

revolving around the attachment to earth and nation as mother; 72–74. Besançon's brilliantly argued thesis reflects the Western masculine obsession, expressed in Freud's writings, with the break from the mother as the foundation for male self-expression.

18. Zenkovsky, 85.

19. Cross and Sherbowitz-Wetzor, 127–128. For Western parallels, see N. W. Ingham, "The Sovereign as Martyr: East and West," *Slavic and East European Journal*, vol. 17, no. 1, 1973, 1–12.

20. Cross and Sherbowitz-Wetzor, 128–130.

21. This official version of the legend has many variations in popular lore, for the princes were beloved by the Russians of later times. In one clerical account, the body of Gleb was placed on a birch by the banks of the Dnieper—a burial testifying to the pagan veneration of tree and river. See E. E: Golubinskii, *Istoriia kanonizatsii sviatykh v russkoi tserkvi* (Moscow, 1903), 43–49.

22. Bezsonov, vol. 3, 634.

23. Ibid., 639.

24. Ibid., 628. See also F. Sciacca, "Royal Farmers: A Folkloric Investigation into the Pagan Origins of the Cult of Boris and Gleb," *Ulbandus Review*, vol. 1, no. 1, 1978, 9. For an illustration of one such icon, see Voyce, plate 119.

25. Eliade, *Patterns*, 98. Leto Phytia, called the "creator," was associated with the ability to change the sex of children. In the case of Leukippus, son of Galatea, this led to incest. See R. E. Bell, *Dictionary of Classical Mythology: Symbols, Attributes, and Associations* (Oxford, 1982), 135. See also F. Chapoutier, *Les Dioscures au service d'une déesse* (Paris, 1935), 3–5; J. Rendel-Harris, *The Cult of the Heavenly Twins* (Cambridge, 1906), 4–8; O'Flaherty, *Women, Androgynes*, 203–204. For rituals associated with the twins, see M. Wenzel, "The Dioscuri in the Balkans," *American Slavic and East European Review*, vol. 26, no. 3, 1967, 363–381.

26. Helen is linked to Kybele, Demeter, and Hekate. See Chapoutier, 143–146, 172; O'Flaherty, *Women, Androgynes*, 211–212.

27. The first day of November in the Russian farming calendar is Kozma and Demian Day. But it is called *Matushka* (Little Mother) Kozma-Demian, as well. Like the Dioscuri serving Helen, the two saints appear to serve other mothers who bring men and women together, Mary and Paraskeva. On *Matushka* Kozma-Demian day, women take the initiative to seek out their future mates. See Chicherov, 46–47. On the gods assimilated with grain and with the day of Boris and Gleb, see ibid., 48–50; and Sciacca, 7–8.

28. Sciacca, 9. Sciacca argues that the murder was a defilement of clan solidarity and thus a threat to the continuance of the farming cycle under the aegis of Mother Earth.

29. Reisman, 142–143.

30. There is an archaic tradition in the north of Russia of wrapping babies and children (like Boris and Gleb) in birch bark or in hollow trees. See Tertz, 71.

31. On the nature of that collaboration in Russia, see D. S. Likhachev, *Chelovek v literature drevnei Rusi* (Moscow-Leningrad, 1958); and for Western traditions, see Ingham, 1–17.

32. On Russian monasticism, see R. de Journel, Monachisme et

monastères russes (Paris, 1952); and P. Kazanskii, *Istoriia pravoslavoga russkogo monashestva* (Moscow, 1855). For Theodosius's escape from his mother, described as an evil *polianitsa* by the ecclesiastical chronicler, see G. P. Fedotov, *A Treasury of Russian Spirituality* (London, 1950), 18–20. On the strong mother figure, see A. Glasse, "The Formidable Woman: Portrait and Original," *Russian Literature Triquarterly*, vol. 9, 1974, 433–453. For the Greek and Byzantine sources of Russian monasticism, see A. Sipiaguine, "Aux sources de la piété russe," *Irenikon*, vol. 2, 1927, 3–10. And on Theodosius's teachings, see Fedotov, *Russian Religious Mind*, vol. 2, 129.

33. Saint Nicholas and Saint George often share attributes—particularly in regard to fertility functions. See B. A. Uspenskii, 99.

34. See Cherniavsky, *Tsar and People*, 43, note 97.

35. H. Delehaye, *Les Légendes hagiographiques* (Brussels, 1927), 162. In Russia the custom of linking George and Demetrius, like the Kievan princely brothers, occurs also in the naming of churches in their honor. The twelfth-century Church of Saint Dmitrii in the province of Dimitrov was changed in the sixteenth century to that of Saint George. An illustration of a George-Dmitrii icon is found in Rice, *A Concise History*, 136.

36. A. Leroy-Beaulieu, *The Empire of the Tsars and the Russians*, A. Rogozin, trans. (London-New York, 1905), vol. 3, 31.

37. See B. A. Uspenskii, 104–105; Gasparini, *Il matriarcato slavo*, 637, for the name of the Moscow church. On the link of Nicholas to Baba Yaga, see B. A. Uspenskii, 117.

38. See Tereshchenko, vol. 6, 3–85, for a complete description of the Russian saints' calendar, which, like that of other nations, was integrated into the pagan fertility cults of the farming populations. Masculine saints outnumber female ones (18 to 11), to suggest that the male is the more potent bringer of fertility, while woman is merely his adjunct. But even in this Christianization of the farming year, women still initiate the year.

39. Tereshchenko, 29–32. George is assimilated to Svarog, to whom the wolf was sacred. See B. A. Uspenskii, 95; Gimbutas, *The Slavs*, 163. For the first associations of Saint George with the Georgians, see D. M. Lang, *The Georgians* (New York, 1966), 112. For the myths of the Ossetians (seen as the direct descendants of the Scythians), see Dumézil, "Les 'Enarées,' " 249–255; and G. Charachidze, *Le Système religieux de la Géorgie païenne* (Paris, 1968).

40. Afanas'ev, *Poeticheskie vozzreniia*, vol. 1, 706: vol. 2, 402, trans. mine.

41. Frazer, 126–127.

42. See Bezsonov, vol. 2, 393–523, for the many versions of his legend; Rambaud, 374–376; and D. Chizhevsky, "Yaroslav the Wise in East Slavic Epic Poetry," in *Slavic Folklore: A Symposium*, American Folklore Society, (Richmond, Virginia, 1956), 9–13, on historical associations with Kievan Rus' and the possible dating of the cycle to the thirteenth century.

43. In other versions of the legend in the *Dukhovnye stikhi*, we find the Western dragon fight more fully articulated (and reflecting the Greek conflict of Perseus and the snake-haired Gorgon). There, the will of the pagan princess saved by the saint determines the success of the conversion of her people.

44. The restriction of George's powers in popular thought seems to

contradict the representation of the saint as the symbol of the autonomous and powerful Muscovite tsardom. See Bezsonov, vol. 2, 523, for the role of the woman as a missionary for George's faith. For a glimpse at the vast literature surrounding the origins of the autocratic ideology in Russia, see D. Obolensky, "Russia's Byzantine Heritage," in M. Cherniavsky, ed., *The Structure of Russian History* (New York, 1970), 3–28; and M. Cherniavsky, "Khan or Basileus: An Aspect of Russian Medieval Theory," in ibid., 65–79. For a summary of the effects of the Mongol yoke on Russia, see V. D. Grekov and A. I. Iakubovskii, *Zolotaia orda i ee padenie* (Moscow, 1950), 247–262. On the myth and ritual surrounding archaic forms of kingship, see S. H. Hooke, *Myth and Kingship* (Oxford, 1958). And on west European kingship, E. H. Kanzer, *The King's Two Bodies* (Princeton, 1957). For the relationship of kingship, priesthood, and initiation in both Eastern and Western traditions, see H. Zimmer, *The King and the Corpse: Tales of the Soul's Conquest of Evil* (Princeton, 1971).

45. On the church's encouragement of the prince to assume more control in the governance of its affairs, see V. E. Val'denberg, *Drevnerusskie ucheniia o predelakh tsarskoi vlasti: Ocherki russkoi politicheskoi literatury ot Vladimira Sviatogo do kontsa XVII veka* (St. Petersburg, 1916), 132; and Cherniavsky, "Khan or Basileus," 73–74.

46. Indeed, Moskva, or Moscow, had been in the territory of the Uralic-Finnish and Altaic tribes who gave Moscow and the rivers Volga and Oka their names. The word *ka* means "water"; *mosk* means "turbulent"; *o* means "clear"; and *vol* means "holy." A fit shrine for a goddess associated with holy waters. See V. Alexandrov, *Les Mystères du Kremlin: Mille ans d'histoire* (Paris, 1960), 15–18, 21.

47. On the word *tsar'*, see P. Miliukov, *Outlines of Russian Culture: Religion and the Church in Russia*, V. Ughet and E. Davis, trans. (New York, 1960), 18–19, note 4.

48. Cherniavsky, *Tsar and People*, 43, 71.

49. See D. Stremoukhoff, "Moscow the Third Rome: Sources of the Doctrine," in Cherniavsky, *The Structure of Russian History*, 108–125.

50. On the life of the upper classes in the seventeenth century, see G. Kotoshikhin, *O Rossii v tsarstvovanii Alekseia Mikhailovicha* (St. Petersburg, 1859), 12, 122–123.

51. See D. Atkinson, "Society and the Sexes in the Russian Past," in Atkinson et al., *Women in Russia*, 20; and M. F. Vladimirskii-Budanov, *Obzor istorii russkogo prava* (Kiev, 1886), 86. For an account of Ivan's murder of his son, see V. Kliuchevskii, *Kurs russkoi istorii*, vol. 3 (Moscow, 1937), 17.

52. See A. Orlov, ed., *Domostroi po kosinskomu spisku* (Moscow, 1908); and A. P. Shchapov, 111–112. For the proverb, Dal', vol. 1, 469, 470, 490.

53. For the continuing debate on the nature and aims of the *oprichnina*, see L. Yaresh, "Ivan the Terrible and the *Oprichnina*," in C. Black, ed., *Rewriting Russian History* (New York, 1962), 216–232; A. A. Zimin, *Oprichnina Ivana Groznogo* (Moscow, 1964); M. Cherniavsky, "Ivan the Terrible as Renaissance Prince," *Slavic Review*, vol. 27, no. 2, 1968; and a recent study critical of Western historians' attitudes, A. Yanov, *The Origins of Autocracy: Ivan the Terrible in Russian History*, S. Dunn, trans. (Berkeley, 1982). Yanov contends that historians have been dominated by the hegemony of the "state school" born of Hegelian assumptions about

the centricity of the nation in the evolution of the human spirit. This orientation has blinded them to the democratic elements in Kievan and Muscovite societies and has prevented them from questioning the "inevitability" of a centralized autocratic state.

54. J. L. I. Fennell, ed. and trans., *The Correspondence between Prince Kurbsky and Tsar Ivan IV of Russia, 1564–1579* (Cambridge, Massachusetts, 1963), 19; and Kurbsky, *History of the Prince of Moscow*, cited in Cherniavsky, *Tsar and People*, 108–109. The recent controversy over the authenticity of the correspondence has little relevance to my argument, since an early-seventeenth-century origin would not affect it. See R. G. Skrynnikov, "On the Authenticity of the Kurbskii-Groznyi Correspondence: A Summary of the Discussion," *Slavic Review*, vol. 37, no. 1, 1978, 107–115. On the schism between "Holy *Rus'*" and its ruler, see M. Cherniavsky, "Holy Russia: A Study in the History of an Idea," *American Historical Review*, vol. 63, no. 3, 1958, 621.

55. Cherniavsky, *Tsar and People*, 51–52, describes the popular view of the ruler during the reign of Ivan the Terrible.

56. Ibid., 112, 115. Cherniavsky does not discuss the pagan aspects of the epithet, though he refers to the notion of a common motherland in pre-Muscovite Russia. See "Holy Russia," 620, note 15.

57. See Dal', 329.

58. I. Golovine, *Russia under the Autocrat Nicholas the First*, vol. 1 (London, 1846), 131; E. V. Barsov, *Drevnerusskie pamiatniki sviashchennogo venchaniia tsarei na tsarstvo* (Moscow, 1883), ii–iii, xxxii.

59. See the Koliada songs to the tsar in Zabylin, 582–583.

60. Olearius, cited in Snegirev, vol. 1, 161–163, trans. mine.

61. Zabylin, 103–104.

62. Tereshchenko, vol. 2, 57–66.

63. For legends associated with the feminine source of tsarist authority, see E. A. Tudorovskaia, "Skazka o Borme Laryzhke," *Russkii fol'klor*, vol. 6, 1976, 173–185.

64. Dal', 240 (1878 edition), trans. mine.

65. R. Pipes, *Russia under the Old Regime* (New York, 1974), 115; and Besançon, 130, points to the psychological dislocations out of which emerges the myth of "Holy Russia."

66. Besançon, 77–87.

67. See B. N. Putilov, "Pesnia o gneve Ivana Groznogo na syna," *Russkii fol'klor*, vol. 4, 1959, 5–32. For a translation of the *bylina*, see Chadwick, *Russian Heroic*, 195–196.

68. Chadwick, *Russian Heroic*, 196–198.

69. K. V. Chistov, *Russkie narodnye sotsial'no-utopicheskie legendy XVII–XIX vv.* (Moscow, 1967); A. Field, *Rebels in the Name of the Tsar* (Boston, 1976), 6; and B. A. Uspenskij, "Tsar and Pretender: Samozvančestvo or Royal Imposture in Russia as a Cultural-Historical Phenomenon," in Ju. M. Lotman and B. A. Uspenskij, *The Semiotics of Russian Culture*, A. Shukman, ed. (Ann Arbor, 1984), 259–292. On the sign of the cross to be found on the body of the pretender, see Chistov, 44, 66–67, 126–127, 148–149, 210.

70. Field, 6–7, 23–24. On the notion of the inauthenticity of the ruling tsars, see Uspenskij, "Tsar and Pretender," 277.

71. See Kologrivof, 261–273; E. Behr-Sigel, *Prière et sainteté dans*

l'église russe (Paris, 1950), 92–120; Fedotov, *Russian Religious Mind*, vol. 2, 316–344. Fedotov also attributes divine folly to Saint Theodosius and suggests that the *Kievan Caves Paterikon* bears hints of the beginnings of the tradition in Russia. See R. W. F. Pope, "Fools and Folly in Old Russia," *Slavic Review*, vol. 39, no. 3, 1980, 480–481.

72. Fedotov, *Russian Religious Mind*, vol. 2, 317–324; Kologrivof, 263; Gasparini, *Il matriarcato slavo*, 650.

73. On the simpleton, see Meletinskii, 236–247.

74. Fedotov, *Russian Religious Mind*, vol. 2, 329; Kologrivof, 266; and for stories about other Holy Fools, see L. A. Dimitrieva, *Povesti o zhitii Mikhaila Klopskogo* (Moscow-Leningrad, 1958), 100–110. On the feminine associations with the left hand, see Ivanov and Toporov, *Slavianskie iazykovye*, 94.

75. Fedotov, *Russian Religious Mind*, vol. 2, 337–338.

76. Kologrivof, 262, 269–270. On the relationship between the *Iurodivye* and shamanism, see E. Thompson, "Russian Holy Fools and Shamanism," *American Contributions to the Eighth International Congress of Slavists* (Zagreb-Ljubljana, 1978), vol. 2, 694–703. See also D. S. Likhachev and A. M. Panchenko, *"Smekhovoi mir" drevnei Rusi* (Leningrad, 1976), 93–183, on divine folly as social protest.

77. Savva, Archbishop of Tver, *Sacristie patriarcale, dit synodale de Moscou* (Moscow, 1865), 9–10.

78. See M. Cherniavsky, "Old Believers and the New Religion," in Cherniavsky, *The Structure of Russian History*, 146; Leroy-Beaulieu, vol. 3, 289. On the symbolism of two and three, see P. S. Smirnov, *O perestolzhenii* (St. Petersburg, 1904).

79. Kliuchevskii, vol. 3, 336, trans. mine.

80. F. Conybeare, *Russian Dissenters* (New York, 1962), 17.

81. Leroy-Beaulieu, vol. 3, 462–463, on the importance of women in the Old Believer and sectarian movements; A. P. Shchapov, 113–114, on Avvakum.

82. *Povest' o boiarine Morozovoi*, A. I. Mazunina, ed. (Leningrad, 1979), 152. On Feodos'ia Morozova and her sister Princess Evdokiia Urusov, see P. Pascal, *Avvakum et les débuts du raskol* (Paris, 1938), 35ff; and P. Smirnov, "Znachenie zhenshchiny v istorii vozniknoveniia raskola," *Missionerskii sbornik*, 1891, 330–365.

83. Miliukov, 40–55.

84. See S. Smirnov, "Drevnerusskii dukhovnik," 280–281; A. Shchapov, *Russkii raskol staroobriadchestva* (Kazan, 1859), 163; and S. Bolshakoff, *Russian Nonconformity* (Philadelphia, 1956), 73. The radical *stranniki* (wanderers) had such a close link with the earth that they buried their children, like seeds, in plowed fields and gardens. Conybeare, 160.

85. Shchapov, *Russkii raskol*, 189, 191–194.

86. The importance of the Schism in alienating a considerable segment of the population from the autocracy is underscored in S. A. Zenkovsky, "The Russian Church Schism," *Russian Review*, vol. 16, no. 4, 1957, 37–58. On Western influences, see Billington, 175–180; and Miliukov, 77–121. The ethnographers of the nineteenth century found the richest store of folklore and epic among the Old Believers, who continued to pratice the *dvoeverie* in the ancient manner. See Leroy-Beaulieu, 293, 315–316. On the burial in the woods and marriage by a tree or lake among

the "Priestless" Old Believers and sectarians, see P. I. Mel'nikov, "O sovremennom sostoianii raskola v Nizhnegorodskoi gubernii," *Deistviia Nizhnegorodskoi gubernskoi uchenoi arkhivnoi komissii*, vol. 7, *Sbornik v pamiat' P. I. Mel'nikova (Andreia Pecherskogo)*, pt. 2 (Nizhnii Novgorod, 1910), 275; and D. K. Zelenin, *Opisanie rukopisei uchenogo arkhiva imp. russkogo geograficheskogo obshchestva*, no. 2 (Prague, 1915), 581. On the ancient Slavs' custom of burying the dead in fields and forests, see Koz'ma Prazhskii, *Cheshskaia khronika* (Moscow, 1962), 107, 173. See Iu. Lotman and B. A. Uspenskii, "Rol' dual'nykh modelei v dinamike russkoi kul'tury," *Trudy po russkoi i slavianskoi filologii*, no. 28 (Tartu, 1977), 3–36, on the continuance of pagan beliefs and rituals in Russian culture, accounting for aspects of its "binary" form.

86. Miliukov, 89–91; Conybeare, 342–343. On Western influences, see Bolshakoff, 87–88.

87. Leroy-Beaulieu, vol. 3, 411, 404. For a hymn admonishing believers to "pray for your soul / Your soul which emerges from Mother Moist Earth," see T. S. Rozhdetsvenskii and M. I. Uspenskii, eds., *Pesni russkikh sektantov mistikov* (St. Petersburg, 1912), 561, trans. mine. As in the epics and *Dukhovnye stikhi*, the hymns of the *Khlysty* reflected the peasant notion of the mother's hegemony over her (Christ) son. See, for example, hymn no. 151, 217–218.

88. An offshoot of the *Khlysty*, the *Skakuny* (Jumpers), whose activities brought them still closer to Slavic pagan rites, stressed the agrarian and erotic nature of their cult. See Leroy-Beaulieu, vol. 3, 417–418. On the *Skoptsy* leader Selivanov, see 429.

89. For a foreigner's impressions of the havoc Peter created among his people, see J. Perry, *The State of Russia under the Present Tsar* (London, 1716), 1–13.

90. This illustration is from Besançon, plate 8.

91. See Cherniavsky, "The Old Believers," 171–172.

92. M. T. Florinsky, *Russia: A History and an Interpretation* (New York, 1953), 423–427.

93. On the position of women in Peter's new society, see Elnett, 46–53; Shashkov, 191–267.

94. See I. Golovine, *Russia under the Autocrat Nicholas the First*, vol. 1 (London, 1846) 111–112, on the contrast between a "foreign" St. Petersburg and a "native" Moscow.

95. Cherniavsky, *Tsar and People*, 83–85; See F. Prokopovich, "Slovo o vlasti i chesti tsarskoi . . .", in *Feofan Prokopovich: Sochineniia*, I. P. Eremin, ed. (Moscow, 1961), 91; and P. N. Krekshin, "Kratkoe opisanie Blazhennykh del Imperatora Petra Velikogo," in N. Sakharov, ed., *Zapiski russkikh liudei: Sobytiia vremen Petra Velikogo* (St. Petersburg, 1841), 4, trans. mine.

96. Dal', 329, trans. mine.

97. Rambaud, 295–306.

98. Ibid., 306.

99. Ibid., 319, trans. mine.

100. Chistov, 102.

101. See R. Tucker, *The Soviet Political Mind* (New York, 1963): "The relation between the state and society is seen as one between conqueror and conquered" (70).

CHAPTER SEVEN: PUSHKIN AND OTHER CHAMPIONS
FROM THE INTELLIGENTSIA

1. A. Blok, "Russia and I," *The Twelve and Other Poems*, J. Stallworthy and P. France, trans. (London, 1970), 101.
2. Cherniavsky, "Holy Russia," 637. "Mother Earth, for the Russian *narod*, is Russia," wrote D. Samarin in 1918 (2).
3. See Besançon, 42–46, for a psychoanalytic perspective.
4. For an overview of the education of the gentry, see M. Raeff, *Origins of the Russian Intelligentsia: The Eighteenth Century Nobility* (New York, 1966), 122–147; P. Dunn, "That Enemy Is the Baby: Childhood in Imperial Russia," in L. deMause, ed., *The History of Childhood* (New York, 1975), 385–405. The literature on the "kindly nurse" begins with one of the first intellectual rebels, A. Radishchev, in *A Journey from St. Petersburg to Moscow*, L. Wiener, trans. (Cambridge, Massachusetts, 1958), 188–189, who denounces the institution of serfdom by invoking the suffering peasant mother. The emotional attachment of Russians to their childhood results, according to the psychoanalyst G. Gorer, from the pratice of swaddling infants, a custom which was continued through the nineteenth century. For the "Swaddling Hypothesis," see G. Gorer and J. Rickman, *The People of Great Russia: A Psychological Study* (New York, 1962), 93–236.
5. Raeff, 132–139.
6. Ibid., 129.
7. M. Raeff, "Home, School, and Service in the Life of the Eighteenth Century Nobleman," in Cherniavsky, *The Structure of Russian History*, 216; and J. Hubbs, "An Analysis of Martinism in the Last Quarter of the Eighteenth Century," (Ph.D. dissertation), Ann Arbor, Michigan, 1971, 264–265.
8. Russian prose tales of the previous two centuries reflected the attempts to unite folk themes with the changes which the gradual process of modernization was bringing to a traditional society. See G. Cox, "Fairy Tale Plots and Contemporary Heroes in Early Russian Prose Fiction," *Slavic Review*, vol. 39, no. 1, 1980, 96; and D. S. Likhachev, *Poetika drevnerusskoi literatury* (Leningrad, 1967), 63–64, on the schism between peasantry and educated classes deepened by the introduction of a literary tradition.
9. Besançon, 188; and S. Monas, "The Revelation of St. Boris: Russian Literature and Individual Autonomy," in Cherniavsky, *The Structure of Russian History*, 416–418.
10. See Pushkin, *Sochineniia*, vol. 1, 310. Roughly translated, the poem begins: "I remember at the beginning of my life in school. . . A humble, wretchedly dressed but majestic woman / Hovered over the well-being of the school—and protected us . . . / I was troubled by her stern beauty. . . / But I did not heed her advice and reproaches."
11. S. F. Eleonskii, *Literatura i narodnoe tvorchestvo* (Moscow, 1956), 117.
12. Pushkin, *Sochineniia*, vol. 1, 91, trans. mine.
13. Ibid., 99, 104–105.
14. See E. J. Simmons, *Pushkin* (New York, 1964), 220–221; G. A. Pelisov, "O fol'klornykh osnovakh 'Skazok' A. S. Pushkina," *Sovetskaia etnografiia*, no. 4, 1950, 94; and R. Jakobson, *Pushkin and His Sculptural*

Myth, J. Burbank, trans. (The Hague, 1975), 61–62. On Pushkin's wearing of peasant clothing, a habit that became *de rigueur* among the Slavophiles and the Populists of later decades, see H. Rogger, *National Consciousness in Eighteenth Century Russia* (Cambridge, Massachusetts, 1969), 138.

15. Eleonskii, 128, 135. Pushkin's library yielded not only the first collection of Russian folklore by K. Danilov, but also compilations of folklore from other countries—notably Grimm's tales and those of Washington Irving.

16. F. M. Dostoevsky, *The Dream of a Queer Fellow and the Pushkin Speech*, S. Koteliansky and J. Middleton Murry, trans. (London, 1972), 82.

17. A. S. Pushkin, *Eugene Onegin*, C. Johnston, trans. (Harmondsworth, Middlesex, 1979), 63. On the theme of seasonal changes, see R. Gustafson, "The Metaphor of the Seasons in *Eugene Onegin*," *Slavic and East European Journal*, vol. 6, no. 1, 1962, 6–20.

18. Pushkin, *Eugene Onegin*, 70, italics mine.

19. Ibid., 87, 90.

20. Ibid., 91.

21. Ibid., 134. On Tatiana's dream, see R. A. Gregg, "Tatyana's Two Dreams: The Unwanted Spouse and the Demonic Lover," *Slavonic and East European Review*, vol. 48, no. 113, 1970, 492–505.

22. Pushkin, *Eugene Onegin*, 173.

23. Ibid., 186.

24. Ibid., 202.

25. Ibid., 227.

26. A. S. Pushkin, "The Queen of Spades," in *The Complete Prose Tales of Alexander Sergeyevitch Pushkin*, G. R. Aitken, trans. (New York, 1966), 278.

27. Ibid., 279.

28. Ibid., 281.

29. Ibid., 286.

30. See N. Frye, *Fables of Identity: Studies in Poetic Mythology* (New York, 1963), 16, for a schematization of his theory regarding the association of literary genres with the cycles of nature. P. Debreczeny, "Poeetry and Prose in 'The Queen of Spades,'" *Canadian-American Slavic Studies*, vol. 2, no. 1, 1977, 91–113, alludes to this theme, as well as to the rituals of Masonry.

31. Pushkin, "The Queen of Spades," 291.

32. Ibid., 292.

33. Ibid., 293.

34. Ibid., 294.

35. Ibid., 295.

36. See J. E. Cirlot, *A Dictionary of Symbols*, J. Sage, trans. (New York, 1962), 221–222. See Debreczeny, 96–99, on the numbers two, three, and seven.

37. Pushkin, "The Queen of Spades," 297.

38. Ibid., 301–302.

39. See N. Rosen, "The Magic Cards in the Queen of Spades," *Slavic and East European Journal*, vol. 19, no. 3, 1975, 261–263; and H. B. Weber, "*Pikovaia Dama*: A Case Study for Freemasonry in Russian Literature," *Slavic and East European Journal*, vol. 12, no. 4, 1968, 439–442.

40. Pushkin, "The Queen of Spades," 305.

41. Rosen, 268–270.

42. In his folktale drawn from Russian sources, "Skazka o tsare Saltane, o syne ego . . . Gvidone . . ." (1831), a story he heard from his nurse, all the forms of the goddess are apparent: There are a *rusalka*, a Yaga, and a Wise Vasilisa; and all are invoked to illustrate the moral that only those who live within their laws stand to prosper. The tale provides a counterpoint to "The Queen of Spades," for it is infused with the peasant ethos found in popular folktales such as "Three Kingdoms" and "Ivan and the Witch." See Afanas'ev, *Narodnye russkie skazki*, vol. 1, 228–243, 173–182. For Pushkin's *skazka*, see *Sochineniia*, vol. 1, 411435. The folklore background for this story is explored by Pelisov, 96; and V. de Gerard, "The Folktales of Pushkin," in S. H. Cross and E. J. Simmons, eds., *Centennial Essays for Pushkin* (Cambridge, Massachusetts, 1937), 138. On Russia's becoming a "service" state, see Cherniavsky, *Tsar and People*, 137, who points to Paul I's substitution of the term *gosudarstvo* (state) for Peter's *otechestvo* (fatherland).

43. On the uprising, see A. Mazour, *The First Russian Revolution* (Berkeley, 1937).

44. On *The Captain's Daughter*, see G. E. Mikkelson, "The Mythopoetic Element in Pushkin's Historical Novel, *The Captain's Daughter*," *Slavonic and East European Review*, vol. 7, no. 3, 1973, 296–313.

45. Cited in Jakobson, *Pushkin*, 24.

46. For a traditional view which shows Pushkin praising Peter and his work, see M. Slonim, *The Epic of Russian Literature* (New York, 1975), 92–93. A number of scholars continue to hold this opinion of the poem. For example, R. Gregg, "The Nature of Nature and the Nature of Eugene in 'The Bronze Horseman,'" *Slavic and East European Journal*, vol. 21, no. 2, 1977, 167–179; and J. Bayley, "Looking at Pushkin," *New York Review of Books*, vol. 30, no. 1, 1983, 36. There is, however, another view of the meaning of the poem. W. Lednicki, *Pushkin's 'Bronze Horseman': The History of a Masterpiece* (Berkeley, 1955), 71, argues that Eugene's rebellion is a "democratic Galilean revolt" against the "giant" of the bureaucratic state. A. D. P. Briggs, "The Hidden Qualities of Pushkin's '*Mednyi vsadnik*,'" *Canadian-American Slavic Studies*, vol. 10, no. 2, 1976, 228–241, points out that Peter's statue is singularly graceless and that the squat figure on the rearing mount does not appear to be in command!

47. Jakobson, 40. Pushkin's poem, entitled, "Unto Myself I Raised a Monument," is a sardonic comment on hubris and the cult of self-importance. On the belief in vampires, see Oinas, "Heretics as Vampires," 433–434.

48. A. S. Pushkin, "The Bronze Horseman," in *Poems, Prose, and Plays of Pushkin*, O. Elton, trans., A. Yarmolinsky, ed. (New York, 1964), 95. The tone is regarded as ironic by a number of scholars, among them the Soviet critic V. Briusov, *Moi Pushkin* (Moscow-Leningrad, 1929), 63–94, who argues that Pushkin shares the Polish poet Adam Mickiewicz's denigration of the tsarist regime and predicts its eventual demise.

49. Pushkin, "The Bronze Horseman," 98.

50. Ibid., 101.

51. Pushkin, "The Bronze Horseman," 102.

52. Ibid., 107–108.

53. See Besançon, 77–144.

CONCLUSION: THE MOTHER AS RUSSIA

1. N. A. Nekrasov, "Rodina," in *N. A. Nekrasov: Izbrannoe* (Kiev, 1954), 12, trans. mine.
2. Pushkin, *Eugene Onegin*, 156.
3. Dostoevsky, *Dream of a Queer Fellow and the Pushkin Speech*, 47–48, 51–52.
4. F. M. Dostoevsky, *The Notebooks for "A Raw Youth,"* E. Wasiolek, ed., V. Terras, trans. (Chicago, 1969), 307; and *The Diary of a Writer*, B. Brasol, trans. (New York, 1949), vol. 1, 418; vol. 2, 845–856.
5. F. M. Dostoevsky, *The Possessed*, A. R. MacAndrew, trans. (New York, 1962), 138, 140.
6. On the theme of the intellectual as a Christ figure, see N. Gorodetsky, *The Humiliated Christ in Modern Russian Thought* (London, 1938), 175–176.
7. V. Dunham, "The Strong Woman Motif," in C. Black, ed., *The Transformation of Russian Society* (Cambridge, 1960), 462. The sense of *lichnost'* as wholeness and community among Soviet women is discussed in C. Shulman, "The Individual and the Collective," in Atkinson et al., *Women in Russia*, 383.
8. N. S. Arsen'ev, *Iz russkoi kul'turnoi tvorcheskoi traditsii* (Frankfurt, 1959), 34, argues for the importance of the mother in Russian culture generally and in Tolstoi's work in particular.
9. L. N. Tolstoi, "Father Sergius," in *"Master and Man" and Other Stories*, I. P. Foote, trans. (Harmondsworth, Middlesex, 1984), 56.
10. Ibid., 64.
11. M. Gorky, *The Autobiography of Maxim Gorky* (New York, 1962), 89–90.
12. Ibid., 94.
13. See M. Schwartz Rosenhan, "Images of Male and Female in Children's Readers," in Atkinson et al., *Women in Russia*, 301, who points to the official cult of motherhood and suggests that it expresses pre-Revolutionary themes as well as the opportunism of the regime in saddling its women with the duties of both worker and producer of more workers.
14. See H. Smith, *The Russians* (New York, 1976), 426–427.
15. D. E. Peterson, "Solzhenitsyn Back in the USSR: Anti-Modernism in Contemporary Soviet Prose," *Berkshire Review*, vol. 16, 1981, 69; and H. Smith, 417–438, on the resurgence of nationalism among intellectuals, artists, party leaders, and the public, linked to a revival of interest in past traditions, including Orthodoxy and village life.
16. Peterson, 66; and H. Smith, 434.
17. R. L. Jackson, " 'Matryona's House': The Making of a Russian Icon," in *Solzhenitsyn: a Collection of Critical Essays*, K. Feuer, ed. (Englewood Cliffs, 1976), 62. My analysis below draws on this and on D. E. Peterson's article.
18. A. Solzhenitsyn, "Matryona's Home," H. T. Willets, trans., *Encounter*, vol. 20, no. 5, May, 1963, 27.
19. Ibid., 31.
20. Ibid., 34, 39.
21. Ibid., 45.

Selected Bibliography

Abramova, Z. A. "Paleolithic Art in the USSR." *Arctic Anthropology*, vol. 4, 1967, 1–179.

Afanas'ev, A. N. *Narodnye russkie legendy*. Vol. 1. Kazan, 1914.

———. *Narodnye russkie skazki A. N. Afanas'eva*. 3 vols. Moscow, 1957.

———. *Poeticheskie vozzreniia slavian na prirodu*. 3 vols. Moscow, 18651869.

———. *Russian Fairy Tales*. N. Guterman, ed. and trans. New York, 1974.

Alexander, A. E. *Bylina and Fairy Tale: The Origins of Russian Heroic Poetry*. The Hague, 1973.

Alexandrov, V. *Les Mystères du Kremlin: Mille ans d'histoire*. Paris, 1960.

Alpatov, N. W. *Art Treasures of Russia*. N. Guterman, trans. New York, n.d.

Ambroz, A. K. "O simvolike russkoi krest'ianskoi vyshivki arkhaicheskogo tipa." *Sovetskaia arkheologiia*, no. 1, 1966, 61–76.

Anchikov, E. *Iazychestvo i drevniaia Rus'*. St. Petersburg, 1914.

Anisimov, A. F. *Kosmologicheskie predstavleniia narodov-severa*. Moscow-Leningrad, 1959.

Arbatskii, Iu. *Etiudy po istorii russkoi muzyki*. New York, 1956.

Aristov, N. "Sud'ba russkoi zhenshchiny v do-petrovskoe vremia." *Zaria*, no. 3, 1871, 190–211.

Arsen'ev, N. S. *Iz russkoi kul'turnoi i tvorcheskoi traditsii*. Frankfurt, 1959.

Ashe, G. *The Virgin*. London, 1976.

Astakhova, A. M. *Byliny severa*. 2 vols. Moscow-Leningrad, 1938–1951.

Atkinson, D.; Dallin, A.; and Warshofsky Lapidus, G., eds. *Women in Russia*. Stanford, 1977.

Azadovskii, M. K. *Russkaia skazka*. 2 vols. Leningrad, 1931–1932.

Barker, A. M. *The Mother Syndrome in the Russian Folk Imagination*. Columbus, Ohio, 1986.

Baroja, J. C. "Witchcraft amongst the German and Slavonic Peoples." In M. Marwick, ed., *Witchcraft and Sorcery*, 88–100. Harmondsworth, Middlesex, 1970.

Barsov, E. V. *Drevnerusskie pamiatniki sviashchennogo venchaniia tsarei na tsarstvo*. Moscow, 1883.

Behr-Sigel, E. *Prière et sainteté russe dans l'église russe*. Paris, 1950.

Benet, S., ed. and trans. *The Village of Viriatino*. New York, 1970.

Benz, E. *The Eastern Orthodox Church: Its Thought and Life*. R. and C. Winston, trans. Garden City, New York, 1963.

Berdiaev, N. *The Russian Idea*. R. M. French, trans. Boston, 1962.

Besançon, A. *Le Tsarévitch immolé*. Paris, 1967.

Bezsonov, P., ed. *Kalieki perekhozhie*. Moscow, 1861.

Bibikov, S. N. "Khoziaistvenno-ekonomicheskii kompleks razvitogo Tripoliia." *Sovetskaia arkheologiia*, no. 1, 1965, 48–62.

———. "Rannetripol'skoe poselenie Luka-Vrublevetskaia na Dnestre." *Materialy i issledovaniia po arkheologii SSSR*, no. 38, 1952, 191–274.

Billington, J. *The Icon and the Axe*. New York, 1966.

Blakely, K. "Folktales of Ancient Russia: *Byliny* of Lord Novgorod the Great." *Slavonic Review*, vol. 3, no. 7, 1924, 52–62.

Bleichsteiner, R. "Iranische Entsprechungen zu Frau Hölle und Baba Yaga." *Mitra*, no. 3, 1914, 66–71.

Boba, I. *Nomads, Northmen, and Slavs in Eastern Europe in the Ninth Century*. The Hague, 1967.

Bobula, I. "The Symbol of the Magna Mater." *American Journal of Archeology*, vol. 62, no. 2, 1958, 221–222.

Boguslavskaia, I. Ia. "O transformatsii ornamental'nykh motivov sviazannykh s drevnei mifologiei v russkoi narodnoi vyshivke." *Report of the Seventh International Congress of Anthropological and Ethnographic Sciences*, Moscow, vol. 7, 1964, 74–82.

Boissevain, E. "A Tentative Typology, Chronology, and Distribution Study of the Human Figurines of Eastern Europe and the Near East in Early Farming Levels." *Actes du 7e congrès international des sciences préhistoriques et proto-historiques*, Prague, vol. 1, 1970, 384388.

Bolshakoff, S. *Russian Nonconformity*. Philadelphia, 1956.

Bridenthal, R., and Koonz, C., eds. *Becoming Visible: Women in European History*. New York, 1977.

Briffault, R. *The Mothers: A Study of the Origins of Sentiments and Institutions*. 3 vols. New York, 1927.

Brückner, A. *Mitologia slava*. J. Dicksteinowna, trans. Bologna, 1923.

Brudnyi, V. I. *Obriady vchera i segodnia*. Moscow, 1968.

Bulgakov, S. *The Orthodox Church*. E. S. Cram, trans. London, 1944.

Burtsev, A. *Materialy dlia istorii russkogo raskola*. N. d.

Bushkovitch, P. "'Rus' in the Ethnic Nomenclature of the *Povest' vremennykh let*." *Cahiers du monde russe et soviétique*, vol. 12, no. 3, 1972, 296–306.

Bystron, J. "Les Rites agraires chez les peuples slaves et l'origine du culte agraire." *Actes du congrès international d'histoire des religions*, vol. 2, 203–220. Paris, 1925.

Caillois, R. "Les Spectres du midi dans la mythologie slave." *Revue des études slaves*, vol. 16, no. 1–2, 1936, 18–37.

Chadwick, N. K. *The Beginning of Russian History*. Cambridge, 1946.

———. *Russian Heroic Poetry*. New York, 1964.

Chalus, P. *L'Homme et la religion: Recherches sur les sources psychologiques des croyances du paléolithique au premier millénaire avant notre ère*. Paris, 1963.

Chapoutier, F. *Les Dioscures au service d'une déesse*. Paris, 1935.

Charachidze, G. *Le Système religieux de la Géorgie paienne*. Paris, 1968.

Cherniavsky, M. "Holy Russia: A Study in the History of an Idea." *American Historical Review*, vol. 63, 1958, 617–637.

———. "Old Believers and the New Religion." In M. Cherniavsky, ed., *The Structure of Russian History*, 140–188. New York, 1970.

———. *Tsar and People: Studies in Russian Myths.* New York, 1969.
Chicherov, V. I. *Zimnii period russkogo narodnogo zemledel'cheskogo kalendaria XVI–XIX vekov.* Moscow, 1957.
Chistov, K. V. *Russkie narodnye sotsial'no-utopicheskie legendy XVII–XIX vv.* Moscow, 1967.
Chizhevsky, D. "Yaroslav the Wise in East Slavic Epic Poetry." In *Slavic Folklore: A Symposium,* American Folklore Society, vol. 6, 3–17. Richmond, Virginia, 1956.
Chodorow, N. *The Reproduction of Mothering.* Berkeley, 1978.
Clark, K. *The Soviet Novel: History as Ritual.* Chicago, 1981.
Conybeare, F. *Russian Dissenters.* New York, 1962.
Copeland, F. "The Golden-Horned Hind (Zlatorog), a Slovenian Legend." *Slavonic and East European Review,* vol. 11, 1933, 651–654.
Cox, G. "Fairy Tale Plots and Contemporary Heroes of Early Russian Prose Fiction." *Slavic Review,* vol. 39, no. 1, 1980, 85–96.
Crawford, O. G. S. *The Eye Goddess.* New York, 1957.
Cross, S. H., and Sherbowitz-Wetzor, O. P., eds. and trans. *The Russian Primary Chronicle: Laurentian Text.* Cambridge, 1953.
Dal', V. I. *Poslovitsy russkogo naroda.* Moscow, 1878. Reprint, Moscow, 1957.
Delehaye, H. *Les Légendes hagiographiques.* Brussels, 1927.
Dieterich, A. *Mutter Erde.* Berlin, 1925.
Dintses, L. A. "Drevnie cherty v russkom narodnom iskusstve." In B. A. Rybakov, *Istoriia kul'tury drevnei Rusi: Domongol'skii period,* vol. 2 : *Obshchestvennyi stroi i dukhovnaia kul'tura,* 465–491. Moscow-Leningrad, 1951.
Dittrich, Z. R. "Zur religiösen Ur and Frühgeschichte der Slaven. *Jahrbücher für Geschichte Osteuropas,* vol. 9, 481–510. Wiesbaden, 1961.
Dostoevsky, F. M. *The Diary of a Writer.* B. Brasol, trans. New York, 1954.
———. *The Dream of a Queer Fellow and the Pushkin Speech.* S. Koteliansky and J. Middleton Murry, trans. London, 1972.
———. *The Possessed.* A. R. MacAndrew, trans. New York, 1962.
Dumézil, G. *Déesses latines et mythes védiques.* Brussels, 1956.
———. "Les 'Enarées' scythiques et la grossesse du Narte Hamyc." *Latomus,* vol. 5, 1946, 249–255.
———. Mythe et épopée: L'Ideologie des trois fonctions dans les épopées des peuples indo-européens. Paris, 1968.
Dunham, V. "The Strong Woman Motif." In C. Black, ed., *The Transformation of Russian Society,* 459–483. Cambridge, Massachusetts, 1960.
Dunn, S. P. "The Family as Reflected in Russian Folklore." In D. S. Ransel, ed., *The Family in Imperial Russia,* 153–170. Urbana, Illinois, 1978.
Dvornik, F. *The Slavs: Their Early History and Civilization.* Boston, 1956.
Efimenko, P. I. "Sud nad ved'mani." *Kievskaia starina,* vol. 7, 1883, 374–401.
Eisner, J. "Les Origines des slaves d'après les préhistoriens tchecques." *Revue des études slaves,* vol. 24, nos. 1–4, 1948, 129–142.
Eleonskii, S. F. *Literatura i narodnoe tvorchestvo.* Moscow, 1956.

Eleonskoi, E. H. "Nekotorye zamechaniia o perezhitkakh kul'tury v russkikh narodnykh skazkakh." *Etnograficheskoe obozrenie*, vol. 68-69, nos. 1–2, 1906, 63–72.

Eliade, M. *Patterns in Comparative Religions*. R. Sheed, trans. New York, 1970.

———. *Shamanism: Archaic Techniques of Ecstasy*. W. R. Trask, trans. Princeton, 1972.

Elnett, E. *Historic Origins and Social Development of Family Life in Russia*. New York, 1926.

Elnitskii, L. A. "Skifskie legendy kak kul'turno-istoricheskie materialy." *Sovetskaia arkheologiia*, no. 2, 1970, 64–74.

Erickson, E. *Childhood and Society*. New York, 1963.

Evgen'eva, A. P., and Putilov, B. I., eds. *Drevnie rossiiskie stikhotvoreniia sobrannye Kirsheiu Danilovym*. Moscow, 1977.

Fedotov, G. P. *The Russian Religious Mind*. Vol. 1, New York, 1960. Vol. 2, New York, 1966.

Field, D. *Rebels in the Name of the Tsar*. Boston, 1976.

Firsov, N. *Pugachevshchina: Opyt sotsiologo-psikhologicheskoi kharakteristiki*. Moscow-St. Petersburg, n.d.

Franz, M.-L. *Problems of the Feminine in Fairy Tales*. Irving, Texas, 1977.

Frazer, J. G. *The New Golden Bough*. T. H. Gaster, ed. New York, 1964.

Frye, N. *Fables of Identity: Studies in Poetic Mythology*. New York, 1963.

Gal'kovskii, N. "Drevnie russkie slova i poucheniia napravlennye protiv ostatkov iazychestva v narode." *Moskovskii arkheologicheskii institut, zapiski*, vol. 18, 1913, 1–307.

Garnett, L. M. J. *Balkan Home Life*. New York, 1917.

Gasparini, E. *Il matriarcato slavo*. Florence, 1973.

———. "Studies in Old Slavic Religion: *Ubrus*." *History of Religions*, vol. 2, no. 1, 1962, 112–139.

Gaster, H. "The Child-Stealing Witch among the Hittites." *Studi e materiali di storia delle religioni*, vol. 23, 1951–1952, 134–137.

Giedion, S. *The Eternal Present: The Beginnings of Architecture*. Vol. 1. Princeton, 1964.

Gil'ferding, A. P. *Onezhskie byliny zapisannye A. P. Gil'ferdingom letom 1871*. Moscow, 1951.

Gimbutas, M. *Ancient Symbolism in Lithuanian Folk Art*. Philadelphia, 1958.

———. *The Gods and Goddesses of Old Europe, 7000–3500: Myths, Legends, and Cult Images*. London, 1974.

———. *The Slavs*. New York, 1971.

Girard, R. *Violence and the Sacred*. P. Gregory, trans. Baltimore, 1977.

Glasse, A. "The Formidable Woman: Portrait and Original." *Russian Literature Triquarterly*, vol. 9, 1974, 433–453.

Goldman, B. "Typology of the Mother-Goddess Figurines." *Jahrbuch für Prähistorische und Ethnographische Kunst*, vol. 20, 1963, 8–15.

Golubinskii, E. E. *Istoriia kanonizatsii sviatykh v russkoi tserkvi*. Moscow, 1903.

Gorer, G., and Rickman, J. *The People of Great Russia: A Psychological Study*. New York, 1957.

Gorkii, M. *Byliny*. Leningrad, 1957.

Gorky, M. *The Autobiography of Maxim Gorky*. New York, 1962.

———. *Mother*. M. Wettlin, trans. New York, 1966.

Gorodetsky, N. *The Humiliated Christ in Modern Russian Thought*. London, 1938.

Gorodtsov, V. A. "Dakosarmatskie religioznye elementy v russkom narodnom tvorchestve." *Trudy Gosudarstvennogo istoricheskogo muzeia*, no. 1, 23, 1926, 7–36.

Graham, S. *Undiscovered Russia*. London, 1914.

Grakov, B. N. "TYNAIKOKPATOYMENOI: Perezhitki matriarkhata u Sarmatov." *Vestnik drevnei istorii*, no. 3, 1947, 100–121.

Graves, R. *The Greek Myths*. 2 vols. Harmondsworth, Middlesex, 1955.

Grekov, B. D. *Kiev Rus'*. Moscow, 1959.

Griaznov, M. P. "Minusinskie kamennye baby v sviazi s nekotorymi novymi materialami." *Sovetskaia arkheologiia*, vol. 12, 1959, 128–156.

Groot, A. D. de. *Saint Nicholas: A Psychoanalytic Study of His History and Myth*. The Hague, 1965.

Grossman, J. D. "Feminine Images in Old Russian Literature and Art." *California Slavic Studies*, vol. 11, 1980, 33–70.

Gudzii, N. K. *Khrestomatiia po drevnei russkoi literature XI–XVII vv.* Moscow, 1962.

Haase, F. *Volksglaube und Brauchtum der Ostslaven*. Breslau, 1939.

Hancar, F. "Zum Problem der Venusstatuetten in eurasiatischen Jungpäläolithikum." *Prähistorische Zeitschrift*, vol. 30–31, 1939–1940, 85–156.

Haney, J. V. "On the 'Tale of Peter and Fevroniia, Wonderworkers of Murom.'" *Canadian-American Slavic Studies*, vol. 13, nos. 1–2, 1979, 139–162.

Hapgood, I. *Service Book of the Holy Orthodox Church*. Boston, 1906.

Harkins, W. E. "Does Russia Have a Tragic Epos?" *Slavic and East European Journal*, vol. 21, no. 3, 1977, 307–317.

Hawkes, J. *Prehistory*. New York, 1965.

Haxthausen, A. von. *Studies in the Interior of Russia*. S. F. Starr, ed. and trans. Chicago, 1972.

Hayes, H. R. *The Dangerous Sex: The Myth of Feminine Evil*. New York, 1972.

Heiler, F. "The Madonna as a Religious Symbol." In *The Mystic Vision: Papers from The Eranos Yearbooks*. R. Mannheim, trans., 348–374. Princeton, 1968.

Herodotus. *The History of Herodotus*. G. Rawlinson, trans. New York, 1956.

Holmberg, U. "Finno-Ugric Mythology." In *Mythology of All Races*, J. A. MacCulloch, ed., vol. 4, 3–298. New York, 1964.

Hooke, S. H. *Myth, Ritual, and Kingship*. Oxford, 1958.

Howey, M. O. *The Horse in Magic and Myth*. London, 1923.

Hubbs, J. "The Worship of Mother Earth in Russian Culture." In J. Preston, ed., *Mother Worship: Theme and Variations*, 123–144. Chapel Hill, North Carolina, 1982.

Ingham, N. W. "The Sovereign as Martyr: East and West." *Slavic and East European Journal*, vol. 17, no. 1, 1973, 1–17.

Ivanitskii, N. A. *Pesni, skazki, poslovitsy, pogovorki, i zagadki*. Vologda, 1960.

Ivanov V. V., and Toporov, V. N. *Slavianskie iazykovye modelirushchie semioticheskie sistemy*, Moscow, 1965.

Jakobson, R. "La Geste du Prince Igor'." *Selected Writings*, vol. 4, 106–300. The Hague, 1966.

————. *Pushkin and His Sculptural Myth*. J. Burbank, trans. The Hague, 1975.

————. "Slavic Mythology." In *Funk and Wagnalls Standard Dictionary of Folklore, Mythology, and Legend*, 1025–1028. New York, 1949.

————, and Szeftel, M. "The Vseslav Epos." In *Selected Writings*, vol. 4, 301–368. The Hague, 1966.

James, E. O. *The Cult of the Mother Goddess*. New York, 1959.

Journel, R. de. *Monachisme et monastères russes*. Paris, 1952.

Kalmykov, A. "Iranians and Slavs in South Russia." *Journal of the American-Oriental Society*, vol. 45, no. 1, 1925, 68–71.

Kantorowicz, E. H. *The King's Two Bodies*. Princeton, 1957.

Kharuzina, V. N. "K voprosu o pochitanii ognia." *Etnograficheskoe obozrenie*, vol. 70–71, nos. 3–4, 1906, 68–205.

————. "Neskol'ko slov o rodil'nykh krest'ianskikh obriadakh i ob ukhode za det'mi v Pydozhskom uezde." *Etnograficheskoe obozrenie*, vol. 68–69, nos. 1–2, 1906, 88–95.

Khazanov, A. M. "Obychai pobratimstva u Skifov." *Sovetskaia arkheologiia*, no. 3, 1972, 68–75.

Khudiakov, I. A. *Velikorusskie skazki v zapisiakh I. A. Khudiakova*. V. G. Bazanov, ed. Leningrad, 1964.

Kliuchevskii, V. *Kurs russkoi istorii*. Vol. 3. Moscow, 1937.

Koleva, T. A. "Vesenie devich'i obychai u nekotorykh iuzhnoslavianskikh narodov." *Sovetskaia etnografiia*, no 5, 1974, 74–85.

Kologrivof, I. *Essai sur la sainteté en Russiè*. Bruges, 1953.

Kolpakova, N. P., ed. *Liriki russkoi svad'by*. Leningrad, 1962.

Komarovich, V. "Kul't roda i zemli v kniazheskoi srede XI–XIII vv." *Akademiia nauk SSSR: Trudy otdela drevnerusskoi literatury*, vol. 16, 84–101.

Kondakov, N. P. *Ikonografiia Bogomateri*. 2 vols. St. Petersburg, 1914–1915.

Kosven, M. O. "Amazonki: Istoriia legendy." *Sovetskaia etnografiia*, nos. 2–3, 1947, 33–49, 3–33.

Kovalevsky, M. *Modern Customs and Ancient Laws of Russia*. London, 1891.

Kushkin, V. A. "Zakhoroneniie Ivana Groznogo." *Sovetskaia arkheologiia*, no. 1, 1967, 289–295.

Laming, A. *Lascaux*. Harmondsworth, Middlesex, 1959.

Laming-Emperaire, A. *La Signification de l'art rupestre paléolithique*. Paris 1962.

Lannoy, R. *The Speaking Tree: A Study of Indian Culture and Society*. Oxford, 1971.

Laroche, E. "Koubaba, déesse anatolienne et le problème des origines de Cybèle." *Elements orientaux dans la religion grecque ancienne*, 120–142. Paris, 1960.

Laufer, B. "Origin of the Word 'Shaman.'" *American Anthropologist*, vol. 19, no. 3, 1917, 361–371.

Lebedev, A. *Razlichie v uchenii vostochnoi i zapadnoi tserkvei o Presviatoi Deve Marii*. Moscow, 1881.

Lebedeva, N. I., and Maslova, G. G. "Russkaia krest'ianskaia odezhda, XIX-nachala XX veka kak material k eticheskoi istorii naroda." *Sovetskaia etnografiia*, no. 4, 1956, 81–131.

Lederer, W. *Fear of Women*. New York, 1968.

Léger, L. *Les Anciennes civilization slaves*. Paris, 1921.

Leicht, P. S. "Tracce di paganesimo fra gli slavi dell'Isonzo nel sec. XIV." *Studi i materiali di storia della religione*, vol. 1, 1925, 247–250.

Leroy-Beaulieu, A. *The Empire of the Tsars and the Russians*. Z. A. Rogosin, trans. London, 1905.

Levy, G. R. *The Gate of Horn*. New York, 1946.

Likhachev, D. S. *Chelovek v literature drevnei Rusi*. Moscow-Leningrad, 1958.

———, and Panchenko, A. M. *"Smekhovoi mir" drevnei Rusi*. Leningrad, 1976.

Linforth, I. M. "Greek Gods and Foreign Gods in Herodotus." *University of California Publications in Classical Philology*, vol. 9, no. 1, 1926, 1–25.

Loorits, O. "The Development of the Uralian Culture-Area." *Slavonic and East European Review*, vol. 31, 1957, 1–19.

Lot-Borodina, M. "Religioznye legendy XII i XIII vekov." *Russkaia mysl'*, nos. 1–2, 1922, 91–119.

Machal, J. "Slavic Mythology." In L. H. Gray, ed., *The Mythology of All Races*, vol. 3, 217–398. New York, 1964.

Mann, R. "Is There a Passage Missing at the Beginning of the Igor Tale?" *Slavic Review*, vol. 41, no. 4, 1982, 666–672.

———. *The Song of Prince Igor: A Great Medieval Epic*. Eugene, Oregon, 1979.

Mansikka, V. J. *Die Religion der Ostslaven*. Helsinki, 1922.

Marshack, A. *The Roots of Civilization*. New York, 1972.

Martin, M. K., and Voorhies, R. *The Female of the Species*. New York, 1975.

Martynova, A. "Life in the Pre-Revolutionary Village as Reflected in Popular Lullabies." In D. L. Ransel, ed., *The Family in Imperial Russia*. 171–185. Urbana, Illinois, 1978.

Masse, H. *Persian Beliefs and Customs*. New Haven, 1954.

Matorin, N. *Zhenskoe bozhestvo v pravoslavnom kul'te*. Moscow, 1931.

Matossian, M. "When God Was a Woman." *Journal of Social History*, vol. 6, no. 3, 1973, 325–343.

———. "The Peasant Way of Life." In W. S. Vucinich, ed., *The Peasant in Nineteenth Century Russia*, 1–40. Stanford, 1968.

Megas, G. *Greek Calendar Customs*. Athens, 1963.

Meletinskii, E. M. "The Low Hero of the Fairy Tale." In F. Oinas and S. Soudakoff, eds., *The Study of Russian Folklore*, 236–254. The Hague, 1975.

Melkov, A. L. "Nekotorye detskie igry v Kurskoi gubernii." *Etnograficheskoe obozrenie*, nos. 3–4, 1914, 181–184.

Mellaart, J. *Çatal Hüyük*. London, 1967.

———. "Çatal Hüyük, A Neolithic City in Anatolia." *Proceedings of the British Academy*, vol. 51, 1965–1966, 201–213.

Meriggi, B. "Il concetto del Dio nelle religione dei popoli slavi." *Ricerche slavistiche*, vol. 1, 1952, 148–176.

Meuli, K. "Scythica." *Hermes*, vol. 70, 1935, 121–176.
Miliukov, P. *Outlines of Russian Culture*. V. Ughet and E. Davis, trans. 3 vols. New York, 1960.
Miller, W. W. *Russians as People*. New York, 1961.
Minns, E. H. *Scythians and Greeks*. Cambridge, 1913.
Moshkova, M. G. *Proiskhozhdenie rannesarmatskoi (prokhorovskoi) kul'tury*. Moscow, 1974.
Moszynski, K. *Kultura ludowo slowian*. 2 vols. Warsaw, 1967.
Movsha, T. G. "Goncharnyi tsentr tripol'skoi kul'tury na Dnestre." *Sovetskaia arkheologiia*, no. 3, 1971, 228–234.
———. "Ob antropomorfnoi plastike tripol'skoikul'tury." *Sovetskaia arkheologiia*, no. 2, 1969, 15–34.
———. "Sviatilishcha tripol'skoi kul'tury." *Sovetskaia arkheologiia*, 1971, 201–205.
Mur'ianov, M. F. "Mif o Lade." *Russkii fol'klor*, vol. 12, 220–225.
Nahodil, H. "The Mother Cult in Siberia." In V. Dioszegi, ed., *Popular Beliefs and Folklore Traditions of Siberia*, 459–477. Bloomington, Indiana, 1968.
Nechaev, A. A., and Rybakov, N., eds. *Russkie narodnye skazki*. Moscow, 1959.
Netting, A. "Images and Ideas in Russian Peasant Art." *Slavic Review*, vol. 35, no. 1, 1976, 48–68.
Neumann, E. *The Great Mother: An Analysis of the Archetype*. R. Mannheim, trans. Princeton, 1963.
Niederle, L. *Byt' i kul'tura drevnikh slavian*. Prague, 1924.
———. *Slavianskiie drevnosti*. T. Kovaleva and M. Khazanova, trans., Moscow, 1956.
Nikol'skii, N. K. "O drevnerusskom khristianstve." *Russkaia mysl'*, no. 6, 1913, 1–23.
Nosova, L. S. *Iazychestvo v pravoslavi*. Moscow, 1975.
———. "Mapping the Shrovetide Ritual." *Soviet Anthropology and Archeology*, vol. 14, nos. 1–2, 50–70.
Novgorod-Severskii, I. I. *Skazki sibirskie i legendy o Bozhei Materi*. Munich, n.d.
O'Flaherty, W. D. *Women, Androgynes, and Other Mythical Beasts*. Chicago, 1980.
Oinas, F. J. "Heretics as Vampires and Demons in Russia." *Slavic and East European Journal*, vol. 22, no. 4, 1978, 433–441.
———. "The Problem of the Aristocratic Origin of Russian *Byliny*." *Slavic Review*, vol. 30, no. 3, 1971, 513–522.
———, and Soudakoff, S. *The Study of Russian Folklore*. The Hague, 1975.
Onasch, K. "Paraskeva Studien." *Ostkirchliche Studien*, vol. 6, nos. 2–3, 1957, 121–141.
Pagels, E. *The Gnostic Gospels*. New York, 1981.
Paulson, I. *The Old Estonian Folk Religion*. Bloomington, Indiana, 1971.
Pelisov, G. A. "O fol'klornykh osnovakh 'Skazok' A. S. Pushkina." *Sovetskaia etnografiia*, no. 4, 1950, 92–106.
Perets, V. N. *Materialy k istorii apokrifa i legendy*. St. Petersburg, 1899.
Perkowski, J. *Vampires of the Slavs*. Cambridge, 1976.

Petrov, V. P., and Makarevich, M. L. "Skifskaia genealogicheskaia legenda." *Sovetskaia arkheologiia*, no. 1, 1963, 20–31.
Pomerantseva, E. V. *Mifologicheskie personazhi v russkom fol'klore.* Moscow, 1975.
———. and Mints, S. I. *Russkoe narodnoe poeticheskoe tvorchestvo, Khrestomatiia.* Moscow, 1963.
Pomeroy, S. B. *Goddesses, Whores, Wives, and Slaves: Women in Classical Antiquity.* New York, 1975.
Popov, A. A. "Tavgiitsy: Materialy po etnografii Avamskikh i Vedeievskikh Tavgiitsev." *Trudy Instituta antropologii i etnografii Akademii nauk SSSR*, vol. 1, no. 5, 1936, 80–128.
Popova, T. A. "Zoomorfnaia plastika tripol'skogo poseleniia Polivanov Yar." *Kratkie soobshcheniia Instituta arkheologii SSSR*, vol. 123, 1970, 8–14.
Potebnia, A. A. "O mificheskom znachenii nekotorykh obriadov i poverii." *Chteniia obshchestva istorii i drevnostei rossiiskikh*, nos. 2, 3, 4, 1865, 1–310.
Procopius. *History of the Wars.* H. B. Dewing, trans. Vol. 4. Cambridge, 1924.
Pronin, A. and B. *Russian Folk Arts.* New York, 1975.
Propp, V. Iy. *Russkie agrarnae prazdniki.* Leningrad, 1963.
Puhvel, J. *Myth and Law among the Indo-Europeans: Studies in Indo-European Comparative Mythology.* Berkeley, 1970.
Pushkin, A. S. *The Complete Prose Tales of Alexander Sergeyevitch Pushkin.* G. R. Aitken, trans. New York, 1966.
———. *Eugene Onegin.* C. Johnston, trans. Harmondsworth, Middlesex, 1979.
———. *The Poems, Prose, and Plays of Alexander Pushkin.* A. Yarmolinsky, ed. New York, 1964.
———. *Sochineniia.* 3 vols. Moscow, 1964.
Putilov, B. N. "Pesnia o gneve Ivana Groznogo na syna." *Russkii fol'klor*, vol. 4, 1959, 5–32.
———. "Russian and South Slavic Epic Songs about Contests with Serpents." *Soviet Anthropology and Archeology*, vol. 8, no. 1, 1969, 43–69.
Raeff, M. *Origins of the Russian Intelligentsia: The Eighteenth Century Nobility.* New York, 1966.
Raevskii, D. S. "Skifskii mifologicheskii siuzhet v iskusstve i ideologii tsarstva Ateia." *Sovetskaia arkheologiia*, no. 3, 1970, 90–101.
Ralston, W. R. S. *Russian Folktales.* New York, 1880.
———. *Songs of the Russian People.* London, 1872.
Rambaud, A. *La Russie épique.* Paris, 1879.
Reeder, R. *Down along the Mother Volga.* Philadelphia, 1975.
Reinach, S. "Le Souper chez la sorcière." *Actes du congrès international d'histoire des religions*, Paris, vol. 1, 1925, 493–498.
Reisman, E. S. "The Cult of Boris and Gleb: A Remnant of Varangian Tradition?" *Russian Review*, vol. 37, 141–157.
Rendel-Harris, J. *The Cult of the Heavenly Twins.* Cambridge, 1906.
Rice, T. T. *The Ancient Arts of Central Asia.* New York, 1965.
———. *A Concise History of Russian Art.* New York, 1967.
———. *The Scythians.* New York, 1957.

Rohrlich-Leavitt, R. "Women in Transition: Crete and Sumer." In R. Bridenthal and C. Koontz, eds., *Becoming Visible: Women in European History.* New York, 1977.

Rostovtzeff, M. I. "Le Culte de la Grande Déesse dans la Russie méridionale." *Revue des études grecques,* vol. 32, 1919, 462–481.

———. *Iranians and Greeks in South Russia.* Oxford, 1922.

Rozhdestvenskii, T. S., and Uspenskii, M. I. *Pesni russkikh sektantov mistikov.* St. Petersburg, 1912.

Rudenko, S. I. *Frozen Tombs of Siberia: The Pazyryk Burials of Iron Age Horsemen.* M. W. Thompson, trans. Berkeley, 1970.

Rybakov, B. A. "Cosmology and Mythology of the Agriculturalists of the Eneolithic." Pts. 1 and 2. *Soviet Anthropology and Archeology,* vol. 4, nos. 2–3, 1965–1966, 16–36, 33–52.

———. "Drevnie elementy v russkom narodnom tvorchestve." *Sovetskaia etnografiia, no. 1, 1948, 90–106.*

———. "Kalendar' IV veka iz zemli Polian." *Sovetskaia arkheologiia,* no. 4, 1962, 66–89.

———. "Rusalii i bog Simargl-Pereplut." *Sovetskaia arkheologiia,* no. 2, 1967, 91–116.

Ryndina, N. V. "Rannetripol'skaia obrabotka medi." *Sovetskaia arkheologiia,* no. 3, 1969, 21–24.

Sadnik, L. "Ancient Slavic Religion in the Light of Recent Research." *Eastern Review,* vol. 1, no. 1, 1948, 36–43.

Samarin, D. "Bogoroditsa v russkom narodnom pravoslavii." *Russkaia mysl',* vol. 39, 1918, 1–38.

Sanday, P. R. *Female Power and Male Dominance: On the Origins of Sexual Inequality.* Cambridge, Massachusetts, 1981.

Savitsch, E. de. "Religious Amulets of Early Russian Christendom." *Gazette des beaux-arts,* vol. 23, 1943, 111–116.

Schwoeffermann, C., project supervisor. *Goddesses and Their Offspring: Ninteenth and Twentieth Century East European Embroideries.* Exhibition catalogue, Roberson Center for the Arts and Sciences, Binghamton, New York, 1986.

Sciacca, F. "Royal Farmers: A Folklore Investigation into Pagan Origins of the Cult of Boris and Gleb." *Ulbandus Review,* vol. 1, no. 1, 1978, 3–14.

Shangina, I. I. "Izobrazheniie konia i ptitsei v russkoi krest'ianskoi vyshivke XIX-nachala XX veka." *Sovetskaia etnografiia,* no. 3, 1972, 116–126.

Shashkov, S. S. *Istoriia russkoi zhenshchiny.* St. Petersburg, 1879.

Shchapov, A. P. "Vliianie obshchestvennogo mirosozertsaniia na sotsial'noe polozhenie zhenshchiny v Rossii. *Sochineniia,* vol. 2, 55–104. St. Petersburg, 1906.

Shchapov, Ia. N. "Brak i sem'ia v drevnei Rusi." *Voprosy istorii,* vol. 10, 1970, 216–219.

Shein, P. *Velikorusy v svoikh pesniakh, obriadakh, obychaiakh, verovaniakh, skazkakh, legendakh.* Vol. 1. St. Petersburg, 1900–1902.

Shinn, W. T. "The Law of the Russian Peasant Household." *Slavic Review,* vol. 20, no. 4, 1961, 604–612.

Shternberg, L. Ia. *Pervobytnaia religiia v svete etnografii.* Moscow, 1936.

Sipiaguine, A. "Aux Sources de la piété russe." *Irenikon,* vol. 2, 1927, 1–30.

Smirnov, P. "Znachenie zhenshchiny v istorii vozniknoveniia raskola." *Missionerskii sbornik, 1891,* 330–365.

Smirnov, S. "Baby bogomerzkiia." *Sbornik statei posvulshchennykh Vasiliu Kliuchevskomu,* 217–243. Moscow, 1909.

————. "Drevnerusskii dukhovnik." *Chteniia obshchestva istorii i drevnostei Moskovskogo universiteta,* April-June, 1914, 255–283.

Smith, H. *The Russians.* New York, 1976.

Smith, R. E. F. *The Origins of Farming in Russia.* Paris, 1959.

Smolitsch, I. "Die Verehrung der Göttesmutter in der Russischen Frommigkeit und Volksreligiösitat. *Kyrios,* vol. 5, 1940–1941, 194–211.

Snegirev, I. M. *Russkie protonarodnye prazdniki i obriady.* 2 vols. Moscow, 1837–1839.

Sokolov, Yu. *Le Folklore russe.* G. Welter, trans. Paris, 1945.

Soloviev, A. V. *Holy Russia: The History of a Religious-Social Idea.* The Hague, 1959.

Solzhenitsyn, A. "Matryona's Home." H. T. Willetts, trans. *Encounter,* vol. 20, no. 5, May, 1963, 27–45.

Speranskii, M., ed. *Russkaia ustnaia slovesnost' byliny.* Moscow, 1916.

Stepanov, V. "Svedeniia o rodil'nykh i krest'ianskikh obriadakh v Klinskom uezde Moskovskoi gubernii." *Etnograficheskoe obozrenie,* vol. 70–71, nos. 3–4, 1906, 221–234.

Stratilesco, T. *From Carpathians to Pindus.* Boston, 1907.

Strotmann, D. "Quelques aperçus historiques sur le culte marial en Russie." *Irenikon,* vol. 32, 1959, 178–202.

Stscherbakiwskyj, W. "The Early Ukrainian Social Order as Reflected in Ukrainian Wedding Customs." *Slavonic and East European Review,* vol. 31, 1952, 325–351.

Sulimirski, T. *Prehistoric Russia.* New York, 1970.

————. *The Sarmatians.* New York, 1970.

Svirin, A. N. *Drevnerusskoe shit'e.* Moscow, 1963.

Tchetverikoff, S. "Piété Orthodoxe: De l'esprit religieux russe et de la dévotion du peuple russe pour la Mère de Dieu." *Irenikon,* vol. 3, no. 7, 385–390; and no. 8, 459–467.

Tereshchenko, A. V. *Byt' russkogo naroda.* 7 vols. St. Petersburg, 1848.

Thompson, E. "Russian Holy Fools and Shamanism." *American Contributions to the Eighth International Congress of Slavists,* Zagreb-Ljubljana, 1978, vol. 2, 691–706.

Tokarev, S. A. *Religioznye verovaniia vostochno-slavianskikh narodov XIX–nachala XX veka.* Moscow, 1957.

————. "K voprosu o znachenii zhenskikh izobrazhenii epokhi paleolita." *Sovetskaia arkheologiia,* no. 2, 1961, 12–20.

Tolstoi, L. *Master and Man and Other Stories.* P. Foote, trans. Harmondsworth, Middlesex, 1984.

Tolstov, S. P. "The Central Asian Scythians in the Light of the Most Recent Archeological Discoveries." *Soviet Anthropology and Archeology,* vol. 2, no. 4, 1964, 15–31.

Toporov, V. N. "Fragment slavianskoi mifologii." *Akademiia nauk SSSR, Institut slavianovedeniia, kratkie soobshcheniia,* vol. 38, 1961, 32–36.

————. "Khettskaia Salgusi i slavianskaia Baba-Yaga." *Akademiia nauk SSSR, Institut slavianovedeniia, kratkie soobshcheniia,* vol. 38, 1963, 14–32.

Trever, K. *The Dog-Bird Senmurv-Paskudj: The Dog-Bird of Persian Mythology.* Leningrad, 1938.

Tringham, R. *Hunters, Fishers, and Farmers of Eastern Europe, 6000-3000 B.C.* London, 1971.

Trubetskoi, I. S. "K voprosu o 'Zolotoi Babe.'" *Etnograficheskoe obozrenie,* vol. 68–69, nos. 1–2, 1906, 52–62.

Tudorovskaia, E. A. "Skazka o Borme Iaryzhke." *Russkii fol'klor,* vol. 6, 1976, 173–185.

Tul'tseva, L. A. "Kalendarnye religioznye prazdniki v byty sovremennogo krest'ianstva." *Sovetskaia etnografiia,* no. 6, 1970, 111–118.

Ukhov, P. D. *Byliny.* Moscow, 1957.

Uspenskii, B. A. "Kul't Nikoly na Rusi v istoriko-kul'turnom osveshchenii." *Trudy po znakovym sistemam,* no. 10, 86–140. Tartu, 1978.

Uspenskii, D. I. "Narodnye verovaniia v tserkovnoi zhivopisi." *Etnograficheskoe obozrenie,* vol 68–69, nos. 1–2, 1906, 73–87.

———. "Svadebnye velichal'nye pesni." *Etnograficheskoe obozrenie,* vol. 70–71, nos. 3–4, 1906, 234–242.

Valashov, D. M. "Dunai." *Russkii fol'klor,* vol. 16, 1976, 95–114.

Val'denberg, V. E. *Drevnerusskie ucheniia o predelakh tsarskoi vlasti: Ocherki russkoi politicheskoi literatury ot Vladimira Sviatogo do kontsa XVII veka.* St. Petersburg, 1916.

Vasilenko, V. M. *Russkaia narodnaia rez'ba i rospis' po derevu XVIII—XX vv.* Moscow, 1960.

Veletskaia, I. I. "O novgorodnikh rusaliiakh." In B. A. Rybakov, ed., *Slavianie i Rus',* 394–400. Moscow, 1968.

Vernadsky, G. *Ancient Russia.* New Haven, 1943.

———. *Kievan Russia.* London, 1973.

———. *The Origins of Russia.* Oxford, 1959.

Veselovskii, A. N. "Opyty po istorii razvitiia khristianskoi legendy." *Zhurnal ministerstva narodnogo prosveshcheniia,* vol. 189, 1877, 186–252.

Volkov, T. "Rites et usages nuptiaux en Ukraine." *L'Anthropologie,* vol. 2, 1891, 539–587.

Voyce, A. *Art and Architecture of Medieval Russia.* Norman, Oklahoma, 1967.

Vsevolodskii-Gerngross, V. N. *Istoriia russkogo teatra.* Moscow-Leningrad, 1929.

Warner, E. "Work and Play: Some Aspects of Folk Drama in Russia." *Comparative Drama,* vol. 12, no. 2, 151–169.

Warner, M. *Alone of All Her Sex: The Myth and Cult of the Virgin Mary.* New York, 1976.

Weidlé, W. *Russia: Absent and Present.* New York, 1961.

Wenzel, M. "The Dioscuri in the Balkans." *American Slavic and East European Review,* vol. 26, no. 3, 1967, 363–381.

Witt, R. E. *Isis in the Graeco-Roman World.* Ithaca, New York, 1971.

Wosien, M. G. *The Russian Folktale.* Munich, 1969.

Yadrintsev, N., and Kulikovski, G. I. "O kul'te medvedia, preimushchestvenno u suevernykh inorodtsev." *Etnograficheskoe obozrenie,* vol. 1, 1890, 101–115.

Zabylin (Zabelin), M. *Russkii narod: Ego obychai, obriady, predaniia, sueveriia, i poeziia.* Moscow, 1880.

Zavoiko, G. K. "Verovaniia, obriady i obychai velikorussov Vladimirskoi gubernii." *Etnograficheskoe obozrenie*, nos. 3–4, 1914, 81–178.

Zelenin, D. K. *Le Culte des idoles en Sibérie*. Paris, 1952.

————. "Istolkovanie perezhitochnykh obriadov." *Sovetskaia etnografiia*, no. 5, 1934, 3–16.

————. "Totemicheskii kul't derev'ev u russkikh i u belorussov." *Izvestiia Akademii nauk SSSR, otdelenie obshchestvennykh nauk*, no. 6, 1933, 591–629.

Zemtsovskii, I. I., ed. *Poezii krest'ianskikh prazdnikov*. Leningrad, 1970.

Zenkovsky, A., ed. *Medieval Russia's Epics, Chronicles, and Tales*. New York, 1963.

Zguta, R. "The Ordeal by Water (Swimming Witches) in the East Slavic World." *Slavic Review*, vol. 36, no. 2, 1977, 219–230.

————. "The Pagan Priests of Early Russia: Some New Insights." *Slavic Review*, vol. 33, no. 2, 1974, 259–266.

Znayenko, M. T. *The Gods of the Ancient Slavs: Tatishchev and the Beginnings of Slavic Mythology*, Columbus, Ohio, 1980.

Index

Agrarian Festivals: Mother Earth cult, 61–86; Mary's holy days, 114–15; Saint George, 180–81; role of tsar, 188–89

Agriculture: neolithic goddess cult, 5–6; transition to and *rusalki*, 34–35; Mother Earth cult, 53, 55, 254n. *See also* Plow

Ahura Mazda: Bosphoran kingdom and goddess cult, 10

Alexander I: exile of Pushkin, 211–12

Alexis: *Raskol*, 195–97

Alkonost': Persian origin, 30; women and the dead, 31

Amazons: Greeks and goddess cult, 8; image of Olga, 90; *polianitsa* of epic, 149

Ancestors: women and cult of, 14; veneration of and *rusalki*, 30–31; amulets and Mary, 107–108; Orthodox Christianity, 173–74; *pech'*, 256n. *See also* Rod

Animals: Sarmatians and goddess cult, 9; *rusalki*, 31–32; symbols of Baba Yaga, 43; Mother Earth as guardian, 56; Mary as patron, 113; Paraskeva, 120; symbolism in Muscovite epic, 163

Anti-Christ: tsar and *Raskol*, 196–97, 198–99; Peter the Great as, 201, 202; Nicholas as in *The Possessed*, 229

Apollo: and Mother Earth, 54

Architecture: early Russian church, 101–102

Aristocracy: goddess cult in Kiev, 94–95; Peter the Great, 202–203

Artemis: *vily*, 29; *rusalki*, 36; and Mother Earth, 54; Saint Nicholas, 95

Avvakum: *Raskol*, 197–98.

Baba Yaga: motif and symbolism in folktale, 3, 147; folklore and goddess cult, 24; image of goddess as elder, 36–51; parthenogenetic mother, 52; Demeter-Kore myth, 53; compared to Mother Earth, 55, 57, 58; Kupalo Night, 77; wedding customs, 84; Mary and icons, 104; compared with Mary, 106–107; Mary and folktales,

109; compared to Paraskeva, 116; Kievan-Vladimir epic cycle, 156, 159; symbolism and Peter the Great, 201; "The Queen of Spades," 217, 218; "Matriona's Home," 236; evil nature and male ethnologists, 252n; folktales and spinning, 254n; and Solovei, 268n

Bab'e Leto: agrarian cycle and Mother Earth cult, 79; role of tsar, 189

Bereginy: early Slav religion, 14–15

Birch: veneration of, 33; *rusalki* and bride, 83; plow and *rusalki*, 251n; burial of Gleb, 271n

Birds: images of Mary, 113; tsar and imagery of folklore, 184. *See also* Dove; Firebird; Swan

Birth: Mother Earth cult, 59–60; Semik, 72; Paraskeva, 121

Bogoroditsa: Mary and goddess cult, 101

Boris: Christianity and *rod*, 173–74; popular version of legend and feminine power, 174–75; twin motif, 175–77. *See also* Divine Twins; Gleb

Bosphoran Kingdom: displacement of goddess cult, 10; goddess cult and coinage, 244n

"The Bronze Horseman": themes and motifs, 222–27. *See also* Pushkin, Alexander

Buslaev, Vasilii: feminine power in Novgorod epic cycle, 161–62

Byliny. See Epic

Byzantium: Vladimir and Christianity, 87; trade with Kiev, 88, 89, 90; origins of Russian icon, 103; conquered by Turks, 183

Çatal Hüyük: goddess cult and agriculture, 5; Baba Yaga, 47; link to Mary, 110; symbolism and goddess cult, 240n. *See also* Neolithic

Childhood: theme of return to motherland, 233–34. *See also* Gorky, Maxim

Children: rites of initiation and Baba Yaga, 47–51; intelligentsia and peasantry, 208

Christianity: goddess cult, 21; witch-

Lightning Source UK Ltd.
Milton Keynes UK
UKHW022058050821
387960UK00023B/570